Georgina Campbell

MEALS
for all
SEASONS

The Best of Contemporary Irish Cooking

WOLFHOUND PRESS

First published 1992 by
WOLFHOUND PRESS
68 Mountjoy Square, Dublin 1
© 1992
Text copyright Georgina Campbell. Photographs © Irish Sugar plc /
Wolfhound Press. Design, typography and other material © Wolfhound Press

British Library Cataloguing in Publication Data
Campbell, Georgina
    Meals for All Seasons: The Best of Contemporary Irish Cooking
    I. Title
    641.5
    ISBN 0-86327-322-X

Acknowledgements
We are pleased to acknowledge
Irish Sugar, plc whose support has
made it possible to produce and
publish this comprehensive book
on contemporary Irish cookery
with its full range of recipes and
to illustrate it in colour with
specially commissioned
photographs. Author Georgina
Campbell, whose idea this book
was, joins with the publisher in
this acknowledgement.

Credits
Book Design: Jan de Fouw
Photography: Rai Uhlemann
Food Stylist: Kevin Thornton
Index: Julitta Clancy
Thanks to Brian Morland and
Rose Sevastopulo for providing
cakes and decorations

Editorial: Wolfhound Press
Printed in the Republic of Ireland
by Colour Books, Dublin

Preface

This is a book I very much wanted to write for some time, because I believe so strongly in the *enjoyment* of food. Ever since the basics of cookery were taught to me as a child in our farmhouse kitchen, using produce straight from the field or garden, I have had a passion for food. Today's growing emphasis on its negative aspects is the antithesis of everything which makes working in this field such a joy. I don't believe in food taboos and feel strongly that the ever-increasing stress on why we shouldn't eat certain things is not only built on very shaky foundations at a time when life expectancy in the western world is at an all-time high but, in the long run, bound to be counter-productive.

Never having believed in the philosophy of 'good' and 'bad' foods, rather that all quality ingredients are potentially good in a balanced diet, I suggest that it is time to go back to first principles: eat as wide-ranging a diet as possible and make the most of food in season, both for the pleasure it brings and as a natural guarantee of variety.

Conflicting theories on health and diet abound, but the one thing missing is common sense, which involves a healthy interest in and enjoyment of well-balanced, interesting food. When good meals and good company coincide, especially, this is truly living and the stuff of which life-long memories are made. The French have it just about right, with food a key to the wider enjoyment of life.

Inspiration for this book came from a number of sources, but the catalyst was a conversation with representatives of Irish Sugar plc, whose own products have so often (and, in my view, unfairly) been in the firing line. Sugar is an essential ingredient in a surprisingly wide variety of dishes, not only as a major ingredient in a range of cakes, desserts and other sweet dishes but also as a preservative, in small but vital quantities in yeast cookery and as a seasoning in a huge variety of savoury dishes, including many oriental ones — but its main role is that it makes other nutritious foods more enjoyable to eat. Where would a good cook be without it?

I am very pleased that Irish Sugar not only shared my views, but supported them through the generous sponsorship which has helped to make this book possible. My thanks go to them, and also to Wolfhound Press who agreed with such encouraging enthusiasm to publish the book.

Many favourite recipes collected over the years are here — both my own and others generously passed on by cooks from all over the country as mementos of memorable meals — so I hope that you will enjoy not only the book but, perhaps even more, the dishes, as much as I have enjoyed them myself.

Read, cook and enjoy!

Georgina Campbell.

Contents

Where the recipe text includes '[Microwave]', consider using your microwave —at least part of the recipe is suitable.

Above: Mother's Day: Breakfast in Bed, page 13

Previous Pictures
Title Page: Cassoulet, page 115
Page 2: Soups, including Tomato and Golden Pumpkin, page 103
Page 3: Crystallised Rose Petals, page 100
Page 4: Twice-baked Cheese Soufflé, page 104
Page 7: Whole Glazed Ham, page 145

CHRISTMAS 134

CONVERSION TABLES

Spoon Measurements

All of the measurements given are for levelled spoonfuls
(British Imperial Standard)
1 teaspoon = 5 millilitres (ml.)
1 dessertspoon = 10 ml.
1 tablespoon = 15 ml.
Use the spoon measurements below to obtain
approximately 1 oz. (25 g.) of the following everyday
foods:

Tablespoons needed for approx.

1 oz. or 25 g.

Breadcrumbs, dried	3
Breadcrumbs, fresh	7
Butter, lard, margarine	2
Cheese, grated (Cheddar type)	3
Cheese, grated (Parmesan)	4
Cocoa	4
Coffee, ground	4½
Coffee, instant	6½
Cornflour, custard powder	2¾
Flour, unsifted	3
Gelatine, powdered	3
Milk powder, dried skimmed	5
Parsley, freshly chopped	10
Rice, uncooked	2
Suet, shredded	3
Sugar (caster, Demerara, granulated)	2
Sugar, icing	3
Syrup and honey	1
Yeast, dried	2

Weight

The Imperial pound (lb.) approx equals 450g. —
slightly less than ½ kilogram (500 g.).

Imperial	*(Approx)* Metric	Imperial	*(Approx)* Metric
1 oz.	25 g.	2 lb.	900 g.
2 oz.	50 g.	2½ lb.	1.1 kg.
3 oz.	75 g.	3 lb.	1.4 kg.
4 oz.	**100**-125 g.	3½ lb.	1.6 kg.
5 oz.	150 g.	4 lb.	1.8 kg.
6 oz.	175 g.	4½ lb.	2 kg.
7 oz.	200 g.	5 lb.	2.3 kg.
8 oz.	225 g.	5½ lb.	2.5 kg.
9 oz.	250 g.	6 lb.	2.7 kg.
10 oz.	275 g.	6½ lb.	3 kg.
11 oz.	300 g.	7 lb.	3.2 kg.
12 oz.	325-**350** g.	7½ lb.	3.4 kg.
13 oz.	375 g.	8 lb.	3.6 kg.
14 oz.	400 g.	8½ lb.	3.9 kg.
15 oz.	425 g.	9 lb.	4.1 kg.
16 oz. (1 lb.)	450 g.	9½ lb.	4.3 kg.
1½ lb.	700g.	10 lb.	4.5 kg.

Oven Temperatures

Thermostatic dials on cookers marked in Centigrade
correspond to Fahrenheit and gas markings as follows:
(Fan ovens operate at slightly lower temperatures.
Consult your manufacturer's manual for details.)

°F	°C	Gas Mark	Temperature
250	130	½	Very cool
275	140	1	Very cool
300	150	2	Cool
325	160 or 170	3	Warm
350	180	4	Moderate
375	190	5	Fairly hot
400	200	6	Fairly hot
425	210 or 220	7	Hot
450	230	8	Very hot
475	240	9	Very hot

Liquid Capacity

The Imperial pint (20 fluid oz.) measures slightly more
than ½ litre — approximately 575 millilitres (ml.).

Imperial	Approx. metric equivalent
1 fluid oz.	25 ml.
2 fluid oz.	50 ml.
3 fluid oz.	75 ml.
4 fluid oz.	**100**-125 ml.
5 fluid oz.	150 ml.
6 fluid oz.	175 ml.
7 fluid oz.	200 ml.
8 fluid oz.	225 ml.
9 fluid oz.	250 ml.
10 fluid oz. (½ pint)	275-**300** ml.
15 fluid oz. (¾ pint)	425 ml.
20 fluid oz. (1 pint)	575-**600** ml.
30 fluid oz. (1½ pint)	850 ml.
40 fluid oz. (2 pint)	1.15 litre

Length

The Imperial yard (36 in.) is slightly shorter than the
metre (m.) (or 100 centimetres (cm.))

Imperial	Approx. metric equivalent
⅛ in.	0.3 cm.
¼ in.	0.6 cm.
½ in.	1.2 cm.
¾ in.	1.9 cm.
1 in.	2.5 cm.
1¼ in.	3.2 cm.
1½ in.	3.8 cm.
1¾ in.	4.5 cm.
2 in.	5 cm.
2½ in.	6.3 cm.
3 in.	7.6 cm.
3½ in.	8.9 cm.
4 in.	10 cm.
4½ in.	11.4 cm.
5 in.	12.7 cm.
6 in.	15 cm.
7 in.	17.8 cm.
8 in.	20.3 cm.

9 in. . . . . 22.8 cm.
10 in. . . . . 25.4 cm.
11 in. . . . . 27.9 cm.
12 in. (1 ft) . . . . 30.5 cm.
36 in. (1 yd) . . . . 91.5 cm.

A Guide for American Users

Imperial	*American*
1 lb. butter or other fat	2 cups
1 lb. flour	4 cups
1 lb. granulated or caster sugar	2 cups
1 lb. icing or confectioners' sugar	3½ cups
1 lb. brown (moist) sugar	2 cups
. . . .	(firmly packed)
12 oz. golden syrup or treacle	1 cup
14 oz. rice	2 cups
1 lb. dried fruit	3 cups
1 lb. chopped or minced meat	2 cups
. . . .	(firmly packed)
1 lb. lentils or split peas	2 cups
2 oz. soft breadcrumbs	1 cup
½ oz. flour	2 tablespoons
1 oz. flour	¼ cup
1 oz. sugar	2 tablespoons
½ oz. butter	1 tablespoon
1 oz. golden syrup or treacle	1 tablespoon
1 oz. jam or jelly	1 tablespoon
4 oz. grated cheese	1 cup
4 oz. button mushrooms	1 cup
4 oz. chopped nuts (most kinds)	1 cup

Liquid Measures

¼ pint water, milk, etc. . . . . ⅔ cup
½ pint water . . . . 1¼ cups
1 pint water . . . . 2½ cups
2 pints water . . . . 5 cups
The British pint is 20 fl oz: the American pint is 16 fl oz.

Pastry/Filling guide for tarts/flans

Flan rings, tins and ceramic dishes vary in depth as well as width, so estimates of the amount of pastry needed are approximate. To allow for this, amounts given are generous: if there are leftovers, use to make a lid, pasty of turnover, some tartlet cases or simply some decorative extras, such as a lattice top, for the flan being made.

Size of Tin	*Amount of Pastry Needed*
6"/15cm.	4oz/100g flour etc
7"/18cm	5oz/150g four etc
8"/20cm	7oz/200g flour etc
9"/23cm	9oz/250g flour etc
10"/25.5cm	11oz/300g flour etc
11"/28cm	12oz/350g flour etc.

Fillings:
A 6"/15cm flan needs half as much as an 8"/20cm one
A 7"/18cm flan needs half as much a 9"/23cm oneA 10"/25.5cm flan needs half as much as an 8"/20cm one/
HINT: Although ceramic flan dishes are pretty and useful as oven-to-table ware they are best kept for other dishes, such as gratins, as pastry cooks much better in metal, which is a good conductor of heat and produces a crisper finish.

MEALS FOR ALL SEASONS

In the kaleidoscope of the constantly changing seasons, the cook's year is governed by a variety of influences: the arrival of fresh young local produce moving towards the peak of its season brings with it a sense of excitement unknown to the cosmopolitan shopper who has given in to the sales hype on all-year availability of seasonal foods. The ebb and flow of the seasons also brings the challenge of making the best possible use of the good things so abundant in Ireland and of blending new ideas with old traditions: in recent years, especially, the public interest in good food has blossomed into something approaching a celebration of our good fortune in having such wonderful natural produce on our doorstep. In food, as in other aspects of our social life, we are especially blessed in Ireland — working with the rhythm of the seasons and moving smoothly from one culinary highlight to the next comes naturally to us. **Christmas** is the major peak for any cook, of course — and provides a fifth season for the purposes of this book — but **St Patrick's Day, Easter** and **Hallowe'en** are not far behind and, in addition to private celebrations like weddings, birthdays and anniversaries, there are many other dates of public significance, such as **St Valentine's Day, Shrove Tuesday** and even the **Chinese New Year** which seem to have growing culinary importance as social patterns change. But it is perhaps to the steady core of good cooking as, for example, it has developed in the kitchens of our best country houses that we owe our good reputation for food today — ever since President and Madame de Gaulle paid a holiday visit to Ireland in 1968 it has been a valued destination for discerning continental visitors, people who care about the purity of our ingredients and the respect for local, seasonal produce shown by our leading cooks — many of whom have been kind enough to contribute recipes to this book. So here's to the wonderful variety of our seasonal foods and the good things we can make of them.

SPRING

March, April, May

SPRING is a cruel season in the kitchen, as cooks are frustrated by what gardeners call 'the hungry gap'. As spring progresses, longer, brighter days with a hint of the warmth to come signal a change of appetite to lighter, more colourful food and the delicate flavours of the new season's produce. But winter vegetables come to an end early in spring, while the growing season is barely under way, and we must wait for summer before most local crops mature. The weather is often fickle and on many a day the best place to be is in a warm kitchen. This can be a particularly satisfying time of year for baking — a comforting activity for a cold early spring day which fills the house with wonderful aromas and is not dependent on seasonal produce except, of course, for eggs, traditionally symbolic of spring and at their best. My 'seasons' vary slightly from the traditional, so spring recipes here are for March, April and May: summer for June, July and August: autumn for September, October and November: Christmas recipes for December, and winter for January and February.

HIGHLIGHTS of the season include Mother's Day, St Patrick's Day and Easter.

SUGGESTED MENUS

Mother's Day Breakfast in Bed
Spiced Fruit Compôte (see Winter recipes);
Marmalade Popovers; Dundee Marmalade.

St Patrick's Day Lunch
Carrot Soup with Tarragon, Hot Yeast Rolls;
Baked 'Limerick' Ham with Orange & Red-
currant Sauce and Glazed Jerusalem Artichokes;
Tangy Lemon Tart.

Easter Lunch or Dinner
Avocado & Citrus Salad;
Glazed Easter Chicken with Fresh Herb &
Pine Kernel Stuffing, Baked Cherry Tomatoes;
Chocolate Marquise with Crème Anglaise.

Easter Tea
Wholemeal Bread and Butter, Smoked Salmon;
Drop Scones with Strawberry Jam (Summer)
Easter Biscuits; Simnel Cake; Lemon Cake.

Dinner Party for Friends
Leek & Tomato Soup with Olive Bread;
Guard of Honour with Button Onions and
Spring Vegetables;
Gâteau Diane or Rhubarb with Orange.

Casual Bank Holiday Brunch
Lamb Sausages with Tomato Coulis;
Onion & Walnut Bread;
Green Salad with Orange Dressing;
Gooseberry Crumble Cake, Crème Fraîche.

Pre- or Post-Theatre Supper
Grilled Grapefruit;
Stir-Fried Chicken & Walnuts with Wild Rice;
Chocolate Roulade.

PRODUCE IN SEASON includes:

Vegetables: In addition to basic vegetables such as potatoes, carrots and onions which are available from one source or another all year round, those with more limited availability which are currently in season include artichokes (Jerusalem ending in March, globe starting the new season), asparagus (from May), broccoli, chicory, leeks, parsnips, spinach and the last of the brussels sprouts. Lettuce and other salads are either imported or grown under glass early in the season, although outdoor lettuce and other fast-growing produce such as spring onions gradually come in as the season progresses. In late May, the new season's produce begins to come in — the first new potatoes (imported or grown under glass), baby carrots, early broad beans and spinach. Fresh herbs are doing better, too. As well as the shrubby ones like rosemary, thyme and bay which have been available throughout the winter, fresh shoots are growing fast and, by late spring, there are plenty to choose from: chives, fennel, lovage, marjoram, sage and savory should all be cropping well. Parsley will be growing strongly and rosemary and thyme are putting out new, tender and aromatic growth. Mint is growing also, although, like tarragon, it isn't yet ready for picking.

Fruit: Gooseberries, from May; forced rhubarb is available from very early in the year; by April garden rhubarb appears. Imported apricots are welcome in late spring.

Fish: Most fish can be bought all year round, but particularly good or plentiful for at least part of spring are: brill, haddock, hake, halibut, herring, lobster, mackerel, mullet, mussels, native oyster, pike, plaice, salmon, salmon trout, scallops, skate, sole, turbot and whitebait.

Poultry and Game: Chicken, duck, goose (March), turkey, pigeon.

When the winter vegetables have finished and we are waiting impatiently for the new season's produce to start coming in, we have to use our imaginations to get the best out of basics, whether home-produced or imported. Salads grown under glass and the best of dried, frozen and tinned produce tide us over 'the hungry gap'. These are generally very simple products: dried pulses, rice and pasta are indispensable at this time of year, as is the ubiquitous frozen pea although there is an enormous difference between the qualities available, and buying the cheapest is usually a false economy. Tinned 'petits pois' are deservedly popular with the French — although not at all like fresh peas, they are excellent in their own way. Similarly tinned tomatoes, both whole and chopped, are essential to many a family meal for most of the year, and tinned beans — red kidney beans, butter beans, haricot beans, chick peas etc — are ideal when time is too short for lengthy soaking and cooking of the dry variety. They are equally good in both hot dishes and salads. As the days get brighter we feel the need for lighter, more colourful dishes than the ones we relished earlier in the year but, particularly in the early part of the season, they still need to provide warmth and comfort.

Spring can be a very deceptive season in our climate and, while longer days and brighter light make us feel the need for more colour, the weather can often be harsh so warming soups are very welcome.

Carrot Soup with Tarragon

Serves 4:
1½ lb/700g carrots
1 onion
2 medium-sized potatoes
1½ oz/40g butter
1 tablespoon olive oil
1 tablespoon freshly
  chopped tarragon
2½ pints/ 1.5 litres chicken
  or vegetable stock
Sea salt, freshly ground
  pepper and 2 teaspoons
  sugar
4 tablespoons cream or
  soured cream
Extra freshly chopped
  tarragon to garnish.

Carrot Soup with Tarragon is bright, nourishing and easy to make. Tarragon marries well with carrots and is now available fresh all year round from specialist growers. If in short supply, use a mixture of tarragon and parsley. [Microwave]

Peel and trim the carrots then grate coarsely, using a food processor if available. Chop the onion and peel and dice the potatoes. Heat the butter and oil in a large, heavy-based pan and cook the onion in it over gentle heat until soft and transparent, then add the carrots and potatoes and turn with a wooden spoon to coat the vegetables in butter and oil. Add the tarragon, cover and cook over very gentle heat for 15 minutes. Add the stock and seasonings, then simmer for 20 minutes, or until the vegetables are tender. Put through a mouli-légumes food mill, or blend in a food processor or liquidiser to make a purée. Return to the rinsed pan, stir in the cream and reheat gently. Serve with a scattering of freshly chopped tarragon and crusty home-baked bread.

Leek & Tomato Soup

Serves 6:
3 large leeks
1 oz/25g butter
1 tbsp olive oil
1 lb/450g tomatoes *or tinned tomatoes*
Sea salt, freshly ground
  black pepper and 1
  teaspoon sugar
2 medium potatoes
1¾ pints/ 1 litre chicken
  stock.

Leek & Tomato Soup makes the most of large, maincrop leeks which are at their best in late winter and early spring. If fresh tomatoes are too expensive or flavourless, use a tin of Italian chopped tomatoes instead. [Microwave]

Trim the leeks at the base and remove any coarse or damaged parts from the tops of the green leaves. Slit the leeks open lengthways, wash throughly under cold running water to remove all traces of grit, shake dry and slice finely. Reserve a handful of the finely-sliced leek to use as a garnish, then heat the butter and oil in a large, heavy-based pan. Add the rest of the leeks, cover and cook gently for 5-10 minutes until just softening but not browned. Add the peeled and roughly chopped tomatoes (or the contents of the tin, including juice), a good seasoning of salt and pepper and the sugar. Cover and leave to simmer while you peel and dice the potatoes, then add them together with the stock. Bring back up to the boil, cover and simmer for 20-30 minutes, until the potatoes are soft. Meanwhile, blanch the reserved sliced leeks by plunging them into boiling water for a couple of minutes, then refresh them in a colander under the cold tap so that they keep their bright colour. When the soup is ready, remove from the heat, pass through a mouli-légumes food mill or purée in a food processor or blender and return to the rinsed pan. Adjust the seasoning if necessary, bring back up to boiling point and serve very hot garnished with the reserved blanched leeks. Served with home-made brown bread, cheese and chutney or pickles, this makes a delicious, wholesome snack.

Green Lentil & Sorrel Soup

When the herbs are growing strongly in the late spring, try this Green Lentil & Sorrel Soup — an unfamiliar combination to Irish tastes, but a common country dish in France. It is an interesting soup with an earthy texture that is balanced up by a surprisingly subtle flavour — a great conversation piece. Make it with the delicious little mottled green Lentilles du Puy if possible, or similar small green or brown lentils from France that are often simply labelled 'rustique'. The more ordinary lentils benefit from an hour or two soaking in cold water before cooking, but the delicate Puy lentils can be cooked straight away. [Microwave]

Lay the lentils out on a tray and check through for bits of grit. Put into a large pan with the water and bring slowly to the boil. Simmer, partially covered, for about half an hour, or until the lentils are very tender and beginning to break up. Season lightly with salt. Meanwhile, wash the sorrel and shake it dry; remove any coarse stalks and chop the leaves roughly. Melt a good lump of butter, about 1-2 oz/25-50g, in a shallow pan and cook the sorrel in it gently, until it melts down to a creamy mush. Turn into the pan of lentils, stir in, then put the contents of the pan through a mouli-légumes or, in several batches, liquidise it in a blender. Return to the rinsed pan and, if necessary, thin it down a little with some extra water or stock. Season with salt, freshly ground pepper and a little sugar. Serve as a soup course — or, with fresh crusty bread, home-baked ham and chutney, it makes a marvellous casual lunch.

Variations: Ham stock could be used instead of water, if available. Watercress might replace the sorrel.

Homemade Lamb Sausages
with a Tomato Coulis

Once a regular on the menu at the late lamented restaurant, Reveries of Rosses Point, Sligo, Homemade Lamb Sausages with a Tomato Coulis made an especially original first course — and it's easy too. [Microwave]

Grind the lamb in a food processor; add fat and garlic and process until smooth. Add sherry and season well. Shape the meat into sausages with your hands or, using a 12"/30.5 cm long piece of clingfilm, spoon the meat along the length of the film, then roll up into a sausage shape. Remove clingfilm and cut into portions. Roll in bran or oatmeal, then cook as usual. (Better fried than grilled). Makes 12 sausages.

Chop tomatoes and herbs roughly. Combine with all other ingredients in a bowl; leave for 4 hours or overnight if possible. Purée and sieve. Serve warm, with the sausages.

Mushrooms au Gratin

Apart from the ubiquitous Mushrooms in Garlic Butter (which I love, but no deep frying) Mushrooms au Gratin has to be one of the tastiest little hot starters around. This version comes from Roche's Bistro in Malahide and is very more-ish.

Wipe and trim the mushrooms and cook in the butter over fairly high heat for about 8 minutes, turning frequently. Add the sherry and lemon juice and, after a few minutes, the cream. Bring to the boil, season to taste,

Serves 6:
7 oz/200g green or brown French lentils
4 pints/2.25 litres water
A large bunch of sorrel, about 8 oz/225g
Butter
Salt, freshly ground pepper and sugar.

Homemade Lamb Sausages
Serves 4:
1 lb/450g lamb scraps, trimmed of gristle
1/2 lb/225g pork fat
Small clove garlic
1/2 tablespoon sherry
Salt and freshly ground black pepper
Bran or fine oatmeal for rolling.

Tomato Coulis:
1 lb/450g very ripe tomatoes
Bunch mixed herbs, eg basil, tarragon, parsley (about 1 oz/25g)
2 tsp caster sugar
1/2 tsp cayenne
4 fl oz/100 ml olive oil.

Mushrooms au Gratin
Serves 4-6:
1 lb/450g button mushrooms
1 oz/25g butter
Small glass of medium or sweet sherry
Juice of 1/2 lemon
1/2 pint/300 ml cream
Salt and freshly ground pepper
Pinch of grated nutmeg
A little beurre manié (equal parts of flour and butter, worked together)
Grated Parmesan or Regato to finish.

then thicken a little with beurre manié, as required. Divide between six ramekins or four gratin dishes, sprinkle generously with the grated cheese and grill until brown and bubbling. Serve very hot with freshly baked bread.

Peperonata

Serves 4-6:

4 large peppers, preferably a mixture of red and green
1 large onion
8 large, ripe tomatoes, OR 1 tin Italian plum tomatoes
2 or 3 cloves garlic, or to taste
1 oz/25g butter
2 tablespooons olive oil
Sea salt and freshly ground black pepper
1 dessertspoon caster sugar.

Sweet peppers are also particularly useful in spicy cooked dishes which can be served hot as an accompaniment to simple roasts or grilled food or cold as a side salad or first course, such as Ratatouille (see Summer Soups etc) and its simpler cousin Peperonata, which depends less on seasonal ingredients and is ideal for this time of year. When tomatoes are over-priced and flavourless, use tinned instead. [Microwave]

Halve and deseed the peppers, then slice fairly finely. Peel and chop the onion. If using fresh tomatoes, plunge briefly in boiling water to loosen the skins, then peel, remove the core if it is tough, and chop the flesh roughly. Peel the garlic and chop finely or crush in a little salt. Heat the butter and oil in a flameproof casserole, add the peppers and onion, cover and cook gently for about 10 minutes, until softening but not brown. Add the tomatoes (with their juices) and garlic, season with salt, pepper and sugar, cover and cook gently for another half hour or until the vegetables are soft and most of the tomato juice has evaporated. Check the seasoning, adjust if necessary, transfer to a serving dish and serve hot or cold.

Soused Seatrout Canapés

Serves 6:

For every 4 oz/100g sea trout trimmings, you need:
$1/2$ teaspoon fine sea salt
$1/2$ teaspoon brown sugar
3 good pinches of freshly ground black pepper
$1/2$ teaspoon freshly chopped fennel
2 teaspoons of chive flowers
3 teaspoons of lemon juice.

The Old Rectory in Wicklow is well known for the originality and pretty presentation of its food — and this lovely quick recipe for Soused Seatrout Canapés is no exception. It is an ideal way to use up fresh sea trout trimmings and can be served as a buffet dish or, in suitable salad wrappings, as a delicious canapé before dinner.

Before weighing the fish, remove the skin by scraping under the flesh with a sharp knife, then use tweezers to remove any bones. Chop the prepared fish into $1/4$"/0.6 cm cubes. Toss in a bowl with all the other ingredients — the resulting mixture is 'cured' by the salt and lemon juice and does not need cooking. It can be served immediately, when the fish is still translucent, the flavour vibrant and the texture soft, or it can be kept in the fridge for up to 24 hours, when the lemon juice will have made the flesh opaque, firmer and the flavour more founded. To serve, divide the mixture into 12 portions and pile onto rounds of cucumber or toast, or wrap in softened lettuce leaves. (To soften, place in a polythene bag and microwave for a few seconds until they wilt.) Serves 2 canapés per person.

Avocado Salad with Citrus Fruits

Serves 6-8:

3-4 large ripe avocados
Juice of 1 lemon
2 large grapefruit
2 large oranges
Caster sugar
Mint leaves to garnish.

Avocado flesh discolours very easily: always use a stainless steel knife for preparation and sprinkle with lemon juice or another suitable acid as soon as the flesh has been cut, or it will become unattractive almost immediately.

Use slightly over-ripe avocados in a colourful and refreshing first course. This salad is served immediately, but all ingredients should be well chilled before use if possible.

Using a stainless steel knife, peel and halve the avocados, remove the stones, then cut into quarters and slice thinly. Sprinkle thoroughly with the lemon juice. Cut a slice from the top and bottom of the grapefruit and oranges so that they will stand steadily on a board then, using a sharp serrated knife, cut through peel and pith in strips from all round each fruit and remove; discard the peel. Working over a bowl to catch both segments and juice, segment the oranges and grapefruit by cutting between the flesh and segment membranes. When all the segments have been removed, squeeze out any remaining juice from the membranes before discarding them. Arrange the drained avocado slices and citrus segments on individual serving dishes. Mix all the juices together and sweeten lightly with a little caster sugar, then sprinkle this mixture over the salads, garnish with little mint leaves and serve immediately.

Green Salad with Orange Dressing

Another variation on the citrus and avocado theme, this is a mouthwateringly piquant starter to serve with hot herb bread.

Prepare all the salad vegetables except the avocado — shred the lettuce, remove coarse stems from the watercress and chop the leaves roughly and cut the cucumber into matchsticks, leaving the skin on if you like it — and put them into a large salad bowl. Toast the almond flakes, watching carefully as they burn very suddenly. Make the dressing by whisking together the grated orange rind, juice and olive oil; season to taste with salt, pepper and turmeric, if using. Lastly, using a stainless steel knife, peel the avocado, remove the stone and slice the flesh thinly. Add to the salad bowl with the almond flakes and immediately add the dressing. Toss lightly and serve at once.

Serves 4:

8 leaves cos lettuce or other crunchy lettuce
1/2 bunch of watercress, washed
1/4 cucumber
l small green pepper
l avocado (optional)
l oz/25 g almond flakes

Dressing:

Grated rind of l small orange
2 tbsp orange juice
2 fl oz/50 ml olive oil
Pinch turmeric (optional)
Sea salt, sugar and freshly ground black pepper.

Crunchy Spring Coleslaw

It seems incredible that sweet peppers were unusual enough to be regarded as exotics only a decade ago — now they're one of our most reliable all-year vegetables, usually available in a range of colours as well as the more common green, and particularly useful in the spring and early summer when the winter vegetables are coming to an end and the next season's are still a long way from maturity. Peppers give a special piquancy to this Crunchy Spring Coleslaw which, with its tangy mixture of dressings, will liven up any meal, especially a cold lunch or supper — serve with cold meat or poultry and crusty bread and butter.

Trim the cabbage, halve and remove core. Put one half aside and cut the remaining one into quarters, then slice finely against the grain to shred and put into a large salad bowl. Peel and coarsely grate the carrot; add to the bowl. Quarter, de-seed and finely slice the peppers, then add to the bowl along with the raisins and walnuts. Next make the dressing by putting the dry ingredients into a small bowl or jug, then whisking in the vinegar and, when the seasonings have dissolved, the oil. Add the dressing to the salad bowl, mix everything well and chill for half an hour. Before serving, mix in a few tablespoons of single cream to the mayonnaise to thin it down to a fairly thick pouring consistency, then add it to the salad and toss well. Taste for seasoning and sharpness, and sprinkle with freshly chopped herbs.

Note: If soured cream is used instead of mayonnaise, it should not need thinning. A good sharp natural yogurt is another possible alternative if a lighter dressing is preferred.

Crunchy Spring Coleslaw: Serves 6

1/2 small white cabbage
l large carrot
l green and l red pepper
2 tablespoons raisins
l tablespoon roughly chopped walnuts
3 tablespoons home-made mayonnaise or soured cream
A little single cream/top of the milk to thin the mayonnaise
l tablespoon freshly chopped herbs, eg chives and parsley

Dressing:

Sea salt and freshly ground black pepper
l teaspoon caster sugar and a good pinch of paprika
2 tablespoons white wine vinegar or sherry vinegar
4 tablespoons olive oil or a mixture of olive and sunflower oils.

Sugar-Browned Potatoes

A traditional Danish method of cooking the first new potatoes.

Wash the potatoes thoroughly in cold water and cook in boiling salted water for about 10 minutes, until just tender. Drain the potatoes, leave until cool enough to handle, then peel off the skins (unless the potatoes are very fresh and the skins have already come off in the washing). Put the sugar in a frying pan over low heat and stir occasionally until the sugar has melted and is a golden caramel colour. Add the butter and stir until thoroughly blended with the sugar. Rinse the potatoes in cold water to make it easier to coat them with the caramel, then add them to the pan and continue cooking over low heat, shaking the pan gently from time to time, until they are evenly glazed and golden brown. Arrange immediately in a warm serving dish, or around a joint of roast meat or poultry.

Variation: **Glazed Jerusalem Artichokes** can be prepared in the same way: peel them immediately before cooking (to prevent discoloration) and cut up as necessary to give even-sized pieces, then be careful to remove

Sugar-Browned Potatoes: Serves 4

2 lb/900g small, new potatoes
l oz/25g caster sugar
2 oz/50g unsalted butter.

them from the cooking water while they are still quite firm or they will break up in the frying pan. Do not discard the water in which artichokes are cooked, as it makes a good jellied stock.

Sweet & Sour Onions

Serves 6:
6 even-sized onions
Sea salt and freshly ground
  black pepper
2 oz/50g light golden
  brown sugar
½ pint/300 ml chicken or
  vegetable stock
1 level tablespoon cornflour
  or arrowroot
1 tablespoon cider vinegar.

Although they have now been in storage for a long time and you have to be careful to avoid buying soft onions at this time of year, good keepers are always available and onions make another of the great year-round stand-bys which are so useful during the between-season gap when winter vegetables are finishing and the new spring ones still have a long way to go before harvest. This recipe for Sweet & Sour Onions makes a lively accompaniment for any plainly grilled or fried meat or poultry.

Preheat a moderate oven, 350°F, 180°C, Gas mark 4. Peel the onions and put them into a flameproof casserole. Cover with cold water, bring to the boil, cover and simmer for 10 minutes. Drain, season with salt and pepper and sprinkle the sugar over. Add the stock, cover and bake in the oven for about half an hour, until tender. Transfer the onions to a serving dish and keep warm. Blend the cornflour or arrowroot with the vinegar, stir in a little of the hot juices, then add this mixture to the casserole and bring up to the boil, stirring, and cook for a minute or two until the sauce is smooth and clear. Check the seasoning, pour the sauce over onions and serve with any plainly cooked meat or poultry, especially pork chops or chicken portions.

Glazed Carrots

Serves 4:
1 lb/450g young carrots
1 oz/25g butter
Sea salt and freshly ground
  black pepper
1 teaspoon caster sugar
1 level tablespoon freshly
  chopped tarragon.

When the first young carrots start to come onto the market in the late spring, make the most of their delicate flavour by cooking them in a lovely buttery coating. Tarragon is especially delicious with carrots, particularly if you are serving them with fish or poultry, but parsley can be used instead if tarragon is unavailable — flat-leafed French parsley is a particularly good substitute, as it has a much better flavour than the more common curly parsley.

Wash and scrape the carrots and slice quite thinly. Melt the butter in a pan, add the carrots and season with freshly ground pepper and the sugar. Add just enough cold water to cover the carrots, bring to the boil, cover and cook gently for about 15 minutes or until the carrots are tender. Remove the lid, raise the heat and cook briskly until the water has evaporated and only the butter remains — but watch closely to prevent burning. Remove from the heat, add the freshly chopped tarragon (or parsley), sprinkle lightly with sea salt and toss to mix well.

Despite its frustrations, spring is a very interesting season for the cook as our tastes and the ingredients available change dramatically over quite a short period, ranging from the roasts and casseroles which still suit cold and blustery March through to the light, colourful May meals which herald the summer. Food for St Patrick's Day, for example, tends to be hearty, with baked ham and cabbage or spring greens especially appropriate, while Easter food signals a change of mood as poultry or lamb is served in colourful combinations with fresh herbs and young vegetables, often including new potatoes. Everyday food changes character gradually, influenced as much by the weather as the availability of fresh produce, but sauces are enlivened by fresh fruit, especially rhubarb and later gooseberries, and salads benefit from the pep of young herbs. Mention spring and the first meat to come to mind is lamb, but joints are small and expensive until later in the season, making it very much a special occasion meat meanwhile, ideal for a dinner party or as an alternative to poultry at Easter for a small number. Traditionally, of course, spring is the season for poultry, especially chicken, and fresh young free-range chickens are particularly good. If you entertain large numbers at Easter, turkey is the ideal choice and fast becoming traditional.

Baked 'Limerick' Ham
with Juniper Berries and Glazed Jerusalem Artichokes served with Orange & Redcurrant Sauce

This is the kind of heart-warming dish I make often in the late winter and early spring but, although it is more economical than most special-occasion meals (especially if you use inexpensive shoulder of bacon) it is quite impressive and could be useful when Easter falls very early or — as can sometimes happen — when the weather is particularly grim and not at all spring-like. The idea is based on the old eighteenth-century speciality, Limerick Ham, which was flavoured with the juniper berries that grew wild in the area — hence the inclusion of juniper berries in the glaze and gin, which is juniper-based, in the sauce.

Soak the joint in cold water overnight. When ready to cook, drain and weigh the joint. Return to a pan of fresh cold water, add a bayleaf if you like, cover tightly and bring gently to the boil, then reduce the heat to a gentle simmer and cook for 15 minutes to the lb/450g and 15 minutes over, about 1-1½ hours. When the time is up, remove the joint from the pan and set the stock aside for making soup. Preheat a fairly hot oven, about 400°F, 200°C, Gas mark 6. Peel the skin and any thick fat off the joint with a sharp knife. Mix the mustard, sugar and juniper; spread evenly all over the surface of the meat, put the joint into a roasting tin and finish cooking in the hot oven for another 10 minutes per lb/450g and 10 minutes over (i.e. an hour for a 5 lb/2.3 Kg joint) until it is a crunchy golden brown. Remove from the oven and leave in a warm place to relax for 15 minutes before carving.

Meanwhile, prepare the **Glazed Jerusalem Artichokes:** peel the artichokes and cut up to about the same size so they will cook evenly. (If this preparation is done ahead, make sure the artichokes are kept in acidulated water before cooking, to prevent discoloration.) Boil for 5-10 minutes until just tender, then drain but reserve the cooking liquor which has a delicious flavour and forms a clear jelly when cold. Put the roasting tin over a moderate heat on the hob, tip the boiled artichokes into it and turn them in the sugar-and-mustard flavoured juices from the baked ham until they are golden brown and glazed all over. Keep warm while making the sauce: finely grate the zest from one of the oranges and blanch it in a jug of boiling water for 1 minute then turn into a sieve and refresh under

Serves 6-8:

1 good joint of ham or bacon, 4-5 lb/1.8-2.3 Kg weight

1 rounded tablespoon Dijon mustard

1 rounded tablespoon Demerara sugar

1 teaspoon juniper berries, crushed

2-3 lb/900g-1.4 Kg Jerusalem artichokes

Sauce:

Finely grated zest of 1 orange

Juice of 2 oranges

3 tablespoons redcurrant jelly

A good dash of Cork gin (optional).

Ham & Pea Soup

To make a wonderfully easy Ham & Pea Soup, soak about 8 oz/225g (half a packet) green split peas in cold water overnight, then rinse and drain. Skim off any fat from the cold stock, then add the soaked peas, and a couple of finely chopped onions. Bring up to the boil, skim and simmer for ½ hour or until tender. Liquidise, add any bits of leftover ham, chopped, and adjust seasoning. Serve with home-made brown bread and farmhouse cheese for a perfect snack lunch.

Glazed Easter Chicken

Serves 6–8:

1 large chicken, 5-6lb/ 2.3-2.7 Kg (or 2 smaller birds)
6-8 slices streaky bacon to bard.

Stuffing:

3 oz/75g pine kernels
6 oz/175g fresh breadcrumbs, preferably wholemeal or a mixture of white and brown
2oz/50g finely chopped mixed fresh herbs, eg parsley, chives, thyme, rosemary, lovage, marjoram, sorrel etc, as available
Finely grated rind and juice of 1 small lemon
Sea salt, freshly ground black pepper and a grating of nutmeg
3 oz/75g softened butter
1 large egg to bind.

Accompaniments:

3-4 lb/1.4-1.8 Kg potatoes, peeled for roasting
12 oz/350g streaky rashers, rolled and strung on skewers
12 oz/350g best quality sausages
A bunch of watercress, washed and trimmed, for garnish.

Continued on facing page

cold running water; drain well. Squeeze the juice from the other two oranges. Melt the redcurrant jelly in a small pan (or in a bowl in the microwave). Stir in the orange juice and rind, then add a good dash of gin and turn into a sauce boat or small jug. Serve the ham with the sauce, the artichokes and all the crusty sediment from the roasting tin, potatoes boiled or baked in their jackets, bâtons of carrot and any lightly cooked green vegetable.

Glazed Easter Chicken with Fresh Herb & Pine Kernel Stuffing

Although modern farming methods have extended the seasons in many ways, there's nothing to rival the pleasure of food when it is just coming to the peak of maturity in its natural time — respecting the succession of the seasons is the surest way to guarantee real variety and balance in the diet and the only way to retain that wonderful element of surprise as each one presents its unique bounty. All of which leads me to the fact that, although chicken is now very much an all-year food, a genuinely free-range bird eaten in spring, at the height of its traditional season, is in a league of its own. So why not bring together all the traditional associations of Easter, especially chickens and eggs, to make a spring feast based on poultry — a large chicken is suggested to serve 6-8, but a capon (average weight 6-8 lb, serves 8-10) or a small turkey would be equally suitable for a larger number. Treat a capon in the same way as the large chicken below. Double the quantities of stuffing for a 10-12lb/4.5-5.4 Kg turkey and see Chistmas Section for cooking instructions. When selecting herbs for the stuffing, be careful to keep the balance in favour of lighter flavours like parsley and chives and go easy on dominant flavours like rosemary and thyme. Including accompaniments such as bacon rolls, sausages, bread sauce and so on will allow for teenage appetites and/or much greater flexibility of numbers.

Wipe the bird out with a clean damp cloth or kitchen paper and remove the two pieces of fat from just inside the body cavity. (Render down for roasting the potatoes.) To make the stuffing, first brown the pine kernels by toasting for a few minutes on a baking tray in a hot oven, or by turning frequently in a heavy cast-iron frying pan over gentle heat. Put the breadcrumbs, finely chopped herbs, grated lemon rind and a good seasoning of sea salt, freshly ground pepper and grated nutmeg into a large bowl and mix well. Add the butter, which needs to be almost runny so that it will blend easily, and the lemon juice and egg, lightly beaten together. Mix well with a fork to bind all ingredients thoroughly together, then use to stuff the chicken. Avoid packing too tightly — if there is any stuffing left over, form it into balls and cook it alongside the chicken for the last 20-30 minutes of cooking time. Secure the chicken with a fine skewer and truss with cotton string for cooking. Put the bird into a deep roasting tin and lay the streaky bacon rashers over the breast and legs to keep them moist during cooking.

Preheat a warm oven, 325°F, 160°C, Gas mark 3.

To calculate the cooking time, weigh the stuffed chicken and allow 25 minutes per lb/450g and 25 minutes over. (If cooking two smaller birds, allow only 20 minutes per lb/450g and 20 minutes over, and cook at a higher temperature, 375°F,190°C, gas mark 5.) Put the chicken on a low-to-middle shelf in the preheated oven and put the two cushions of fat, removed earlier, into another roasting tin and leave them to render down — the fat will give excellent flavour to roast potatoes, which can be put in the oven about ¾-1 hour before the chicken will be ready.

While the chicken is cooking, prepare the glaze — for a good, free-range chicken this is purely optional, but it gives the bird a festive appearance and is very useful for making mass-produced poultry more interesting.

Put the granulated sugar into a heavy-based pan over moderate heat and stir until the sugar has dissolved. Boil until the sugar has turned to a caramel colour, then remove from the heat immediately, cool slightly, then add the water and vinegar. (Be careful, as adding water will make the hot caramel boil up.) Return to the heat and stir to dissolve the caramel. Using a vegetable peeler, peel the zest from one of the oranges and cut it up into fine julienne strips. Squeeze and strain the juice from both oranges and add to the caramel mixture with the shredded peel. Blend the cornflour with the cider or wine and mix this into the caramel mixture. Bring to the boil, stirring, and simmer, uncovered, for 5 minutes. Keep warm.

Half an hour before the chicken is due to be served, move it to another roasting tin; remove (and reserve) the streaky rashers and brush the chicken all over with the caramel glaze. Reserve any remaining glaze and keep warm. Raise the oven temperature to 375°F, 190°C, Gas mark 5 and return the chicken to the oven, along with any balls of leftover stuffing, bacon rolls and sausages. Meanwhile, pour off most of the fat from the tin the chicken was cooked in (and reserve for use in cooking). Finely chop a small onion, scatter it into the roasting tin and fry on the hob, over gentle heat, until softened and golden brown. Sprinkle in about a tablespoonful of flour and cook, stirring, for a few minutes, then add chicken or vegetable stock as required to make a gravy to the thickness you like. If you have some spare wine or cider include it to enrich the flavour. Season to taste with sea salt, freshly ground pepper and, if you like, a light grating of nutmeg. Pour into a bowl or gravy boat and keep warm. When the chicken is cooked, remove to a warmed serving dish, pour over any remaining glaze and serve surrounded by the bacon rolls, sausages, stuffing balls and a garnish of fresh watercress. In addition to the accompaniments given above, bread sauce and cranberry sauce or redcurrant jelly are suitable: other vegetables might include whole young carrots and very lightly cooked spring cabbage.

Continued from previous page

Glaze:

4 oz/100g granulated sugar
1 tablespoon water
1 tablespoon vinegar
2 oranges
1 level tablespoon cornflour
1/4 pint/150 ml dry cider or white wine.

Guard of Honour with Button Onions and Spring Vegetables

Apart from poultry, lamb is the most traditional festive meat for Easter and a dramatic presentation such as Guard of Honour with Button Onions and Spring Vegetables is particularly appropriate to herald the change of season.

Get the butcher to chine the joints and remove the fat and skin from the top 2"/5 cm of the rib bones. Preheat a moderate oven, 350°F. 180°C, Gas mark 4. Arrange the two joints, skin side outwards, with the cutlet bones interlacing the top like a guard of honour. Tie with cotton string between every two or three cutlets and sprinkle with salt and pepper. Wrap foil around the cutlet bones to prevent them from charring. Weigh the joint and calculate the cooking time, allowing 20 minutes per lb/450g and 20 minutes over. Melt the lard or dripping in a roasting tin, add the meat and put in the centre of the oven. Meanwhile, peel the onions or shallots: put them into a large pan of boiling water, bring back up to the boil and blanch for about 30 seconds; at the sink, tip into a colander and cool under the cold tap, then trim the stalk and root and slip off the skins with your fingers, like peeling tomatoes. Leave the onions or shallots whole and add to a fresh pan of lightly salted boiling water; cover and simmer for 20 minutes, then drain and keep hot. Put the shelled peas or topped and tailed mangetout into a pan with the sugar and barely enough water to cover. Bring to the boil, simmer until just tender, then drain and mix with the onions. Likewise, scrape the carrots and trim, leaving a little of the green stalk on. Put into a pan with a little water and cook until just tender, then drain and mix with the other vegetables.

Serves 6-8:

2 fair ends of lamb (8 cutlets each)
Sea salt and freshly ground black pepper
2 oz/50g white fat or dripping
2 lb/900g button onions or shallots
2 lb/900g peas (shelled weight) or mangetout
1/2 teaspoon caster sugar
2 lb/900g young carrots
New potatoes (accompaniment)

When the joint is cooked, remove from the roasting tin, take off the string and foil and dress each bone with a cutlet frill. Pour off any excess fat from the roasting tin and either make a thickened gravy, or pour off the pan juices and any sediment and serve them in a sauce boat. Arrange the vegetables around the meat and serve with the gravy, mint or redcurrant jelly and potatoes — if you can get new potatoes grown under glass for Easter, they are a real treat, otherwise a garlicky Potato Gratin is simple and delicious.

Variation: Guard of Honour can also be served as a stuffed roast by filling the cavity with any suitable stuffing mixture. The stuffing given above for Easter Chicken, for example, could easily be adapted for lamb by omitting the mixture of fresh herbs and substituting 1 tablespoon rosemary (or to taste) and 2 good cloves garlic, peeled and slivered. Otherwise make the stuffing as above and use to fill the arch underneath the Guard of Honour; any leftover stuffing can be formed into balls and cooked around the joint for the last 30-40 minutes. To calculate the cooking time, remember to weigh the joint *after* stuffing. The same recipe can be also be adapted to make a simpler **Rack of Lamb**.

Pork Chops with Orange Sauce

Serves 4:

4 pork chops
l orange
1/2 pint/300 ml orange juice
l oz/25g demerara sugar
1/2 teaspoon ground ginger
l teaspoon arrowroot
A little sunflower oil for
   frying.

There is more to spring meals than one or two grand menus over the Easter holidays. For a simple meal that is slightly out of the ordinary and would equally well suit a family dinner or casual entertaining, try this delicious recipe for Pork Chops with Orange Sauce.

Heat a little oil in a heavy frying pan over fairly high heat, add the chops and cook quickly on each side to brown, then reduce the heat to moderate and cook for about 8-10 minutes on each side. Meanwhile, finely grate about a teaspoon of zest from the orange rind, then peel the orange and divide it into segments. Put the grated zest into a small pan with the orange juice, sugar and ginger, then bring up to the boil and simmer for 10 minutes. Blend the arrowroot with a little water to make a thin cream and add to the orange juice mixture. Drain any surplus fat from the chop pan, leaving any crusty bits. Add the orange sauce and segments, mix well, cover, and simmer for 5 minutes before pouring over the chops. Serve with rice.

Stuffed Mackerel with Rhubarb Sauce

Stuffed Mackerel: Serves 4

4 whole mackerel, cleaned
l onion
1 oz/25g butter
4 heaped tablespoons fresh
   white breadcrumbs
l rounded tablespoon
   freshly chopped parsley
Finely grated zest of l lemon
Sea salt, freshly ground
   pepper and grated
   nutmeg to taste
l egg, lightly beaten
Melted butter or olive oil
   for grilling.

Sauce:

8 oz/225g rhubarb
   (trimmed weight)
3 fl oz/75 ml water
1-2 oz/25-50g caster sugar,
   or to taste
l oz/25g butter
l tablespoon freshly
   chopped tarragon or 2
   teaspoons dried.
   (Optional)

For farmers and gardeners alike, things are on the move and, however slow it seems at first, new season's produce is beginning to inch its way into the kitchen, bringing with it a freshness and lightness of touch which heralds summer. Rhubarb, for example, although technically a vegetable, is generally treated as a fruit and much appreciated at this time of year when most of the native fruits are out of season. Like other sharply-flavoured fruits — gooseberry is the classic, a little later in the season — rhubarb makes an ideal accompaniment to balance up the richness of oily fish. This recipe for Stuffed Mackerel with Rhubarb Sauce is as delicious as it is economical — a winning combination. [Microwave]

Ask the fishmonger to bone the mackerel, or do it yourself: open out the body of the cleaned fish, turn flesh side down on a board and run your thumb firmly down the back bone — when you turn the fish over, the bones should lift out in one complete section. Peel and finely chop the onion, melt the butter in a pan and cook the onion gently in it for 5-10 minutes, until softening but not browning. Add the breadcrumbs, parsley, lemon zest, salt, freshly ground pepper and a little grated nutmeg. Mix well, then add the beaten egg to bind. Divide the mixture between the four fish, secure with cocktail sticks and brush with melted butter or olive oil. Preheat the grill and cook under moderate heat for about 8 minutes on each side.

Meanwhile, make the sauce: Cut the rhubarb up into short lengths, about ½"/1.2 cm, and put into a saucepan with the water, about 1 oz/25g sugar, the butter and tarragon, if using. Cook over gentle heat until the rhubarb is tender, but do not allow it to become mushy. Taste for sweetness and add extra sugar if necessary, bearing in mind that the sauce needs to be quite sharp. Serve the stuffed mackerel with the hot sauce, accompanied by potatoes boiled in their jackets, or creamed potato, and a salad.

Prawns Provençale

Shellfish are often quite good value in the late winter and early spring and this recipe for Prawns Provençale is both easy and versatile. [Microwave]

If the prawns have been bought raw, cook them in boiling water for about 5 minutes until bright pink, then tip into a colander and refresh under cold running water to cool. Peel off the shells and, using a sharp knife, make a shallow cut along the back so that the dark intestinal vein can be removed. Peel and finely chop the onion and garlic. Heat the oil and butter in a heavy-based pan and gently cook the onion in it without browning, for 5 minutes until beginning to soften. Add the garlic and stir around over gentle heat for a minute, then add the prawns and cook for about 3 minutes before adding the peeled and roughly chopped tomatoes (with their juices) and the wine. Season to taste with sea salt, freshly ground black pepper and the caster sugar, then bring to the boil and simmer, uncovered, for about 6 minutes. Blend the cornflour or arrowroot with a tablespoon of water or wine and stir into the prawns. Bring back up to the boil and simmer for a few minutes, stirring, until the sauce has thickened and cleared. Remove from the heat, stir in the parsley and serve immediately with rice — a mixture of long-grain and wild rice is interesting and looks attractive — and buttered mangetout or a mixed leaf salad.

Serves 4 as a first course, or 2 as a main course:

1 lb/450g prawn tails, shelled weight
2 onions
4 cloves garlic
2 tablespoons olive oil
1 oz/25g butter
1 lb/450g ripe tomatoes OR a 16 oz/450g tin chopped tomatoes
1 small glass dry white wine
Sea salt and freshly ground black pepper
1 teaspoon caster sugar
1 teaspoon cornflour or arrowroot
1 heaped tablespoon freshly chopped parsley, preferably French flat-leafed.

Lambs' Liver with Dubonnet & Orange, served with Glazed Onions

If you leave lambs' liver soaking in milk until you are ready to cook it, it has a tenderising effect and makes the flavour more subtle, almost like calves' liver (which is much more expensive). Try this classic combination: Lambs' Liver with Dubonnet & Orange, served with Glazed Onions. The suggested accompaniments — creamed potatoes and grilled tomatoes and mushrooms — make this a colourful and well-balanced meal, requiring nothing more than a refreshing green salad and perhaps a piece of fresh fruit to be served afterwards.

Rinse the lambs' liver, pat dry and lay in a shallow dish; add just enough milk to cover, cover with a lid or clingfilm and refrigerate overnight or for several hours before use. Heat the olive oil and butter together very gently in a large, deep frying pan and cook the finely chopped shallots and the crushed garlic in it over very low heat, covered, until soft and just beginning to colour. Drain the liver and discard the milk. Pat dry with kitchen paper, then cut into even slices about ½"/1.2 cm thick and coat lightly with flour which has been seasoned with salt and pepper. Add the liver to the pan containing the shallots and garlic in one layer and continue to cook gently. When you see the blood rise in it, turn over and cook the second side over even lower heat for a slightly shorter time. Remove to a warmed plate and cover with as much of the shallots and garlic as you can remove from the pan with a slotted spoon. Add the orange juice and the Dubonnet to the juices left in the pan, scraping the base well with a wooden spatula. Bring to the boil and cook briskly for a couple of minutes to reduce by about half. Remove from the heat, add the parsley, orange and lemon zests (keep

Serves 4:

1 lb/450g lambs' liver
Milk for soaking (optional)
1 tablespoon olive oil
1½ oz/40g butter
2 shallots
2 cloves garlic
Seasoned flour
Juice of 1 orange
5 fl oz/125 ml red Dubonnet
2 -3 tablespoons freshly chopped parsley
Coarsely grated zest of 1 orange, blanched
1 teaspoon finely grated lemon zest
Sea salt, freshly ground black pepper.

a bit back for garnish if you like) and stir in. Check the seasoning and add sea salt, freshly ground black pepper and a pinch of caster sugar if necessary. Pour over the liver and serve with mashed potato, glazed onions and grilled tomatoes and mushrooms. Scatter any remaining parsley and orange zest over the liver just before serving.

For the **Glazed Onions:** To a large pan of boiling water, add 1 lb/450g button onions or shallots and boil for 1 minute, then drain and peel. (The skins will come off easily, like blanched tomatoes.) Melt 2 oz/50g butter (preferably unsalted) in the empty pan, add the onions and turn over low heat for 5-10 minutes until beginning to soften, then sprinkle over 2 tablespoons caster sugar and continue cooking, turning the onions all the time, for another few minutes until they are evenly glazed and tender. Serve with any remaining glaze scraped from the pan onto the onions.

Kidneys in Mustard Sauce with Mixed Leaf & Fresh Herb Salad

This is a colourful and piquant dish, which is wonderfully delicious as long as the kidneys are really fresh — keep refrigerated, of course, and use them within 24 hours.

Remove the cushion of fat from around the kidneys, snip out the core with scissors and remove the skin. Put the kidneys into a basin, cover with cold water and a splash of vinegar, and leave to soak for an hour. Meanwhile, prepare the salad: trim any coarse outer leaves from the curly endive and break the leaves up into manageable sections; trim the Belgian endive and cut quite thickly into slices about 1/2"/1 cm wide. Trim the watercress, removing any damaged leaves and coarse lower stems. Put all the leaves into a large bowl of cold water, rinse well, dry in a salad spinner and put into a salad bowl with the chopped herbs. Put the vinegar, mustard, salt, pepper and sugar into a small jug and whisk vigorously to dissolve the seasonings, then whisk in the oil(s); taste and adjust sharpness to taste; set aside until required.

When ready to cook the kidneys, drain them, pat dry with kitchen paper and slice thickly. Heat the butter and olive oil in a frying pan until foaming, then add the kidneys and cook gently for 5 minutes. Be careful not to overcook. Season well with salt and pepper, sprinkle over the flour and stir well, then add the soured cream and mustard to taste — the sauce should have quite a piquant flavour. Bring up to the boil, stir until thick and smooth, then remove from the heat and serve immediately with the tossed salad and creamed potatoes or rice — or serve simply with buttered toast as a snack. *Variation:* Don't be tempted to make the Mixed Leaf Salad too complicated, but do consider adding a few broken walnuts and including a tablespoonful of walnut oil in the dressing — the robust flavours and textures work well together.

Chicken & Walnut Stir-Fry

Nuts, especially walnuts, also marry well with chicken as in this oriental-style Chicken & Walnut Stir-Fry which makes an ideal midweek meal for two as it is so quick and easy. If speed is an essential ingredient of this meal, make sure you have the rice cooking and the salad prepared before you start cooking — then allow about 15 minutes.

Peel and finely chop the onion. Heat the oil in a wok or frying pan, add the onion and cook gently for a couple of minutes, stirring occasionally, then add the roughly chopped walnut pieces. Meanwhile, dice the chicken into 1/2"/1.2 cm pieces and toss in the cornflour and salt; shake off and

---

Serves 4:

8 lambs' kidneys
A splash of vinegar (see method)
1 1/2 oz/40g butter
1 tablespoon olive oil
Salt and pepper
1 rounded teaspoon flour
1 carton (5 fl oz/ 125 ml) soured cream
1 tablespoon wholegrain or smooth Dijon mustard, or to taste

Mixed Leaf & Fresh Herb Salad:

1/2 head curly endive ('frisee')
1 head Belgian endive
1 bunch watercress
2 tablespoons freshly chopped herbs: eg chives, parsley, thyme
1 tablespoon balsamic or sherry vinegar
1 rounded teaspoon Dijon mustard, smooth or grainy
Salt, freshly ground black pepper, caster sugar
3 tablespoons olive oil, or a mixture of oils.

Chicken and Walnut: Serves 2

1 onion
3 tablespoons sunflower oil
2-3 oz/50-75g walnut pieces
2 chicken breasts, boned and skinned
1 level tablespoon cornflour
Pinch of salt
2-3 tablespoons dry sherry
1 teaspoon caster sugar
2 teaspoons soy sauce, or to taste
A little stock or water, if required.

Facing page: Stuffed Mackerel with Rhubarb Sauce, page 22
Overleaf: Filo Chicken Parcels with Tarragon, page 27

discard any excess cornflour. Remove the onions and walnuts from the pan with a slotted spoon and keep warm. Add a little extra oil to the pan if required (a tablespoon of olive or walnut oil would not go amiss for the flavour) and cook the chicken pieces in it over fairly brisk heat for several minutes, keeping it moving all the time. Add the sherry, sugar, and soy sauce to taste, return the onions and walnuts to the pan and cook, stirring, for another minute to heat through. Add a little stock or water to the sauce if required. Serve with boiled rice and a simple green salad.

Filo Chicken Parcels with Tarragon

These take a bit longer to prepare, but they make quite an impressive and delicious light meal with very little effort. Serve with a Beurre Blanc or Blue Cheese Sauce, if a sauce is required.

Mash the cream cheese with the tarragon, season well with salt and pepper and chill until required. Season the chicken breasts on both sides with salt and pepper. Heat the oil and butter in a heavy frying pan and quickly brown the chicken breasts on both sides, then put aside on a rack to cool. Preheat a fairly hot oven, 400°F, 200°C, gas mark 6. When the chicken breasts are cold, take the cheese and tarragon mixture from the fridge and, dividing it evenly between them, use to stuff the pockets in the chicken breasts. Keeping the pile of filo pastry covered while you work (because it dries out and becomes unworkable very quickly), brush each filo sheet with melted butter, then fold in half; lay a chicken breast on top and quickly roll up to make a parcel, folding the ends to seal and brushing well all over with melted butter. Place parcels on a greased baking sheet and cook in the preheated oven for about 20 minutes. Serve with **Baked Cherry Tomatoes**: prick about 1 lb/450g cherry tomatoes with the point of a sharp knife, then put into a jug and cover with boiling water. After 1 minute, drain into a colander and cool under the cold tap. Peel and lay the tomatoes in a shallow buttered ovenproof dish. Melt about 2 oz/50g butter in a small pan (or in the microwave) and stir in 2 tablespoons freshly chopped parsely or basil (or a mixture) and a teaspoon of caster sugar. Mix well and brush or drizzle over the tomatoes. Bake in the oven with the Filo Chicken Parcels for 15 minutes, or until just softening. At the same time, brown a handful of pine kernels in the oven (be careful, they burn very easily) and scatter them over the only other accompaniment needed for this delicious light meal, a **Mixed Leaf Salad with Olives & Pine Kernels.** Select, trim, wash and dry your preferred mixture of salad leaves — a little curly endive, radicchio, lamb's lettuce, rocket, watercress etc, as available — put into a salad bowl and add a handful of drained black olives, which can be stoned if you like, scatter in the toasted pine kernels and toss in just enough Olive Oil Dressing to moisten.

Variation: If you have a little leftover Cashel Blue cheese, use all blue cheese, or whatever you have plus plain cream cheese made up to 6 oz/150g. Sometimes a few broken or roughly chopped walnuts creep into this mixture and the Filo Chicken Parcels start to become seriously irresistible. A second salad, based on celery and apples is complementary.

Chicken Fricassée with Sherry

A good choice for a special family meal, or informal entertaining. [Microwave]

Put the chicken into a large pot, add the water, wine, peeled and sliced carrot, onion, bayleaf and salt and pepper. Bring to the boil, then turn down the heat and simmer gently for 1½ hours, or until the meat is tender. Remove the chicken from the stock and cut it into serving-size pieces, removing the skin, breastbone, backbone and wing tips. Arrange in a fairly

Serves 6:

6 oz/175g cream cheese
3 tablespons finely chopped fresh tarragon
Sea salt and freshly ground black pepper
6 chicken breasts, skinned and boned
1 tablespoon olive oil and ½ oz/15g butter
6 full size sheets of filo pastry
2 oz/50g melted butter

Chicken Fricassée: Serves 6
1 whole chicken, 4½lb/2 Kg
26 fl oz/750 ml water
9 fl oz/250 ml white wine (or water)
1 carrot
1 onion, peeled and studded with 4 cloves
1 bay leaf
Salt and freshly ground pepper

Sauce:
1 ½ oz/40g tablespoons butter
2 level tablespoons flour
¼ teaspoon cayenne pepper
1 teaspoon granulated sugar
5 fl oz/125 ml medium sherry
9 oz/250g cooked peas
5 medium-sized carrots, peeled, sliced and cooked
4 stalks celery, chopped and cooked.

deep, warm casserole dish and moisten lightly with a few spoons of stock. Cover tightly and keep warm. Return the skin and bones to the cooking liquid in the pot and boil this stock down until it is reduced by about half. Melt the butter in a saucepan and stir in the flour; cook gently for a minute or two, then gradually add the strained stock, stirring or whisking all the time, to make a fairly thick, smooth sauce. Cook gently for a minute or so, then season with the cayenne, sugar, sherry and add the cooked vegetables. Heat through, then pour the sauce over the chicken pieces and serve immediately with a pilaf of brown rice and a mixed leaf salad.

Roast Pigeon

Pigeons must be one of our most under-rated birds, probably simply because they are plentiful. Although there is no closed season and they can be classified as poultry as well as game, pigeon bought in Ireland is wild, at its best between March and October, used fresh (within 24 hours of shooting) and generally treated as game. Wild birds are inevitably more unreliable in quality than farmyard poultry and, unless you are very sure of their youth, slow, tenderising cooking methods like casseroling, braising and pot-roasting are wise — and, of course, they are excellent on their own or as part of a mixture, in game pies. Young birds have thick necks, supple breastbones and pliable beaks; they can be roasted in a hot oven, 400°F/200°C/ Gas mark 6 — stuff with a rich, fatty stuffing or simply put a lump of butter inside each bird, rub each one well with salt and butter and wrap it in streaky bacon or fat pork to keep it moist, add a grinding of pepper and pour a little medium-dry wine or cider around the birds before cooking in the preheated oven for about 30-45 minutes, depending on size: small birds, making individual servings, will cook in half an hour, but larger ones, serving two, will take about 45 minutes. If you are slightly doubtful about their age, cover the roasting tin with foil to keep the steam in and cook in a moderate oven, 350°F, 180°C, Gas mark 4, for twice as long. Serve with Glazed Button Onions and Cumberland sauce or redcurrant or rowan jelly. Accompaniments suitable for roast chicken work well with pigeon — bacon rolls, chipolata sausages, bread sauce — and the gravy is improved by a dollop of redcurrant or other sweet jelly. Dried fruits also complement pigeon — pigeon and raisins make a classic partnership in a casserole, but stone fruits such as apricots or prunes, pre-soaked in wine, cider or port and cooked in it, also make very good accompaniments. Or you can include fruit in another accompaniment — rice, for example, as in Perfect Pilaf, a delicious combination of brown rice, raisins and toasted almonds and serve fruit chutneys instead of (or as well as) a jelly.

Apart from new season fruit, harbinger of warmer days to come, chocolate is the flavour that dominates the sweet things of spring, especially at Easter. Chocolate eggs of all shapes and sizes are of course the major treat in most families over Easter and the seasonal association has become as good an excuse as any to enjoy all sorts of other chocolate-based cakes, biscuits, desserts and treats of all kinds.

Baked Chocolate Cheesecake

Chocolate desserts are always a winner on restaurant menus and The Red Bank, in Skerries, Co. Dublin, say that this Baked Chocolate Cheesecake is well worth the effort and it serves 6 'but if no one goes for second helpings there could be some left over and it keeps well in the fridge'! Best made the day before it is to be served. These quantities make an 8"/20 cm cheesecake.

Grease and base-line an 8"/20 cm loose-based cake or tart tin.

Preheat a very moderate oven, 300°F, 150°C, Gas mark 2. Crush the biscuits, melt the butter and mix well. Press into the base of the prepared tin. Whisk the cream cheese, caster sugar and egg together until light and creamy, then add the coffee, rum and melted chocolate. Pour the chocolate mixture over the biscuit base and cook for 45 minutes, then turn off the oven and leave undisturbed for at least 4 hours, or overnight. Chill for several hours before serving. The Red Bank recommends a glass of Orange Muscat as accompaniment.

Serves 6: Base:

1 packet (about 8 oz/225g) digestive biscuits
4 oz/100g unsalted butter

Filling:

8 oz/225g cream cheese, preferably Compsey Co-op
4 oz/100g caster sugar
1 egg
2 teaspoons diluted instant coffee
A good measure of dark rum
4 oz/100g dark chocolate, melted
1/3 pint/200 ml cream, lightly whipped.

Foolproof Chocolate Mousse

Chocolate mousse is an all-time top favourite with children and adults alike but it seems to have acquired a (totally unjustified) reputation for being tricky. The important thing, especially if it is for discerning adults, is to use the best quality dark or bitter chocolate available. Although this Foolproof Chocolate Mousse would be equally suitable for any number of occasions throughout the year, it would make a good alternative to serve with a lemon tart for an Easter meal. Although very easy to make, it has a good, rich flavour. [Microwave]

Melt the chocolate with whichever spirit or liqueur you are using. Stir until smooth. Separate the eggs and add the yolks one by one, beating each one well with a wooden spoon before adding the next. The mixture will stiffen at first, then gradually become soft, smooth and glossy. Whip the egg whites until they stand in stiff peaks but are not completely dry. Stir one third of the egg whites into the chocolate mixture until perfectly blended, then lightly fold in the rest with a metal spoon, working lightly but making sure no white specks remain. Pour into a glass dish, or six individual dishes, and refrigerate. Serve with chilled double cream (or, better still, Crème Fraîche) and crisp biscuits.

Foolproof Chocolate Mousse: Serves 6:

6 oz/175g plain or bitter chocolate, eg Menier or Bournville
2 tablespoons brandy or Grand Marnier
6 large eggs.

Note: For an even smoother, richer mousse, omit the egg whites and use 1/2 pint/300 ml whipped cream instead. A finely grated zest of orange can be included, if you like.

Chocolate Roulade

This is another rich chocolate dessert that never fails to impress. The sponge base is fragile and can be rather alarming the first time you make it, but there is no need to worry as it is meant to be cracked and it is actually very easy to make. You do need to plan ahead though, as the baking is best done the day before. [Microwave]

Prepare a large shallow baking tin, about 12"x9"/30x22cm, by brushing lightly with oil and lining the base and short ends with non-stick baking parchment. Preheat a moderate oven, 350°F, 180°C, Gas mark 4. Break

Serves 8:

6 oz/175g plain chocolate
5 eggs
6 oz/175g caster sugar
3 tablespoons hot water
Icing sugar
1/2 pint/300 ml cream.

the chocolate into a small bowl and melt, stirring occasionally, over a pan of hot water. Meanwhile separate the eggs, putting the yolks into a large bowl and the whites into a smaller one. Whisk the yolks and caster sugar until pale and fluffy. Remove the melted chocolate from the heat and stir in 3 tablespoons of hot water taken from the pan. Stir until smooth, then beat into the yolk mixture. Whisk the egg whites until stiff but not dry then fold gently but thoroughly into the chocolate mixture with a metal spoon, losing as little volume as possible. Turn into the prepared tin, spread the mixture out evenly and bake in the preheated oven for 15-20 minutes, or until just set. Remove from the oven but leave in the tin; cover with a sheet of greaseproof paper and a damp cloth and leave until the next day, or until cold. Dust a piece of greaseproof paper generously with icing sugar, loosen the unlined sides of the roulade with a sharp knife and turn it out. Peel off the lining paper. Whip the cream fairly stiffly and spread evenly over the roulade, then roll up like a swiss roll, with the help of the sugared paper. Chill for several hours, then serve dusted with a little extra icing sugar. Using a sharp knife, cut the roulade into diagonal slices to serve.

Variations: Although many people would feel that the simplest chocolate roulade is the best, the filling can be varied to include any flavour that is compatible with chocolate — a couple of ounces (50g) of praline folded into the cream is delicious, for example, or ground or finely chopped toasted hazelnuts or almonds. Orange is always wonderful with chocolate, so try a little grated zest and, perhaps, a dash of any orange-flavoured liqueur in the cream. Coffee is good too: to make a **Mocha Roulade** replace the hot water in the roulade mixture with strong black coffee and flavour the cream with Bailey's Irish Cream, or in summer, fill with fresh raspberries (below).

Chocolate Roulade filled with Fresh Raspberries

Instead of the usual rich wintry fillings for chocolate roulade, try this Chocolate Roulade filled with Fresh Raspberries, a speciality from Gregan's Castle Hotel, Ballyvaughan, Co Clare.

9 fl oz/250ml cream
2 oz/50g sifted icing sugar
9 fl oz/250 ml raspberry
   coulis
2 teaspoons of Framboise
   Liqueur or Kirsch
6 oz/150g fresh raspberries

Make the roulade as in the previous recipe and turn onto a clean tea towel. When it is cool, whip the cream with the sifted icing sugar. Mix the raspberry coulis (sweetened, puréed, sieved fruit) with 2 teaspoons of Framboise Liqueur or Kirsch (or to taste) and brush this mixture liberally all over the sponge. Spread the whipped cream over the sponge, add the evenly distributed raspberries and roll up with the aid of the cloth. Leave for at least 20 minutes to set before slicing. Serve with extra fresh cream.

Chocolate Marquise with Crème Anglaise

But the richest of all the chocolate desserts has to be Chocolate Marquise. There are countless variations of this irresistible classic — this is is a particularly smooth, rich one, with a little coffee to enhance the flavour of the chocolate. It is wonderful served simply in a pool of Crème Anglaise accompanied by Hazelnut Hearts — perfect for Valentine's Day — or with a scoop of home-made vanilla ice cream and a rather sharp fruit coulis such as raspberry or, better still, loganberry or fresh apricot. [Microwave]

Serves 8:
8 oz/225g plain or bitter
   chocolate
4 oz/100g unsalted butter,
   at room temperature
6 oz/175g icing sugar
3 large eggs
½ teaspoon instant coffee
l teaspoon water.

Line a 2 lb/900g loaf tin (about 8½"x4½"/20.5x11.5 cm) generously with clingfilm, leaving plenty of overlap. Break the chocolate into a small bowl and melt, stirring, over a pan of hot water. Remove the bowl from the heat and leave to cool a little. Cut the butter into a mixing bowl and cream with the sifted icing sugar until light and smooth. Separate the eggs and beat in the yolks, one by one, then add the blended coffee and water and, finally, the chocolate. Mix well. Whisk the egg whites until stiff but not dry. Stir a tablespoonful of the egg white into the chocolate mixture to lighten it, then carefully fold in the rest with a metal spoon to mix thoroughly but lose as little volume as possible. Turn into the prepared loaf tin, spread evenly and leave to chill overnight, or for at least 4 hours — when ready, the mixture should be firm enough to slice.

Meanwhile, make 1 pint/600 ml Crème Anglaise (See Sauces, page 222)

To serve: Take the chocolate marquise from the fridge about an hour before serving. Holding the clingfilm, remove from the loaf tin and turn onto a plate. Using a sharp knife, slice fairly thinly. Divide the Crème Anglaise between 8 serving plates and arrange the sliced marquise on the pool of custard. Sprinkle the custard with a light dusting of cocoa powder and serve with Hazelnut Hearts.

Hints: Do not allow egg custard to boil or overcook, as it will curdle. To be on the safe side, have a washing-up bowl full of cold water handy and, if the custard shows the slightest sign of curdling, plunge the pan into the cold water to lower the temperature quickly. Return to a low heat and whisk the sauce vigorously, then it should thicken normally.

The number of egg yolks required is not absolute: 2 per 1/2 pint/300ml milk will thicken the sauce, or the proportion can be increased to 5 for the above quantity to make a richer sauce. A little cornflour or arrowroot can be used to give extra body to the sauce and stabilise it. Custard sauces can be flavoured with other spices (cinnamon is particularly useful), fruit such as orange, or other flavourings such as coffee or chocolate. There will be a number of egg whites left over after making the Crème Anglaise. Ways in which these might be used include making meringues or macaroons, soufflés or gâteaux.

Hint: Vanilla pods are re-usable: rinse and dry after use, then store as usual.

Gâteau Diane

What better way could there be to round off a dinner in the season of chocolate indulgence than with the magnificent classic multi-layered meringue and chocolate party sweet, Gâteau Diane? Make this rich dessert the day before to allow the flavours and texture to develop.

Preheat a cool oven 300°F, 150°C, Gas mark 2. Prepare two large baking sheets by lining with non-stick parchment. (A dot of cooking fat under each corner will hold it in place.) Whisk the egg whites stiffly, then whisk in about 2 oz/50g of the sugar and carefully but thoroughly fold in the rest with a metal spoon. Quarter the mixture and spread into four equal circles about 1/4"/0.6 cm thick, as if making a vacherin with four thin layers. Bake in the preheated oven for about 30 minutes, or until just colouring, then reduce the temperature to 275°F, 140°C, Gas mark 1, turn the meringue circles over and leave until they have dried out. Cool on wire racks.

Meanwhile, make the filling: put the 2 egg whites and the sifted icing sugar into a bowl over a pan of hot water and whisk until thick. Cream the butter well. Melt the chocolate over gentle heat and allow to cool. Beat the meringue into the butter a little at a time, then beat in the chocolate. Toast the almonds under the grill, until they are an even golden brown.

Select a suitable flat plate or board for the gâteau and sandwich the circles of cooked meringue with the chocolate cream to make a 4-layered cake. Cover the top and sides completely with the remaining chocolate cream and finish with the toasted almonds. Dust the top lightly with sifted icing sugar and store the gâteau in a cool place until required.

Variations: If preferred, cocoa powder can be used instead of block chocolate to flavour the filling: blend 3 tablespoons cocoa powder with 3

Serves 8-10:

Meringue:
4 egg whites
8 oz/225g caster sugar

Filling:
2 egg whites
4 1/2 oz/125g icing sugar
8 oz/225g unsalted butter, at room temperature
3 1/2 oz/90g dark dessert or bitter chocolate
4 oz/100g nibbed almonds
Icing sugar for dusting.

tablespoons boiling water to make a thick cream and allow to cool before use; a little instant coffee included with the cocoa enhances its flavour. Although not a classic ingredient, a dash of brandy or any appropriate liqueur will not go amiss in the chocolate cream.

Tangy Lemon Tart (Tarte au Citron)

Serves 8-10:

Pastry:
7 oz/200g plain flour
Pinch of salt
4 oz/100g butter or block margarine, at room temperature
2 level tablespoons caster sugar
1 small egg, lightly beaten
A little very cold water, if necessary

Filling:
2 large, juicy lemons
2 large eggs
4 oz/100g caster sugar
2 oz/50g ground almonds
4 oz/100g butter, preferably unsalted, well softened
¼ pint/150 ml double cream
Icing sugar for dusting.

This makes a perfect dinner party dessert at any time of year but, with its fresh golden colour and zingy flavour, it also seems especially appropriate in spring — particularly for an Easter meal and perhaps as an alternative to one of the chocolate temptations above. Although rich, this is a particularly easy version — the pastry shell does not need to be pre-baked before filling and the filling itself is very simple to make. Like other tarts, it is best eaten on the day of making if possible, but this one comes to little harm if prepared ahead and gently re-warmed before serving.

Sift the flour and salt into a mixing bowl, cut in the fat and rub in to make a mixture like fine breadcrumbs. Using a fork, work in the caster sugar, the lightly beaten egg and, if necessary, a little very cold water to make a smooth dough. Roll into a ball, wrap in clingfilm and chill for half an hour before use, if possible. When ready to cook, roll the pastry out fairly thinly and use to line a 10"/25 cm loose-bottomed tart tin. Prick the base lightly with a fork and leave in the fridge while you prepare the filling. Preheat a very moderate oven, 325°F, 170°C, Gas mark 3. Finely grate the zest from one of the lemons; squeeze the juice from both and strain. Using an electric mixer if possible, whisk together the eggs and sugar until very light and fluffy, add the ground almonds, the softened butter, the cream, lemon juice and zest. Whisk together gently until the mixture is smooth and creamy, but take care not to overbeat as it may curdle. Pour into the pastry case and bake in the preheated oven for about 40 minutes or until the filling is set and a light golden brown. Serve warm or cold, dusted with icing sugar.

Lemon Whip

Serves 6:
4 large eggs
1 sachet gelatine
2 tablespoons cold water
8 oz/225g caster sugar
2 large juicy lemons
2 tablespoons hot water.

Then there is my old friend, Lemon Whip, made so often on my mother's instructions and still a great favourite. After a filling main course this is the perfect light and refreshing uncooked sweet. Make it the day before if possible to get the best lemon flavour and don't worry if it separates into layers — it's almost better that way.

Separate the eggs, putting the yolks into a larger bowl. Put the gelatine and cold water into a small jug or cup to soak. Add the caster sugar to the egg yolks and whisk together, preferably with an electric mixer, until very light and fluffy. Meanwhile, finely grate the zest from the lemons. Squeeze the juice and measure it — if there is less than ¼ pint/150 ml, make up with extra fresh lemon juice or water. Mix the lemon rind and juice with the whisked yolk mixture. Pour the hot (not boiling) water over the gelatine and stir until dissolved, then add to the yolk mixture and mix thoroughly. Whisk the egg whites until stiff but not dry and fold lightly into the lemon mixture with a metal spoon to blend the whites in thoroughly without loss of volume.

Turn into a bowl, or individual dishes, and chill until set. Decorate with whipped cream and, perhaps, a few chopped pistachio nuts and hand some crisp biscuits, such as Almond Tuiles separately.

Variation: The volume can be increased considerably by including a small (6 oz/175 ml) tin of well-chilled evaporated milk — add to the well-whisked yolks and sugar and continue whisking, at high speed, for a further 5 minutes until the mixture is very pale and the volume has greatly increased then continue as above. The flavour is not quite as lemony, but this is a useful family variation, or for large numbers.

Rhubarb with Orange

Rhubarb is the first native fruit of the new season and deserves a special welcome for that. Early stalks are forced so the texture is tender and the colour a lovely delicate pink. The pretty pink sticks look lovely floating whole in a delicate orange-flavoured syrup. Orange and rhubarb make a perfect partnership, as the orange highlights the flavour of the rhubarb and takes the edge off its sharpness. [Microwave]

Wash and trim the rhubarb; cut the stalks into 1"/2.5 cm lengths. Measure the water and sugar into a large pan, stir over low heat until the sugar has dissolved, then bring to the boil. Add the prepared rhubarb, bring back up to a gentle simmer and cook for 5 minutes, or until the rhubarb pieces are barely tender. Take the pan off the heat, cover with a lid and leave undisturbed for 10 minutes, so the rhubarb pieces will become tender without losing their shape. Test with the tip of a knife to see if they are ready, then add the finely grated zest and juice of the orange, and the Cointreau or Grand Marnier, if using. Transfer the rhubarb and juices to a glass serving bowl and leave until cold. Chill for several hours or overnight before serving. The flavour improves if it is made 24 hours ahead.

Serves 6:
2 lb/900g rhubarb
1/2 pint/300ml water
6 oz/175g caster sugar
Finely grated zest and juice of 1 orange
Dash of Cointreau or Grand Marnier (optional).

Rhubarb & Orange Crumble

It is surprising how often the simplest dishes are best and classic partnerships prove themselves time and again — as in this recipe, from Enniscoe House near Ballina, Co. Mayo, which makes a delicious spring pudding. [Microwave]

Preheat a moderate oven, 350°F, 180°C, Gas mark 4. Put the rhubarb into a 2 pint/1.15 litre pie dish. Grate the zest from both oranges, sprinkle half over the rhubarb and reserve the remainder. Add 3 oz/75g sugar and 2 tablespoons of water to the fruit. Cover and bake in the preheated oven for 10-15 minutes. Meanwhile peel the oranges and cut into segments, discarding pith and membranes. Mix the remaining orange zest with the flour, rub in the butter and mix in the sugar. Arrange the orange segments over the rhubarb, sprinkle the topping over the fruit and return to the oven for 35-40 minutes, until golden brown. Serve hot or cold, with cream.

Serves 4–6:
1 lb/450g rhubarb, in 1"/2.5 cm lengths
2 oranges
3 oz/75g sugar

Crumble:
6 oz/150g flour
3 oz/75g butter
4-5 oz/100-125g sugar.

Rhubarb Fool

An old-fashioned, simple and wonderfully refreshing way to round off a meal. [Microwave]

Cut the rhubarb into 2-3" lengths and put into a pan with the sugar, a very little water and the orange rind. Resist the temptation to over-sweeten as it is the tartness of the fruit which is refreshing. Simmer very gently for a few minutes until tender, taking care not to overcook so that the bright colour isn't lost. Drain and purée. Add a little of the cooking juice if necessary, but make sure it isn't too sloppy. Leave to cool, then whip the cream lightly and stir in with the Pernod if using — it's not essential but enhances the flavour of the fool without being recognisable.

Variation: Use 1/2 custard, 1/2 cream.
Variation 2: If frozen, the fool makes a good no-stir ice-cream.

Rhubarb Fool: Serves 4-6
1 1/2 lb/700g rhubarb
4-5 oz/100-125g Demerara sugar
A little water
Finely grated rind of 1 orange
1/2 pint/300 ml cream
2-3 teaspoons Pernod (optional).

Gooseberry Layer Cake

Serves 6–8:

1½ lb/700g gooseberries

Crumble Topping:

3 oz/75g self-raising flour,
  preferably wholemeal
1 oz/25g rolled oats
3 oz/75g light golden
  brown sugar
3 oz/75g butter, at room
  temperature
1 tablespoon water
1 or 2 tablespoons
  granulated sugar to
  sprinkle over.

Base:

6 oz/175g self-raising flour
4 oz/100g butter, at room
  temperature
4 oz/100g caster sugar
2 large eggs
A few drops of vanilla
  essence
A little milk to mix.

Gooseberries, the first soft fruit of the year, begin to come on stream in May and, although they are in no way related, rhubarb and gooseberries are very often interchangeable in recipes. Often under-estimated (perhaps simply because they are plentiful and cheap), gooseberries are actually very versatile and most useful in the kitchen at a time when there is very little native fresh fruit available. Like rhubarb, their natural sharpness can be a positive advantage in some ways — making them especially suitable for use in savoury dishes, to offset the richness of oily fish, for example. Their high pectin and acid content means they set easily and make wonderful preserves, either alone or combined with other fruits or herbs in a wide range of jams, chutneys and jellies. For use in desserts, early season green gooseberries need a lot of sweetening to make them palatable, although adding a few leaves of the herb Sweet Cicely (which acts as a natural sweetener) reduces the amount of added sugar required. Careful partnering with blander ingredients offsets their natural sharpness, as in this delicious sweet-sour cake:

Top and tail the gooseberries. Mix all the dry topping ingredients except the granulated sugar in a bowl, cut in the butter and rub in until fine and crumbly. Set aside. Grease the base and sides of a deep 8"-9"/20-22.5 cm loose-based cake tin. Preheat a moderate oven, 350°F, 180°C, Gas mark 4. Sift the flour. Cream the butter and sugar until light and fluffy. Mix the eggs and vanilla essence lightly together, then gradually beat into the creamed mixture, including a little flour with each addition of egg. Finally mix in any remaining flour with just enough milk to keep the consistency fairly soft. Turn this mixture into the prepared tin, spread level and lay the gooseberries on top, in an even layer. Add the tablespoon of water to the topping and mix with a fork so that it forms larger lumps; cover the gooseberries with it, spreading evenly with the back of the fork, then sprinkle fairly generously with granulated sugar to make a crunchy topping and bake in the preheated oven for about an hour, or until the fruit is tender and the top is crisp and golden brown. Serve warm with chilled double cream, Crème Fraîche or ice cream, handing a bowl of caster sugar separately if the fruit is very under-ripe.

Clafoutis à Groseille Verte

Serves 6:

1½ lb/700g gooseberries
3 eggs
1 oz/25g plain flour
Salt
2½ oz/60g caster sugar
¾ pint/450 ml milk
1 tablespoon kirsch
  (optional)
1-1½ oz/25-40g unsalted
  butter.

Clafoutis is a warm pudding based on a sweet pancake batter and baked with fresh fruit. It originates from the Limousin area of France, where it is is made with the black cherries of the region ('Clafoutis Limousin'), but the basic recipe is very versatile and adapts particularly well to gooseberries, hence this Clafoutis à Groseille Verte.

Preheat a hot oven, 425°F, 220°C /Gas mark 7 and generously butter a large, shallow ovenproof dish. Top and tail the gooseberries; wash them and drain well. Beat the eggs lightly together in a mixing bowl (or use a food processor or blender), blend in the sifted flour, a pinch of salt and 3 tablespoons of the caster sugar. Warm the milk to blood temperature and gradually add to the egg mixture, beating all the time. Add the kirsch, if using. Lay the gooseberries in the buttered dish, pour the batter over them and dot with the remaining butter. Bake in the centre of the preheated oven for about half an hour, or until the gooseberries have risen to the top and the batter has set like a baked custard. Sprinkle the pudding with the remaining caster sugar and serve warm with cream.

Gooseberry Fool with Elderflowers

The classic cold sweet based on gooseberries is, of course, the fool — it seems to have been out of fashion recently, but is too good to overlook and definitely deserves a come-back. It is surely no coincidence that produce naturally occurring at the same time and place marries well, but the elderflower and gooseberry are both at their peak in late spring and early summer — and, providing you make sure you have the right kind of elderflower (some smell rank and would destroy any dish they were added to), the combination can be magical. In this fool, as in many preserves based on gooseberries, the aromatic elder flowers combine with gooseberries to produce an almost muscat-like flavour. [Microwave]

To serve 6-8:
2 lb/900g gooseberries
3-4 heads elderflowers
$1/2$- $3/4$ pint/300-450 ml water
1 teaspoon arrowroot, if required
Caster sugar
1 level dessertspoon custard powder
$1/4$ pint/150 ml milk
$1/2$ pint/300 ml double cream.

Top and tail the gooseberries. Wash them and put into a pan with the elderflowers, tied in a square of muslin, and the water. Bring to the boil and simmer gently for 15–20 minutes, or until the gooseberries are soft, then remove the elderflowers and strain the fruit, reserving the juice.

Purée the gooseberries and pass through a nylon sieve to remove the pips. Measure the purée and make up to a pint/600 ml with some of the reserved juice if necessary. If it is very runny, thicken the purée with arrowroot: mix the arrowroot with a little cold water to make a paste; return the purée to the rinsed saucepan and bring up to boiling point, then mix a little of the hot purée with the arrowroot; turn into the pan and cook, stirring, until the purée thickens and clears. Sweeten to taste with the caster sugar and set aside until cold. Meanwhile, make the custard, sweeten lightly and leave to cool. When both gooseberry purée and custard are cold, mix the custard into the purée, then whip the cream lightly and fold it in gently to give a marbled effect. Turn into a serving bowl or individual glasses and serve with sponge fingers or tuiles. Like other fools, the texture is less inclined to be cloying if a mixture of custard and whipped cream is used, but the custard can be omitted and the amount of cream increased if preferred. Egg custard is even more delicious, if time permits.
Variation: The fool can be frozen to make a delicious no-stir ice-cream.

There's a strong emphasis on tea-time treats in traditional Easter cooking, and baking for it is most enjoyable, especially if we happen to be going through a spell of harsh March weather at the time. What better place to be then, than in a cosy kitchen enjoying the unbeatable aroma of good home baking?

Simnel Cake

For the marzipan:

8 oz/225g caster sugar
8 oz/225g icing sugar
1 lb/450g ground almonds
2 eggs (or 4 yolks)
3 teaspoons lemon juice
1 teaspoon almond essence

For the cake:

8 oz/225g plain flour
1/2 teaspoon salt
1 saltspoon each nutmeg,
  cinnamon and allspice
6 oz/175g butter
6 oz/175g rich dark brown
  sugar (Barbados)
3 eggs
1 lb/450g currants
8-12 oz/225-350g sultanas
4 oz/100g chopped candied
  peel
Scant 1/4 pint/150 ml milk
1 level tablespoon black
  treacle.
A little apple jelly or apricot
  jam
1/2 egg yolk beaten up with
  a little oil to glaze.

Simnel Cake was originally associated with Mothering Sunday, but in recent times it has become an Easter speciality and is often decorated as below, with eleven marzipan balls to represent the twelve apostles, less Judas. This is one of our favourite cakes — everyone loves the layer of gooey almond in the centre of the cake.

First make the marzipan: Mix sugars and almonds together in a large bowl, make a hollow in the centre and drop in the lightly beaten eggs (or yolks), lemon juice and almond essence. Mix to a stiff paste, first with a wooden spoon then with hands dusted with icing sugar. Knead well until smooth and free from cracks. (Or do all this very quickly in a Kenwood chef, using the K beater.) If possible, leave the ball in a polythene bag in the fridge overnight, then leave to reach room temperature again before use; it will then be easier to handle.

Preheat a slow oven, 300°F, 150°C, Gas mark 2. Butter and line a deep 8"/20 cm round cake tin, preferably loose-based.

To make the cake: Sift the flour, salt and spices together. Cream butter and sugar until light and fluffy, then add the lightly beaten eggs, a little at a time, including a spoonful of the sifted flour and beating well after each addition. When the mixture is thoroughly beaten, lightly stir in the remaining flour and then the fruit. Add just enough of the milk to make a fairly stiff batter (like a Christmas cake) and the treacle. Divide the marzipan unevenly in half and roll the smaller piece to the exact size of the inside of the cake tin. Turn half of the cake mixture into the tin, level it out and cover with the circle of marzipan. Cover with the rest of the mixture, smooth down with the back of a tablespoon and bake in the centre of the preheated oven for about 3 1/2 hours, or until the top is springy to the touch and the cake is shrinking slightly from the tin. A skewer should come out of the cake clean, but the marzipan in the middle makes this method less reliable than usual, so be careful not to put the skewer through it. Cool the cooked cake in the tin. When cold, turn out, remove papers and brush the top with a little warmed apple jelly or apricot jam, sieved if necessary, and place the second circle of marzipan on top, pressing down well. Mark the top into squares 3/4"–1", 2.5 cm wide with a sharp knife and make eleven small balls from the marzipan trimmings. Arrange these around the edge of the cake, brush the marzipan lightly with beaten egg and put the cake into a hot oven or under the grill for a few minutes until toasted to a deep golden brown. Alternatively, another traditional finish is to run a small pool of pastel coloured icing, preferably yellow, into the centre of the marzipan. In either case, it can also be decorated with a few tiny marzipan or foil-covered chocolate eggs and/or Easter chicks — children love these.

Easter Lemon Cake

Makes a 10"/25 cm cake:

6 oz/175g butter, at room
  temperature
6 oz/175g caster sugar
3 large eggs
3 lemons
6 oz/175g flour
About 8 oz/225g caster
  sugar for the icing
Crystallised violets and
  mimosa balls for
  decorating (optional).

My mother relies on me for the traditional simnel cake at Easter — it's my children's favourite above all others so she knows I'll make several — so, instead, she makes this mouthwateringly delicious Easter Lemon Cake. It's light, moist, sharp and delicately coloured – a real taste of spring.

Preheat a moderate oven, 350°F, 180°C, Gas mark 4.

Cream the butter and sugar until they are light and fluffy. Add the finely grated zest of the lemons. Whip the eggs lightly and add alternately with the sieved flour, beating well. Line a 10"/25 cm shallow cake tin, preferably spring-clip, with greased greaseproof paper and spread in the mixture. Bake in the centre of the preheated oven for 20 minutes, then reduce the heat to 300'F, 150'C, Gas mark 2 and bake for a further 20 minutes, or until a skewer comes out clean from the centre of the cake.

Meanwhile, make the icing from about 8 oz/225g caster sugar dissolved in the juice of two of the lemons. This is spread on the cake when it cools, and it is easier if the icing is allowed to stand for an hour or two to set a little. Stir from time to time, adding more sugar if necessary — but remember that the icing must be rather sharp to give the cake its characteristic tang. When the cake is cool, stand it on a large board or dish and spoon the icing over it in small quantities — when it runs over the side, scoop it up and put it back on top again. It may take a little while, but it should be possible to get all the icing on eventually. Leave for 2 or 3 hours to harden. Decorate in spring colours with crystallised angelica, violets and primroses or mimosa balls as available. Serves 8-10, as a cake or as a dessert.

Easter Nest Cake

*Easter Nest Cake has enormous child appeal and can be based on any cake. As chocolate is so much the flavour of the season and always a winner with children, I've based this one on a good but very **Quick Chocolate Sponge**. Another pretty alternative would be a Victoria sponge marbled with yellow and chocolate brown.*

Preheat a moderate oven, 350°F, 180°C, Gas mark 4, and grease and base-line a round 7"/18 cm cake tin, at least 2"/5 cm deep.

Mix the cocoa, coffee and hot water together in a small bowl. Put the sieved flour and baking powder, sugar, soft margarine and eggs into a mixing bowl. Add the cocoa mixture and beat everything together for about a minute, until well-mixed and of a soft consistency. Turn the mixture into the prepared tin and bake in the centre of the oven for 45 minutes, or until the cake is springy to the touch and shrinking slightly from the tin. Leave to cool in the tins for 5 minutes, then turn out onto a wire rack and leave until cold.

Sieve the icing sugar into a bowl, blend in the soft margarine with a fork and mix to a smooth, spreading icing with the milk. Colour and flavour to taste, carefully adding drops one at a time off the end of a skewer. Spread the icing over the top and sides of the cake and leave to set a little, then melt the chocolate in a medium-sized bowl over hot water and stir in the breakfast cereals. Mix to coat well, then turn half of the mixture onto the cake and spread to make a circle covering at least two-thirds of the cake. Use the rest of the chocolate mixture to build up the wall of the nest until you have a convincing nest-like structure that is not too deep. Leave to set, then fill with the miniature eggs and one or two yellow chicks.

Variation: If preferred, the cake could be covered with ready-to-roll fondant icing. Leftovers can easily be coloured and moulded to make decorative flowers etc.

Easter Biscuits

Other tea-time treats that are traditional for Easter include, of course, Hot Cross Buns for Good Friday (see Yeast Baking) and these big spiced Easter Biscuits, that my mother has made for many years. There is a tradition in some families of piping a cross of glacé icing on top, but ours were always left plain.

Sift the flour, salt and spices together. Cream the butter and sugar until

For the cake — ingredients should be at room temperature:

3 level tablespoons cocoa
l teaspoon instant coffee
3 tablespoons hot water.
4 oz/100g self-raising flour
l level teaspoon baking powder
4 oz/100g caster sugar
4 oz/100g soft tub margarine
2 large eggs

For the Icing and Nest

8 oz/225g icing sugar:
3 oz/75g soft margarine or butter
4 tbsp top of the milk
2-3 drops yellow colouring
1-2 drops lemon flavouring
4 oz/100g plain coating chocolate
4 oz/100g All-Bran or Shredded Wheat
About a dozen each miniature sugar-coated and foil-wrapped eggs
l or 2 fluffy Easter chicks.

Makes about 3 dozen:

1 lb/450g plain flour
1 level teaspoon salt
1 level teaspoon each
  ground cinnamon and
  mixed spice
8 oz/225g butter, at room
  temperature
8 oz/225g caster sugar
2 large eggs, beaten
6 oz/175g currants
2 oz/50g candied peel,
  chopped
Milk, as required
1 egg white, lightly beaten,
  OR a little extra milk
Granulated sugar to
  sprinkle over.

Jap Cakes: 12-18 small cakes

2 egg whites
4 oz/100g hazelnuts,
  ground with their skins on
4 oz/100g caster sugar

Icing:

4 oz/100g icing sugar,
  sieved
4 oz/100g unsalted butter,
  at room temperature
Coffee essence to flavour

Glacé Icing (optional):

4 oz/100g icing sugar,
  sieved
1 teaspoon lemon juice
About 1 tablespoon warm
  water.

Decorations (optional)
  Hazelnuts, almonds,
  angelica etc.

Nutty: Makes about 12 slices:

Shortcrust Pastry:

8 oz/225g plain flour
Pinch of salt
2 oz/50g butter / margarine
2 oz/50g white fat
1 egg yolk
About 2 tablespoons cold
  water.

Filling:

2 or 3 tablespoons raspberry
  jam
2 egg whites
8 oz/225g caster sugar
8 oz/225g ground almonds
1-1½ oz/25-40g flaked
  almonds to decorate
  (optional).

light and fluffy, then beat in the eggs and add alternately the currants and chopped peel and dry ingredients. Mix to a stiff dough, adding a little milk if necessary. Make a ball with the dough, wrap in clingfilm and chill for at least an hour if possible. Preheat a fairly hot oven, 400°F, 200°C, Gas mark 6. Flour a work surface and roll out the dough quite thinly, then prick all over with a fork and stamp into rounds with a large fluted cutter, 3½ -4"/9-10cm diameter. Lay them on greased baking trays (they should not spread much, but leave a little room between them) and bake in the preheated oven for 15-20 minutes, or until they are just beginning to brown. Remove from the oven, brush the biscuits quickly with the lightly beaten egg white or milk and sprinkle with granulated sugar. Return to the oven for a few minutes until pale golden and crisp. Allow to cool on the trays for 5 minutes, then transfer to a wire rack. When completely cold, store in an airtight tin.

Jap Cakes

Although they have nothing whatsoever to do with Easter customs generally, any special occasion in our family called for a batch of Jap Cakes and dates like Christmas or Easter would be a better excuse than most. For Jap read 'Japonnais', of which there are many versions varying from a large formal gâteau, based on meringue discs made with ground almonds and covered with praline, to little individual cakes containing hazelnuts and sandwiched with coffee cream. This simplified version is made with hazelnuts and an easier alternative to the praline.

Line a shallow baking tray about 11"x7"/28x18cm with non-stick baking parchment.

Preheat a moderate oven, 350°F, 180°C, Gas mark 4. Whisk the egg whites until stiff. Whisk in half the sugar and continue whisking until stiff again, then fold in the remaining sugar with the nuts. Spread the mixture out evenly on the lined tray and bake in the preheated oven for about 15 minutes, or until pale golden brown, then remove from the oven and use a small cutter, 1–1½"/2.5-3.8 cm diameter, to mark out rounds. Return the tray to the oven to finish cooking, for another 10 minutes, or until crisp and medium-brown. Remove the rounds with a palette knife and cool on a rack. Meanwhile, return the scraps, well broken, to the oven to dry out. Cool and roll out to make fine crumbs. Make the butter icing by creaming the butter with the sieved icing sugar, then beat in coffee essence to taste. Use to sandwich rounds in pairs, then spread over the tops and sides and roll in the toasted crumbs. Finally, if using glacé icing, sift the icing sugar into a deep bowl, add the lemon juice and the water, a little at a time, until the mixture is thick enough to coat the back of a wooden spoon and use to decorate the tops of the Jap Cakes, before adding nuts etc. Serve the cakes in small paper cases. If stored in a cool place in an airtight tin, Jap Cakes will keep for several weeks. Forgotten at the back of the freezer, they have been known to keep several years ....

Hint: Ground almonds can be used instead of hazelnuts, if preferred. Shelled nuts in their brown skins are easy to grind in a blender or coffee grinder.

Nutty

Another family favourite which goes back further than my own memory is simply called Nutty — presumably it once had a more elegantly descriptive title but, if so, nobody can remember it. We usually made it with hazelnuts, ground in their skins, in combination with home-made jam as available (preferably Dried Apricot Jam) but it can also be made with almonds as given here, in which case raspberry jam makes the best partnership.

Sift the flour and salt into a bowl, cut in the fats and rub in lightly to make a mixture like fine breadcrumbs. Fork in the egg yolk and just enough cold water to hold the dough together. Form into a ball, wrap in clingfilm and set aside in the fridge to rest for at least half an hour.

Preheat a fairly hot oven, 400°F, 200°C, Gas mark 6. Grease a shallow baking tin about 11"x7"/28x18 cm. On a floured work surface, roll out the pastry to fit the greased tin, then use it to line the base and ½"/1.25 cm up the side of the tin. Spread the pastry evenly with raspberry jam. Whisk the egg whites until quite stiff, then whisk in half of the sugar and continue beating until thick and glossy. Mix the remaining sugar with the ground nuts and fold carefully into the beaten egg whites with a metal spoon, to mix thoroughly with as little loss of volume as possible. Turn the nutty meringue mixture into the lined baking tray and spread out evenly with the back of a fork. Sprinkle with flaked almonds, if using, and bake in the preheated oven for about 30 minutes, until the topping is golden brown and the pastry is crisp. Leave in the tin to cool, then cut into slices.

Quick Chocolate Cake with Orange Fudge Icing

This recipe is one I come back to time and again. Always in demand for birthdays, it makes a good alternative to Simnel Cake at Easter and is ideal when you need a cake that looks special but haven't much time to spare. [Microwave]

Preheat a moderate oven, 350°F, 180°C, Gas mark 4. Butter two 7"/18 cm sandwich tins. Sift the flour, cocoa and salt into a mixing bowl, cut in the butter or margarine and add the sugar, almonds and eggs. Mix with a wooden spoon for 2-3 minutes, until thoroughly mixed and no traces of butter remain. Divide the mixture between the prepared tins and bake in the centre of the oven for 25-30 minutes, or until springy to the touch and just beginning to shrink from the tins. Turn out and cool on a wire rack.

Meanwhile make the icing. Put the butter, brown sugar, orange zest and juice into a small saucepan and heat together gently, stirring, until the sugar dissolves. Remove from the heat, add the roughly broken chocolate, and stir until melted. Gradually stir in the icing sugar and beat until smooth.

When the cakes are cold and the icing has cooled enough to begin thickening and will spread easily without running off the cake, use some to sandwich the two layers together and the remainder to cover the top and, if liked, the sides — a good layer on top which is allowed to drip unevenly down the sides can be attractive. Decorate with crystallised violets and skinned fresh orange segments or, if short of time, tinned mandarin segments, well-drained.

Hazelnut Coffee Cake

Coffee cakes always go down well, especially when combined with nuts. Walnuts are most usual, but I prefer the combination in this simple, attractive cake. [Microwave]

Preheat a moderate oven, 350°F, 180°C, Gas mark 4. Grease two 7"/18 cm sandwich tins. Cream the butter and sugar until light and fluffy, then beat in the eggs, one at a time, adding a spoonful of flour with each one. When thoroughly mixed, combine the remaining flour and the nuts; mix in well, but do not over-beat. Divide the mixture between the prepared sandwich tins, smooth the tops and bake in the centre of the preheated oven for about 30 minutes, or until springy to the touch and just shrinking from the tins. Turn out onto a wire rack to cool.

To make the icing, cream the softened butter well, then gradually beat in the sifted sugar and the coffee essence. Sandwich the sponges together with some of the icing and use the rest to cover the top and sides — any

---

6 oz/175g self-raising flour
1 rounded tablespoon cocoa powder
Pinch of salt
6 oz/175g soft butter or margarine
6 oz/175g rich dark brown sugar
2 oz/50g ground almonds
3 large eggs, lightly beaten.

Orange Fudge Icing:
2 oz/50g butter
6 oz/175g rich dark brown sugar
Finely grated zest and juice of 1 orange
1 oz/25g good dark chocolate, eg Bournville
6 oz/175g icing sugar, sifted.

To decorate:
Crystallised violets and fresh orange segments.

Hazelnut Coffee Cake:
6 oz/175g softened butter or margarine
6 oz/175g caster or light golden brown sugar
3 large eggs
6 oz/175g self-raising flour, sifted
2 oz/50g ground hazelnuts.

Butter Cream Icing:
6 oz/175g softened butter, preferably unsalted
12 oz/350g sifted icing sugar
2 tablespoons coffee essence
Whole hazelnuts to decorate.

Variation: For a more adult version, try a couple of tablespoons of Bailey's Irish Cream in the icing.

8 oz/225g flour
Pinch of salt
½ teaspoon baking powder
2 oz/50g ground almonds
8 oz/225g glacé cherries
6 oz/175 g butter, at room temperature
6 oz/175 g caster, or light golden brown sugar
2 large eggs
Milk to mix
A few drops each of vanilla and almond essences
1 oz/25g granulated sugar.

remaining icing can be piped around the top in rosettes, a whole hazelnut decorating each one.

Cherry Cake

Plainer looking cakes, without decoration, are particularly useful to have in the house as they usually keep better (possibly because they are slightly less tempting, although often just as delicious) and they are more versatile, as they lend themselves to packing up for picnics and packed lunches. This rich, moist Cherry Cake with its lovely crunchy top has a generous allocation of cherries and keeps well, although it is irresistible when fresh so it may not get the chance to prove it!

Preheat a moderate oven, 350°F, 180°C, Gas mark 4. Grease and base-line a deep 7"-8"/18-20 cm cake tin, preferably loose-based. Sieve the flour, salt and baking powder into a basin; quarter 7 oz/200g of the cherries and add them to the flour. Halve the remaining 1 oz/25g and set aside. Cream the butter and sugar until light and fluffy, then beat in the eggs, one by one, including a little of the flour with each one. Mix well, then stir in the dry ingredients lightly, adding a little milk to mix, and lastly add the essences. Blend the mixture thoroughly, turn into the prepared tin and smooth the top. Press the reserved cherries lightly into the top of the cake, sprinkle with the granulated sugar and bake in the preheated oven for an hour, or until firm to the touch and golden brown. Cool in the tin for 10-15 minutes until the cake is shrinking away from the sides, then turn out onto a rack and leave to cool. When cold, remove the papers and store in an airtight tin until required.

Date Cake

8 oz/225g self-raising flour
A pinch of salt
A pinch of mixed spice
4 oz/100g butter
4 oz/100g sugar
8 oz/225g pressed (cooking) dates
1 egg
Milk to mix
1 tablespoon granulated sugar.

*This Date Cake is quick to make and, although rubbed-in mixtures are generally best eaten fresh, the dates tend to keep this cake moist for longer in the same way as cherries do — in fact, the same recipe can be used to make a **Plain Cherry Cake**.*

Preheat a moderate oven, 350°F, 180°C, Gas mark 4. Grease and base-line a 7-8", 18-20 cm deep cake tin, preferably loose-based. Sieve together the flour, salt and spice and rub in the butter. Add the stoned and chopped dates and mix with the beaten egg and enough milk to give a dropping consistency. Turn into the prepared tin and sprinkle the granulated sugar over the top. Bake in the preheated oven for about 1½ hours, or until firm and golden brown.

Newport Fruit Cake

1 lb/450g plain flour
8 oz/225g butter
8 oz/225g rich dark brown sugar
1 lb/450g sultanas
1 teaspoon bread soda
A little chopped chocolate (eg half a small bar of Bournville)
2 eggs
½ - ¾ pint/300-450 ml Guinness (see note).

At Newport House in Co. Mayo everyone is always impressed by the wonderful picnics, put up in real old-fashioned wicker hampers. This moist Fruit Cake is the pièce de résistance — it has an unusual bitter-sweet flavour and (given the chance) it keeps for ages. I've made it successfully at home since visiting Newport, but found ½ pint/300 ml Guinness enough — I suggest you use as much as needed to make a good wet mixture.

Butter and base-line a deep 8"/20 cm cake tin. Preheat a moderate oven, 350°F, 180°C, Gas mark 4. Sift the flour into a mixing bowl, cut in the butter and rub in until the mixture is like fine breadcrumbs. Add all the remaining dry ingredients and mix well. Blend the eggs with half of the Guinness and add, together with enough of the remaining Guinness to make a wet dropping consistency. Turn into the tin and bake in the centre of the preheated oven for 1½ hours, or until the top is springy to the touch and the sides are shrinking slightly from the tin. Cool in the tin before turning out and peeling off the lining paper. Stored in an airtight tin, it will keep for weeks.

Dundee Cake

One of the best of all traditional cakes, it keeps well and is best kept at least a week before cutting. With its attractive topping of split almonds it makes a great present.

Grease and base-line a deep 7"/18cm round cake tin, preferably loose-based. Preheat a fairly slow oven, 325°F/170°C/Gas mark 3. Cream the butter and sugar until light and fluffy. Gradually beat in the eggs and grated zest. Sift the flour, baking powder, salt and spice into the bowl and fold in gently with the mixed fruit, peel and ground almonds. (If the cherries are very sticky, wash and dry them before quartering). The mixture should be fairly stiff, but add a little milk if it is difficult to stir. Spoon into the prepared tin and level the top of the cake with the back of a tablespoon. Then, starting at the outside, arrange the split almonds in rings, not too close together, finishing with just 3 or 4 split almonds in the centre. Bake in the middle of the very moderate oven for 2 hours, or until the cake is shrinking slightly from the tin and when tested with a skewer, it comes out clean. Remove the cake from the oven and leave to cool in the tin. When cold, peel off the lining paper on the base, wrap in fresh greaseproof paper and store in an airtight tin.

6 oz/170g soft butter
6 oz/170g light golden brown sugar or caster sugar
3 eggs
Finely grated zest of 1 orange or lemon
8 oz/225g plain flour
1/2 level teaspoon baking powder
A good pinch of salt
1 teaspoon mixed spice
6 oz/175g sultanas
6 oz/175g raisins
6 oz/175g currants
3 oz/75g glacé cherries, quartered
2 oz/50g chopped candied peel
1 oz/25g ground almonds
A little milk (if required)
1-2 oz/25-50g blanched split almonds.

Swiss Rolls

Swiss Rolls seem to be unfashionable at the moment, but are delicious, light, fun to make and versatile — after all, in the unlikely event of having any leftovers, it's a great excuse to make a trifle.

For a swiss roll tin about 12"x8"/30x20cm, take a piece of greaseproof paper big enough to line the base and ends; brush both tin and paper thoroughly with melted butter or margarine.

Preheat a fairly hot oven, 400°F, 200°C, Gas mark 6.

Whisk the eggs and sugar in an electric mixer at high speed until thick and creamy. (OR, whisk by hand in a bowl over hot water until frothy, then remove and continue whisking until cool.) Lightly but thoroughly, fold in the flour with a metal spoon, including the baking powder if using, with the last spoonful. Pour into the greased and papered tin and bake in the hot oven for about 10 minutes, or until the sponge is light golden brown and springy to the touch. Meanwhile, lay out a sheet of greaseproof paper on top of a damp tea towel and scatter it with caster sugar. Turn the cake out onto the sugared paper, trim off the crisp edges and spread quickly with the jam. Roll up quickly, using the greaseproof paper as a guide. When completely rolled, leave the paper around it for a minute or two, then remove and put the swiss roll on a rack to cool. Sprinkle with caster sugar and eat very fresh.

Variations: For **Chocolate Swiss Roll** simply substitute a heaped table-spoonful of cocoa powder for the same amount of flour and sift flour and cocoa together thoroughly. Fill with whipped cream and dust with icing sugar to serve.

Other variations are endless. The cake base can be flavoured in all kinds of ways, with coffee essence, or finely grated lemon or orange zest, and/or the filling can be varied by flavouring whipped cream (orange flower water or rose water makes a charming addition) or by including other ingredients such as chopped nuts or, perhaps, soft fruit.

Serves 8-10 slices:

3 large eggs
3 1/2 oz/90g caster sugar
3 oz/75g flour
1/4 tsp baking powder (optional)
2 tablespoons home-made raspberry jam, warmed if stiffly set
Caster sugar for rolling.

Date Slices

Date Slices used to be a great treat in our family in the '50s and I remember how delicious they were also from a home-made cake shop when we were on holiday, so I was delighted to find the recipe in an old note-book recently.

Date Slices: Makes 16:

12 oz/350g pressed dates,
  stoned and chopped
6 tbsp water
Grated zest of 1/2 large
  lemon
8 oz/225g fine wholemeal flour
4 oz/100g flaked oats
3 oz/75g light golden
  brown or Demerara sugar
5 oz/150g butter or
  margarine, melted.

Put the dates, water and lemon zest in a saucepan. Heat gently, stirring occasionally until the mixture is soft. Combine the remaining ingredients and sprinkle half the mixture into an 11" x 7"/28 cm x 18 cm shallow cake tin and press down well. Cover with the dates, sprinkle the remaining oat mixture over and press down firmly. Bake in a preheated oven, 400°F, 200°C, Gas mark 6 for 20 minutes, or until golden. Cool in the tin, then cut into slices.

Variations: Figs can be used instead of dates to give a very similar result. Other fruit, such as apricots, are also good but have quite a different, tarter, flavour.

Cherry Buns

Cherry Buns are very quick to make (especially if you use a food processor for the rubbing-in) and the basic recipe is almost endlessly variable, so they're ideal if people drop in for tea unexpectedly or for children coming in hungry from school. [Microwave]

Cherry Buns: Makes 12

8 oz/225g self-raising flour
1/4 teaspoon salt
3 oz/75g butter
4 oz/100g glacé cherries,
  chopped
4 oz/100g granulated sugar
1 egg
Milk to mix
Extra cherries for
  decoration (optional).

Preheat a hot oven, 425°F, 220°C, Gas mark 7. Sieve together the flour and salt and rub in the butter. Add the chopped cherries and half of the sugar and mix with the lightly beaten egg and enough milk to give a soft dropping consistency. Lightly grease a tray of deep bun tins and three-quarters fill them with the mixture. Lay a half cherry lightly on top of each if you like, then sprinkle the remaining sugar on top and bake in the hot oven for about 20 minutes, until well-risen and golden brown. Turn out and cool on a rack.

Variations: **Sultana, Raisin** or **Currant Buns** are made in exactly the same way. **Date Buns** are made using 4 oz/100g stoned, chopped dates.

Drop Scones

On a different tack entirely, it might be nice to make something quick but more-ish for tea, such as Drop Scones. More a pancake than a scone, they're absolutely delicious eaten straight from the pan with butter and jam and not at all tricky to make. Although traditionally made on a griddle, a heavy cast-iron pan is fine.

8 oz/225g plain (cream)
  flour
1/2 level teaspoon salt
2 level teaspoons cream of
  tartar
1 level tsp bread soda
2 level tablespoons caster
  sugar or 1 tablespoon
  sugar and 1 tablespoon
  golden syrup
2 large eggs
Scant 1/2 pint/275 ml milk.

If you don't have cream of tartar and bread soda, leave these out and use self-raising flour instead of plain.

Sift together the dry ingredients; make a well in the centre and add sugar, syrup and eggs. Gradually add the milk, then beat well to make a thick, smooth batter. (Use a processor or blender to do this very quickly if you have one.) Heat the griddle or frying pan until very hot, grease the surface lightly with a white fat as for pancakes and dot dessertspoons of the mixture onto the smoking surface — cook a test one first to get the heat right, then do batches, spacing well apart. When bubbles start to rise to the surface and the pancakes are brown underneath, flip them over, then cook for a few seconds on the other side. Keep warm in a low oven, wrapped in a clean tea towel, until all the pancakes are ready, then serve warm with butter and jam. Makes about 30 scones.

Marmalade Popovers

Incredibly quick and easy if you have a processor or blender, as they are based on a batter like the pancake mixture used for drop scones. They're ideal for weekend guests — it's an easy way to impress everyone at breakfast, because the batter can be made the night before and you just pop them into the oven to bake while everyone is getting up. For the same reasons, they're perfect for children to make for a surprise breakfast in bed on Mother's Day or any other special occasion. You need deep bun/muffin tins for this recipe, which is just right for a tray of 12:

3 eggs
6 oz/175g plain flour
1/2 teaspoon salt
Good half pint/325 ml milk
1 teaspoon finely grated
  orange rind
1 1/2 tablespoons melted
  butter or oil
12 teaspoons marmalade,
  preferably home-made.

Make a batter with the eggs, flour, salt and milk — use a processor or blender, put the eggs in first to prevent the flour from sticking to the bowl and mix until smooth. Add the orange zest and melted butter or oil and

Above: Guard of Honour, page 21
Right: Chocolate Marquise with Crème
Anglaise, page 30

A selection of breads, page 48

Whether you mix and knead the dough by hand or machine, bread-making is a most satisfying activity. Not only is handling the dough reckoned to be highly therapeutic, but there is a very primitive pleasure to be gained by making such a basic food for your family and friends. It also impresses people out of all proportion to the degree of skill involved — more power to the growing number of restaurateurs who are making good bread, or a selection of breads, a house speciality: they've definitely got the psychology right. Once you've got into the way of it, you will find it very hard to go back to bought bread because it really isn't time-consuming and the quality is so good — better even than the greatly improved breads we can now buy from in-store bakeries, although they certainly have their place.

blend again until thoroughly mixed and smooth, with bubbles rising. Pour into a jug, cover and put aside in a cool place until required.

Preheat a hot oven, 425°F/220°C/Gas mark 7. Grease the deep bun/muffin tins well and put into the oven until really hot. Divide the batter evenly between them, filling each one about two-thirds full, then stir a small spoonful of marmalade into each one (the marmalade can be warmed slightly if it is too stiff) and put straight into the hot oven. After about 10 minutes, reduce the temperature to 350°F/180°C/Gas mark 4 and bake for another 20 minutes or until well risen and golden brown. Eat hot with butter and more marmalade if you like.

Basic Brown Soda Bread

This simple, traditional bread is very wholesome and best eaten fresh with butter, farmhouse cheese and a bowl of home-made soup or some crisp sticks of celery. All sorts of flours and other grains — pinhead oatmeal, wheatgerm and bran for example, can be used in brown soda bread, giving a very versatile loaf. Although delicious eaten warm from the oven, it slices better if left to cool and 'set' for at least four hours.

Makes one large loaf:
1 lb/450g coarse wholemeal flour
6 oz/175g plain white flour
1 rounded teaspoon bread soda
1 teaspoon salt
About ¾ pint/425 ml buttermilk or sour milk.

Preheat a hot oven 400°F, 200°C, Gas mark 6.

Mix the dry ingredients in a mixing bowl and stir in enough buttermilk to make a fairly soft dough. Turn onto a work surface dusted with wholemeal flour and knead lightly until smooth underneath. Form into a circle about 1½"/3.8cm thick, and put onto a baking sheet. Mark a deep cross on the top with a floured knife. Bake for about 45 minutes, or until the bread is browned and sounds hollow when tapped on the base. Cool on a wire rack, wrapped in a tea towel if you want to keep a soft crust.

Variation: **Dillisk**, or **Dulce, Bread** can be made using this recipe. Add a small handful of the washed and finely chopped seaweed to the flour with the buttermilk. It's an attractive loaf and a good accompaniment to cheese.

Traditional White Soda Bread

A basic mixture which can be adapted to make a sweet fruited version (see below). White soda bread is less varied than brown because the ingredients are more restricted, but it is very delicious and, like scones, should be eaten on the day of baking.

1 lb/450g plain flour
½ teaspoon salt
1 teaspoon caster sugar
1 teaspoon bread soda
1 oz/25g butter
½ pint/300ml buttermilk

Preheat a hot oven, 425°F, 220°C, Gas mark 7. Mix the flour, salt, sugar and soda together, then cut in the butter and rub in lightly. Stir in enough buttermilk to make a soft dough. Turn onto a floured worktop and knead quickly and lightly. Form the dough into a flat, round cake about 2"/5cm high, and cut a deep cross in it to ensure that it cooks evenly. Put onto a floured baking tray and bake in the hot oven for 30-40 minutes or until well risen and lightly browned. When cooked, it will sound hollow when tapped on the base. Cool on a wire rack and eat very fresh with butter and home-made jam. Makes one loaf or four farls (quarters).

Variation: To make **Fruit Soda Bread**, increase the sugar to 1 tablespoonful and add 4 to 6 oz/100-150g sultanas or a mixture of currants, sultanas and chopped candied peel to the rubbed-in ingredients.

Note: The butter, which can be rubbed into the dry ingredients or melted and added with the buttermilk, is optional but it enriches the bread and helps it to keep better.

Golden Crunch

Golden Crunch is very easy for kids to make and it makes a good big batch, which is just as well as they enjoy eating it at least as much as making it. It is very like flapjack, but without the syrup.

Makes at least 2 dozen pieces:
12 oz/350g butter or block margarine
12 oz/350g brown sugar, Demerara or light golden brown
1 lb/450g oatflakes.

Grease a very large shallow baking/swiss roll tin, about 16"x10½"/40cm x 27 cm. Preheat a moderately hot oven, 375°F, 190°C, Gas mark 5. Put the butter and sugar into a large heavy-based saucepan and warm through together over gentle heat until they have both melted. Add the oatflakes, stir to mix thoroughly and cook together for a minute or two. Turn into the prepared tin and spread out evenly. Flatten down with the back of a tablespoon, working well into the corners. Put into the oven and reduce the temperature to moderate, 350°F,180°C, Gas mark 4. Bake for about half an hour until golden-brown. Remove from the oven, allow to cool a little and then mark into squares or fingers. Leave in the tin until cold, then cut where marked. Store in an airtight tin.

Chocolate Chip Cookies

Version 1: makes about 18

8 oz/225g flour
l tsp baking powder
4 oz/100g (block) margarine
4 oz/100g sugar
2 oz/50g dark cooking
   chocolate
l egg
l teaspoon vanilla essence.

Version 2

4 oz/100g butter or
   margarine, at room
   temperature
2 oz/50g light golden
   brown sugar
2 oz/50g granulated sugar
1 egg
A few drops of vanilla
   essence (optional)
5 oz/150g flour
1/2 teaspoon bread soda
Pinch of salt
4 oz/100g chocolate chips
2 oz/50g walnuts, or other
   chopped nuts (optional).

Another good little number for the kids to make, either for themselves or for the picnic basket, is Chocolate Chip Cookies. This Mark 1 version is based on a rolled dough and makes quite big, flat biscuits — it is very popular with my youngest son, but being very more-ish, it's difficult to say if they keep well.

Preheat a moderate oven, 350°F/ 180°C/Gas mark 4.

Sieve flour and baking powder into a bowl and rub in margarine. Add sugar and chopped chocolate. Beat the egg lightly with the vanilla, add to the dry ingredients and mix well to make a stiff dough. Turn onto a floured work surface, knead until smooth, then roll out to 1/2"/1.2 cm thick. Stamp out with 21/2"–3"/6.5–7.5 cm cutters, place well spaced out on greased baking trays and bake in the preheated oven for 20 minutes or until nicely browned.

Chocolate Chip Cookies (2) is a chewier version and quicker to make as there is no rolling out involved.

Preheat a moderately hot oven, 375°F, 190°C, Gas mark 5.

Beat the butter with both sugars until pale and fluffy, then beat in the egg and vanilla essence. Sift flour, soda and salt and beat into the mixture. Stir in the chocolate chips and finely chopped nuts. Place small spoonsful of the mixture onto greased or non-stick baking trays, leaving plenty of room for the cookies to spread. Bake for 10-15 minutes, until the little heaps have become thick cookies and are just turning golden brown. Lift off the baking sheets and leave to cool and harden on wire racks.

Chocolate Saucepan Cake

*Makes an 8"/20cm cake,
   serving 8 good wedges:*

Basic Mixture:

8 oz/225g digestive or other
   plain biscuits
2 oz/50g butter
2 tablespoons golden syrup
41/2 oz/125g chocolate,
   preferably a plain dessert
   chocolate such as
   Bournville

Optional extras: Depending
   on taste and availability,
   add raisins, glacé cherries,
   chopped nuts etc,
   including as much as the
   mixture can hold.

Chocolate Saucepan Cake is another long-time favourite in our house and, apart from being delicious, it has many virtues. It's a great way to use up all those oddments of broken biscuits that collect at the bottom of the tin and need to be cleared out every now and then — anything fairly plain can be used — and, as there's virtually no cooking involved, even quite young children can do it almost by themselves. It travels well too, making it useful for picnics. [Microwave]

Oil an 8"/20 cm sandwich tin, or flan ring (set on a greased baking sheet).

Put the biscuits into a heavy duty freezer bag and crush roughly with a rolling pin — not too finely, as there should still be a bit of crunch. Put the butter, syrup and chocolate into a large, heavy-based pan and warm through over gentle heat until everything has melted. Stir well, then add the crushed biscuits and mix until they are well coated. Now add any extras, remembering that a good coating of the chocolate mixture is needed to hold everything together. Turn the mixture into the prepared tin or flan ring and smooth the top down firmly with the back of a tablespoon. If convenient, pat down all over with the cut surface of half a lemon — this will give the cake a smooth and shiny surface. Leave until cold and set, then remove from the tin, wrap in greaseproof and store in an airtight tin, or double-wrap in foil. Cut into wedges to serve.

CHOCOLATE HINTS

★ Chopping chocolate: chips can be made very successfully in the food processor. However, it is hard to make chocolate chips by hand. If you have to, grate coarsely instead of chopping.

★ When baking, sift cocoa and drinking chocolate with the other dry ingredients. But when using in icing, the starch must be cooked, so blend the powder with very hot water — not boiling, though, as it makes a lump which is difficult to use.

★ If you need bitter chocolate, ordinary plain chocolate, such as Bournville, can be made slightly 'bitter' by adding a little strong black coffee, a little instant coffee powder/granules or 1 teaspoon cocoa powder per 2 oz chocolate.

★ If using a mould, make sure it is scrupulously clean, or the chocolate will stick to the mould and crack.

CHOCOLATE DECORATIONS

★ Make decorative Chocolate Cups for serving scoops of home-made ice cream or mousse-textured sweets: Break 4 oz/100g dark dessert chocolate, eg Bournville, into a mixing bowl set over a pan of hot water. Set 16 bun baking cases in pairs on a baking tray (i.e. double thickness to make 8 shells). Drop a spoonful of the melted chocolate into each one, then tilt to run the chocolate over the base and sides of the case, to make a cup. As it is finished, turn each one upside down so that the chcolate runs to the edge and forms a rim. Chill until firm, (or until required) then peel the paper cases away. Citrus mousses complement the cups especially well and the dramatic presentation can make a very simple dessert seem special — try it with Lemon Whip, perhaps (See Winter Desserts.). *Variations*: Can also make a large shell in the same way.

★ Although special metal leaf moulds can be bought at specialist kitchen shops, chocolate leaves can easily be made using real leaves, especially firm, well-defined ones such as rose leaves: paint melted chocolate onto the underside of the leaves, chill until firm, then peel away and you will be left with a perfect leaf shape.

★ To make chocolate caraque, spread a thin layer of melted chocolate onto a cold smooth surface, preferably marble. When it has lost its shine and has almost set, scrape a sharp kitchen knife across it at an angle to make rolls like ragged scrolls. Caraque makes a glamorous decoration for desserts and party gateaux. Shorter, less dramatic rolls can be taken straight off a block of dessert chocolate using a vegetable peeler.

★ For sweets and petits fours: using a fork to hold them individually, dip whole nuts — blanched almonds, brazil nuts, hazelnuts — into melted chocolate, then lay out on non-stick baking parchment to set. Fruit such as strawberries, cherries, grapes or orange segments or crystallised peel look and taste marvellous if half-dipped in chocolate, providing visual contrast as well as flavour.

SPRING   Yeast Baking

Yeast cookery is outside the Irish tradition but it seems to be catching on with the success of the easy-mix dried yeasts and easier availability of fresh yeast. Fresh yeast takes more time and patience, but it does make a loaf with better texture and flavour which dries out less easily. In any case, the time involved should not be exaggerated: most of the time the yeast and dough work away on their own, leaving the cook free to get on with other things except for a few brief intervals when the dough requires attention.

Whether you mix and knead the dough by hand or machine — a Kenwood Chef with a dough hook is undoubtedly the single greatest asset for an enthusiastic yeast baker — bread-making is a most satisfying activity. Not only is handling the dough reckoned to be highly therapeutic, but there is a very primitive pleasure to be gained by making such a basic food for your family and friends. It also impresses people out of all proportion to the degree of skill involved — more power to the growing number of restaurateurs who are making good bread, or a selection of breads, a house speciality: they've definitely got the psychology right. Once you've got into the way of it, you will find it very hard to go back to bought bread because it really isn't time-consuming and the quality is so good — better even than the greatly improved breads we can now buy from in-store bakeries, though they certainly have their place.

Some Hints on Yeast Baking

★ Although quick breads have obvious advantages and are in fact very good if eaten fresh, the more slowly yeast bread is made the better it is, so try not to rush it — flavour, texture and keeping qualities will all be improved by patience.

★ Yeast is an extremely nutritious ingredient, rich in the B vitamins which are killed by the bicarbonate of soda in soda bread. It is a live organism which works by transforming the natural sugars in the flour into tiny bubbles of carbon dioxide that expand during baking to give the bread its texture and taste. Yeast thrives and multiplies in warmth, can survive cold (for storage) but is killed by high temperatures, so yeast dough cannot be hurried by heating it prematurely — the back of an Aga is just about perfect for getting the best out of yeast and, having seen it work so well throughout my childhood is certainly the explanation for my own love of yeast cookery. Now, with a modern fan oven, the charm is less obvious — but the magic is still there. Use fresh yeast if possible. It is now available quite easily through the various in-store bakeries, is not expensive and keeps very well. Providing it is well-wrapped but allowed to breathe a little (wrapped in greaseproof paper and kept in a snap-top plastic box, for example) fresh yeast will keep for several weeks in the coldest part of the fridge. Better still, it keeps for months in the freezer — just divide into 1 oz/25g pieces, wrap in clingfilm and store in a freezer bag or box.

★ 1 oz/25g fresh yeast should be enough to rise a 3 lb/1.4 Kg batch of plain dough, to make four l lb/450g loaves. If the yeast is stale (it will look brown and crumbly instead of pale and creamy), or if it has been in the freezer for a long time, allow a little extra. In my experience wholemeal bread also benefits from extra yeast, as the gluten content of the flour is lower. Yeast works more efficiently in a large quantity of dough, so when doubling a recipe it is not usually necessary to double the amount of yeast. On the other hand, when the dough is enriched with fruit or other ingredients, the proportion of yeast required is higher.

★ Sugar is vital, along with liquid and warmth, to feed the yeast and enable it to grow. For white bread, ordinary white sugar is used in small quantities, about 2 teaspooons per 1 oz/25g fresh yeast. Wholemeal loaves need only the same amount to make the dough rise, but a larger quantity of a brown sugar — say a tablespoonful of rich dark brown sugar per 1 oz/25g yeast — improves the colour and character of the bread. Black treacle can also be included to give a more interesting, moister loaf.

★ For white bread, use strong white flour, preferably unbleached, as ordinary plain (cream) flour lacks flavour and is made from softer wheat with a lower gluten content — it is gluten that gives the dough its elasticity, vital to a good, light texture. Because wholemeal flour has less gluten it can be a good idea to include a proportion of strong white flour in your brown bread: two thirds wholemeal to one third strong white makes a good loaf. Fine ground wholemeal is generally more satisfactory for yeast baking than the coarser types that suit soda breads.

★ Salt is essential to good bread and using too little is one of the most common beginners' mistakes. Salt gives flavour, strengthens the gluten content of the dough and prevents the yeast from fermenting too quickly. The exact amount required depends on the bread being made, but an average 3lb/1.4 Kg batch needs a tablespoonful of salt, preferably cooking salt, or sea salt.

★ Storage of bread can be a problem in the modern kitchen — builders no longer consider a cool larder, with external ventilation a necessity (why not, one wonders?). The atmosphere in the kitchen is usually too warm and dry and space is too limited for the earthenware crocks that provide both insulation and ventilation. Assuming a batch of four loaves (which must be absolutely cold before wrapping), the best solution is to keep one loaf in the bread bin for immediate use, the next well wrapped in the fridge for use within the following two days and the other two in the freezer. Fortunately, bread freezes extremely well. It is best left to defrost naturally, in which case it will age at the same rate as a fresh loaf. If urgently required it can be defrosted by microwave, but it should be used fairly quickly as there will be a tendency to dry out much more quickly.

Note: Where instructions are given for fresh yeast, any of the recipes can easily be adapted to using the easy-blend yeast (sold as Fast Action Dried Yeast). It is extremely simple to use, as the dried yeast mixture is simply blended into the other dry ingredients before liquid is added and, as it requires only one kneading and proving, time is certainly saved. However, although the results are good if eaten when very fresh, bread made with dried yeast doesn't have quite the same moist, doughy texture or keep as well as bread made with fresh yeast. In my experience you also need to use more than recommended by the manufacturers: although it will work with the amount suggested, i.e. 1 sachet per 1½ lb/700g flour, to make two loaves, increasing the proportion to 1 sachet per 1 lb/450g flour works better, especially for wholemeal flour.

Basic White Bread

This makes four loaves, or it can be made into plaits, cottage loaves or rolls.

Cream the yeast and caster sugar together in a measuring jug, add about ¼ pint/150 ml of the measured liquid and leave in a warm place for about 10 minutes to froth up. Meanwhile, mix the salt into the flour and rub in the fat. Using a Kenwood Chef with a dough hook attachment, or working by hand in a mixing bowl, add the yeast mixture and remaining liquid to the flour and work it in to make a firm dough which leaves the bowl clean. Knead well, either by hand on a floured surface, or in the mixer, until the dough has become firm and elastic — with experience it is easy to tell when the texture is right, but it is better to knead too much rather than too little as it is impossible to over-knead bread. Return to the bowl, cover lightly with a tea towel and leave in a warmish (but not hot) place to rise for an hour or until it has doubled in size. The dough will now be very springy and full of air. Turn it out onto a floured work surface and 'knock back', flattening it out with your knuckles to knock the air out. Knead lightly into shape again, divide into four and form into loaf shapes. Lay the dough into four oiled 1 lb/450g loaf tins, pushing down well to fit into the corners, then leave to rise again for another 20-30 minutes, or until the dough is rising just above the rims of the tins. Meanwhile, preheat a very hot oven, 450°F, 230°C, Gas mark 8. Bake the loaves in the centre of the oven for about half an hour, or until well browned and shrinking from their tins — when turned out and rapped on the base they should sound hollow. For a crusty finish all round, the loaves can be removed from the tins and returned to the oven for a few minutes to crispen up. Cool on wire racks.

Variations: If you have no loaf tins, you can form the Basic White Bread dough into rolls or any suitable loaf shapes and bake on greased baking trays. Baking time will be shorter for rolls, only 15-20 minutes.

Olive Bread

Olive Bread is a delicious variation on white bread and has found its way into many an exclusive restaurant recently, where it is usually made into rolls.

Sift the flour, salt and rosemary into the bowl of an electric mixer and put in a warm place until required. Cream the yeast with the light golden

Makes four 1 lb/450 g loaves:
1 oz/25g fresh yeast
2 teaspoons caster sugar
1½ pints/900 ml tepid water or milk and water mixed
1 tablespoon (15 ml) salt
3 lb/1.4 Kg strong white flour, preferably unbleached
2 oz/50g lard or white cooking fat.

Olive Bread: Makes two 1 lb/ 450 g loaves, or at least 18 rolls:
1½ lb/700g strong white flour, preferably unbleached
2 teaspoons salt
½ teaspoon ground rosemary (optional)
½ oz/15g fresh yeast
1 teaspoon light golden brown sugar, or caster sugar
¾ pint/450 ml tepid water
2 tablespoons olive oil
6 oz/175g pitted black olives, drained and chopped.

brown sugar in a small bowl or measuring jug and add about ¼ pint/150 ml of the tepid water. Leave in a warm place for about 10 minutes until frothy. Make a well in the middle of the flour and pour in the yeast mixture, remaining tepid water and the olive oil. Using a dough hook, mix at very low speed (1) until combined then, when it is no longer likely to splash, gradually increase the speed to medium (3) and knead for 10-15 minutes until a ball of elastic dough has formed around the dough hook. Add the chopped olives and continue to knead until they are thoroughly mixed in. Turn the dough out onto a lightly floured surface, shape it into a ball and return it to the bowl. Cover with a cloth and leave in a fairly warm place for about 20 minutes, or until doubled in bulk. Meanwhile, grease two or three baking sheets. Knock the dough back, divide into three, then cut each portion into six equal pieces. Knead each one by hand to make a roll, tucking the 'corners' underneath. Lay out on the baking trays, leaving space between the rolls to allow for expansion. Cover lightly with tea towels and leave at room temperature for another 20-30 minutes or until well-risen. Meanwhile, preheat a hot oven, 425°F, 220°C, Gas mark 7. When the rolls are ready, bake near the top of the oven for about 15 minutes, or until golden brown and crisp — like bread loaves, the cooked rolls will sound hollow when tapped on the base. Cool on a wire rack.

Hint: If you want a shiny finish, the rolls can be brushed with melted butter just as they are coming out of the oven.

Onion & Walnut Bread

Makes two 1 lb/450g loaves, or at least 18 rolls:

2 large onions
3 tablespoons olive oil
6 oz/175g walnuts
1 oz/25g fresh yeast
l teaspoon caster sugar
¾ pint/450 ml warm water
1½ lb/700g strong white flour, preferably unbleached
2 teaspoons salt
3 tablespoons walnut oil.

Like the Olive Bread, this Onion & Walnut Bread is another which might find its way into a few restaurant bread baskets and, although very practical with lashings of butter and a big vegetable soup to make a delicious light lunch or supper, small rolls would also be a great conversation piece on the table at a dinner party.

Chop the onions quite finely and fry them crisp in the olive oil. Chop the walnuts fairly finely. Cream the yeast with the sugar in a measuring jug, add the warm water and leave until frothy. Sift the flour and salt into a large basin, make a well in the centre and add the yeast mixture and the walnut oil. Mix to make a dough, cover the bowl with a tea towel and leave to rise. Turn out onto a floured work surface, knock back and knead the dough again. Knuckle back to flatten, spread over the onions and walnuts and knead them into the dough. Either divide in half and place into two oiled loaf tins, then leave in a warm place to rise again for half an hour, or divide the dough up into 18 or more rolls and lay out on oiled baking sheets. Preheat a fairly hot oven, 400°F, 200°C, Gas mark 6. When the rolls have risen, bake them in the preheated oven for 10 minutes, then reduce the temperature to 375°F, 190°C, Gas mark 5 and bake for another 10-15 minutes, or until they are a crisp golden-brown and sound hollow when tapped on the base. As with the Olive Bread, the Onion & Walnut rolls can be glazed with melted butter as they come out of the oven. Cool on wire racks. If baking loaves, reduce the temperature of the preheated oven to 375°F, 190°C, Gas mark 5 as they go into the oven and bake at that temperature for 50 minutes to l hour. If, when you turn out the loaves to test them, the sides and base are soft and damp, remove them from their tins and return to the oven, upside down, for 5-10 minutes until crisp and hollow-sounding. Cool on wire racks.

Basic Wholemeal Bread

This is a recipe for a genuinely rich and chewy Basic Wholemeal Bread although you could lighten the texture by including a third to half strong white flour to wholemeal. Although you can make rolls and other simple variations on this recipe, loaves are best made in tins as the dough is too heavy to make into fancy shapes.

Put the flour into a large bowl and mix in the salt. Put into a low oven to warm through for a few minutes. Meanwhile, put the yeast into a small basin or measuring jug with the sugar. Cream together and stir in about 1/4 pint/150 ml of the measured liquid; leave to froth up. Remove the mixing bowl from the oven. Rub in the lard, then make a well in the centre and add the yeast mixture and, gradually, the rest of the liquid. Knead well, by hand or machine, adding a little extra flour if the dough is too sticky to come away from the bowl and form a ball. Cover and leave to rise for an hour or until doubled in size, then knock back, knead again briefly and divide into four portions. Form into loaf shapes and lay into four greased 1 lb/450g loaf tins, tucking well into the corners. Leave for another 20 minutes or so to rise again. Meanwhile, heat a very hot oven, 450°F, 230°C, Gas mark 8. When the bread is coming up over the top of the tins, bake in the centre of the preheated oven for 20 minutes, then reduce the temperature to 400°F, 200°C, Gas mark 6 and bake for another 15-20 minutes, or until the loaves are well browned and shrinking from the tins. When baked, the bases will sound hollow when tapped. Turn out and cool on a wire rack.

Makes four 1 lb/450g loaves or two larger ones:

3 lb/1.4 Kg fine wholemeal flour
1 tablespoon salt
1 oz/25g fresh yeast
2 heaped teaspoons rich dark brown sugar
1¾ pints/1 litre tepid water or milk and water
1 oz/25g lard.

Quick Wholemeal Yeast Bread

This popular, much-requested recipe for Quick Wholemeal Yeast Bread is a compromise between the various methods, as it is kneaded but only has one rising, in the tin. It takes very little time or attention and this version, using dried yeast, is particularly simple although the same recipe can very easily be used with fresh yeast instead, using 1-1½oz/25-40g fresh yeast and 2 teaspoons rich dark brown sugar instead of the dried yeast.

Mix flour, salt and yeast well in the bowl of a Kenwood Chef. Measure milk, hot water and oil into a jug. Using a dough hook, start on a low speed and add the tepid milk, water and oil mixture. When the liquid has been absorbed into the flour and is unlikely to splash, increase to a medium speed (3) and mix until the dough forms a ball around the dough hook, leaving the sides of the bowl clean. If the mixture seems too wet, sprinkle a little extra flour down the side of the bowl; if too dry, add a little extra liquid — the absorbency rate of flour varies, so the measured amounts aren't always quite right. (If you aren't using a mixer, mix by hand in a large bowl until manageable, then turn out onto a floured work surface and knead until a smooth, elastic ball of dough is formed.) Turn the dough out onto a floured worktop, knead lightly, then quarter the ball and knead each piece individually until smooth. Form into oblong shapes and put into four oiled 1 lb/450 g loaf tins, pressing well into the corners. Leave in a warm place for about 20-30 minutes to rise. Preheat a very hot oven, 450°F, 230°C, Gas mark 8. When the dough is coming over the tops of the tins, transfer to the centre of the hot oven and bake for 30-40 minutes until well browned and shrinking slightly from the tins; the bases should sound hollow when tapped. Take the loaves out of the tins for the last 5 or 10 minutes if you like a crisp crust. Cool on a wire rack.

Makes four x 1 lb/450g loaves:

3 lb/1.4 Kg fine wholemeal flour (OR 2 lb/900g wholemeal and 1 lb/450g strong white)
3 rounded teaspoons salt
3 sachets easy-blend/fast action dried yeast
3 tablespoons sunflower or groundnut oil
1 pint/600 milk, made up to 1¾ pints/1 litre with boiling water.

Variations: Using any of the basic recipes given, you could divide the basic mixture into three instead of four and make the following:

Cheese Bread: A third of a basic bread dough above; 8 oz/225g grated Cheddar cheese; pinch of mustard powder; 1 beaten egg. Work the cheese, mustard and egg into the dough. Place the dough in a lightly greased large (2 lb/900g) loaf tin, then leave to rise and bake as above.

Garlic Bread: A third of a basic bread dough above; 3 cloves garlic, crushed in a little salt. Knead the crushed garlic into the dough and continue as above. Serve hot with soups and salads.

Herb Bread: A third of a basic bread dough above; 2 tsp oregano;

$1^1/_2$ tsp rosemary; 1 tsp turmeric; $^1/_2$ tsp sage. Knead the herbs into the dough until evenly distributed, then continue as above.

Cheese Baps are another slightly more complicated variation, good for packed lunches and picnics or with soup, served split, buttered and filled with mustard and cress. A third of a basic bread dough above; 1 egg, beaten; 9 oz/250 g grated Cheddar cheese. Work the egg into the dough until evenly mixed. Roll out the dough on a lightly floured surface to a rectangle 15"x10"/38cmx25cm. Sprinkle a third of the cheese over the centre third of the dough. Fold the left-hand third of the dough over the cheese. Sprinkle another third of the cheese over the double thickness of dough, then fold the right-hand side of the dough towards the centre to cover the cheese completely. Press down well. Stamp out 4"/10 cm rounds, folding and rolling trimmings to make the last baps. Place on a floured baking tray and brush lightly with milk. Sprinkle with the remaining cheese and bake in a hot oven, 200°C, 400°F, Gas mark 6, for about 25 minutes. Cool on a wire tray. Makes 6 baps.

Pizza Base & Toppings

For 4 pizzas:

1 lb/450g strong white flour
1 teaspoon salt
1 sachet easy-blend/fast
  action dried yeast
2 tablespoons olive oil
Scant 10 fl oz/300 ml
  lukewarm water.

The correct dough for a real pizza base is made with yeast and, although it takes time, it is much quicker using easy-blend dried yeast which requires only one kneading and proving. Although not, perhaps, totally authentic, this is a lot nearer to the perfect pizza than the usual short-cut scone base.

Mix dry ingredients together in a mixing bowl (or, better still, in the bowl of a mixer with a dough hook), add the oil and water and mix well. Knead by hand or machine for 5-10 minutes until smooth, then divide the ball of dough into four and stretch with the hands so that the dough makes a fairly thin base on the pizza tins (or flat tin pie plates), leaving a raised rim around the edge to contain the filling. Brush the rim with olive oil and leave to prove in a warm place for 15-20 minutes while you prepare the topping.

Hints for better/faster Pizzas

For a really crisp base, heat a baking sheet in the oven and slide the prepared pizzas straight onto it for baking.

Although ready-made bases are very useful to have in the freezer or store cupboard, a simple scone mixture makes an acceptable fresh base if you're in a hurry. A mixture based on 2 oz/50 g butter or margarine rubbed into 8 oz/225 g self-raising flour will make one large or 2 small pizzas.

Even simpler is the option of using French bread as a base. Not very Italian, admittedly, but extremely quick.

Topping: The simplest tomato base is well-drained chopped tomatoes; tinned Italian plum tomatoes are 'correct' and they can be puréed and seasoned to make a sauce if preferred. Alternatively, when fresh tomatoes are cheap, you can make a thick sauce with ripe tomatoes, onion, garlic, seasonings and perhaps some concentrated tomato purée to give it a boost. The traditional pizza herbs are oregano (or its cousin, marjoram) and basil, which can be used generously if fresh, more cautiously if dried. Either stir the herbs into the tomato sauce, if using, or scatter them over. The classic cheese for pizza is mozzarella which melts to make delicious creamy white 'strings'; it is best if diced and scattered over the pizza to make a contrast of colour and flavour between the dough and the tomato. Other ingredients such as anchovies, olives, grilled peppers or mushrooms can be added to taste, but olive oil is essential for drizzling over the top.

Baking: Before assembling the pizzas, par-cook the bases for 7-10 minutes in a very hot oven, 450°F, 230°C, Gas mark 8. Prick any puffy bits with a fork, then spread with tomato topping and the other ingredients, finishing with the cheese and finally a drizzle of olive oil. Return to the oven and cook for another 7-10 minutes until the cheese is just beginning to bubble. Drizzle over a little extra olive oil and serve immediately, with a green salad on the side.

Hint: Once fresh herbs come on stream in the garden, they can be chopped and kept in a freezer box so they're always handy. They keep their flavour surprisingly well and it's a useful way to preserve them for the winter at the end of the season. Simply use by the teaspoon and crumble as required.

Below: Tangy Lemon Tart, page 32
Previous page: Simnel Cake, page 36
Top right: Hazelnut Coffee Cake, page 39
Bottom right: Lemon Sponge, page 79
Page 56: Home-Made Wedding Cake, page 59

(Photo courtesy of the author)

Hot Cross Buns

Although they are very much a fleeting, seasonal thing Hot Cross Buns are fun. This quick version using easy-blend yeast might encourage the faint-hearted to give them a try and brighten Good Friday with their spicy aroma.

Sift flour, salt and mixed spice into a bowl. Mix in the yeast and caster sugar and rub in the butter. Beat the egg lightly. Make a well in the middle of the dry ingredients and mix in the egg and the tepid milk and water. Mix with a fork to make a rough dough, then turn onto a floured work surface and knead until it changes from being soft and sticky to make a smooth dough. Knuckle out the dough to flatten, then spread the currants and chopped peel over it. Gather up and knead lightly until the fruit is evenly dispersed through the dough. Shape the dough into a long sausage shape, divide into 12 equal portions and form each one into a neat roll. Place, well spaced apart, on greased baking sheets and leave in a warm place to rise. Meanwhile, preheat a hot oven, 425°F, 220°C, Gas mark 7.

To make the paste for the crosses, mix together the oil, milk and water and sift in the flour and salt. Whisk until smooth. Put into a paper piping bag, snip off the end and pipe over the buns. *or*, if all this sounds like too much trouble, simply slash the buns before baking to make a cross shape in the top. When the buns are puffy-looking, bake in the preheated oven for 15-20 minutes. To give them a glaze, brush with melted butter in the same way as for the Olive Bread, given above.

Makes 12:

12 oz/350g strong white
  flour
1 teaspoon salt
1 level teaspoon mixed spice
1 sachet fast-action
  /easy-blend dried yeast
1 teaspoon caster sugar
1 oz/25g butter
1 egg
1/4 pint/150 ml warm milk
  and water mixed
1 1/2 oz/40g currants
1/2 oz/15g chopped mixed
  peel

For the crosses:

2 teaspoons oil
2 teaspoons milk
2 tablespoons water
1 oz/25g self-raising flour
Pinch of salt.

Crumpets

Nothing whatsoever to do with Easter, but great fun to make, wickedly delicious when eaten by the fire just dripping with butter and somehow evocative of a more carefree era when calories and cholesterol didn't count — Crumpets say all that to me and more. Not surprisingly, children love them. They are baked in rings on a griddle or heavy frying pan, almost like a well-disciplined drop scone. The rings are available from specialist kitchen shops, or you can use egg-poaching rings.

Sift flour and salt into a bowl and leave in a warm place. Cream the yeast and sugar together in a mixing bowl, add the warm milk and water and leave for about 10 minutes until frothy. Make a well in the flour, add the yeast mixture and beat with a wooden spoon to make a smooth, thick batter. Cover the basin with a cloth and leave in a warm place for 30-40 minutes until light and frothy, then pour into a measuring jug and leave beside the hob. Heat the griddle thoroughly over moderate heat. Grease the rings and lightly grease the griddle with white fat, as for pancakes. Half-fill the rings with mixture ladled in from the jug. Cook steadily over moderate heat for about 5 minutes, until bubbles start coming to the surface, then lower the heat and cook gently until the bubbles have burst and the rings can be slipped off the crumpets; remove, turn the crumpets over and cook for a few minutes on the other side. Continue in batches until all the mixture has been used up — if you are using a griddle and have six rings, two batches should be enough but it will take longer in a frying pan. Either serve immediately, with lashings of butter and a sprinkling of salt or home-made jam, or cool on a wire rack and store: then toast them before serving — a toasting fork before the fire is the traditionally idyllic method, but they do very well under the grill or in an electric toaster.

Makes about a dozen:

8 oz/225g strong white flour
1/2 teaspoon salt
1 oz/25g fresh yeast
1 teaspoon caster sugar
1/4 pint/150 ml milk,
  warmed
7 fl oz/200 ml water.

Quick Barm Brack

This is basically the traditional yeasted brack mainly associated with Hallowe'en, but it's a much simpler version made with easy-blend yeast. Make it in loaf tins, as it's a more convenient shape for slicing, especially if you want to toast it.

Makes two 1 lb/450g loaves:

1 lb/450g plain flour
1/2 tsp ground cinnamon
1/4 tsp ground nutmeg
1/2 tsp salt
2 sachets easy-mix dried
  yeast
3 oz/75g rich dark brown
  sugar
4 oz/100g butter
1/2 pint/300 ml tepid milk
1 egg
8 oz/225g sultanas
4 oz/100g currants
2 oz/50g mixed chopped
  peel
Rings (optional).

*Gooseberry Bread: Makes two
  1 lb/450g loaves:*

8 oz/225g gooseberries
1 1/2 lb/700g strong plain
  flour
1/2 teaspoon salt
1/2 oz/15g fresh yeast
1 teaspoon sugar.

Mix the dry ingredients in a large bowl and make a well in the centre. Melt the butter, mix with the tepid milk and lightly beaten egg and turn into the bowl. Add the fruit and peel and mix thoroughly. Turn the mixture into two buttered 1 lb/450g loaf tins and, if it's for Hallowe'en, press a ring wrapped in foil into each one. Leave in a warm place for about half an hour to rise. Meanwhile, preheat a hot oven, 400°F, 200°C, Gas mark 6. When the dough has doubled in size and is showing above the rims of the tins, bake in the hot oven for about 45 minutes, or until they are shrinking slightly from the tins. When ready, they will sound hollow when tapped. Remove from the oven and brush over with a glaze made from 1 tablespoon of sugar dissolved in 2 tablespoons of boiling water, then return to the oven for about 3 minutes until the tops are a rich shiny brown. Turn onto a wire rack to cool. Serve sliced and buttered. The brack keeps well, but is delicious toasted and served hot-buttered. Makes two 1 lb/450g loaves.

Gooseberry Bread

Gooseberry Bread would make an unusual addition to the tea table — or an even more unusual accompaniment to an oily fish dish, such as grilled mackerel.

Simmer the gooseberries in very little water until soft enough to sieve. Put the flour and salt into a warm bowl. Cream the yeast with the sugar and add to the flour, together with the gooseberry purée. Knead well and leave in a fairly warm place to rise, until doubled in size, then turn out onto a floured surface, knock back and knead again before shaping into two loaves and pressing into two greased 1 lb/450g loaf tins. Leave to rise again until the dough has risen over the top of the tins. Bake in a preheated oven, 425°F, 220°C, Gas mark 7 for 15 minutes then reduce the temperature to 375°F, 190°C, Gas mark 5 and bake for another 45 minutes or until cooked — when upturned, the loaves will leave the tins easily and should sound hollow when rapped with the knuckles. If the fruit content has made the sides and base soft and moist, turn out of the tins and cook, upside down, for a further 5-10 minutes until crisp. Turn out onto racks to cool. *Variation:* Try other tart fruits, such as rhubarb, instead.

WEDDING CAKE

Ingredients:	6"/15cm tin	9"/22cm tin	12"/30cm tin
Currants	8 oz/225g	1 lb/450g	1 lb 12oz/800g
Sultanas	5 oz/150g	11 oz/300g	1 lb/450g
Raisins	3 oz/75g	6 oz/175g	9 oz/250g
Almonds, shredded	2 oz/50g	4 oz/100g	7 oz/200g
Glacé cherries	3 oz/75g	4 oz/100g	7 oz/200g
Peel, cut mixed	3 oz/75g	4 oz/100g	7 oz/200g
Plain flour	6 oz/175g	11 oz/300g	1 lb 3 oz/525g
Salt	Pinch	1 coffeespoon	1 teaspoon
Spices, mixed	3/4 tsp	1 1/2 tsp	2 1/2 tsp
Butter	5 oz/150g	10 oz/275g	1 lb/450g
Rich dark sugar	5 oz/150g	10 oz/275g	1 lb/450g
Black treacle	1 tbsp	1 1/2 tbsp	2 tbsp
Orange & lemon zest	1/2 tsp	1 tsp each	1 1/2 tsp each
Eggs	3 large	6 large	8 large
Vanilla essence	1/2 tsp	1 tsp	1 1/2 tsp
Brandy	2 tbsp	3 tbsp	4 tbsp
Approx cooking time	3-3 1/2 hrs	3 1/2-4 hrs	4 1/2-5 1/2 hrs.

▶

Home-Made Wedding Cake

Making a wedding cake isn't really any harder than making Christmas cakes. If there are several tiers to deal with it's a longer job, admittedly, but the basic baking is just the same. The bit which most home cooks do find too difficult is the icing, although even that can be done successfully without too much trouble if you keep it simple. Fondant icing is much easier to apply than traditional royal icing — you just roll it out and enfold the whole of each tier in a sheet of it in a single operation — and it can also be used by quite inexperienced cooks for moulding decorations. Alternatively, you can bake the cakes yourself and get a specialist to finish it.

The recipe given here makes a 3-tier square cake using 6"/15cm, 9"/22 cm and 12"/30 cm square tins and the same quantities would make a round one, using 7"/18cm, 10"/25cm and 13"/33cm tins. This makes a fairly shallow cake, about 2"/5 cm deep before almond paste or icing have been applied. If you like a deeper cake, use tins one size smaller and allow for the extra depth in longer baking time. If you are nervous about the job in hand, try making the smallest cake first and build up your confidence gradually.

The method used is the same as for any rich fruit cake. Prepare the tins by greasing and lining with three layers of greaseproof paper, extending at least 2"/5cm above the top of the tin. Tie a thick band of folded newspaper around the outside of the tin to protect the edge of the cake from over-cooking. Have ready some brown paper or foil to protect the top of the cake if it is in danger of over-browning. Handling the large cake can be daunting and must be done with great care — the weight may take you by surprise when lifting it from the oven. Judging when it is cooked can also be tricky. Cooked cakes shrink slightly from the tins and a skewer thrust into the centre will come out clean, without any trace of uncooked mixture on it. However, if you are in any doubt, take a test plug from the centre so you can see for yourself that it is fully cooked.

Sort through the fruit and remove any stalks etc, then mix in a large bowl with the halved cherries, peel and a tablespoon or two of flour (depending on the size of the cake) taken from the measured amount. Sift flour, salt and spices. Cream the butter and sugar until light and fluffy, then add the treacle, zests and essences. Beat well. Add the eggs, one by one, including a dessertspoonful of flour from the measured amount with each one and beating well between additions. Fold in the fruit and remaining flour, plus the measured amount of brandy. Mix well.

Turn the mixture into the prepared tin and smooth down well with the back of a tablespoon, leaving slightly hollow in the centre. The prepared cake may now be left overnight or until it is convenient to start baking. When you are ready to bake, preheat a slow oven, 300°F, 150°C, Gas mark 2 and bake the cake in the centre of the oven for 1-1½ hours according to size, then reduce to 275°F, 140°C, Gas mark 1 for the remaining baking time until the top of the cake feels firm to the touch and a skewer thrust into the centre comes out clean and dry. Keep an eye on the cake throughout and be prepared to protect the top from over-browning by covering loosely with brown paper or foil. If you have a fan oven, consult the manufacturer's leaflet for the correct temperature. They work at lower temperatures than conventional ovens and, as the heat is evenly distributed, the shelf selected is less important. This may mean you could cook the two smaller cakes at the same time. Just keep a close eye on progress and use your common sense. Cool the cooked cakes in the tins, then remove the papers and turn upside down onto a board. Make a lot of small holes all over the base with a skewer, then pour in some extra brandy — about ⅛ pint/75 ml for the small cake, a scant ¼ pint for the medium one and ⅓ pint/200 ml for the big one. When the brandy has been thoroughly absorbed, wrap the cakes in a double layer of greaseproof paper, then a layer of foil. Seal and store in an airtight tin, or a heavy-duty polythene bag, in a cool place for at least a month, until you are ready to finish the cake about a fortnight before the wedding.

Hints: For a 3-tier cake, a 3"/7.5 cm difference between tiers looks well-balanced, as given above. For a 4-tier cake, 2"/5cm difference is enough, eg 6"/15cm, 8"/20cm, 10"/25cm, 12"/30cm. Cake boards need to be 3"/7.5cm bigger than the cake.

If you have a favourite Christmas cake recipe and want to make a simple 2-tier cake, it can be adapted quite easily. Use the quantities given for an 8"/20cm square or 9"/22cm round cake for the base and halve them to make a square 6"/15 cm or round 7"/17.5 cm one for the top layer.

SUMMER

June, July, August

Lazy, hazy days are what we all hope for in summer and, when Mother Nature obliges, they are indeed a gift to be relished. But perhaps the charm of an Irish summer is its unpredictable, ephemeral nature as characterised by the wonderful flow of seasonal produce which can all too easily pass us by unless we are determined to make the most of its short season: broad beans, baby carrots, courgettes, peas and beans, new potatoes, outdoor tomatoes and fresh herbs are just a few examples of kitchen garden treats which are theoretically available (from other sources) throughout the year but can never have the crisp tenderness of texture or depth of flavour of local produce harvested at the peak of its natural season and transported a minimum distance from field or garden to the kitchen. Then there are the luscious, richly coloured, fragrant soft fruits — strawberries, raspberries, loganberries, currants of every hue, cherries and bilberries — which appear so briefly that they must almost be snatched into the kitchen before they disappear again — although, by a lucky stroke of fortune, these most perishable of fruits are often the very ones which can best be used to preserve the taste of summer and bring a shaft of sunlight to the winter table. Then there are the the pleasures of eating out of doors — picnic sites carefully chosen to allow the wine to chill in a crystal clear stream, the aroma of barbecueing food wafting across the garden, afternoon tea outdoors. Just occasionally these *al fresco* feasts measure up to the dreams we all have of them, and remain in our memories, the essence of summer.

HIGHLIGHTS OF THE SEASON include:

Father's Day (mid-June), Longest Day (21st June) and Midsummer's Day (24th June). None of these has any particular culinary tradition attached and, except for special occasions such as a family wedding or anniversary, food throughout the season tends to be very casual in preparation and presentation. If you have American guests, Independence Day (4th July) is a cause for celebration.

PRODUCE AT ITS PEAK THIS SEASON

Vegetables: Aubergines, avocados, beetroot, broad beans, cabbages, carrots, cauliflowers, celery, chicory, corn-on-the-cob, courgettes, cucumber, fennel, French and runner beans, garlic, globe artichokes, lettuces, mangetout, mushrooms (culti-vated), onions, peas, peppers, potatoes, radishes, shallots, spinach, scallions, tomatoes, turnips, watercress. **Herbs** — all plentiful and at their best; preserve when peaking if possible. **Fruit**: Apples, apricots, bilberries, blackcurrants, cherries, damsons, gooseberries, figs, grapes, loganberries, plums, melons, nectarines, peaches, pears, pineapples, raspberries, redcurrants, rhubarb, strawberries, whitecurrants. **Poultry and Game**: Chicken, duck, grouse, guinea fowl, hare, pigeon, quail, rabbit, snipe, turkey, venison. **Fish**: Most are available throughout the year, but some of the best during this season include: Brill, brown trout, clams, cod, coley, conger eel, crab, Dover (black) sole, Dublin Bay prawns, haddock, herring, lemon sole, lobster, mackerel, (Portuguese) oysters, plaice, prawns, sea trout, salmon, turbot.

SUGGESTED MENUS

Father's Day Dinner
Gravad Lax with Home-made Brown Bread;
Shoulder of Lamb with Redcurrant Sauce, New Potatoes, French Peas and Carrots;
A Trio of Home-made Ices — Vanilla, Straw berry and Orange — in Brandysnap Baskets.

Saturday Evening Barbecue
Crudités, Lime- and Curry-flavoured Mayonnaise;
Sweet Corn on the Cob with Melted Butter;
Grilled Whiting, Oriental Style;
Steak Rolls with Mustard Sauce;
Hot French Bread with Herb Butter;
Baked Potatoes;
Assortment of Salads. Terrine of Summer Fruit;
Raspberry Vacherin.

Afternoon Tea in the Garden
Cucumber Sandwiches; Tomato Sandwiches;
Tea Scones with Strawberry Jam;
Raspberry Sponge Cake with Fresh Cream;
Strawberry Shortcake, Lemon Cake;
Tea, Iced Tea or Home-made Lemonade.

Informal Supper on the Patio
Gazpacho with Hot Garlic Bread;
Chicken with Pineapple and Almonds, Rice and a Mixed Leaf Salad with Nasturtiums;
Strawberry Tart with Raspberry & Redcurrant Glaze

American Independence Day Lunch
Ginger and Coriander Salmon in Filo Flowers;
Baked Pork Chops with Raspberry and Cider Sauce, accompanied by Summer Salad;
Fresh Apricot Trifle; Petits Fours

Light, colourful first courses to tempt the appetite are perfect for the warmer months and there's an abundance of tender young produce to choose from for side dishes and salads. Salmon and, if you are lucky, its cousin the sea trout are at their best and make wonderful starters or light meals. From a wide choice of native vegetables, the very best use can be made of flavoursome outdoor tomatoes, prolific courgettes and peas or mangetout which are at the height of their season and very good value.

Tossed Salad Leaves with Fresh Crabmeat
and Pink Grapefruit, with a Walnut & Lime Vinaigrette

For a special occasion in summer, it would be hard to imagine a prettier or tastier first course than this recipe for Tossed Salad Leaves with Fresh Crabmeat and Pink Grapefruit, with a Walnut & Lime Vinaigrette. It comes from St Ernan's House Hotel, restfully situated on its own tidal island, just outside Donegal town.

Wash salad leaves under gently running cold water; drain well and refrigerate. Place wine vinegar, mustard and lime juice in a bowl and whisk together then slowly add the walnut oil, whisking all the time; add the mayonnaise, chives and dill, whisk together to blend thoroughly and season to taste. Pick through the crabmeat to make sure that no small pieces of shell remain. Cut the peel off the grapefruit with a sharp knife and, holding over a bowl, cut the segments out from their connecting membrane. Add any juice collected to the dressing and set the segments aside. Put a quarter of the prepared salad leaves into a large bowl, season with salt and freshly ground black pepper and lightly toss with 4 tablespoons of the prepared dressing and 2 oz/50g of the crabmeat. Lift onto a serving plate and sprinkle with a further 2oz/50g crabmeat and a quarter of the pink grapefruit segments. Repeat the process for the other three salads and serve with freshly baked brown bread and butter.

Serves 4:
Assorted salad leaves, such as lamb's lettuce, curly endive, radicchio, oakleaf, lollo rossa
2 tablespoons wine vinegar
1½ teaspoons smooth Dijon mustard
2 teaspoons lime juice or to taste
8 tablespoons/120 ml walnut oil
2 tablespoons mayonnaise
1 teaspoon chopped chives
½ teaspoon chopped dill
Seasoning: salt, freshly ground pepper and caster sugar, to taste
1 lb/450g crabmeat
2 pink grapefruit

Gravad Lax

This Scandinavian dish is 'cooked' in a curing mixture which has a chemical effect on the flesh without any heat — and the effect is a fish which can be used in the same way as smoked salmon, thinly sliced as a first course, but has quite a different flavour.

Wash the salmon fillets and pat dry. Combine all the ingredients for the curing mixture. Put a few sprigs of dill in a shallow dish and put half of the fish, skin side down, on top of it. Scatter over half of the curing mixture and rub this into the flesh. Top with plenty of dill sprigs. Rub the other half of the fish with the remaining curing mixture and put it, skin side up, on the first fillet to make a sandwich. Cover with foil, then put a weighted plate or basin on top. Refrigerate for at least 36 hours, turning the fish every 12 hours. During the 'curing' process, the pale pink salmon flesh is compressed and deepens to the colour of smoked salmon.

To serve: Scrape off the curing mixture and dill from the fish and, using a very sharp knife, cut on the bias to make paper-thin slices. Arrange the delicate slices on plain, elegant plates and garnish with sprigs of dill. Serve with mayonnaise — which can be flavoured with dill and mustard — and freshly made wholemeal bread and butter.

Gravad Lax: Serves 8–10
1½lb/700g tailpiece or middle cut salmon, de-scaled and filleted
1 large bunch fresh dill
Dill sprigs or wild flowers to garnish.

Curing mixture:
2 teaspoons black peppercorns, roughly crushed
2 tbsp sea salt
1 tbsp caster or light golden brown sugar
1 tbsp brandy.

Marinated Salmon with Mint

Marinated Salmon: Serves 2.
4 oz/100g very fresh raw
  salmon, boned, skinned
Juice of 1 lemon
Juice of 1 orange
Pinch of caster sugar
Salt and pepper to taste
1 tbsp finely sliced fresh
  mint.

This refreshing dish is based on the same principle as Carpaccio and depends on absolute freshness and very thin slicing for its success. The citrus juices tenderise the fish in a similar way to cooking as in Gravad Lax and give a good sharp flavour.

Slice the salmon as thinly as possible with a very sharp knife. Arrange in a serving dish and pour over the juices mixed with the sugar and a little salt. Grind over some black pepper and sprinkle over the mint. Leave to marinate overnight. Serve with crisp brown bread rolls.

Three-Fish Terrine

1 lb/450g spinach
1 lb/450g cod fillet
3 eggs
4 oz/100g fresh
  breadcrumbs
10 fl oz (1/2 pint)/300 ml
  fromage blanc
Pinch of salt; freshly ground
  black pepper
Freshly grated nutmeg
1 lb/450g salmon fillet
1 lb/450g ray or skate wing,
  skinned by angler or
  fishmonger
Sprigs of fresh dill or fennel
  to garnish.

A pretty striped fishy first course, much easier to make than it looks. [Microwave]

Preheat the oven to 325°F, 170°C, Gas mark 3. Wash spinach, remove stalks and ribs and cook leaves briskly, without adding water but shaking the pan occasionally, until just tender. Drain, squeeze out excess water and put into the bowl of a food processor along with the skinned and chopped cod, eggs, breadcrumbs, fromage blanc, salt, pepper and nutmeg. Process until smooth.

Skin salmon fillet and cut into long thin strips; cut flesh away from between the pieces of cartilage in the ray or skate to give similar pieces; mix them together and season lightly with salt and pepper. (Don't attempt to skin ray or skate yourself unless you know you can do it, by the way, as it's very hard to handle.)

Oil a 2 lb/900g loaf tin or terrine carefully and line the base with a piece of oiled greaseproof paper or foil cut to fit. Make layers with the spinach mixture and the strips of salmon and ray, starting and finishing with the spinach. Press down carefully but firmly to eliminate air pockets and cover the tin or terrine with lightly oiled greaseproof paper; prick a few holes in it to allow steam to escape, then put the terrine into a roasting tin and pour enough boiling water around it to come 2/3 of the way up. Bake in the pre-heated oven for 1-1½ hours until risen, firm and set. Leave to cool, then chill well before serving. To serve, turn the terrine out onto a flat oval or oblong serving dish — the base lining should make this easy, but you can ease a sharp knife down the sides to loosen the terrine if necessary. Carefully cut into slices with a sharp knife and serve against a background of the Fresh Tomato Sauce with Basil, given below; garnish with lemon wedges and fresh basil leaves or, if you prefer, with a seasonal salad.

Offer freshly made brown bread or Melba toast and butter with the terrine.

Fresh Tomato Sauce with Basil

1-1½lb/450-700g juicy red
  tomatoes, peeled and
  de-seeded
1 tbsp olive oil
1/2 tbsp finely chopped
  fresh basil
1-2 tbsp tomato purée
Sugar and freshly ground
  black pepper to taste.

Simmer all ingredients together in a large heavy pan for 15 minutes, stirring occasionally, until the sauce has reduced to the right thickness. If it looks too pale, add a little extra tomato purée. Adjust seasoning if necessary and blend in a food processor until smooth. Serve hot or cold.

NB: If fresh basil is unavailable, frozen basil can be used if it is still aromatic, but dried basil does not make a good substitute. If dried herbs must be used, try marjoram or oregano instead. *[Microwave]*

Ginger and Coriander Salmon in Filo Flowers

Ginger and Coriander Salmon in Filo Flowers is as pretty a dish as you will find, fragrant with oriental flavourings and much easier to make than it sounds. You can make little ones for starters, or double quantities to make a light main course.

Filo pastry is available, frozen, from delicatessens and good supermarkets and is very versatile — any leftovers can be refrozen for another time, but do keep the pile covered with oiled greaseproof or a damp cloth to prevent it drying out, which it does very quickly and then becomes too brittle to handle.

Brush the insides of four flan tins about 4"/10 cm diameter with melted butter. (If you don't have suitable tins, try alternatives such as Yorkshire Pudding tins or any other ovenproof dish about the right size.) Quarter each filo sheet and layer into the tins, brushing liberally with butter or oil and arranging so that corners alternate, forming a flower shape. Bake in a preheated oven, 375°F, 190°C, Gas mark 5 for 7-10 minutes until golden and crisp, being careful not to burn the edges. Cool in the tins. The cases can now be stored in an airtight tin until required.

Filling: Heat the oil and fry the ginger, garlic and shallot for about 5 minutes, until softened but not coloured. Add the salmon pieces, then the coriander and courgette. Stir carefully, then cover and cook gently for a few minutes, until the salmon is cooked and the courgette is just softened. Season well. Stir in the thinned yogurt off the heat and reheat gently without boiling. Spoon the filling into the warmed filo cases and scatter with the chopped coriander or parsley. Serve warm.

Variation: Try using a diced green pepper instead of the courgette, but cook the pepper with the garlic and shallot or onion. Chicken breast fillets can be used instead of salmon.

Avocado with Redcurrant Vinaigrette

This is a speciality at lovely Cashel House Hotel in Connemara, Co. Galway. It makes a striking but easy first course and, although especially appropriate in summer when redcurrants are in season, it can be made with (defrosted) frozen berries at other times of year.

In a blender, combine four parts of oil to one part of lemon juice and add enough redcurrants to colour the sauce pink, thicken it and give a good sharp flavour. Season to taste with sugar, salt and pepper. Put two or three tablespoons of the sauce onto each plate. Just before serving, peel, halve and slice the avocado and arrange in a fan shape on top of the sauce. Garnish with a sprig of fresh young currant or mint leaves and a few whole berries, and serve immediately with fresh brown bread and butter or yeasted rolls.

NB: If there is likely to be any delay between preparation and serving, sprinkle the avocado with lemon juice to prevent discoloration.

Pear and Blue Cheese Salad with Tarragon Dressing

This unusual first course is especially good in the late summer and early autumn when tarragon is abundant and Irish pears are coming into season. The cheese should be slightly under-ripe, not at the runny stage.

Blend the mustard and soured cream together, then beat in the vinegar and the chopped tarragon; season to taste with salt, pepper and sugar. Peel the pears and dice the flesh, coating in the dressing quickly to prevent browning. Fold in half of the nuts and all the cheese. Select 6 large cup-shaped lettuce leaves, or a number of smaller ones, and arrange them on individual plates, then pile the pear and cheese mixture onto them. Scatter with the reserved nuts and some extra chopped tarragon, then chill until required. Serve with freshly baked brown bread and butter.

Makes four 4"/10 cm tartlets
4 sheets filo pastry
1½ oz/40g melted butter or 4 tbsp olive oil

Filling:
2 tbsp olive oil
About ½"/1 cm root ginger, peeled and finely chopped
2 cloves garlic, crushed
2 shallots or 1 small onion, peeled and finely chopped
1 lb/450g salmon fillet, skinned and sliced thinly in strips
2 tsp crushed coriander seeds
1 medium courgette, diced
8 oz/225g carton Greek or set yogurt, thinned with 3 tbsp milk or fish stock
Salt, freshly ground black pepper, pinch of caster sugar
Freshly chopped coriander leaves or flat leaf parsley to garnish.

Avocado with vinaigrette
To serve any number:
Salad oil
Lemon juice
Redcurrants
Caster sugar, salt and freshly ground black pepper
1 avocado per person.

Pear Salad: Serves 6
1 tablespoon smooth Dijon mustard
6 tablespoons soured cream
1 tablespoon tarragon or white wine vinegar
1 tablespoon freshly chopped tarragon, or to taste
Sea salt, freshly ground pepper and a pinch of caster sugar
6 good-sized, firm pears, preferably Conference
4 tablespoons roughly chopped walnuts
6 oz/175g firm Cashel Blue cheese, diced
To serve: 6 large, cup-shaped lettuce leaves
Chopped tarragon (garnish)

Southern Tomato Salad

Serves 4

4 well-ripened Italian plum
    tomatoes or beef tomatoes
8 oz/225g mozzarella cheese
4 oz/100g black olives
Good quality olive oil,
    preferably Italian
Salt, freshly ground black
    pepper and a little caster
    sugar
1 tablespoon freshly
    chopped basil
A few whole basil leaves to
    garnish (optional).

If you have a good supply of fresh basil — the perfect partner for red sun-ripened tomatoes — remember that Southern Tomato Salad is not only pretty but also very easy to prepare. As with all of these summery tomato dishes, the most important thing is to choose well-ripened tomatoes with a good flavour.

Slice the tomatoes and the mozzarella thinly and arrange alternately around four individual serving dishes. Scatter with the black olives, drizzle with olive oil and season with a little sea salt, plenty of freshly ground black pepper and a pinch of caster sugar on the tomatoes. Scatter with the basil and serve as a starter, a side dish for barbecues or any plainly cooked main dish or, with fresh crusty bread, as a light meal. It really is a very versatile salad and, as with all simple dishes, absolutely delicious if the ingredients are top quality.

Iced Tomato Soup

We generally think of soups as warming winter comfort food and, presumably because of the unreliability of our summers, we tend to undervalue chilled soups despite their popularity in other European countries with climates just as tricky as our own. Since we happily eat so many other first courses cold, perhaps it is time for a re-appraisal.

If you are very sure of the quality of your tomatoes, the simplest way to make Iced Tomato Soup, (for 2–3) is to blanch 1 lb/450g tomatoes to loosen their skins, peel them and put into a food processor or blender with just enough water to cover the base of the bowl. Add a generous seasoning of salt and pepper, a pinch of sugar, a few fresh herbs (basil, oregano, marjoram or whatever) and 2 tablespoons olive oil. Liquidise, sieve, chill and serve with crusty French bread.

Chilled Tomato Soup with Basil

Serves 6:

2 lb/450g tomatoes
Salt and freshly ground
    black pepper
1 teaspoon caster sugar
1½ pints/900ml good
    chicken stock
Soured cream or natural
    yogurt (optional)
1 tablespoon finely chopped
    fresh basil.

This cooked version, Chilled Tomato Soup with Basil, has a stronger tomato flavour and if it is based on a good home-made stock with plenty of natural gelatine in it, the soup will thicken and have plenty of body when it is chilled. If the weather turns nasty it can be heated up to serve as a very good, light hot soup. [Microwave[

Preheat a moderate oven, 350°F, 180°C, Gas mark 4.

Halve the tomatoes horizontally and lay them out, cut side up, in a shallow baking dish. Sprinkle with salt, freshly ground pepper and sugar, then cover with foil and bake for 40 minutes, or until the tomatoes are really soft. Push through a nylon sieve, add the stock (melted, if it has jelled), adjust the seasoning and chill. To serve, divide between six chilled soup bowls and top each one with a swirl of cream or yogurt (optional) and a scattering of finely chopped basil.

Gazpacho

Serves 6-10:

2½ lbs/1.1 Kg ripe
    tomatoes
Flesh of 1 large red pepper
    (no seeds)
½ large cucumber or
    melon
2 large cloves garlic
4 tablespoons olive oil
5 fl oz/150 ml flavoured
    wine vinegar
1 tablespoon brown sugar
1½ teaspoon coarse sea salt
½ teaspoon freshly ground
    black pepper

Iced Spanish Soup is traditionally served with individual bowls of raw vegetables — diced tomatoes, onion, cucumber, green pepper — and fried garlic croûtons to which guests help themselves, although it can also be served quite simply, without embellishment. This Classic Gazpacho Roja de Sevilla appears regularly at The Old Rectory, Wicklow. Not only is it very easy to make but it keeps for at least a week in the fridge — ideal for a summer dinner party (Iced Borage Flowers make the presentation really special) — and any unused portions can be frozen.

Liquidise all ingredients together until smooth, then sieve to remove bits of tomato skin and seeds. Cover carefully to prevent garlic from affecting other food and chill for at least 6 hours. To serve, pour into chilled glass bowls with a scattering of tiny cubes of cucumber, one or two fresh

Mixed Leaf Salad with Nasturtiums, page 69

Just as the range of salad leaves available has widened tremendously in recent years — and, indeed, encouraged us to make better use of edible 'weeds' in our own gardens, such as dandelions or nettles — so our minds have also been broadened when it comes to the use of flowers. Although a policy of 'flowers with everything' can very quickly pall, there's no doubt that the judicious use of flowers in salads and as garnishes for both sweet and savoury dishes, can lend great drama to food. And flowers can taste very good too — scented rose petals and violets can lift some very simple sweet dishes onto a different plane, while more characterful, spicy flowers such as nasturtiums, bring colour and a unique peppery flavour to salads.

Gravad Lax, page 61

This Scandinavian dish is 'cooked' in a curing mixture which has a chemical effect
on the flesh without any heat — and the result is a fish which can be used in the
same way as smoked salmon, thinly sliced as a first course, but has quite a different
flavour.

borage flowers and a **Borage Flower Ice Cube**. To make the ice cubes, place a borage flower in each cube of an ice tray and cover with cooled boiled water — this removes the bubbles which would otherwise obscure the flower. Also offer separately the traditional accompaniment of fried croûtons of white bread.

Tomato Granita

Sorbets have been back for a while now, but it looks as if the bid to make vegetable ice creams fashionable was just a bit too eccentric to take off. Looked at logically, though, there are very good reasons for basing a refreshing mid-meal sorbet — or, for that matter, a starter — on savoury ingredients, as in this Tomato Granita. [Microwave]

Serves 6
3 lb/1.4 kg ripe, well-flavoured tomatoes
1 onion
1 dessertspoon freshly chopped marjoram or basil
1 level tablespoon tomato purée
Juice of 1 lemon
Caster sugar to taste
Sprigs of mint to garnish.

Chop the tomatoes roughly and put them into a saucepan with the chopped onion and the marjoram or basil. Bring to the boil over moderate heat, cover and simmer gently for about 25 minutes, stirring occasionally to prevent sticking, until the tomatoes are soft. Rub through a nylon sieve into a mixing bowl, stir in the tomato purée, lemon juice and just enough caster sugar to bring out the flavour of the tomatoes and offset any excess acidity. Leave to cool, then turn into a freezer container, cover and freeze for at least 4 hours. To serve, turn the frozen mixture out, crush it with a rolling pin and pile into serving glasses. Serve garnished with sprigs of mint.

Courgettes with Tomatoes and Garlic

Although it's only a few years since they were regarded as exotics, courgettes grow very easily and, if you don't have your own they are usually cheap and plentiful throughout a long summer season. Cooked gently with onions and garlic, they combine well with tomatoes in this versatile dish which can be served cold as a first course or hot to accompany any simply cooked main course, especially grilled fish or poultry. [Microwave]

Serves 4:
1 lb/450g courgettes
2 large onions
2 tablespoons olive oil
1 oz/25g butter
2 large cloves garlic, or to taste, crushed
1 lb/450 g ripe tomatoes
Sea salt, freshly ground black pepper and caster sugar.

Slice the courgettes, sprinkle with salt and leave in a colander for an hour to remove excess water. Rinse, drain and shake in a cloth to dry. Peel and slice the onions, cook gently in the oil and butter until just softening, then add the crushed garlic. Add the courgettes, cover and cook gently for 10 minutes, shaking occasionally. Meanwhile, scald the tomatoes and remove the skins. Slice, removing the core if it is tough, and add to the pan. Cook, uncovered, over moderate heat for another 10 minutes, or until the courgettes are just tender and most of the excess tomato juice has evaporated. Season well with salt, freshly ground pepper and a pinch of caster sugar.

Ratatouille

Ratatouille is probably the most useful and adaptable of all the mixed vegetable summer dishes and the name is simply provençal for a vegetable stew, so it's hardly surprising that there's no such thing as a 'correct' recipe for it. This one is probably the kind of combination most people expect of ratatouille, but the ingredients can be varied to suit individual tastes, or the availability of produce. [Microwave]

Serves 8-10:
1 lb/450g courgettes
1 lb/450g aubergines
1 lb/450g ripe tomatoes
3 or 4 sweet peppers, any colour
3 large onions
4 tablespoons olive oil
4 large cloves garlic
Sea salt, freshly ground black pepper, caster sugar
1 teaspoon coriander seeds, crushed
Freshly chopped basil, oregano or marjoram

Slice the unpeeled courgettes and aubergines, put into a colander and sprinkle with salt; leave for an hour to drain, then rinse and pat dry. Dip the tomatoes in boiling water to loosen the skins, then peel and chop roughly, discarding the core if it is tough. Halve the peppers, remove seeds and membranes and slice.

Peel and slice the onions and put into a fairly big, heavy-based pan with the oil. Add the crushed or finely chopped garlic and cook gently, without browning, for about 10 minutes, until the onions are softening, then add the peppers and aubergines. Cover and simmer for 20 minutes, then add the courgettes and tomatoes. Season with salt, a good grinding of black pepper and a little sugar. Cook gently and steadily, uncovered, for about 45 minutes, or until the mixture is no longer watery. Stir well from time to time to prevent sticking, but don't crush the vegetables. About 10 minutes before serving, add the coriander. Check the seasoning before serving hot or cold, scattered with freshly chopped basil, oregano or marjoram.

Variation: **Quick Slimmer's Ratatouille** is a cheat's version of the above and, while not as richly flavoured, it does have obvious advantages. Base the dish on a tin of chopped Italian tomatoes, with their juices. Add whichever of the ratatouille vegetables you like, in the same order — I would be inclined to give the aubergines a miss and skip the salting and draining session for the courgettes, but otherwise add the rest. There is, of course, no frying — the onion and garlic go straight into the pot with the tomatoes. Cook gently, on the hob or in the oven, until the vegetables are tender and the juice reduced to a sauce.

French Peas and Carrots

French Peas and Carrots: Serves 8

2 oz/50g butter
1 onion
1 small lettuce
1 lb/450g whole baby carrots
1 lb/450g peas (shelled weight)
¼ pint/150 ml chicken stock or water
Salt, freshly ground black pepper, caster sugar.

Peas, fresh from the pod, must be one of the great joys of summer for most people. At their simplest — and, I suspect, most delicious — tender young peas are wonderful cooked lightly in a little boiling water flavoured with a sprig of mint and a pinch of salt and sugar. For variety, try them in this time-honoured partnership with baby carrots. [Microwave]

Melt the butter over gentle heat in a wide, heavy-based pan. Chop the onion finely and cook it, covered, for a minute or two without allowing it to brown. Shred the lettuce quite finely and add half of it to the pan. Add the washed and trimmed carrots and heat through for about 5 minutes, then add the peas and stock. Season with salt, freshly ground pepper and about a teaspoon of caster sugar, then cover and cook for about 20 minutes, or until the vegetables are tender. Check the seasoning before serving.

Minted Pea Soup

Minted Pea Soup: Serves 4-6

1 onion
A little chicken fat or butter for frying
2 lb/900g peas (podded weight)
1½ pints/900 ml good chicken stock
Sprig of mint
Salt, freshly ground black pepper, caster sugar
A little cream and freshly chopped mint to garnish.

Once past their best, peas make very good soup — this Minted Pea Soup is very easy, thickened simply by the peas themselves but none the worse for that. [Microwave]

Peel and slice the onion. Melt the chicken fat or butter in a large heavy-based pan over gentle heat and cook the onion in it without browning for 5-10 minutes or until it is softening. Add the prepared peas, stock and mint. Bring up to the boil and season with a little salt, a grinding of pepper and a teaspoonful of caster sugar. Cook for 10-15 minutes, or until the peas are soft, then remove the sprig of mint and purée the soup in a food processor or blender, or put through the fine blade of a mouli-légumes. Return the purée to the rinsed pan, bring back up to the boil and check the seasoning. Pour into bowls, add a swirl of cream to each and top with a scattering of freshly chopped mint.

Mangetout and Cucumber Salad with Mint Vinaigrette

Mangetout, or Sugar Peas suddenly came into vogue a few years ago and, like courgettes and peppers, were widely regarded as being 'exotic'. In fact they have been grown in Ireland for a very long time and only fell into disfavour from the '50s onwards, when convenience foods became all the rage. They are extremely easy to grow — dwarf varieties that need no support will even crop prolifically in small gardens — and, although the home-grown ones may not be as large and even-sized as the commercial ones, they have flavour (and availability) on their side. If you don't have them in the garden, they are easy to get over a long season and at reasonable prices. Early in the season, when they are young and very tender, mangetout are good in salads and, unlike most salad greens, they will stay crisp for ages. This Mangetout and Cucumber Salad with Mint Vinaigrette makes a refreshing side salad and a practical choice for a picnic, as it travels well.

Top and tail the mangetout and blanch in boiling water for 1 minute, then refresh in a colander under the cold tap and leave to drain. Wipe the cucumber and cut into fairly thick slices, about $1/4$"/0.5 cm, without peeling. Cut the endive into $1/2$"/1 cm slices and separate the leaves. Put the mangetout, cucumber and endive into a salad bowl. Whisk the mustard, lemon juice and sugar together in a small bowl, then gradually whisk in the oil to form an emulsion. Taste and season with salt, freshly ground pepper and, if necessary, extra caster sugar, then stir in the mint. Pour the dressing over the vegetables in the salad bowl, toss well and chill until required.

Mangetout Salad: Serves 4

8 oz/225g mangetout
1 cucumber
1 head Belgian endive

Dressing:

1 teaspoon smooth Dijon
   mustard
1 tablespoon lemon juice
1 teaspoon caster sugar, or
   to taste
3 tablespoons olive oil
Sea salt and freshly ground
   black pepper
1 tablespoon freshly
   chopped mint leaves.

Stir-Fry of Mangetout with Ginger and Pine Kernels

Although they can be cooked traditionally like any other vegetable by boiling or steaming, the tender, crisp texture of the sugar pea is especially well suited to stir-frying as in this Mangetout with Ginger and Pine Kernels, a delicious summery combination which would enhance many a meal.

Brown the pine kernels under the grill, or toast them in a hot oven for a few minutes — watch carefully as they turn colour quite suddenly and burn easily. Top and tail the mangetout and remove any tough strings. Peel the ginger and chop very finely. Heat the oil in a wok or large frying pan and stir-fry the mangetout and ginger in it for 3-4 minutes until the peas are tender but still slightly crisp. Add the browned pine nuts, stir together and season with sea salt, a grinding of black pepper and $1/2$ teaspoonful caster sugar. Serve immediately.

Serves 4

2-3 oz/50-75g pine kernels
1 lb/450g mangetout
A small piece, about $1/2$"/
   1cm, root ginger
4 tbsp olive oil
Sea salt, freshly ground
   black pepper, caster sugar.

Mixed Leaf Salad with Nasturtiums

Just as the range of salad leaves available has widened tremendously in recent years — and, indeed, encouraged us to make better use of edible 'weeds' in our own gardens, such as dandelions or nettles — so our minds have also been broadened when it comes to the use of flowers. Although a policy of 'flowers with everything' can very quickly pall, there's no doubt that the judicious use of flowers in salads and as garnishes for both sweet and savoury dishes, can lend great drama to food. And flowers can taste very good too — scented rose petals and violets can lift some very simple sweet dishes onto a different plane, while more characterful, spicy flowers such as nasturtiums, bring colour and a unique peppery flavour to salads.

Wash and dry the salad leaves, trim and tear into manageable pieces as required. Put into a bowl with the nasturtium leaves.

Whisk the mustard, sugar and vinegar together, then gradually whisk in the oil to form an emulsion. Add the freshly chopped herbs to taste and season the dressing with salt and pepper. Taste and adjust the seasoning or sharpness if required. Pour the dressing over the prepared leaves and toss well. Lastly, add the nasturtium flowers.

Variation: As with many strongly-flavoured salads, I like a handful of roughly broken walnuts in this salad — and if you can replace some of the olive oil with walnut oil so much the better as the flavours are very robust.

Serves 4

1 bunch watercress OR $1/2$
   small head radicchio
$1\frac{1}{2}$ head curly endive
   (frisée)
$1/2$ small crisp green lettuce
Small handful of
   nasturtium leaves,
   preferably variegated
About a dozen mixed
   nasturtium flowers.

Dressing:

1 teaspoon mild Dijon
   mustard
1 teaspoon caster or soft
   brown sugar
$1\frac{1}{2}$ tablespoons wine or
   cider vinegar
5 tablespoons olive oil
1 tablespoon freshly
   chopped herbs, eg parsley,
   chives, a little thyme
Sea salt and freshly ground
   pepper.

Glazed Baby Turnips

Serves 4

1 lb/450g baby white turnips
½ pint/300 ml water
1 oz/25g butter
1 oz/25g sugar
Sea salt and freshly ground
  black pepper.

Another vegetable that has been under-estimated for a long time and is now becoming popular again is the delightful little white turnip. Very much a summer vegetable, it has a sharp, peppery flavour that is mellowed by serving as Glazed Baby Turnips.

Wash the turnips and trim, but leave a little of the green stalk. Put the water, butter and sugar into a small pan and heat through to dissolve the butter and sugar, then add the turnips, season with salt and pepper and bring up to simmering point. Cook very gently, until the turnips are tender and the water has reduced down to leave a rich golden glaze on them. Check the seasoning before serving.

Note: If the turnips are past the baby stage, they should be halved, or even quartered, to reduce the cooking time, and may need to be peeled.

Summer Salad

1 head Tom Thumb lettuce
A few leaves of Lollo Rossa
A few young spinach leaves
4-6 young dandelion leaves
Small bunch of lemon balm
  leaves
1 tablespoon freshly
  chopped mixed herbs, eg.
  parsley, summer savory,
  chervil and basil
1 small bunch of chives
2 tomatoes
Pinch of caster sugar
1 dessertspoon toasted pine
  kernels

Dressing:

1 tablespoon white wine
  vinegar or champagne
  vinegar
½ teaspoon Dijon mustard
1 clove garlic, crushed
½ teaspoon light golden
  brown sugar
Salt and freshly ground
  black pepper to taste
3-4 tablespoons best quality
  olive oil.

At Rathsallagh House, Dunlavin, Co. Wicklow, the garden produces an abundance of fresh fruit, vegetables, herbs and saladings for the kitchen, so they make up glorious treasure chests of salads to accompany just about anything — this one is often served as suggested with the famous Twice-Baked Cheese Soufflé but it can, of course, be served simply as a side salad for any suitable dish.

Wash and dry all the leaves. Cut the tomatoes into eight slices each and sprinkle lightly with the caster sugar. Mix the vinegar and all the flavourings and seasonings together, then beat in the olive oil. Taste and adjust if necessary. Arrange a mixture of leaves on individual plates to one side. Place tomatoes on the leaves, sprinkle with chopped herbs and pine kernels, then lay some whole chives over the top. Lightly spoon the dressing over and serve immediately with the Cheese Soufflé on the other side of the plate.

(See pages 101, 183, 211, 231 and 239-40 for further information on sugar and its history.)

SUGAR

Sugar is incredibly versatile. Its uses in the kitchen are far more varied than most people realise. Apart from its obvious uses, both as a major ingredient and decoration in baking and desserts, and its essential quality as a preservative, sugar has an interesting and much more subtle role to play in a wide range of less predictable dishes, many of them savoury. Used as a seasoning, small quantities of sugar enhance the natural flavours of many foods, for example, and for the same reasons it is an important, if minor, ingredient in marinades, sauces and a wide range of oriental dishes. It has been used in this way for thousands of years in Chinese cuisine, for example, and in the Middle Ages, when Arab influences crept into European kitchens, sugar joined a whole range of other condiments, spices and seasonings as a flavouring in savoury foods. Then there is yeast cookery, which is something of an enigma to many Irish cooks, but it is fascinating rather than difficult and a perfect example of the miracle that a tiny spoonful of sugar can achieve — it forms such a very small proportion of the ingredients in yeast cookery and yet it is vital to feed the yeast and allow it to multiply. Absolutely magical — no wonder sugar has caused such an upheaval throughout its history.

Easy Holiday Cooking, Picnics, Barbecues, Afternoon Teas and Summer Drinks

While we all rejoice in the good things of summer, it is only natural to want to avoid spending time in the kitchen as much as possible. Fortunately, nature has anticipated this by providing an abundance of produce which either needs no cooking at all or, by a happy chance, takes well to being cooked over a barbecue in the open air. Even those foods which need a little advance preparation tend to be very undemanding. It is hardly troublesome to rustle up a batch of scones or a sponge cake, or to make a quiche or two in the cool of the evening for the following day's picnic in the hills. So, keep the summer holiday cooking as simple as possible, eat out of doors whenever you can, and enjoy it while lasts.

Warm Salad of Salmon with Toasted Pine Kernels

Warm Salad of Salmon with Toasted Pine Kernels is one of my favourite dishes and I often make it, either as a starter if there are guests, or as a light meal for two as a treat. It is easy, healthy and very beautiful.

Preheat a very hot oven, 450°F, 230°C, Gas mark 8. Cut the skinned salmon into quite thin slices. Toast the pine kernels in the oven until golden-brown and crunchy. Make a sauce with the oil, vinegar and mustard; season to taste. Break up salads; wash well and dry without bruising in a spinner. Heat the l–2 tbsp oil in a frying pan, add the $\frac{1}{2}$ oz/15g butter. Season the fish and, as soon as the butter starts to sizzle, quickly fry it for about 15 seconds on each side, turning only once — it should have just become opaque. Remove from the pan and keep warm.

Put the salad leaves into a large Pyrex or stainless mixing bowl, with the pine kernels and the vinaigrette. Toss well. Put into the hot oven and leave for about 30 seconds, until just warmed through. When warm, toss again and divide between four plates. Arrange the slices of fish in the salads, sprinkle with fresh chervil leaves (or another herb) and serve immediately. The secret is to warm the leaves without making them limp and to get them to table before they cool. Serves 4 as a starter, 2 as a light main course.

Variations: Use any firm-fleshed fish, such as turbot or monkfish instead of salmon. If you haven't got pine kernels, try toasted sesame seeds instead for 'crunch'. It's also nearly as good with the salad served cold and only the pine kernels and fish cooked — better than overheated or 'gone cold' if you have to make a choice.

Stir-Fried Mackerel

Mackerel is one of our most plentiful fish and probably at its best cooked very simply fresh out of the sea, but you do need to ring the changes with everyday foods and this stir-fry is always a winner even with self-confessed mackerel haters, which confirms my theory that the best way to get people to like something is to present it in a dish they have already enjoyed using other ingredients — garlic butter, for instance, is enough to get most people to try anything.

First of all, make sure you have all ingredients prepared and arranged close at hand in the order you want to cook them, as the actual cooking is done very quickly and there's no time to pause once you've started. Ingredients can be varied according to availability, but the basic rule is to try to have everything of a similar size and shape for even cooking and, of

l lb/450g salmon fillets
1 oz/15g pine kernels
2 tbsp olive oil
l tbsp sherry vinegar
l scant tsp Dijon mustard
Salt, freshly ground pepper and a pinch of sugar
Mixed salad leaves such as:
$\frac{1}{2}$ small radicchio, $\frac{1}{2}$ head bright green curly endive, $\frac{1}{2}$ head oakleaf lettuce, 2 heads lamb's lettuce, l bunch watercress
l-2 tablespoons oil
$\frac{1}{2}$ oz/15g butter
Garnish with fresh chervil.

Stir Fried Mackerel: Serves 4–6

l onion, finely sliced
Equivalent of l sweet pepper (green, red, yellow or mixed), de-seeded and sliced to match the onion
1"/2.5 cm root ginger, peeled and grated or finely chopped
l good clove garlic, crushed or finely chopped
$\frac{1}{4}$–$\frac{1}{2}$lb/100-225g babycorn
2 oz/50g mangetout
2 oz/50g mushrooms, sliced
l lb/450g mackerel fillets, skinned and sliced
4 oz/100g beansprouts
Oil to fry.

Sauce:

$1\frac{1}{2}$ tbsp light golden brown sugar
1 rounded tbsp cornflour
l tbsp dark soy sauce
3-4 tbsp vinegar
Pinch sugar and freshly ground black pepper
$\frac{1}{4}$ pint/150 ml each fish stock and cider.

Stir-Fried Chicken with cashew

Serves 4: (or stretch to 6 with a good selection of side dishes.)

Oil for frying
2 chicken breasts, boned and skinned, about 12 oz/350g total weight, cut into 1/2"/1.2 cm dice
1 large onion, peeled and chopped
1-2 cloves garlic, peeled and crushed
4 oz/100g trimmed and sliced button mushrooms
1 green pepper, de-seeded and chopped
1 pack fresh beansprouts, about 8 oz/225g weight
4 oz/100g cashew nuts, toasted

Sauce:

2 tbsp dark soy sauce
1 heaped teaspoon cornflour
3 tbsp dry sherry
1/4 pint/150 ml chicken stock or water
Freshly ground pepper to taste
1 teaspoon sugar.

Sweet & Sour Chicken: Serves 4-6:

1 medium chicken, 3-3 1/2 lb/1.4-1.6 Kg, boned (keep the bones)
1 heaped tablespoon flour seasoned with salt and pepper
2 1/2 oz/65g butter
1 tablespoon olive oil
2 carrots, thinly shredded
1 green pepper, deseeded and thinly sliced
1 small tin pineapple pieces, in natural juice
1 bunch scallions, trimmed and chopped
Juice from the pineapple (about 3 fl oz/75 ml)
1 tablespoon soy sauce
2 tablespoons light golden brown sugar
3 fl oz/75 ml wine- or cider vinegar
1 rounded tablespoon cornflour
1/2 pint/300 ml chicken stock
Salt, freshly ground black pepper and sugar to taste
2 oz/50g flaked almonds.

[Stir-Fried Mackerel, continued]

course, to put the pieces which need longest cooking in first. Use a wok if possible, otherwise a large shallow saucepan, preferably with sloping sides.

Combine all sauce ingredients and have ready in a jug. Heat a good pool of oil, about 1/2"–3/4"/1–2 cm deep, in a wok over high gas or an electric ring preheated on high.

Add the onion and toss briefly with two wooden spatulas or spoons, then the pepper, ginger and garlic. Keep stir-frying all the time and continue adding the next ingredient every 30 seconds or so, keeping the beansprouts back until last and adding the fish after the other vegetables. When the mackerel has been added, stir-fry for 1-2 minutes, carefully watching to see when the texture begins to change, then add the sauce ingredients immediately and bring up to the boil. Continue stir-frying for 1 minute to cook the sauce, then add the beansprouts and mix thoroughly. Serve immediately on a bed of boiled rice or noodles.

Note: The timing is only given as a guide — it will vary according to the utensil used and the source of power. The fastest cooking — with a wok and a strong gas flame — gives best results.

Optional garnish: Frilly spring onions make a pretty garnish for any oriental dish: Trim off the green parts and the bulb to leave a section about 3" long. With a sharp knife, cut a cross down about 1" into each end. Soak in iced water: the ends will curl up to make frills.

Stir-Fried Chicken with Cashews

This quick dish is perfect for holiday cooking — light but nourishing, delicious but very quickly cooked.

Prepare all ingredients before starting; mix all the sauce ingredients together in a jug and make sure that accompanying rice or noodles will be ready. Heat some oil in a wok or large pan and stir-fry the diced chicken in it over high heat, for 2-3 minutes. Add the onion and garlic and continue stir-frying for another 2 minutes, then add the mushrooms and green pepper and cook for a further 2 minutes. Finally add the beansprouts and the nuts and mix in quickly. Add the sauce ingredients and bring to the boil; reduce the heat and allow the mixture to cook for a minute or two, stirring, until the sauce is smooth and thick. Taste, adjust seasoning if necessary and serve immediately with Chinese noodles or rice.

Sweet & Sour Chicken with Almonds

An easy one-pot dish suitable for family and friends. [Microwave]

Get your butcher to bone the chicken for you, but ask for the bones for stock. If you have time, start the stock before cooking so you have the use of it, otherwise use it later and keep for soup. Cut up the chicken flesh into bite-sized pieces, toss in the seasoned flour and fry in 2 oz/50g of the butter and the oil until tender. Remove from the pan and keep in a warm oven. Add the carrots to the pan with the pepper, pineapple and scallions. Stir in the pineapple juice, soy sauce, sugar and vinegar. Simmer for 3 minutes. Blend the cornflour with the chicken stock and add to the pan. Stir or whisk until boiling, then simmer for a minute until the sauce thickens and clears. Taste and adjust the seasoning if necessary, then pour the sauce over the reserved chicken. Brown the almonds in the remaining 1/2 oz/15g butter and scatter over the top. Serve with rice and a green salad.

Hint: Chicken Stock is very quick to make in a microwave.

Savoury Bake with Tomato Coulis

What could be more appropriate at this time of year than a luscious meal based on fresh garden produce and served with a colourful tomato sauce and a lively side salad? This mouthwatering Savoury Bake with Tomato Coulis comes from Cashel House in Co. Galway, where it is a popular vegetarian main course. [Microwave]

Slice the onion, courgette and tomatoes and arrange in a buttered ovenproof dish. Sprinkle with the chopped herbs and season with salt and pepper. Preheat a moderate oven, 350°F, 180°C, Gas mark 4. Melt the butter in a pan, add the flour and mix well to make a roux, then gradually add the milk and whisk over high heat until the sauce thickens. Remove from the heat, season to taste and pour over the vegetables. Grate the cheese, mix with the breadcrumbs, add the olive oil and mix well. Spread this mixture over the top of the sauce and bake in the preheated oven for 45-50 minutes, until golden brown and cooked through.

Meanwhile, make the coulis: Chop the tomatoes roughly, peel and chop the onion and chop the garlic finely. Put tomatoes, onion, garlic, rosemary and vinegar into a heavy pot, cover and cook over low heat for about 15 minutes, then remove the sprig of rosemary, add the sugar and season with salt and pepper. Liquidise and pass through a sieve to remove tomato pips and skin. Taste, adjust seasoning if necessary and serve with the Savoury Bake.

Serves 6

1 large onion
1 courgette
8 oz/225g tomatoes
Freshly chopped mixed herbs, eg. chives, parsley and thyme
Salt and freshly ground black pepper
2 oz/50g butter
1½ oz/40g plain flour
¾ pint/450 ml milk
4 oz/100g white cheddar cheese
4 oz/100g fresh white breadcrumbs
1 tablespoon olive oil

Tomato Coulis:

4 ripe tomatoes
1 small onion
1 clove garlic
1 sprig of rosemary
2 tablespoons white wine vinegar
2 teaspoons sugar
Salt and freshly ground black pepper.

Peaches Sweet and Savoury

While it is well known that most fruits are equally at home in a sweet or savoury role, it was intriguing to discover this pair of recipes from Blackheath House in Co Londonderry, for Peaches Sweet and Savoury. First the sweet — Peaches in Pastry:

Sift the flour, cut in butter or margarine, rub in to make a mixture like fine breadcrumbs then add the sugar and cinnamon. Mix with a little very cold water to make a stiff dough, roll into a ball, cover and rest in the fridge for at least half an hour. When ready, preheat a moderately hot oven,375°F, 190°C, Gas mark 5. Roll the pastry out to make a large square, then cut into quarters. Fill each peach with redcurrant jelly, then wrap the pastry around the peaches, decorate the top with pastry leaves and glaze. Bake in the preheated oven for 20-25 minutes until golden brown and crisp. Serve warm with thick cream.

Then the **Savoury Peaches**: Put the tongue, cream cheese. parsley, mustard, redcurrant jelly and walnuts into a liquidiser and blend until smooth. Fold in the stiffly beaten egg white, then pipe or pile the mixture on top of the peach halves and serve with a mixed leaf salad tossed lightly in walnut oil dressing. Garnish with a sprig of redcurrants if available, or chopped walnuts and a drizzling of Cumberland Sauce.

Peaches in Pastry: Serves 4
Cinnamon Pastry

8 oz/225g flour
4 oz/100g butter or margarine
2 oz/50g caster sugar
½ teaspoon ground cinnamon
4 peaches, stoned
4 dessertspoons redcurrant jelly

Savoury Peaches

6 oz/175g cooked tongue
2 oz/50g cream cheese
1 dessertspoon freshly chopped parsley
½ teaspoon mustard
½ teaspoon redcurrant jelly
8 chopped walnut halves
1 egg white.
4 peaches, halved and stoned

Baked Pork Chops with Raspberry and Cider Sauce

Baked Pork Chops with Raspberry Sauce is definitely a talking point if served to guests, but very easy to make. [Microwave]

Preheat a fairly hot oven, 425°F, 220°C, Gas mark 7. Trim any excess fat off the chops and pat them dry with kitchen paper. Put the butter into a bowl, crush the spices and add to it, then crush the garlic in the sea salt and add them to the bowl. Mix to a paste. Spread this paste all over the chops, meanly on the underside, generously on top, then lay the chops in a buttered baking dish — together with small whole onions for baking if you like — and cook them in the preheated oven for about 20 minutes,

Baked Pork Chops: Serves 4

4 lean loin pork chops
2 oz/50g butter
1 tablespoon mixed whole
  spices: coriander seeds,
  juniper berries, allspice
  and black pepper corns
2 or 3 large cloves garlic;
  sea salt

Sauce:

8 oz/225g raspberries
½ pint/300 ml dry cider
1 tablespoon red wine
  vinegar
4 each of all the spices used
  above
1 small onion, chopped.

or until just cooked through. (This depends on the thickness of the chops.) They will be golden brown and crunchy on top.

Meanwhile, make the sauce: Put all the sauce ingredients into a pan, bring to the boil and simmer for 15-20 minutes. The sauce can be left as it is if you like the texture, or sieved or liquidised to make a smooth sauce. Spoon some of the sauce over the chops and cook them for another 10 minutes or until thoroughly cooked, then serve with rice and salad; hand the remaining sauce separately.

Variation: The chops can be grilled, pan-fried or barbecued if preferred. The sauce need not be added during cooking, although it moistens the rather dry meat as well as flavouring it. See variation, Grilled Pork Chops with Cranberry Sauce (Autumn).

PICNICS

Ideas for good, wholesome picnic food which is portable enough to taste as good at its destination as it did in the kitchen at home are hard to come by. Early on the morning of our summer expeditions, my mother used to spend hours making pasties which were wrapped in greaseproof paper and then layers of newspaper to keep them warm in biscuit tins until lunch time. The system worked remarkably well, but work was the operative word and far too much of it for my liking. Then along came the quiche, which tasted as good cold as hot and was made in one big tin. All you need to help quiches along is a bowl of tossed salad and, perhaps, some herb or garlic bread.

Cream Cheese & Tomato Quiche

Serves 8:

10 oz/275g plain flour
Salt, pepper and a pinch of
  dry mustard or cayenne
  pepper
5 oz/125g butter, at room
  temperature
6 oz/175g finely grated
  Cheddar cheese
2 egg yolks or 1 whole egg.

Filling:

2 onions, peeled and finely
  chopped
2 cloves garlic, peeled and
  crushed or finely chopped
1 oz/25g butter and 1
  tablespoonful oil
8 oz/225g cream cheese
4 eggs, beaten
½ pint/300 ml milk
Sea salt and freshly ground
  black pepper.
About 1 lb/450g tomatoes,
  peeled if the skins are
  tough

Makes two 8"/20 cm flans, or one big 10-11"/25-28cm one. Quantities required for filling may vary according to the depth of the tin.

Pastry: If you have a food processor, use it to make the pastry. Otherwise, sift flour and seasonings into a bowl, cut in the butter and rub in until like fine breadcrumbs. Add the finely grated cheese and mix well, then blend in the egg and just enough cold water to make a firm dough. Turn onto a floured work surface, knead lightly into a ball and leave, wrapped, in the fridge, for 15-30 minutes to rest. Turn out onto the floured surface, knead lightly, divide in half and roll each piece out just enough to line the quiche tins or flan rings. Trim to neaten, then prick the bases lightly with a fork and leave in the fridge while preparing the filling.

Preheat a fairly hot oven, 425°F, 220°C, Gas mark 7.

Fry the onions and garlic gently in the butter and oil until just softening but not colouring. Meanwhile, mash the cream cheese with a fork, then beat in the eggs; when smooth, stir in the milk. (As for the pastry, use a food processor for this if available.) Season well with pepper and a little salt. Divide the onion mixture between the two flans, spread evenly, then cover with the custard. Slice the tomatoes and arrange over the mixture, then scatter lightly with grated cheese to give a crisp, well-browned top. Bake in the preheated oven for 10-15 minutes until the pastry is colouring a little, then reduce the temperature to 375°F,190°C, Gas mark 5 and bake for another 20-30 minutes, or until the custard has set and the top is golden brown. Be prepared to reverse the position of the two flans or reduce the temperature towards the end of the cooking time if they are cooking unevenly or too quickly — or, if the pastry is over-browning, lay a piece of greaseproof paper or foil loosely over the top to protect it. Serve hot or cold, with a salad.

Blue Cheese & Walnut Quiche

This more sophisticated quiche can be very quickly made using frozen pastry.

Preheat a fairly hot oven, 400°F, 200°C, Gas mark 6. Roll out the pastry and use to line an 8"-8½"/20-21 cm flan ring or loose-based tart tin. Set aside in a cool place while you prepare the filling. Select about seven perfect walnut halves for decoration, then chop the remainder. Mash the cheeses together with a fork in a mixing bowl, then add the beaten eggs, cream, chopped nuts and seasoning. Taste — only add salt if necessary, as blue cheese is often very salty. Spread the finely chopped onion and garlic over the base, pour over the cheese mixture and bake in the preheated oven for 30 minutes, then reduce the heat to 350°F, 180°C, Gas mark 4 and cook for another 10 minutes, until the filling is set and the pastry crisp and golden brown. Decorate with the reserved walnuts and serve hot or cold. Variations of Waldorf salad go well with this flan and carry well for picnics.

Serves 4-6:

1 x 12 oz/ 350g packet frozen shortcrust pastry, or equivalent home-made
8 oz/225g cream cheese
2 oz/50g blue cheese, eg Cashel Blue
3 large eggs, lightly beaten
¼ pint/ 150 ml cream or top of the milk
Freshly ground black pepper and a pinch of cayenne pepper or mustard powder.
4–6 oz/100–175 g walnuts
1 onion, finely chopped
1 large clove garlic, crushed

Cheese and Apple Pie

An interesting alternative to a quiche which also travels well is this double-crust plate pie based on a duo which has always made a natural partnership. Choose a good mature cheese and rather sour apples if possible — windfalls would do at the end of the holidays — as the tartness of the fruit will bring out the full flavour of the cheese. Serves 4, although it would stretch to 6 if there are plenty of salads and crusty fresh bread or rolls.

Sift flour, mustard and a grinding of pepper into a mixing bowl, cut in the butter and rub in to make a mixture like fine breadcrumbs. Blend in the grated cheese. Beat the eggs lightly and fork in just enough to hold the dough together. Gather it up into a ball, knead lightly on a floured surface, wrap in clingfilm and chill while you peel, core and slice the apples and grate or chop the second batch of cheese. Preheat a hot oven, 425°F, 220°C, Gas mark 7. Halve the pastry slightly unevenly and use the larger piece to line a 7"-8"/18-20 cm pie plate or flan tin. Mix the sugar through the apple slices and pile onto the pastry base. Scatter the coarsely grated or cubed cheese over the apples. Roll out the remaining pastry to make a lid. Moisten the edge of the base pastry, cover with the lid and press down well around the edge. Flute the edges between thumb and forefinger, trim the edge neatly, make an air vent in the centre of the lid and use any pastry trimmings to make decorative leaves around it if you like. Mix the remaining beaten egg with a little milk to make a glaze and brush it evenly over the pastry. Bake in the preheated oven for 35-40 minutes, or until the pastry is crisp and golden-brown. Serve cold — it is delicious with home-made chutney.

Variations: Grated Parmesan or Regato could be used in the pastry instead of Cheddar. Small individual pies or pasties could be made instead.

Serves 4-6:

6 oz/225g plain flour
½ teaspoon powdered mustard, freshly ground pepper
4 oz/100g butter
2 oz/50g mature Cheddar cheese, finely grated

Filling:

2 eggs
2 lb/900g cooking apples
4 oz/100g mature Cheddar cheese, coarsely grated or chopped
1 tablespoon caster sugar.
1-2 tablespoons milk.

Middle-Eastern Picnic Bread

This picnic bread is based on minced meat and would be equally popular for adult packed lunches. Tone down the flavourings for the kids, if you like. Microwave]

Wrap the pitta breads in foil and warm in a low oven. Melt the butter or margarine in a large frying pan and cook the mince in it fairly briskly for about 5 minutes, until brown and crumbly. Stir in the garlic and cumin, then reduce the heat and add the tomatoes. Cook over moderate heat, stirring from time to time, until the tomatoes are soft and their juice has evaporated, then season to taste, remove from the heat and stir in the mint and lettuce. Cut the bread open with a sharp knife to make a pocket and stuff the mixture into them. Re-wrap in their foil parcels, sealing well for carrying. Makes 6.

Middle Eastern Picnic Bread

6 pitta breads (fresh or frozen)
1 oz/25g butter or margarine
1 lb/450g lamb or beef mince
2-3 cloves garlic, finely chopped
2 teaspoons ground cumin (optional, see method)
12oz/350g tomatoes, roughly sliced
Small handful freshly chopped mint (optional, see method)
½ a small iceberg lettuce, or equivalent, shredded finely
Salt, freshly ground black pepper and sugar.

Variation: The cumin and mint marry especially well with minced lamb, making an authentic Middle Eastern combination. If you feel this might be unpopular, use beef instead and flavour with mixed dried herbs and freshly chopped parsley.

Wholemeal Picnic Scone

Serves 8 wedges:

12 oz/350g fine ground self-raising wholemeal flour
1 rounded teaspoon baking powder
Good pinch of salt
3 oz/75g butter
¼ pint/150 ml milk.

This Wholemeal Picnic Scone is very easy to make and serve, as it is made in one piece with divisions ready cut, like Strawberry Shortcake. It can be filled with cream cheese and tomatoes or salad to make a juicy picnic sandwich, or with cream and home-made jam as a tea-time treat.

Preheat a hot oven, 425°F, 220°C, Gas mark 7. Grease a baking sheet. Mix the dry ingredients together thoroughly, cut in the butter and rub in to make a mixture like fine breadcrumbs. Add the milk and mix with a fork to make a dough, then turn out onto a floured work surface and knead lightly to make a ball of dough with no cracks through it. Roll out to make a circle about 8-9"/20-23 cm across and slide onto the prepared baking sheet. Using a sharp knife, cut about halfway through the dough to divide into eight sections, then brush with a little extra milk if you want a glaze, and bake in the hot oven for about 20-25 minutes or until well-risen and golden-brown with a crisp base and crust. Cool on a wire rack, wrapped in a tea towel if you prefer a soft crust. When cool, halve horizontally, fill in any way you like and replace the marked-out top half. Press gently together and, if it is for a picnic, wrap well with a layer of greaseproof paper and then foil, or carry it in an airtight tin. Use on the day of baking.

Savoury Pizza Pie

Savoury Pizza Pie: Serves 6

Tomato Sauce:

1 x 14 oz/400g can chopped tomatoes
1 onion, chopped
1 clove garlic, crushed
2 level teaspoons sugar
Salt and freshly ground black pepper
Good pinch of dried oregano or mixed herbs,

Scone base:

8 oz/225g self-raising flour
1 level teaspoon baking powder
1 level teaspoon salt
2 oz/50g butter/margarine
Freshly ground black pepper
1 level teaspoon dried oregano or mixed herbs
1 large egg
5-6 tablespoons milk

Topping:

6 oz/175g grated Cheddar cheese
2 oz/50g grated parmesan
4 oz/100g cooked ham, cut into strips
2 oz/50g mushrooms, wiped, trimmed and thickly sliced
½ level teaspoon oregano
Salt and freshly ground black pepper
A little olive oil.

Savoury Pizza Pie is a simple, scone-based pizza that makes a tasty hot meal for about six. [Microwave]

First make the sauce: Empty the can of chopped tomatoes into a pan, add the onion, garlic and sugar, seasoning to taste and the herbs. Simmer uncovered for about half an hour until the mixture thickens, then leave to cool. Meanwhile, make the base and prepare the topping: Sieve the flour, baking powder and salt into a mixing bowl; cut in the butter or margarine and rub in until the mixture looks like fine breadrumbs. Add the pepper and stir in the herbs. Make a well in the centre and stir in the beaten egg and enough milk to make a soft dough. Turn out onto a floured worktop, knead lightly and roll out to make a 9"/22 cm diameter circle. Turn on the oven and set at 400°F, 200°C, Gas mark 6. Transfer the dough base to a greased baking sheet, build up an edge with the fingers to contain the filling and spread the sauce evenly over the base. Mix the two cheeses together and sprinkle the sauce generously with about three-quarters of it. Arrange the ham over the top, then sprinkle with the remaining cheese. Finally arrange the sliced mushrooms on top, sprinkle with herbs, seasoning and a light drizzle of olive oil, then bake in the hot oven for 30-40 minutes until the base is well-risen and crisp and the topping is bubbling and golden. Serve with a crisp green side salad.

BARBECUES

How extremely carnivorous the barbecue habit is — most of us eat as much meat at one barbecue as we would normally get through in a week. By contrast, the protein in a vegetarian diet — eggs, dairy products, pulses — is generally unsuitable for barbecueing. Vegetables barbecue well, though, if carefully chosen, and vegetable kebabs would make a very tasty hot dish to go with a protein-rich bean salad, for instance. Courgettes, peppers, mushrooms, tomatoes, baby corn, onion — any of those normally used for meat-based kebabs are suitable. Select vegetables so that all those on one skewer will take about the same cooking time, keep them fairly small for quick cooking and add freshly chopped herbs to the oil with which they are brushed if possible for extra flavour. Larger vegetables are best partly pre-cooked and wrapped in foil before cooking over the barbecue. Whatever your ingredients, the absolute essential for barbecue success is advance preparation: make sure all the necessary tools and accessories are to hand before beginning, have salads and accompaniments prepared beforehand and everything needed for serving and eating laid out ready.

Universal Marinade / Barbecue Sauce

Most barbecue recipes come complete with a special marinade without which that dish would not be genuine, but it can be useful to have a basic recipe or two to hand, such as this Universal Marinade, which is suitable for any meat or poultry, and a basic Barbecue Sauce, which can be used on any food to baste it during cooking.

Marinade: Simply, put all ingredients into a screw-top jar and shake well. Pour over the food to be cooked and marinate for about an hour.

Barbecue Sauce: Blend all ingredients thoroughly in a bowl and use to brush onto food during grillling to flavour it and prevent burning. Suits most barbecued food and is especially useful for everyday things like burgers and sausages that have no special recipes.

Universal Marinade:

2 tablespoons each of olive oil, lemon juice, tomato juice,
2 teaspoons each of Worcestershire sauce and soy sauce.

Universal Barbecue Sauce:

1 level teaspooon chilli powder and celery salt
2 tablespoons each of: light golden brown sugar, wine vinegar or cider vinegar, Worcestershire sauce
3 tablespoons tomato ketchup
$1/4$ pint/150 ml stock or water
Tabasco sauce, to taste.

Chicken Drumsticks with Brown Sugar & Mustard

Inexpensive, quick to cook through and easy to eat with the fingers — drumsticks make ideal barbecue food. Allow two each.

Wipe and trim the drumsticks and cut two or three deep gashes in the thickest parts of the flesh. Put them into a deep bowl. Melt the butter and mix with the mustard, sugar and lemon juice. Spread over the chicken. Leave to marinate in a cool place, turning occasionally, for several hours or overnight. To cook, remove from the marinade and barbecue over moderately hot coals, turning as required and basting occasionally with the marinade. Test with a skewer — the drumsticks are cooked when the juices run clear, without any trace of blood. If preferred, they can be cooked ahead, or partly cooked, for 15-30 minutes in a fairly hot oven, then served hot or cold.

Note: In the wake of recent scares connecting poultry and salmonella, it is wiser to pre-cook all poultry conventionally in the kitchen rather than relying on the barbecue alone.

Serves 4:

8 chicken drumsticks
1 oz/25 g butter
2 tablespoons smooth Dijon mustard
2 tablespoons light golden brown sugar
2 tablespoons lemon juice
Coriander or parsley leaves to serve.

Grilled Whiting Oriental Style

This is a tasty, quickly cooked dish using one of our cheapest and most under-rated fish.

Make three parallel diagonal cuts on both sides of the fish. Wash thoroughly and pat dry with kitchen paper. Combine the shallots, root ginger, sugar, salt, soy, saké or sherry and oil. Rub each fish inside and out with this mixture. Allow to stand for 30 minutes. Place the fish into a greased flat hinged wire basket or directly onto a well-greased grill rack. Cook over hot coals for about 6 minutes on each side, basting frequently with oil. When the first side is nicely browned, turn and lay the fish on a fresh spot on the grill.

Variations: Other fairly small fish, such as herrings, mackerel, fresh sardines or trout can be cooked in the same way. Serves 4.

★ Many of the more interesting — and, especially, exotic — recipes for

Serves 4:

4 whole whiting, cleaned
2 shallots, finely chopped
2 slices root ginger, finely chopped
$1/2$ teaspoon sugar
$1/2$ teaspoon salt
1 tablespoon soy sauce
1 tablespoon saké or dry sherry
1 tablespoon arachide or sunflower oil
Extra oil for basting.

barbecued dishes have off-puttingly long lists of ingredients and complicated, instructions which are both time-consuming and difficult because so many utensils are needed for each dish. The discerning cheat can get around this by careful scrutiny of the appropriate supermarket shelves: the range of prepared products for easier barbecues is growing all the time. Oriental makes are usually worth investigating, also any in-store 'home-made' sauces, otherwise stick to the top of the market — a well-known quality brand shouldn't let you down. Oriental ranges are growing all the time and there is now an excellent selection of marinades, oils and sauces specially designed to make barbecueing easier and more successful.

★ Greek style yogurt is thicker than ordinary yogurt and, because of its slightly higher fat content and lower acidity, has a rich and creamy flavour with a tang which is not at all bitter. For your next barbecue, try it in a **Mint Yogurt Sauce** to use as a dip with kebabs (especially lamb) or pitta bread — just blend 8 oz/225 g of the yogurt with 4 tablespoons freshly chopped mint, a crushed clove of garlic, a tablespoon of honey and season to taste with salt and pepper.

Steak Rolls with Mustard Sauce

Steak Rolls: Serves 6

12 thin steaks about 4 oz /100g each/¼"/ 0.6 cm thick
2 teaspoons wholegrain mustard
1 teaspoon smooth Dijon mustard
Coarse sea salt
Freshly ground black pepper
¼ pint/150 ml good mayonnaise, preferably home-made
3 tbsp thick natural yogurt
1 tbsp wine vinegar
l level teaspoon caster sugar
Lemon wedges and sprigs of fresh herbs to garnish.

Steaks are synonymous with barbecues and this recipe rings the changes from plain grilled meat. It can be cheaper too, as you could use well-beaten quick-fry steak instead of sirloin.

Lay the steaks out on a board, beat if necessary and spread the mixed mustards on one side. Sprinkle lightly with sea salt and pepper. Leave in a cool place for about an hour. When ready to cook, roll up loosely with the mustard inside and thread onto one or two long skewers, leaving gaps between the rolls. To make the sauce, blend all the remaining ingredients together thoroughly, taste and season accordingly, then pour into a bowl or jug to hand separately. Cook the steaks according to taste and serve with the lemon wedges and fresh herbs, accompanied by the mustard sauce and a mixed leaf salad.

Chinese Barbecued Steak

Chinese Barbecued Steak
Serves 3–4
l flank steak

Marinade:
½ tbsp sugar
l teaspoon 5-spice powder
4 large cloves garlic, chopped
3 tablespoons soy sauce
l tbsp dry sherry
2-3 tbsp barbecue sauce.

Although you could equally well use sirloin, fillet or topside steak, the special marinade makes it possible to use a cut which would normally be braised, such as flank.

Trim the flank steak of all fat and membrane. Lay in a shallow dish. Mix all the marinade ingredients well and pour over the meat, rubbing well into the meat. Cover and marinate at room temperature for an hour. When ready to cook, remove the meat from the marinade and shake or dab off excess marinade, then place on the barbecue or under a preheated grill and cook for about 8 minutes on each side. When cooked, remove the meat to a chopping board and let it cool slightly before slicing crosswise, against the grain, into thin slices. Serve with Mixed Leaf Salad with Hazelnut Dressing.

Mixed Leaf Salad with Hazelnut Dressing

Mixed Leaf Salad

A selection of salad leaves, eg lamb's lettuce, oakleaf, radicchio, frisée, lollo rosso etc as available
Fresh large leaf herbs, eg chervil, coriander, basil etc
l tablespoon hazelnuts, roughly chopped
2 tablespoons hazelnut oil
Salt and freshly ground black pepper
1-2 teaspoons sherry vinegar, or good wine vinegar.

Wash and dry the salad leaves; tear any large ones up and put into a salad bowl with the herbs and chopped nuts. Mix oil and vinegar, season to taste with salt and pepper. Just before serving, toss the salad in the dressing.

Variations: Walnuts and walnut oil can be used instead, or any other variation you like. If special oils are hard to get, try using olive oil or any good salad oil enlivened with a dash of sesame oil.

Afternoon Tea: Sandwiches

Tea in the garden is one of the great seasonal treats in our unpredictable climate and it should be taken suitably seriously. Although it is basically an excuse to eat sweet things in the open air, it should begin with a few appropriately delicate sandwiches — very fresh white bread, no crusts; cucumber is traditional, of course, and needs nothing but a sprinkling of sea salt to bring heaven considerably nearer earth and the other very pleasurable filling is tomato, perhaps with a little cream cheese, the tomatoes peeled before slicing, of course and seasoned with a grinding of black pepper and a little caster sugar as well as the sea salt. All served with a choice of teas. Then it's down to the serious business …

Lemon Sponge

Currerevagh House, Oughterard, Co Galway is best known for its fishing but it has a great reputation for afternoon teas and this Lemon Sponge is a speciality.

Preheat a moderate oven, 350°F, 180°C, Gas mark 4. Butter and flour a deep 8"/20 cm cake tin. Put the butter, milk and granulated sugar into a sauce pan and warm over gentle heat until the sugar has dissolved. Allow to cool a little. Separate the eggs and put the yolks into a mixing bowl: beat or whisk together lightly and add the cooled melted mixture, allowing it to fall from a height to cool if it is rather hot for the yolks. Whisk together, or beat with a wooden spoon. In a separate bowl, whisk the egg whites until stiff but not dry. Sift the flour and baking powder together and add to the mixture with the grated lemon zest, blending thoroughly, then fold in the egg whites. Turn the mixture into the prepared tin and bake in the preheated oven for about 30 minutes or until springy to the touch and shrinking slightly from the tin. Turn out and leave on a wire rack to cool. Meanwhile, make the **Butter Icing**: cream the butter with a wooden spoon, then gradually blend in the sifted icing sugar and enough lemon juice to make a smooth, creamy mixture. When the cake has cooled, split it and use half of the mixture as a filling, then swirl the remaining icing on top — no other decoration is needed. This cake will keep for several days.

Spice Bread

Longueville House in Mallow, Co. Cork, is best known for trend-setting cuisine in their Presidents' Restaurant but they also have a great reputation for humbler (but equally important) breakfast and afternoon tea specialities such as this Spice Bread, a good keeper which would be equally useful in the picnic basket or for afternoon tea on the lawn.

Preheat a fairly slow oven, 330°F/170°C/Gas mark 3-4. Sieve flour with mixed spice and ginger. Stir in sugar, sultanas and peel. Melt the butter with the syrup over low heat and stir into the dry ingredients with the milk and beaten egg. Mix well. Pour the mixture into a greased 2 lb/900g loaf tin and bake in the preheated oven for 1½ hours, or until springy to the touch and shrinking slightly from the tin. Turn out and cool on a wire rack. Store in an airtight tin for a day or two before cutting, then serve sliced and buttered.

Caramel Bars

As well as wonderful sandwiches, fresh scones and home-made jam and light-as-a-feather sponge cake, they make these wicked gooey chocolate-topped Caramel Bars at Hunter's Hotel, Rathnew, Co Wicklow.

Preheat a moderate oven 350°F, 180°C, Gas mark 4 and thoroughly grease a 12"x9"/30x23cm swiss roll tin. To make the shortbread: cream

Makes one 8"/20cm sandwich cake.

1½ oz/40g butter
2 tablespoons milk
4½ oz/115g granulated sugar
4 eggs
4 oz/100g plain flour
2 level teaspoons baking powder
Finely grated zest of 1 lemon and a few drops of juice

Butter Icing:

2 oz/50g butter, at room temperature
3½ oz/90g icing sugar
A few drops of lemon juice.

Spice Bread: Makes a 2 lb/900g loaf

10oz/275g self-raising flour
1 teaspoon mixed spice
½ teaspoon ground ginger
4 oz/100g light golden brown sugar
6 oz/175g sultanas
2 oz/50g chopped candied peel
2 oz/50g butter
6 oz/175g golden syrup
6 tablespoons milk
1 large egg.

Caramel Bars: Makes at least 12 bars
Shortbread
5 oz/150g butter
4 oz/100g caster sugar
10 oz/275g flour
4 oz/100g good plain chocolate, for topping

Filling
4 oz/100g butter
4 oz/100g caster sugar
2 tablespoons golden syrup
1 large can condensed milk.

the butter and sugar, then work in the flour and press the mixture into the prepared tin. Bake in the preheated oven for 15-20 minutes, until golden brown. Remove from the oven and leave to cool.

Meanwhile make the filling: Put all the filling ingredients into a pan and heat gently until the sugar has dissolved, stirring occasionally, then increase the heat, bring up to the boil and boil for 5 minutes, stirring all the time. Remove from the heat, leave to cool for 1 minute, then pour onto the cooled shortbread and leave to cool. When the filling has cooled and set, break the chocolate into a small bowl and melt over hot water. Spread over the set filling. Mark out into serving squares or fingers and leave until the chocolate has cooled and set firm before cutting and removing from the tin.

Raspberry Sponge: Makes an 8"/20 cm cake

4 eggs
4 oz/100g caster sugar
3½ oz/90g flour, sifted
Icing sugar for dusting

Filling:

5 fl oz/150 ml double cream
Raspberry jam, home made if possible

Variation: **Strawberry Gâteau.** This cake can very easily be converted into a luscious summer dessert: Omit the jam and double the amount of cream. Hull about 1 lb/450 g strawberries. Select some well-shaped, evenly sized ones for the top of the cake and slice the rest. Whip the cream with a little icing sugar so that it is stiff enough to hold its shape. Divide half of it between the two inner sides of the sandwich. Lay the bottom half on a serving plate and arrange the sliced strawberries on the cream. Cover with the second half of the cake and press down gently so that it all holds together. Spread the remaining cream on top of the cake and arrange the reserved strawberries, whole or halved according to size, on top. Set aside for an hour or so for the flavours to develop, then dust lightly with icing sugar and serve as a dessert. Use on the day of making. Serves 8.

Raspberry Sponge

Raspberry Sponge is a perennial favourite that never seems to date and is especially delicious in the summer, filled with the new season's jam — my mother-in-law remembers it having pride of place on the tea table many years ago when she went to visit her aunts and it's still just as popular today. Like any fatless sponge, it should be eaten on the day it is made but, in the unlikely event of some being left over, it can be used (without the filling) as a trifle base. Have all ingredients at warm room temperature for this recipe. Unless you are using a powerful electric mixer such as a Kenwood Chef, the eggs and sugar will need to be whisked over hot water to get the required volume and consistency.

Grease an 8"/20cm deep cake tin, preferably loose-based, and dust it with a teaspoonful of caster sugar mixed with an equal quantity of flour. Preheat a fairly hot oven, 375°F, 190°C, Gas mark 5.

Put the eggs and sugar into the bowl of an electric mixer and whisk at high speed until it is light and thick and the mixture leaves a good trail as it drops from the whisk. If whisking by hand, or with a hand-held electric whisk, set the bowl over a saucepan or another bowl a quarter filled with hot (not boiling) water and whisk until thick and creamy, then remove from the heat. Sift the flour evenly over the whisked eggs and carefully fold it in with a metal spoon, mixing thoroughly but losing as little volume as possible. Pour the mixture into the prepared tin, level off the top and bake in the preheated oven for 25-30 minutes, until the sponge feels springy to the touch. Leave in the tin for a minute or two to allow the cake to cool a little and shrink slightly from the tin, then loosen the sides gently with a knife and turn out onto a rack to cool. When completely cold, whip the cream until it forms soft peaks, then slice the sponge across the middle and spread the bottom half generously with home-made raspberry jam. Cover with the cream, put the second half of the cake on top and dust with icing sugar. Leave in the fridge, or in a cool larder, for an hour or so, to allow the flavours to blend and the cream to firm up.

Hunter's Tea Scones

Hunter's Hotel is a rambling old coaching inn set in lovely gardens alongside the River Vartry, near Wicklow. The meal they are most famous for is Afternoon Tea which, in summer, is taken in the garden beside a wonderful herbaceous border. These tea scones are always on the menu.

Preheat a hot oven, 425°F, 220°C, Gas mark 7 and grease two baking trays. Cut the fat into the flour and rub in lightly. Mix in the sugar, salt and grated lemon zest then stir in the beaten egg and enough milk to make a loose dough. Turn onto a floured board and knead lightly into shape. Roll out to about ½"/1.25 cm thick and cut out about 12 large or 18 small scones with a fluted cutter. Arrange spaced well apart on the baking trays

Makes 12–18 scones:

1 lb/450g self-raising flour
3 oz/75g butter or margarine
4 oz/100g caster sugar
Pinch of salt
Finely grated zest of ½ lemon
1 egg, lightly beaten
Milk, as required.

and bake in the hot oven for 10-20 minutes (depending on size) until well-risen and golden brown. Cool on wire racks and serve very fresh with butter and home-made jam.

Strawberry Shortcake

Strawberry Shortcake is one of the great classic summer dishes and, although of transatlantic origin, it has a delicate continental cousin, the Sablé (see below) which has been starring in the best restaurants in recent years. First, the shortcake, which serves 8:

First make the pastry: Use a food processor if available, otherwise sift the flour and icing sugar together and put about a third of it into a mixing bowl with the butter, egg yolk, water and lemon juice. Cream this mixture together with a fork until well mixed, then add the remaining flour and sugar and mix to a firm dough. Turn out onto a floured work surface, knead lightly until smooth, then put into a polythene bag and chill for at least an hour. Preheat a fairly hot oven, 400°F, 200°C, Gas mark 6. Butter two baking sheets. Halve the dough and roll out to make two circles about 8"/20 cm diameter. Slide onto the prepared baking sheets, flute the edges with your fingers and mark one into eight triangles. Bake for 20-25 minutes, until the edges begin to brown, exchanging the positions of the baking trays halfway through cooking if necessary. When cooked, remove from the oven but leave them on the trays for a few minutes to cool a little and firm up before transferring them to wire racks to cool completely. Hull the strawberries, select a few of the best ones for the top and set aside, then slice the rest thinly. Whip the cream and caster sugar until thick, then fold in the sliced strawberries. Put the unmarked pastry circle on a flat plate or cake stand and spoon the strawberry mixture onto it, spreading it out neatly. Cut the other circle into triangles and rearrange as a circle on top; decorate with the reserved strawberries and dredge with icing sugar.

Variation: **Strawberry Sablés** are miniature or individual versions of the Shortcake — strictly speaking, the pastry might be a little richer (an extra egg yolk) and sweeter (a little extra icing sugar), but the one given above does very well and is easier to handle. Roll out quite thinly, to about the thickness of a rich tea biscuit, and stamp out circles with a 3"/8 cm fluted pastry cutter. Place on a non-stick baking tray and cook for about 15 minutes or until an even pale golden brown, in an oven pre-heated at 350°F, 180°C, Gas mark 4. Remove from the oven, leave to cool on the trays for a few minutes, then lift off onto wire racks. Allow two or three biscuits per person and arrange in little towers, with one or two layers of filling and just a light dusting of icing sugar on top. Strawberry Sablés are especially attractive and delicious served on a pool of Raspberry Coulis — and Sablés can, of course, be made up with other raw or poached fruit and served with any complementary sauce — Poached Pears, for example, are lovely with a Cinnamon Crème Anglaise.

Serves 8:

Rich sweet pastry:
8 oz/225g plain flour
2 oz/50g icing sugar
5 oz/150g unsalted butter, at room temperature
1 egg yolk
1 tablespoon ice cold water
½ tsp lemon juice.

Filling:
8 oz/225g strawberries
½ pint/300 ml chilled cream
2 heaped tablespoons caster sugar

Decoration:
Whole strawberries, icing sugar for dusting.

Cooling Summer Drinks

Lemon Cordial

This old-fashioned concentrate will keep in the fridge, or in a cool place, for up to 2 weeks.

2 lemons
1½ lb/700g caster sugar
1 oz/25g citric acid (from chemists)
2 pints/1.2 litres boiling water
Lemon slices to garnish.

Squeeze the juice from the lemons and set aside. Put the lemon peel into a large mixing bowl and add the sugar and citric acid. Pour the boiling water over the peel and sugar and stir until dissolved. Leave until cold, squeezing the softening peel occasionally to extract all the flavour. When cold, squeeze the lemon peels thoroughly and discard. Add the reserved fresh lemon juice, mix well and strain the syrup. Put into screw-top bottles and store in a cool place, preferably the fridge. To serve, fill up to a third of a glass with the cordial, add ice and top up with soda or mineral water. Serve with fresh lemon slices.

Variation: **Lime Cordial** can be made in exactly the same way.

Citron Pressé

Less familiar to many, although it is widely used on the continent is Citron Pressé — how I wish this delightfully refreshing bar drink would catch on in Ireland.

For each serving:
Juice of 1 large, juicy lemon
Caster sugar to taste
Still or sparkling water.

Citron Pressé is simplicity itself to make: you serve the lemon juice in a tall glass with some ice and offer caster sugar water separately, so the guest makes the mixture up to his or her own taste. Don't add too much sugar or it won't be refreshing.

Variation: **Orange Pressé** is made in the same way, but with little or no sugar.

Iced Coffee

Iced Coffee seems to have become a rare species these days, but is well worth reviving. Freshly ground coffee, brewed strong and allowed to cool is 'correct' but a good quality instant can be used instead and saves hassle. Serves 6

1½ pints/900 ml strong black coffee
2-3 tablespoons caster sugar
Chilled single cream to serve.

If using fresh coffee, sweeten to taste when hot, then leave to cool. If using instant, dissolve the granules and sugar in just enough hot water to melt them, then top up with cold water. In either case, chill the coffee when cold, To serve, pour into ice-filled glasses, top up with chilled cream and stir to mix. If you keep a jug of black coffee in the fridge, this is very easy to make up at any time.

Variation: For a special occasion, add a dash of rum or brandy.

Summer Wine Cup

A really fruity Summer Wine Cup

Serves 15–20:
8 oz/225 fresh strawberries
1 tablespoon caster sugar
Juice of 3 lemons
1 sherry glass of brandy
1 miniature bottle or 1 large measure Cointreau
1 bottle light red wine, Beaujolais type, well-chilled
1 bottle dessert wine
1 pint/600 ml soda water or sparkling mineral water
Sprigs of mint to decorate.

Slice the strawberries into a large bowl or jug. Add the sugar, lemon juice, brandy and Cointreau. Stir to dissolve the sugar, then leave to chill for awhile. Add the chilled wine and then, immediately before serving, add some ice cubes and the soda water. Garnish with a few sprigs of mint and, if avail-able some pretty blue borage flowers which look enchanting if they are frozen inside individual ice cubes, using boiled water to eliminate air bubbles.

White Wine Cup

Cool and soothing.

Makes 12 glasses:
12 lumps sugar
1 lemon
2 bottles dry white wine
¼ pint/150ml dry sherry
1 pint/600 ml soda water or sparkling mineral water.

Rub the sugar lumps all over the lemon skin to remove the zest and impregnate it into the sugar. Squeeze the lemons and strain the juice. Put the sugar into a large bowl or jug and crush, then add the lemon juice and sherry. Stir until the sugar has dissolved. Stir in the wine and, just before serving, add some ice cubes and lemon or cucumber slices for decoration.

Iced Tea

Very simple and refreshing.

Serves 10–12:
2 lemons
3 pints/1.8 litres of hot tea (China or Jasmine is nice)
2 tablespoons sugar.

Remove thin strips of rind from one of the lemons with a vegetable peeler. Pour the hot tea over the peel, sweeten to taste and leave until cold. Strain into a jug and chill. Serve with slices of lemon.

Sangria

A very popular red wine cup.

Serves 12-16 glasses
2 oranges and 1 lemon
1 or 2 tablespoons caster sugar
1 small glass brandy
2 bottles red wine
Large bottle (1 litre/1¾ pint size) soda or mineral water
Ice.

Slice the oranges and lemons into a bowl or large jug and sprinkle with the caster sugar and brandy. Pour in the 2 bottles of wine and refrigerate for at least an hour. Just before serving, add a large bottle of soda or sparkling mineral water and plenty of ice.

Savoury Bake with Tomato Coulis, page 73
Right: Baked Pork Chops with Raspberry and Cider Sauce, page 73

Luscious desserts and creamy ice creams are, for many people, the essence of summer. Whether it's formally glazed tarts for a wedding party, a shimmering fruit terrine on a buffet table, the casual chic of summer pudding or strawberries and cream or a trio of ice creams in brandysnap baskets, the images summoned up are of langorous days and special occasions — and, although some of the most glamorous desserts take time and care to prepare, the good news is that so many of our best summer sweets are the simplest. Ice creams, too, are much easier than their reputation would imply — and, although the texture of commercial ices can never be matched (especially using quick and easy no-stir methods) the incomparable flavour of home-made ices outweigh any technical disadvantages.

Barbara's Strawberry Tart
with Raspberry Glaze

This delicious summer tart is ideal for a special occasion and needs no accompaniment. The pastry case uses an extremely good Magimix recipe — quick to make, producing an easily handled and very light, crisp pastry. Both it and the Confectioner's Custard can be made ahead, but leave the assembly until as near the time of serving as possible, to be sure of a crisp base. The glaze should be applied while it is still warm — it doesn't flow well if reheated.

First make the pastry: Put the flour, salt and butter into the bowl of a food procesor and process with the double bladed knife for a few seconds until the mixture looks like coarse breadcrumbs. Add the caster sugar and then the egg yolks; continue to process until the mixture forms a ball around the centre of the chopping knife. Stop the machine at once, wrap the ball of dough in clingfilm and leave in the fridge to rest for at least 10 minute before use. (*Variation:* using a whole egg instead of the 2 yolks is not quite correct, but it is less wasteful.) When the pastry has rested, roll out to line a 10"/25 cm loose-based tart tin, prick the base with a fork and chill for another 20 minutes. (Use any leftover pastry to make a few individual tartlets.) Preheat a hot oven, 400°F, 200°C, Gas mark 6. Line the pastry shell with a square of greaseproof paper, weight down with baking beans. Bake in the centre of the oven for 15 minutes, then remove the beans and paper and return to the oven for another 5 minutes, or until golden brown — if the rim starts to overcook, protect it with a strip of foil. When cooked, remove from the oven and leave the pastry in the tin until you are ready to fill it.

Meanwhile, make the Confectioner's Custard (See Sauces) and leave to cool.

To make the glaze: Heat the raspberries in a small pan until the juices begin to flow, then add the wine. Sieve to remove the pips, return to the rinsed pan and boil, uncovered, until reduced by half. Add the redcurrant jelly and the cassis and continue to cook until only about 4 tablespoons remain. While it cools, spread the confectioner's custard in the base of the pastry case and cover with the strawberries, which can be sliced, halved or quartered depending on size. Spoon the warm glaze over the strawberries. Leave the flan on the loose metal base of the tin for serving, particularly if your serving plate isn't absolutely flat.

Note: Lengthy reduction is essential for the glaze if it is to set. Alternatively, if time is short it can be thickened with a little arrowroot: cream a rounded teaspoonful of arrowroot in a little cold water and blend into the hot glaze mixture after the redcurrant jelly and cassis have been added. Bring back up to the boil and simmer until the sauce thickens and clears.

Serves 8:

Pate Sucrée:
8oz/225g plain flour
Pinch of salt
4 oz/100g butter, from the refrigerator, roughly chopped
2 oz/50g caster sugar
2 egg yolks

Filling:
1 quantity Confectioner's Custard (see Sauces)
1 lb/450g strawberries

Glaze:
8 oz/225g raspberries
1 glass/150 ml white wine
1 tablespoon redcurrant jelly
Dash of crème de cassis liqueur (optional).

Short-Cut Strawberry Tart
with Redcurrant Glaze

Serves 8:

Sweet shortcrust (8 oz/225g flour etc) OR 1 x 13 oz/375g packet frozen shortcrust pastry, defrosted
½ pint/300 ml fresh cream
A few drops vanilla essence
Caster or sifted icing sugar to taste
1 lb/450g strawberries
3 or 4 tablespoons redcurrant jelly
Lemon juice to taste
Dash of Crème de Cassis (blackcurrant liqueur), optional.

This short-cut version, Strawberry Tart with Redcurrant Glaze — a very simplified dessert based on the previous recipe, but omitting both the Confectioner's Custard and the raspberries — is almost as good for a family treat. Again, the pastry case can be made ahead (and made with frozen pastry if time is a real problem), but leave assembly until as late as possible so that the pastry will be really crisp.

Make the pastry, leave it to rest for at least 15 minutes, then roll out to line a 10"/25cm loose-based tart tin and prick the base with a fork. Chill for 20 minutes. Meanwhile, preheat a hot oven, 400°F, 200°C, Gas mark 6. Line the pastry shell with a square of greaseproof paper, weight down with baking beans and bake in the centre of the oven for 15 minutes, then remove the beans and paper and return to the oven for another 5 minutes or until golden brown, protecting the rim with a strip of foil if necessary. When cooked, remove from the oven and leave the pastry in the tin until you are ready to fill it. Shortly before the meal, whip the cream until soft peaks form, add a few drops of vanilla essence and sweeten to taste with caster or sifted icing sugar. Hull the strawberries and slice them if they are large. Spread the cream over the pastry base and arrange the strawberries on top. Melt the redcurrant jelly, sharpen slightly with a little lemon juice and add a dash of Crème de Cassis, if using. Spoon this mixture over the strawberries to make a glaze.

Variation: Yet another option would be to forget about the pastry case and use the whipped cream, sliced strawberries and glaze to fill a sponge flan, as in the next recipe.

Sponge Flan with Strawberries and Orange

Serves 6:

Sponge flan case:
2 large eggs
2 oz/50g caster sugar
2 oz/50g plain flour

Filling:
4 oranges
4 tablespoons apricot jam
1 teaspoon arrowroot
1 x 5 fl oz/150 ml carton double cream
A little icing sugar to sweeten
2 tablespoons Cointreau or Grand Marnier (optional) OR a little vanilla essence
1 small punnet strawberries.

Oranges and strawberries have a natural affinity and one of my favourite fruit salads is also the simplest imaginable: sliced strawberries sprinkled with freshly squeezed orange juice and a dash of Cointreau — sheer delight. The same combination stars in this featherlight Sponge Flan with Strawberries and Orange, where quantities are given for one 8-9"/20-22 cm sponge flan case but, as they freeze very well when unfilled and are extremely handy for making a small amount of soft fruit go a long way, it is a good idea to make several cases. [Microwave]

Preheat a hot oven, 425°F, 220°C, Gas mark 7. Grease an 8½"/21.5 cm non-stick flan tin thoroughly and dust with an equal mixture of flour and caster sugar. (If the tin is not non-stick, it is advisable to line the raised central section with a disc of baking parchment or greased greaseproof paper.) Put the eggs and caster sugar into the bowl of an electric mixer and whisk at high speed until very light and creamy. Sift over the flour and fold in carefully but thoroughly with a metal spoon, losing as little volume as possible. Turn into the prepared tin, smooth level with the back of the spoon and bake in the hot oven for about 15 minutes until well risen and golden brown. Turn out carefully and cool on a wire rack. Meanwhile, squeeze the juice from one of the oranges into a measuring jug and peel the others, carefully removing all the pith. Holding the oranges over the jug to catch the juices, cut along each side of the dividing membranes and lift out the segments; set aside and squeeze the remaining juice from the membrane into the jug. If necessary, make the juice up to ¼ pint/150 ml. Put the measured juice and apricot jam into a small pan and bring up to boiling point; mix the arrowroot with a little cold water, add to the pan and simmer for a few minutes, stirring, until the sauce thickens and clears. Sieve and leave to cool a little. Whip the cream until soft peaks form, sweeten lightly with a little icing sugar and flavour with a tablespoonful of the liqueur, or a few drops of vanilla essence. Select and slice 3 or 4 even-sized strawberries and set aside. Chop the rest roughly and scatter them over the base of the flan, then sprinkle with the other spoonful of liqueur and spread the whipped cream on top. Arrange the reserved orange segments and sliced strawberries on top of the cream and cover with the warm glaze.

Variation: For an unusual, exotic flavour, try flavouring both the sponge and the whipped cream with orange-flower water: simply whisk ½ teaspoon into the sponge just before adding the flour and add the same amount to the whipped cream instead of the liqueur or vanilla.

Hint: Have you ever tried sliced strawberries with a little freshly ground black pepper instead of the traditional sugar and cream? It's amazing how the spicy pepper enhances the flavour of the fruit. Or try balsamic vinegar, now all the rage in restaurants.

Gratin of Strawberries and Rhubarb

Gratin of Strawberries and Rhubarb is a speciality from Gregan's Castle, Ballyvaughan, Co. Clare and although the chef particularly likes the combination of strawberries and rhubarb, either could be replaced with your favourite fruit — redcurrants or raspberries, for example, when in season. [Microwave]

Wash and dry the strawberries, remove stalks and cut into quarters. Peel the rhubarb sticks, cut into 1"/2.5 cm chunks and simmer with the water, sugar and lemon juice for 3-5 minutes, until just tender. Turn out onto a tray to cool. Drain and reserve the liquid from the rhubarb, mix the fruit with the strawberries and arrange attractively on a shallow flameproof dish, then top with the **Sabayon Sauce**: Put the egg yolks into the bowl of an electric mixer and whisk at high speed until pale and fluffy. Meanwhile, cook the reserved rhubarb syrup for about 2 minutes. Reduce the speed of the mixer and add the hot syrup, pouring in a thin stream down the side of the bowl and into the whisk; continue to whisk until cool. Whip the cream and fold lightly into the egg mixture with a spoon or spatula. To serve: Preheat a very hot grill. Spoon the Sabayon over the fruit, sprinkle with icing sugar and put under the grill for about a minute, or until it is a light, golden brown. Serve immediately.

10 oz/275g strawberries
11 oz/300g rhubarb
5 fl oz/125 ml water
5 oz/125g caster sugar
Juice of ⅛ lemon (1 wedge)
4 egg yolks
4 fl oz/100 ml whipping cream
Icing sugar for dusting.

Fresh Apricot Trifle

Fresh apricots are so light and delicate that they seem like a totally different fruit from the dried ones that are so enjoyable in winter. From June onwards Spanish apricots are usually very plentiful and they are excellent in cooked dishes as well as raw — a treat not to be missed. At their simplest, poach them in a light syrup and serve as a compôte with slivered almonds, or a scattering of toasted almond flakes. Remember to get the delicious kernel out of the stone and add it to the dish too — it's said to have magical health-giving properties. For a special occasion, try this Fresh Apricot Trifle. [Microwave]

First make the custard and set aside to cool. Wash and dry the apricots, halve them and remove the stones. Break the stone open and remove the kernels; set aside. Put the wine and sugar into a pan and dissolve the sugar over gentle heat, then add the apricots and cook gently until just softening. Leave to cool. Lift the apricots from their juice with a slotted spoon and arrange them in a trifle bowl. Reserve a few biscuits for decoration and break the rest up roughly with a rolling pin; scatter over the apricots. Add the kernels and the apricot brandy to the cooking juices, stir to mix, then sprinkle over the crushed biscuits. Allow time for the biscuits to absorb as much liquid as possible, then pour the cold custard over and refrigerate for several hours or until the custard has set. To serve, whip the cream and swirl or pipe it over the custard and spike with the reserved ratafias or amaretti biscuits.

Serves 6:
1 pint/600 ml fresh egg custard (see Sauces)
1½-2 lb/750-900g fresh apricots
7 fl oz/200 ml white wine, medium or sweetish, not dry
3 oz/75 g caster sugar
4 fl oz/100 ml apricot brandy, or kirsch
8-10 oz/225-275g ratafia or amaretti biscuits
⅓ pint/ 175 ml cream, whipping or double.

Fresh Apricot and Almond Flan

Serves 8:

1 baked 10"/25 cm flan case
   (see above)
1 quantity Confectioner's
   Custard (see Sauces)
1½ lb/700g fresh apricots
½ pint/300 ml water
5 oz/125g granulated sugar
1 tablespoon Amaretto di
   Saronno (optional)
1 oz/25g slivered almonds,
   toasted.

Fresh Apricot and Almond Flan is another special occasion dish and can be based on the recipe already given for Strawberry Tart with Raspberry Glaze — prepare and bake the flan case in the same way, make the Confectioner's Custard and leave it to cool then continue as follows. [Microwave]

Halve the apricots, remove the stones and take the kernels out. Put the water and sugar into a fairly big pan and dissolve the sugar over gentle heat. Add the apricots and poach them gently for 10-15 minutes, or until just tender — the timing depends on the ripeness of the fruit. Remove the apricots from the syrup and leave to cool and drain; meanwhile boil the apricot syrup down until thick enough to use as a glaze. Put the baked flan case onto a serving dish. Flavour the Confectioner's Custard with the Amaretto, if using, then spread the custard into the flan case. Arrange the drained apricot halves and their kernels on top of the custard and brush with the reduced syrup glaze. Scatter with the toasted slivered almonds and serve.

Layered Cinnamon Biscuits with Fresh Cherries and a Cherry Brandy Sauce

Cinnamon Biscuits:

4 oz/100g unsalted butter
5 oz/150g caster sugar
5 oz/150 ml egg white
   (c. 4 egg whites)
½ teaspoon ground
   cinnamon
2 oz/50g flour
4 oz/100g fresh cherries

Brandy Syrup:

½ glass (75ml) cherry
   brandy
4 fl oz/100-125 ml stock
   syrup (see below).

Fresh cherries are the essence of Summer. At Marlfield House, Gorey, Co. Wexford their seasonal menu sometimes includes this pretty dessert, Layered Cinnamon Biscuits with Fresh Cherries and a Cherry Brandy Sauce. Although it involves making a number of components, it is not as difficult as it sounds and would round off a dinner party beautifully. Enough for 4, with extra biscuits for another time.

Cream butter and sugar, warm egg whites to blood temperature and add to the butter, beating well. Sift cinnamon and flour together and fold into the mixture. Cover and leave in the fridge for an hour to rest. Preheat a moderate oven, 350°F, 180°C, Gas mark 4. Grease and flour a baking tray and spread the mixture out on it with the back of a spoon. Bake until brown, mark out into shapes (squares or triangles are less wasteful than circles) and remove from the tray immediately. Allow to cool. Meanwhile, make a ½ pint/300 ml quantity of Pastry Cream (Crème Patissière) and leave to cool.

Wash cherries, halve and remove stones. Heat in a pan, add the cherry brandy and 1 oz/25g of the prepared cherries. Set alight to flambé. Add the stock syrup and leave to cook for 10-15 minutes until it reduces and becomes syrupy. [*Note:* **Stock Syrup** is made by dissolving granulated sugar in water (in the proportion of ½ lb/225g sugar to 16 fl oz/450 ml water), then boiling steadily for 10 minutes, or to 220°F/120°C on a sugar themometer. It is a useful ingredient to have ready.]

To Present the Dish:

Pipe a tiny rosette of pastry cream onto a plate, lay a cinnamon biscuit on top and pipe enough pastry cream over it to cover the biscuit. Place half of the remaining fresh cherries on top, cover with another cinnamon biscuit, repeat with another layer as above and finish by pouring the Cherry Brandy syrup around the plate.

Terrine of Summer Fruits

Terrine of Summer Fruits
Serves 8-10:

1 pint/600 ml freshly
   squeezed orange (or other
   fruit) juice
A little Cointreau or other
   fruit-based liqueur
3 oz/ 75g caster sugar, or to
   taste
1 sachet powdered gelatine
About 1½ lb//700g mixed
   soft fruit: strawberries,
   raspberries, redcurrants,
   cherries, grapes etc, all
   perfectly ripe.

If you want a dessert with a bit of drama about it for a summer party — something which is really colourful and, above all, easy both to make and to serve, look no further than this Terrine of Summer Fruits — served in slices, it looks wonderful against a plain white plate. The jelly base can be made of fruit juice — spiked, perhaps, with a dash of Cointreau or other appropriate fruit-based liqueur — or, for a special occasion, with a dessert wine, which will make a sparklingly clear jelly, in which the fruits are suspended like jewels. There are two methods, producing different but, I think, equally attractive results: the 'correct' method is to build up the terrine using layers of individual fruits, to produce a striped effect. This is more formal, but involves waiting for each layer of jelly to set before another fruit can be added. Equally pretty, I think, and much quicker is the random approach, where you put all the fruit in at once and it is all mixed up, like a solid fruit salad .

In order to get as clear a jelly as possible, strain the orange juice into a measuring jug through a very fine nylon sieve, preferably lined with muslin. The quantity will be slightly reduced, so add enough Cointreau to make up to 1 pint/600 ml again. Put half of it into a pan with the sugar and heat gently, stirring to melt the sugar, then sprinkle the gelatine over and stir over gentle heat until it has dissolved. Do not overheat. Turn the contents of the pan into the measuring jug containing the rest of the orange juice and mix well. Pour a thin layer about $\frac{1}{4}$"/0.5 cm, into the base of a 2 lb/ 900g loaf tin, preferably non-stick (approximate measurements 9"/22cm x 5"/12.5 cm x $2\frac{1}{2}$"/6.3 cm deep) or any other suitable container, capacity about 2 pints/1.2 litres. A ring mould is easy to serve and can be dressed up prettily and a heart-shaped mould looks wonderful, although serving even portions is harder. Chill this layer of jelly for about 15 minutes while preparing the fruit. Hull and slice strawberries, sort through raspberries, remove stalks from redcurrants, halve and stone cherries, halve and remove pips from grapes — unless they are exceptionally tough, there should be no need to skin them. Mix the prepared fruit in a bowl so that they are evenly distributed. Take the loaf tin from the fridge and pack the fruit fairly tightly in layers, adding jelly gradually as you go and giving the tin a sharp tap on the worktop occasionally to make sure the jelly finds its way into all the gaps. When the fruit is finished (or the tin is full, whichever comes first) dribble any remaining jelly over the top and shake it down thoroughly. Cover the terrine with clingfilm, and chill for at least 12 hours, until firmly set. To unmould, loosen the edges by running a sharp knife around the top, then invert the tin onto a serving dish and shake sharply — if a non-stick tin has been used the jelly should release without difficulty. If necessary, dip the tin very briefly into a bowl of hot water (for only a couple of seconds), invert on the plate and shake again; the edge of the jelly will now be melted and the terrine will slide out quite easily. Serve in slices, garnished with a little fresh fruit and leaves. Serve with Melba Sauce. *Note:* In very hot weather, extra gelatine may be required.

Hint: If serving the terrine whole is not vital for presentation, the easiest way to slice it neatly is to use an electric carving knife. Arrange on a platter, or on individual plates, surrounded by the sauce.

Summer Pudding

For at least two centuries, Summer Pudding has been one of the great classic dishes that dealt with as much style as practicality with varying amounts of mixed soft fruit as they came in from the garden. It's a wonderful dish, magnificent in its simplicity and, as it freezes extremely well, it's one of those rare ones that ocasionally bring luscious summer fruits and their rich jewel-like colours to brighten winter tables.

Remove the crusts from the bread. Line the base and sides of a $1\frac{1}{2}$-2 pint/850 -1200 ml soufflé dish or pudding basin, cutting the bread to shape if necessary so that there are no gaps. Sort through and prepare the fruit — the greater the mixture the better but don't include too many blackcurrants as their flavour will dominate the pudding. Top and tail currants, roughly slice strawberries, stone cherries. Put the fruit into a large, heavy-based pan and sprinkle the sugar over it. Warm through over very low heat and slowly bring up to the boil, then cook for 2-3 minutes only, until the sugar has dissolved and the juices are running from the fruit. Take the pan off the heat, set aside 1 or 2 tablespoons of the juice and turn the rest of the fruit

Serves 6:

About 8 slices stale white bread, $\frac{1}{2}$"/1.2 cm thick
$1\frac{1}{2}$ lb/700g mixed soft fruits — raspberries, loganberries, various currants, strawberries, cherries etc.
4 oz/100g caster sugar, or to taste

and its juices into the bread-lined dish. Cover with more bread, cut to fit the top neatly, then lay a plate that fits inside the dish on top of the bread lid and weight it down to compress the pudding. Chill for at least 8 hours before use, then turn the pudding out and use the reserved juice to colour any patches of bread which have not been soaked through by the fruit juices. Serve with chilled, whipped cream.

Variation: **Autumn Pudding** is made in the same way using a mixture of stewed apples, pears, blackberries etc.

Summer Fruits in Filo Tartlets

These deliciously light crumbly mouthfuls make a quick but impressive dessert.

Makes 12, to serve 6 as a dessert or 12 as part of a buffet selection:

Filo pastry, as required (see method)
1 oz/25g melted butter
About 12 oz/350g summer berries, as available
A few drops vanilla essence
½ pint/300 ml cream
Icing sugar.

Preheat a moderately hot oven, 375°F, 190°C, Gas mark 5. Using a damp cloth to cover the roll of filo pastry and prevent it drying out as you work, take one sheet at a time and fold it into a long strip about 4"/10 cm wide and cut it into as many 4"/10 cm squares as possible. Fold the next sheet and continue in the same way until you have 48 squares of pastry. Re-wrap the unused filo carefully and return to the fridge or freezer. Butter twelve bun tins and put four layers of pastry in each one, brushing each layer with melted butter before adding the next, and arranging the corners of the squares to make points like petals; finish off the top layer with the remaining melted butter. Bake the pastry cases in the preheated oven for 15-20 minutes until golden brown, then remove and allow to cool in the tins. To serve, whip the cream with the vanilla essence and a little icing sugar until thick. Scoop a tablespoonful into each tartlet and arrange the berries on top; dust with icing sugar and arrange on a serving plate.

Note: To be sure of crisp pastry, don't assemble more than about an hour before serving.

Hot Marinated Berries Gratinated with Grand Marnier

Mixed berries make especially interesting and delicious desserts — Summer Pudding is the classic example, but this gorgeous recipe, from Rosleague Manor, Letterfrack, Co. Galway, is more unusual.

1 punnet raspberries
1 punnet strawberries
1 punnet blackberries
¼ pint/150 ml basic stock syrup
1 fl oz/25 ml good red wine
2 fl oz/50 ml ruby port
2 egg yolks
4 oz/100g caster sugar
1 tablespoon Grand Marnier (approx.)
1 tablespoon water
3 egg whites.

A day in advance of serving, wash all the berries and place on a dry towel to drain. Cut any large strawberries into halves or quarters according to size, mix the berries together and place in a bowl. Put the stock syrup and red wine into a deep-sided pan, bring to the boil and allow to boil for about 1 minute. Add the port and simmer for a minute, then pour the hot wine mixture over the berries and leave to cool. When cold, refrigerate overnight, or for a minimum of 8 hours. Just before serving, whip egg yolks, sugar, Grand Marnier and water in a double saucepan, or in a bowl over a pan of hot water, until cooked and leaving a trail when the whisk is lifted from the mixture. Whisk the egg whites in a mixing bowl until firm but not too stiff, then fold into the yolk mixture. Preheat a moderate grill. Heat the berries until warm, place in a preheated shallow flameproof dish and place under the grill until golden brown. Remove, dust with icing sugar and garnish with a sprig of mint. Serve with home-made ice cream.

Pears with Bilberries

There's nothing to beat the flavour of your own, or locally grown, pears in the summer. If you have access to heathland, such as the Wicklow Hills, you can add the satisfaction of going out to pick your own bilberries — if not, you can use bought (cultured) blueberries instead. They're bigger, fatter cousins of our own native 'fraughans' and combine well with the same top fruits, notably pears and apples. This recipe for Pears with Bilberries makes a healthy dessert which retains the firm, grainy texture of the pears.

Preheat a fairly hot oven, 400°F, 200°C, Gas mark 6. Arrange the pears in a buttered deep ovenproof dish. Add the butter, red wine, sugar, cinnamon stick and bilberries or blueberries. Bake in the preheated oven for 1 hour, covered with a lid and basting occasionally. Serve hot or warm, with crème fraîche or natural yogurt.

Note: If you prefer not to use wine, try apple juice instead.

Plums generally fall into two main categories, dessert and culinary, but the Victoria plum — which grows well against a North or East wall in our climate — is an exception. Although extremely useful for cooking, ripe Victorias make sweet and juicy dessert plums and they have excellent flavour. Cooking plums are best served hot, with cold cream or ice cream providing contrast of colour and temperature — they are good cooked very simply, either baked or poached in a light syrup. Cook for as short a time as possible to keep the fresh summery taste of the fruit, then remove the plums to a serving dish and boil the syrup fast to reduce by half and pour it over them.

Pears with Bilberries: Serves 4

4 large pears, peeled and left whole
2 oz/50g butter, cut into small pieces
About ½ pint/300 ml red wine
3 oz/75g caster sugar
2 x 1 inch /2.5 cm cinnamon sticks
8 oz/225g bilberries or blueberries
Crème Fraîche to serve.

Crusty Plums

Crusty Plums is a descendent of 'Croûtes aux Prunes', a simple sweet which appeared in Elizabeth David's French Country Cooking in 1951 and has been adapted by any number of food writers since then. It is, as Mrs David says, 'Not exactly a dish for a grand party, but, all the same, an excellent countrified sweet'. It has two major advantages: it's quick and easy to make, and always popular with children of all ages.

Preheat a moderately hot oven, 375°F, 190°C, Gas mark 5.

Cut the crusts off the bread. Stone and halve the plums then fill the middle of each one with brown sugar. Arrange them, cut side down, on the bread in a shallow well-buttered ovenproof dish. Dot generously with butter and sprinkle lavishly with the rest of the brown sugar. Cover with a piece of buttered paper and bake in the preheated oven for about 25 minutes, or until the bread is golden and crisp. Sprinkle with a little more sugar and, if liked, a little cinnamon. Serve hot with chilled cream.

Serves 4

4 slices well-buttered white bread
8-10 large dessert plums, eg Victoria
About 4 oz/100g brown sugar
A good ounce/30 g butter
Caster sugar and cinnamon.

MOUTHWATERING ICE CREAMS

Classic ice cream recipes are rich, expensive and time consuming as they are based on egg custard and contain a high proportion of yolks and cream, but some of the short-cut ices are almost as good so don't be put off if you're short of time or prefer a simpler recipe. Always set the freezer at its lowest before beginning.

Vanilla Ice Cream

A good basic Vanilla Ice Cream is the most useful of all ices. It is delicious on its own, or with fresh fruit or a fruit coulis and can easily be dressed up using one of the presentation ideas at the end of this section. Although you need a little patience to make the essential egg custard, this looks after itself from then on, as it does not need to be stirred during freezing:

  6 egg yolks
  4 oz/100g caster sugar
  1 pint/600 ml single cream OR
  half cream, half milk
  1 vanilla pod OR 2 teaspoons
  vanilla sugar (see Basics) OR 1/2
  teaspoon vanilla essence

Beat egg yolks and sugar together until they are thick and creamy. Rinse out a saucepan in cold water and heat the cream, or cream and milk, with the vanilla pod, or vanilla sugar or essence. If using the pod, remove when nearly boiling and scrape out some of the seeds into the cream. (Rinse pod, dry and store for re-use). Pour the very hot, but not quite boiling, cream onto the egg mixture, beating all the time. Put the bowl over a pan of simmering water, or into a double saucepan, and stir or beat gently until the mixture begins to thicken. Cool. When cold, turn the thickened mixture into a container, cover and freeze. Move from freezer to fridge an hour before serving.

Oatmeal with Bailey's

This is another fairly neutral ice. The toasted oats give it a nutty flavour and it's in the same tradition as the more famous Brown Bread Ice Cream, which takes its flavour and texture from toasted crumbs. Interesting enough on its own, it also mixes well.

  3 oz/75g pinhead oatmeal
  1/2 pint/300 ml double or
  whipping cream
  3 oz/75g caster sugar
  1 tbspoon Bailey's Irish Cream

Toast the oatmeal in a moderate oven, 350°F, 180°C, Gas mark 4, for 10-15 minutes or until it is a fragrant rich brown — this could also be done under the grill, or in a heavy frying pan, but needs careful watching and constant turning. Cool. Whip the cream lightly with the sugar, add the Bailey's and fold in the oatmeal. Freeze in a covered freezer container, or in individual serving dishes or ramekins and transfer from freezer to fridge half an hour before serving.

Praline Ice Cream

Praline Ice Cream is one of the most delicious of all, and especially good as an accompaniment to summer fruits:

  4 egg yolks
  4 oz/100g sugar
  1/2 pint/300 ml single cream or
  top of the milk
  8 oz/225 g praline (see below)
  1/2 pint/300 ml double or
  whipping cream.

Beat the yolks and sugar until well blended. Scald the single cream in a small pan and, when it is nearly boiling, slowly whisk in the egg mixture. Put into a double saucepan, or a bowl over hot water, and keep stirring until the mixture begins to thicken. Turn out into a bowl and leave to cool. Stir in the praline. Whip the cream lightly and fold it into the mixture. Freeze. Check the mixture after an hour or two and, when it is beginning to set, fork through to make sure the praline is evenly distributed, then return to the freezer. Take out 15 minutes before serving.

Praline is worth making in some quantity as it keeps well in an airtight tin or jar and is handy for sprinkling over puddings and ice creams, as well as for use as an ingredient:

Put equal quantities of unblanched almonds and granulated sugar into a heavy-based pan and stir with a wooden spoon over a moderate heat until the sugar has melted and turned a gold-brown, watching carefully as it burns easily if cooked too quickly or for too long. Pour onto a lightly oiled baking tray and leave to cool. When cold, break the praline into pieces, then crush the amount needed with a rolling pin or food processor. Leave the rest in pieces and store in a screw-top jar or airtight tin.

No-Stir Strawberry

This ice cream is not only very easy, but has the added virtue of making a little fruit go a long way, especially if you serve it in Brandysnap Baskets or Tuiles Tulips. Serves 6.

  8 oz/225g strawberries, plus a
  few for decoration
  3 oz/75g icing sugar
  1 teaspoon lemon juice
  1/2 pint/300ml whipping cream.

Hull the strawberries, cut up roughly and put into a blender or food processor with the sieved icing sugar and lemon juice. Sieve to remove pips. Whip the cream until thick but not stiff and fold into the strawberry purée. Turn into a plastic freezer box, cover with a lid and leave in the freezer overnight, or for at least 8 hours. About half an hour before serving, transfer from the freezer to the fridge, to allow the ice cream to soften slightly. Scoop into Tuiles Tulips, or into individual serving glasses, and decorate with strawberry slices.

Basic Very Easy No-Stir Ice Cream

This is the family recipe I come back to time and again — instructions are given for gooseberry but it works well with any strongly flavoured fruit purée, especially blackcurrant. A high acid content makes the evaporated milk thicken before freezing, hence its ease and foolproof success.

1 lb/450g gooseberries
2 tablespoons water
6-8 oz/175-225g sugar, to taste
1 large tin evaporated milk, chilled in the fridge overnight (*or*, for a richer ice cream but less volume, 1/2 pint/300 ml cream plus 1 unbeaten egg white)

Wash the fruit but don't bother to top and tail. Simmer in the water for 10 minutes, or until tender. Remove from the heat, stir in the sugar to dissolve, then purée the fruit and rub through a sieve if you want to remove the pips. Discard pips and allow the purée to cool. Whisk the evaporated milk until thick and foamy — this takes 5-10 minutes in a Kenwood Chef on high speed; a splash cover is helpful. If using cream, add the egg white to the cream and whisk both together until thick and light. Fold in the gooseberry purée and turn into a large, lidded freezer box. Freeze. To serve, simply scoop out straight from the freezer as the texture should be light and creamy.

Variation: **Lemon Ice Cream** is even easier: Set the chilled evaporated milk to whisk. Meanwhile, finely grate the zest from 2 or 3 lemons according to size and quality, then squeeze the juice. Sweeten the whipped milk by whisking in about 8 oz/225g caster sugar, then fold in the lemon zest and juice. Mix well, taste for sweetness and freeze as above. *Hint*: It's useful to keep a tin of evaporated milk handy in the fridge for making ice cream.

Gooseberry Elderflower

Gooseberries and elderflowers come into the peak of their season at the same time in June and make a heady combination. This aromatic ice cream comes from Ballylickey Manor House in Co Cork.

1/2 pint/300ml water
12 oz/350g sugar
1 lb/450g gooseberries, topped and tailed
Juice of 1/2 lemon
25 heads of elderflower
1/2 pint/300ml cream

Heat the water and sugar together, stir until the sugar has dissolved then bring up to the boil and boil fast for 3 minutes to make a syrup. Add the gooseberries and lemon juice and boil for 3 minutes. Remove from the heat, add the elderflowers and put them into the saucepan. Leave until cold, then pick out the elderflowers. Turn into a freezer box, cover and freeze until half frozen, then turn out and stir the mushy mixture well. Whip the cream, fold it into the semi-frozen fruit and freeze for several hours, until completely frozen.

No-Stir Blackcurrant

This is an eggless ice cream and one of my favourites as it's easy to make, pretty and full of flavour. Basically it's a fruit fool and can be served that way and, of course, other soft fruits can be used instead. Serves 6.

12 oz/350g blackcurrants
3 tbsp water
6 oz/175g sugar, or to taste
1 teaspoon lemon juice
1/2 pint/300 ml cream.

Put the blackcurrants into a small pan with the water and cook gently over low heat until soft. Remove from the heat, add the sugar and stir until dissolved. Leave to cool a little, then sieve or liquidise to make a purée. Set aside and leave to cool, then add the lemon juice and stir well. Whip the cream fairly stiffly and carefully fold it into the purée with a metal spoon, losing as little volume as possible. Turn the mixture into a snap-top freezer box, freeze quickly at the lowest setting, then return the thermostat to normal. Remove from freezer to fridge 15-20 minutes before serving to allow the ice cream to 'come to' a little, improving both texture and flavour. Serve in slices, with whipped cream and finger biscuits.

Orange Ice Cream

Citrus fruits keep their flavour very well when frozen and this Orange Ice Cream makes a good foil to soft summer fruits, especially strawberries. It would make a good partnership with the strawberry ice cream given above if a selection is being served.

4 egg yolks
2 egg whites
8 oz/225g caster sugar
Juice of 6 oranges
Juice of 2 lemons
2 tablespoons Grand Marnier, Cointreau or Curaçao (optional)
3/4 pint/450 ml double cream

Beat the egg yolks and whites and sugar together until very thick, pale and fluffy. Add the orange and lemon juice. Turn into a double saucepan or set the bowl over a pan of simmering water and heat gently, stirring, until the mixture begins to thicken. Cool. When cold stir in the liqueur, if using, and fold the mixture into the lightly whipped cream. Turn into a freezer container, cover and freeze. Transfer from freezer to refrigerator about 15 minutes before serving.

Bombe Favourite

By complete contrast, Bombe Favourite is an ice cream I make often and one of the easiest. If you have any broken meringues, this is an ideal way of using them up, although a good commercial one such as Sharwood's will do quite well. Despite being simple and foolproof, this looks devastating against a pool of bright red Melba sauce (which is also ridiculously easy) or just served with fresh raspberries or strawberries.

8 half shells of meringue, or equivalent broken meringues
1/2 pint/300 ml double cream
1 or 2 tbsp kirsch or brandy
Caster sugar.

Lightly oil a bombe mould or 7"/18cm cake tin and line the base with a disc of paper. Break the meringues up into fairly big pieces, whip the cream lightly and flavour with the kirsch and a little caster sugar. Cover and freeze for about 2 hours, then return the freezer setting to normal. Remove from freezer about 15 minutes before serving so that it can be served lightly frozen. To serve, unmould onto a plate and pour around a Melba sauce made by rubbing 1/2 lb/225 g raspberries through a nylon sieve then beating in 3-4 tablespoons sifted icing sugar a little at a time, adding enough to thicken the purée. A squeeze of lemon juice will sharpen the flavour.

Summer Ripple Bombe

Summer Ripple Bombe is similar except that the fruit (in this case 6 oz/175g each of raspberries and strawberries) is incorporated into the mixture.

6 oz/175 g each of raspberries and strawberries
8 half shells of meringue, or equivalent broken meringues
1/2 pint/300 ml double cream
1 or 2 tbsp kirsch
Caster sugar.

Liquidise the fruit and sieve it. Whip the cream with caster sugar to taste, add the kirsch (or Grand Marnier, which goes well with strawberries) and lightly fold in the crushed meringues. Carefully fold in the fruit purée to give the rippled effect and freeze as above. Remove from the freezer 15 minutes before serving, unmould onto a plate and serve with Melba sauce or decorated with whipped cream and fresh berries.

Fruit Parfait

This rich and creamy Fruit Parfait recipe was given to me at Tinakilly House, Co Wicklow and it is remarkably simple to make. Serves 6, allowing 2 slices per portion.

3 eggs separated
3 oz/75g caster sugar
1/2 pint/300ml purée (any fruit)
1/2 pint/300ml whipped cream.

Line a 1lb/450g loaf tin with clingfilm. Whisk the egg yolks and 2oz/50g of the caster sugar until light and creamy, then fold into the fruit purée. Whisk up the egg whites with the remaining 1oz/25g sugar until soft peaks form and fold into the mixture, then fold in the whipped cream. Turn into the prepared loaf tin, freeze for 3-4 hours and serve in slices, straight from the freezer

Chocolate Parfait

This easily made and very more-ish Chocolate Parfait comes from MacCloskey's Restaurant, Bunratty, and requires no stirring during freezing.

It is subtly scented with orange and makes a great party sweet — with meringues in winter, or soft fruit, especially strawberries, in summer. Serves 6-8 [Microwave]

9oz/250g dark chocolate
6oz/175g butter, at room temperature
4oz/100g icing sugar
5 eggs, separated
1-2 tablespoons Cointreau or Grand Marnier
Finely grated zest of 1/2 orange.

Melt the chocolate in a bowl over hot water. Sift the icing sugar and beat it in, then add the butter, in pieces, and beat well. Remove from the heat and stir in the egg yolks. Put the zest of orange and the Cointreau or Grand Marnier into a small pan and bring up just to boiling point. Remove from the heat and add to the chocolate mixture. Allow to cool. Whisk the egg whites until stiff but not dry and fold them into the chocolate mixture, then divide up into individual moulds, or turn into a loaf tin or other suitable large container if you prefer to serve the parfait in slices. Cover and freeze until firm. Serve with a Crème Anglaise, with a dash of Tia Maria added.

Raspberry Yogurt Sorbet

As it is set with gelatine before freezing this Raspberry Yogurt Sorbet is something of a hybrid between mousse and ice and does not need stirring during freezing. It is very light and refreshing and, although raspberries are suggested here, any other soft fruit could be used. Try blackberries for example. [Microwave]

1 sachet gelatine
4 tablespoons cold water
8 oz/225g raspberries
Juice of 1/2 lemon
2-3 oz caster sugar to taste
1/2 pint/300 ml natural yogurt
2 egg whites.

Soak the gelatine with the cold water for at least 5 minutes, then dissolve it over hot water, or in the microwave. Meanwhile, liquidise the raspberries, sieve to remove the pips if you like, then stir in the lemon juice. Sweeten to taste, then add the yogurt. Stir in the liquid gelatine and chill

until almost setting. Whisk the egg whites until stiff but not dry, fold into the thick purée and freeze in a covered freezer container until firm. Transfer from freezer to fridge half an hour before serving.

ACCOMPANIMENTS
Brandy Snaps

Brandy Snaps very rarely contain any brandy, although the filling can be flavoured with anything you like. Unfilled, they keep well in an airtight tin and are equally delicious served as a tea time treat filled with whipped cream, or served as they are to accompany ice creams or cold sweets. [Microwave]

Makes about 2 dozen:
3 oz/75g butter
3 oz/75g caster sugar
3 level tablespoons (about 3oz/75g) golden syrup
3 oz/75g plain flour
1/2 level teaspoon ground ginger
Juice and finely grated zest of 1/2 lemon

Line 2 or 3 baking sheets with non-stick baking parchment and preheat a moderate oven, 350°F/ 180°C, Gas mark 4. Put the butter, sugar and syrup into a heavy-based pan and gently melt together over low heat. Off the heat, add the sifted flour, ginger and lemon zest and juice; mix together thoroughly with a wooden spoon. Leave to cool for a minute or two, then put out onto the prepared baking sheets in teaspoonfuls leaving about 4"/10 cm spreading room between them. Bake in the preheated oven for 7-10 minutes, or until the biscuits are bubbly, lacy in texture and golden brown — but arrange the baking so that they won't all be ready at once. Meanwhile, butter the handles of several large wooden spoons. As the biscuits are ready, remove them from the trays with a palette knife and roll each one around a buttered spoon handle; leave until set, then twist off and finish cooling on a wire rack. If any of the biscuits are left too long and set on the trays before rolling, put them back into the oven for a few moments and they will become pliable again. When absolutely cold, the brandysnaps can be stored for several days in an airtight tin. When required, serve them as they are to accompany cold sweets, or fill with whipped cream. The cream can simply be lightly sweetened or flavoured with brandy or a liqueur, or with finely grated orange/lemon zest, or finely chopped stem ginger.

Variation: **Brandysnap Baskets** make a dramatic presentation for ice creams, but are quite easily made. Make the brandysnaps as above but use slightly larger spoons for measuring out the mixture and allow plenty of room (at least 6"/15cm) between the piles. Baking will take a little longer, about 10-12 minutes. Meanwhile, oil the outside of a few ramekins, teacups or jam jars. When the biscuits are ready, drape them carefully over the oiled moulds and shape quickly but gently into a basket shape with your hands. Once set, transfer to a rack to finish cooling and continue in the same way until all the mixture has been used up. It should make about 12 baskets. Can be stored in an airtight container for a day or two.

Brandy Cornets can be made using exactly the same mixture but, instead of moulding them into baskets, cream horn moulds are used to make cone shapes. Cook as for basic brandysnaps, allow the cooked biscuits to cool on the baking trays for 1-2 minutes, then roll around the outside of well-greased cream horn moulds. When hardened, slip them off gently. These Brandy Cornets are delicious served filled with Chantilly Cream, in the same way as rolled brandysnaps, or they can be used to make **Strawberry Cones,** a simple but dramatic cold sweet that would be ideal as the centrepiece for a summer buffet table:

Put a good layer of sugar into an attractive glass bowl and press in the Brandy Cornets, standing them upright in circles to fill the bowl. Select a small but perfectly formed strawberry for each cone (or half of a big one). Whip a mixture of double and whipping cream together (proportion 1/2 pint/300ml double to 1/4 pint/150 ml whipping). Sweeten lightly with a little icing sugar or include a dash of orange-flavoured liqueur such as Cointreau if you like, and spoon or pipe into the cones. Top each one with a strawberry. Superb.

Miniature Brandy Snaps make perfect petits fours. Make half of the quantity for Brandysnaps and put them out with small coffee spoons. Cook for only 3–4 minutes, then roll them around an oiled pencil or the handle of a small wooden spoon. When cold, store in an airtight tin. Serve without filling.

Hint: When using brandysnaps as petits fours, include a few finely chopped almonds in the mixture to give it extra crunch.

Almond Tuiles

Almond Tuiles, named after the traditional curved French roof tiles, are very light and crisp — an ideal accompaniment to ices and a wide variety of cold sweets. Makes about 36 depending on size.

2 whites of egg
4 oz/100g caster sugar
2 oz/50g flour
1/2 teaspoon vanilla essence
1 oz/25g blanched shredded or flaked almonds
2 oz/50g butter, just melted (not hot)

Preheat a moderate oven, 350°F, 180°C, Gas mark 4. Grease several baking sheets with white cooking fat. Break the egg whites into a bowl, beat in the caster sugar with a fork and mix in the flour, vanilla, almonds and melted butter. Blend thoroughly. Lay teaspoons of the mixture out on the greased baking sheets, leaving plenty of room to spread. Bake in the preheated oven until golden brown, then lay over rolling pins to cool. When they are completely cold, store in an airtight tin.

Langues de Chat

These long, narrow biscuits are very light and crisp and make excellent accompaniments to ices and cold sweets.

2 oz/50g butter
2 oz/50g caster sugar
2 egg whites
2 oz/50g plain flour.

Preheat a hot oven, 425°F, 220°C Gas mark 7. Grease several baking sheets with white cooking fat. Cream butter and sugar until light and fluffy, break up the egg whites with a fork and gradually blend into the creamed mixture, adding a little of the flour with the last addition of egg. Fold in remaining flour with a metal spoon. Put the mixture into a nylon piping bag fitted with a plain 1/4"/5 mm nozzle and use to pipe 21/2"/6 cm lengths onto the prepared baking sheets, leaving good gaps (about 1"/2.5 cm) between them. Bake in the centre of the preheated oven in batches, for 4-5 minutes or until the edges are brown, then loosen with a palette knife and transfer to a wire rack. When crisp and completely cold, store in an airtight tin.

Variation (1): **Tuile Tulips** are made in the same way: increase the amount of sugar in the previous recipe to 21/2 oz/60g. Make the baskets two at a time by dropping two teaspoons of the mixture onto greased baking sheets and using the teaspoon to spread them out to make circles about 4"/10 cm across. Bake until tinged with brown, then remove and press around a teacup or ramekin and leave for a minute or two until cool and crisp. Remove and continue in the same way, baking and shaping batches of two, until all the mixture is used.

Variation (2): The mixture can also be moulded around cream horn moulds (as the Brandy Cornets, above). To decorate, try crystallised flowers , or very quick and simple ideas such as strawberries or strips of candied peel half-dipped in melted chocolate.

Strawberry and Redcurrant Jam

2 lb/900g redcurrants
A little water
4 lb/1.8kg small
  strawberries
4 lb/1.8kg granulated sugar.

As the soft fruit season develops, we tend to become blasé about eating bowls of fruit simply with sugar and cream — in fact there isn't the same urgency to enjoy the harvest in desserts at all, so this is the time to think about preserving the taste of summer for the dark days later in the year. It's ideal, too, because fruit tends to get smaller and less luscious as the season progresses, perfect, in fact, for jam-making. Strawberry jam is probably the top favourite with most people but, because strawberries are low in the setting agent pectin, it has a reputation for being difficult. Don't be put off by this (or the mystique which seems to surround the process of preserving) if you haven't tried jam-making before: even strawberries will set easily if you mix them with a high-pectin fruit, such as redcurrants, or use jam sugar which is mixed with pectin and fruit acid to guarantee a good set. Avoid using over-ripe fruit; include some under-ripe fruit, as the pectin content is higher at this point.

Wash and string the redcurrants, put them into a pan with a little water and simmer gently until tender. Then pass them through a nylon sieve or strain through a cloth to obtain the juice. Pick over the strawberries, put them into a pan with the redcurrant juice and boil gently until tender. Add the sugar, stir until dissolved and bring to the boil. Boil briskly for about 10–15 minutes or until setting point is reached. (Put a little of the hot jam onto a cold saucer and allow to cool slightly; if the surface wrinkles when pushed with a teaspoon, setting point has been reached.) Cool for about 15 minutes, to prevent the fruit rising in the jars. Stir gently, then pour into clean, warm jars. Lay a waxed disc on top immediately, then leave until completely cold before sealing with screw tops or cellophane. Store in a cool, dark place. Makes about 7 lb/3.2 kg.

Sure-Set Strawberry Jam

Makes about 2 Kg/ 5½ lb.
1 Kg/2 lb 3 oz Sure-Set
  sugar
1 Kg /2 lb 3 oz strawberries
Juice of ½ lemon, if desired.

Sure-Set sugar provides a foolproof way of making small quantities of jam — the recommended quantity is 1 Kg sugar and an equal weight of fruit. The colour and flavour should be very fresh as the boiling time is only 4 minutes (1 minute for jellies).

Hull and wash the strawberries and drain well. Put into a large saucepan and mash or crush. Lemon juice may be added now. Add the Sure-Set and heat, stirring, until it is dissolved, then bring to the boil and boil *vigorously* for 4 minutes. Allow to cool for a few minutes, stir to distribute the fruit, then pour into clean, warm jars. Cover as above.

Variation: Sure-Set **Raspberry Jam** or **Loganberry Jam** can be made in the same way, omitting the lemon juice.

Sure-Set sugar produces a very well-set jam and, while that is encouraging to anyone who wants to be sure of foolproof results in the shortest possible time when making a small quantity of jam, it is sometimes nicer to take the time to make a batch by the traditional method. For most fruit this produces a softer set and for something as special as Raspberry Jam, for example, this may actually be preferable.

Raspberry Jam

Makes about 10 lb/4.5 Kg:
6 lb/2.7 Kg raspberries
6 lb/2.7 Kg granulated
  sugar.

Along with apricot jam and redcurrant jelly, raspberry jam is one of the most useful preserves to have in the kitchen, so don't let the chance go by during the short season when raspberries are plentiful.

Pick over the raspberries, but don't wash them. Put about a quarter of the fruit into a preserving pan and crush with a wooden spoon to release some of the juices, then add the rest of the fruit and heat gently until the juices run. Add the sugar and stir, still over very gentle heat, until completely dissolved, then bring to the boil, and boil fast until setting point is reached — which could be as little as 3-4 minutes for freshly picked fruit, but is not likely to be more than 6-8 minutes. (Keep testing — shorter boiling time means a fresher flavour.) If there is a scum, skim or stir in a knob of butter to disperse, then pour into warmed jars and cover with waxed discs. Leave until absolutely cold, then seal and label.

Uncooked Raspberry Jam

For absolute freshness of flavour, try making Uncooked Raspberry Jam. Old-fashioned methods for this are based purely on fruit and sugar, dependent on the fruit being absolutely dry and very time-consuming to make. More recently, the easy availability of liquid pectin (a by-product of apple processing) makes it possible to set a mixture of sweetened fruit very easily. As it doesn't have the keeping qualities of a cooked jam, it has to be kept in the freezer — hence the fact that it is often referred to as 'freezer jam'. When required, leave it in the fridge overnight to thaw, then use it from the fridge like any other perishable food; once opened, it should keep about a fortnight.

Put the fruit into a bowl and crush with a wooden spoon, then add the sugar and lemon juice. Leave to stand for about an hour, stirring occasionally, until the sugar has completely dissolved — do not heat, normal room temperature is quite adequate. Add the liquid pectin, stir for a minute or two to ensure that it is evenly distributed, then pour into suitable containers, leaving $1/2$"/1.2 cm headroom in each. (Small containers, such as yogurt pots with lids, are best so that only a little need be defrosted at a time.) Leave the jam for 24 hours to set, still at room temperature, then seal, label and freeze. The fruit may settle, in which case stir well before using on scones or freshly baked bread, or as a sauce with ice cream — sieve to remove pips if you like.

Makes $3 1/2$ lb/1.6 kg:
1 lb/550g raspberries
2 lb/900g caster sugar
2 tablespoons lemon juice
4 fl oz/125ml liquid pectin, eg Certo.

Variation: **Uncooked Strawberry Jam** can be made from the same recipe.

Garden Jam

Soft fruit flourishes in the warm country gardens of West Cork and, after the first flush of early fruit is over, much of it is used for preserves, including mixed fruit jams which are especially useful when supplies are sporadic. From Assolas Country House at Kanturk in Co Cork.

Put the blackcurrants into a preserving pan and simmer in the water until nearly cooked, then add the rest of the fruit and simmer gently for about 10 minutes or until the fruit is soft. Add in the warm sugar and stir over gentle heat until completely dissolved. Bring up to boil and boil hard until setting point is reached. To test: put a spoonful of jam onto a cold saucer, cool, then push the surface of the jam to see if a skin has formed. If not, boil a little longer and keep testing until it sets. Remove any scum from the top of the jam, pour into clean, warm jars, cover and seal.

Makes about 8lb/3.6kg:
1lb/450g blackcurrants (stalks removed)
$1/4$ pint/150ml water
1lb/450g blackberries (or white or redcurrants)
1lb/450g raspberries or loganberries
1lb/450g strawberries
4lb/1.8 kg granulated sugar, warmed.

Gooseberry and Orange Jam

If you have gooseberries in the garden, they tend to be very prolific and it is worth making the effort to use them in a variety of ways so they won't be taken for granted or, worse still, rejected by the family. They freeze very well — just top and tail them and store in freezer bags to use in pies and tarts or for sauces during the winter. Being a naturally 'free-flow' product, they are extremely convenient to use from the freezer. But, as gooseberries need a lot of sugar whatever you do with them, they're absolutely ideal for preserving. They actually have much greater versatility than they are normally given credit for, especially as they have the added virtue of combining

Makes about 6 lb/2.7 Kg:
3 lb/1.4 Kg green
  gooseberries
3/4 pint/450 ml water
Finely grated zest and juice
  of 2 oranges
3½ lb/1.6 Kg granulated
  sugar.

well with other fruits to produce interesting and unusual combinations, as in this *Gooseberry and Orange Jam.*

Top and tail the gooseberries and put them into a preserving pan or other large, heavy-based pan, with the water, orange zest and juice. Simmer gently for about 30 minutes, crushing fruit occasionally with a wooden spoon, until the gooseberries are tender. Add the sugar and stir until dissolved, then bring to the boil and boil hard for about 10 minutes until setting point is reached. Skim, or stir a knob of butter into the jam to disperse any scum, then pour into warmed jars and cover with wax discs. Seal and label when absolutely cold.

Variation: If **Single-fruit Gooseberry Jam** is preferred, omit the orange zest and juice and increase the water to 1 pint/600 ml.

Gooseberry Jelly

4 lb/1.8 Kg green
  gooseberries
1¾ pints/1 litre water.
Granulated sugar (see
  method)

Gooseberry Jelly is less often made than jam, but it is delicious used as a table jelly in the same way as, for example, redcurrant or quince jelly. It can be served with virtually any plainly-cooked meat, poultry or fish but complements oily fish such as mackerel or the salmon family and rich meats like pork especially well.

Wash the gooseberries, but do not top and tail. Put into a preserving pan or large saucepan with the water, bring to the boil, then reduce the heat and simmer to a pulp. Put into a jelly bag (or strain through a double thickness of muslin, rigged up over an upturned stool) and leave to drip overnight. Measure the juice, return to the pan and stir in 1 lb/450g sugar per 1 pint/600 ml of juice. Stir over gentle heat to dissolve, then bring up to the boil and boil hard until setting point is reached. Pot into small warmed jars and leave to cool. Label and seal when absolutely cold.

Variations: **Gooseberry and Elderflower Jelly** is a very subtle preserve, fragrant with the muscat flavour of elderflowers: simply add a bunch of elderflowers while the sugar is dissolving, then remove it when the flavour seems strong enough. Be careful only to use sweet-smelling elderflowers — some varieties have a distinctly offensive odour which will ruin the jelly.

Herb Jellies

3 lb/1.4 Kg windfalls
  (prepared weight)
1¼ pint/750 ml water
¼ pint/150 ml white wine
  or cider vinegar
A good bunch of young
  mint or tarragon, or 2-3
  sprigs of thyme, marjoram
  or sage
Sugar (see method).
Freshly chopped leaves as
  appropriate to type — 3-4
  tablespoons for a
  mild-flavoured herb such
  as parsley, for example,
  much less for
  strongly-flavoured herbs
  (optional).

Herb Jellies based on windfalls can be made at any time during the late summer and early autumn when the availability of ingredients and time coincides. Any herb can be used — mint is most common, but parsley, tarragon, thyme, marjoram and sage all work equally well and it is handy to have a selection.

Cut out any bruises from the apples, then wash them and cut up roughly. Put them into the preserving pan with the water and vinegar, strip the leaves from the herb stalks, put the stalks in with the apples and simmer for 30-40 minutes until mushy. Put into a jelly bag and leave to drip overnight. Measure the liquid and return to the pan to reheat, then add 1 lb/450g sugar per 1 pint/600 ml juice and warm through gently over low heat until the sugar has completely dissolved. Tie the herb leaves into a square of muslin, add to the pan and bring up to the boil. Boil hard until setting point is reached. Squeeze and remove the bag of herbs, skim, stir in the freshly chopped leaves and pour the jelly into small, warmed jars. Leave until cold, then label and seal.

Note: The flavour of the herbs should not be overpowering — taste the jelly occasionally during boiling and remove the bag of leaves at an earlier stage if necessary. A few drops of green food colouring can be stirred in before potting if required.

Redcurrant Jelly

*Of all the soft fruits, redcurrants are probably the most highly-prized by cooks —
not only are they very beautiful and delicately flavoured for use in a wide variety of
sweet and savoury dishes and as a garnish when fresh, but the frozen berries and
preserves are incredibly versatile throughout the year, as an accompaniment to a wide
variety of meat dishes in the winter, for example, and as an ingredient in countless
others. The home-made version is greatly superior to even the best commercial
varieties. Like all currants, redcurrants are high in pectin and set well, so ordinary
sugar works well. This version is based on pure redcurrants and only suitable when
supplies are good and/or prices reasonable, otherwise a less extravagant jelly including
apples can be made instead — see Elderberry and Apple Jelly, Autumn Preserves.*

3 lb/1.4 Kg redcurrants
1 pint/600 ml water
Granulated sugar

Wash the fruit but don't remove the stalks. Place in a pan with the water
and simmer gently until really soft and pulped. Strain through a jelly cloth.
Measure the juice and return to the pan with 1 lb/450g sugar per pint/600
ml. Heat, stirring, until the sugar has completely dissolved, then boil rapidly
until setting point is reached. Skim, then pot and cover as above. Yield
depends on amount of juice produced.

Variations: **Blackcurrant Jelly** is made in the same way; allow 3 lb/1.4
Kg berries per 1 pint/600 ml water. **Raspberry and Redcurrant Jelly** is
a very useful preserve, especially for glazing fruit flans, and a particularly
good combination. Use 4 lb/1.8 Kg fruit per 1 pint/600 ml water, half
raspberrries, half redcurrants.

Rhubarb and Ginger Jam

*Rhubarb and ginger make a classic partnership and this old-fashioned preserve can
be made at any time when rhubarb is in full season, through May and June.*

Makes about 8 lb/3.6 Kg:
4 lb/1.8 Kg rhubarb
  (prepared weight)
4 lb/ 1.8 Kg granulated
  sugar
2 large lemons
1 oz/25g root ginger
2 oz/50g preserved ginger
  in syrup, or crystallised
  ginger.

Trim rhubarb and cut into 1"/2.5 cm lengths before weighing, then put
into a large mixing bowl in layers with the sugar. Finely peel the lemon
with a potato peeler and tie the peel in a square of muslin with the bruised
root ginger. Add to the fruit along with the juice from the two lemons.
Drain the preserved ginger from the syrup in the jar, or wash the crystallised
ginger to remove the sugar. Chop the ginger finely and add to the other
ingredients. Cover the basin with a cloth and leave to stand overnight, so
the sugar begins to dissolve and the juices are drawn out of the rhubarb.
Next day, pour the contents of the bowl into a large preserving pan. Bring
slowly to the boil, stirring occasionally to make sure all the sugar has
dissolved, then boil fast for 10-15 minutes until setting point is reached.
Remove the pan from the heat and take out the muslin bag of flavourings.
Pot up into warmed jars and seal when cold. Store in a cool, dark place.

Blackcurrant Jam

*If you grow blackcurrants, there's usually a time when there are far too many. They
freeze very well for use in winter, but jam is the traditional solution and the flavour
is excellent. This recipe is from Glassdrumman House at Annalong, Co Down.
Reduce the water a little if scaling up the quantities: when cooked, the weight of
fruit pulp should be about the same as the sugar. Blackcurrants have a very high
pectin content and set very easily.*

Makes about 2 lb/1 Kg
1lb/450g blackcurrants,
  stalks removed
1 pint/600ml water
1½ lb/700g granulated.
  sugar, warmed

Cook blackcurrants with the water for about 30 minutes until really soft,
then add the sugar. Stir over very gentle heat to dissolve. When completely
dissolved, boil vigorously for about 10 minutes until the setting point is
reached. Remove any scum (stirring in a knob of butter is often enough
to disperse it), pour into clean warm jars, cover, label and store in a cool
dark place. *Note:* To prepare in a pressure cooker, reduce the water by half
to ½ pint/300ml and cook for only 1 or 2 minutes under pressure.

Confit of Apricots with Mustard Seeds

1 whole onion
1 clove of garlic
Handful of yellow mustard
  seeds
3 oz/75g unsalted butter
2 oranges
10 fresh apricots
Handful of freshly chopped
  sage and thyme,
Salt, freshly ground pepper
  and sugar to taste.

At The Mustard Seed Restaurant, Adare, Co. Limerick, they make this delicious Confit of Apricots with Mustard Seeds to serve warm as a relish with pork or ham. It is a short-term preserve so, although it keeps well in the fridge for several weeks and can probably be used for much longer, it will gradually lose flavour with age. The winter variation using dried apricots will keep and hold its flavour longer than the fresh fruit confit.

Chop the onion finely, crush the garlic and put into a saucepan with the mustard seeds and the butter. Melt the butter, cover tightly and sweat over gentle heat for 5 minutes or until the onions are soft but not coloured. Meanwhile, finely grate the zest from one orange and squeeze the juice from both. Add zest and juice to the softened onions and cook, uncovered, until reduced by half. Halve and stone the apricots (there is no need to peel them), chop roughly and add to the pan with the herbs. Season and sweeten to taste and cook for 5-10 minutes, or until the apricots are just soft. Turn into a clean, warm preserving jar and leave to cool, then store in the fridge and use as required to serve warm with pork or ham. *Note:* Using dried apricots in winter, less sugar will be needed. This recipe should also work successfully with other fruits such as nectarines, peaches or plums, although any with tough skins may need to be peeled.

Candied Angelica

Candied Angelica
Fresh angelica stems
1 teaspoon salt
4 pints/2.3 litres boiling
  water
Sugar (see method).

Angelica is easy to grow and, as well as being useful to have and fun to candy, makes an unusual gift. Although the process is quite lengthy, it is quite simple and not really time-consuming as it requires no attention between stages.

Pick tender young stems from the plants in late spring and early summer and cut into 3-4"/7-10 cm lengths. To retain their natural colour, cover with boiling brine made from 1 teaspoon salt to 4 pints/2.3 litres water. Leave for 10 minutes, then drain and rinse the angelica in cold water. Put into a pan, add enough boiling water to cover, bring back up to the boil and cook for about 7 minutes, or until tender and bright green. Drain, reserving the water, and scrape off the outer skin. Measure the water the angelica was cooked in and note the quantity, then make a syrup, allowing 6 oz/175g granulated sugar per ½ pint/300ml juice. Put the angelica into a bowl and pour the syrup over the stems. Cover and leave for 24 hours. Drain off the syrup and add another 2 oz/50g sugar per ½ pint/300 ml of the original juice; dissolve the sugar in the syrup, bring back up to the boil and pour over the angelica in the bowl. Cover and leave for another 24 hours. Repeat this process each day for 5 days, until the syrup is the consistency of runny honey. On the last day, when the final addition of sugar has dissolved, add the angelica and boil in the syrup for 2-3 minutes, then leave the stems to soak in the syrup for at least 2 days. Dry off in a very cool oven 225°F, 110°C, Gas mark ¼. When quite dry, leave to cool then store in airtight jars.

Crystallised Rose Petals

1 cup small rosebuds (or 2
  cups violets)
4 fl oz/100 ml water
8 oz/225g granulated sugar.

This method of crystallisation is suitable for small rose buds that can be used whole for decorating cakes and desserts and is also ideal for other small flowers, notably violets in spring time. A sugar thermometer is useful, but not essential, for this long-term preserve.

Gather the flowers early in the day, just after the dew has dried. Bring the water to the boil in a heavy-based pan, remove from the heat and add the sugar. Stir until dissolved. Remove the stems, wash the flowers lightly and drain them carefully in a colander without bruising. Put the syrup back onto the heat, carefully stir in the flowers and cook gently until the syrup registers a temperature of 240°F/115°C on a sugar thermometer, or until a soft ball is formed when a little of the syrup is dropped off a teaspoon into a bowl of cold water. Take off the heat and stir gently with a wooden spoon until the syrup begins to granulate. Pour the contents of the pan into a colander and shake off the extra sugar as the flowers cool. When absolutely cold, store in airtight jars.

Crystallised Mint Leaves

Select fresh mint with small, perfectly formed leaves. Beat the egg white lightly and, using a small artist's paint brush, paint all over the leaves, back and front, with the egg white. Be careful to do this really thoroughly, as any bare spots will shrivel and may cause mould. Dredge lightly with caster sugar back and front, then lay out on a sheet of greaseproof paper on a wire rack. Leave in an airing cupboard, or the oven at its coolest setting, for 24 hours to dry out, turning once or twice to prevent sticking. When thoroughly dried out, store in an airtight tin, between layers of greaseproof paper.

Also suitable for primroses, polyanthus, violets, fruit blossom and rose petals. If carefully done the results should keep for several months.

Fresh mint leaves (or flower petals)
Egg white
Caster sugar.

SUGAR IN IRELAND

In Ireland, sugar was first introduced at the end of the twelfth century, shortly after the coming of Strongbow, but it was in the form of a sweetmeat so rare and costly that it was no more than a curiosity. It was only in the seventeenth and eighteenth centuries that cane sugar became widely available to those who could afford it, as in England, but there were far-sighted men who saw that Ireland could be a good place to grow sugar beet. In 1842, in the first attempt to establish a beet-sugar industry, a considerable acreage of beet was planted near Belfast, but there was no factory built. A decade later, a factory that was intended to be the first of several, was built near Port Arlington, but it was only in operation for a short time and, despite many subsequent attempts, the sugar industry we know today only goes back to the late 1920s, when a successful regional enterprise in Carlow led to the eventual founding of Comhlucht Siuicre Eireann Teo, The Irish Sugar Company. Climactically, Ireland proved to be ideal for growing sugar beet: although the beet plant is deep-rooted and can survive periods of drought, rainfall is essential to a good crop- but it also needs adequate sunshine to produce a high sugar content, so our typical weather of sunshine and showers suits it perfectly. The factory at Carlow was built in 1926 and, when it had proved that quality sugar could be produced economically in Ireland, further factories were built in 1933-34 at Mallow, Thurles and Tuam. The development and diversification of the sugar industry in Ireland from that point is well known but there are one or two interesting asides that are a justifiable source of pride to people in the industry. Sugar spearheaded the food industry in Ireland and was the earliest food process to employ chemists, for example. It has always been technically advanced too - the refining process is an excellent example of efficient energy usage through the re-use of the heat in steam in a sequence of operations combined with the vapour produced at various stages of the evaporation process. Even going right back to the beginning, despite the commerical failure of that first plant at Port Arlington, it scored a technical first with a centrifugal machine operating on loaves of sugar in their containers, which was patented in 1849 and the forerunner of several similar successful inventions – proof that success can come of apparent failure.

(*See also pages 183, 211 and 231*)

AUTUMN

September, October, November

What a wonderful feeling September brings when tired, dusty summer comes to a close, evenings are drawing in and the light gradually takes on its rich, golden autumnal glow. This is a magic time in the kitchen, with an unparalleled selection of produce ready to harvest for immediate use or to preserve for the winter ahead and a change of mood that draws us back to home and hearth after the months of mainly outdoor activities.

Preparations for Christmas traditionally begin in September, with the making of plum puddings and, although few cooks nowadays like to start planning for Christmas as soon as the children go back to school, Hallowe'en has plenty of fun to offer in the meantime (and traditional food to go with it) and the Christmas countdown starts in earnest as soon as it is over. It is a time to take pleasure in the changing rhythm of the year with its age-old satisfaction in preserving the produce now available in such abundance and making prudent provision for the lean times which may lie ahead.

Onions, shallots and garlic are ripe and dry, ready to be plaited into ropes and hung up for storage. Tomatoes and herbs are coming to the close of their season but many, like windfall apples, pears and other top fruit will make delicious chutneys, jellies and preserves. Overgrown courgettes compete for size with real vegetable marrows and, towards Hallowe'en, big yellow pumpkins start to appear in the shops alongside edible varieties of wild mushrooms and knobbly nuts in shell. Some produce has always had a problem of success but the over-abundance of, say, apples means that we have an unusually rich vein to mine when it comes to choice of recipes using them. Then there's the fun of collecting food from the wild such as blackberries and sloes — and, as autumn progresses, game comes into its own and specialist poulterers and game shops create a great atmosphere with their crowded rails of furred and feathered game as the Christmas market draws closer.

With the possible exception of the late winter, when the prospect of a party can transform the dreariest grey day, this is probably the best time of year for entertaining, so make the most of it while there is such a wide choice of produce in the shops and before the Christmas party season begins.

HIGHLIGHTS OF THE SEASON

Harvest Festival, Hallowe'en and, if you have American connections, Thanksgiving.

PRODUCE IN SEASON includes:

Vegetables: Aubergines, avocados, beetroot, broccoli, brussels sprouts, cabbages, calabrese, carrots, cauliflower, celeriac, celery, chicory, corn-on-the-cob, courgettes, cucumber, endive, fennel, French beans, garlic, globe artichokes, horseradish, kale, kohl rabi, Jerusalem artichokes, leeks, lettuces, mangetout, mushrooms (wild as well as cultivated), onions, parsnips, peas, peppers, potatoes, pumpkin, radishes, runner beans, salsify, shallots, spinach, scallions, swedes, tomatoes, turnips, vegetable marrows, watercress. **Fruit**: Apples, bilberries, blackberries, blueberries, Chinese gooseberries, damsons, figs, grapes, greengages, melons, peaches, pears, pineapples, plums, pomegranates, raspberries, strawberries, watermelon. **Poultry and Game**: Chicken, duck, goose, grouse, guinea fowl, hare, mallard, partridge, pigeon, quail, rabbit, snipe, teal, turkey, venison, wild duck. **Fish**: Brill, clams, cod, coley, conger eel, crab, Dover (black) sole, Dublin Bay prawns, eels, haddock, hake, herrings, lemon sole, lobster, mackerel, mussels, native oysters (also Portuguese), pike, plaice, prawns, salmon (only in September), shrimps, rainbow trout, turbot.

SUGGESTED MENUS could include:

Harvest Festival Supper
Tomato Soup with Fresh Herbs;
Chicken with Cider and Apples;
Baked Potatoes, Green Salad;
Apple and Hazelnut Crumble, Crème Fraîche.

Hallowe'en
Pork Kebabs with Barbecue Sauce;
Red Cabbage with Apples;
Pumpkin Pie; Barm or Tea Brack.

Autumn Dinner Party
Soufflé Surprise;
Pot-Roast Pheasant Normandy Style;
Game Chips; Pumpkin au Gratin;
Green Salad with Walnut Dressing;
Apple Filo Tart with Calvados.

Thanksgiving Celebration
Pears, Cashel Blue Cream, Walnuts (see Winter)
Roast Turkey and all the trimmings (see Christmas)
Pumpkin Pie

Many of the autumn vegetables are very colourful, a characteristic worth taking advantage of. We're now moving into a season where more comforting, satisfying food is in demand again, but it can also be vibrant with autumn colour: peppers, pumpkins, tomatoes, apples, carrots and nuts are just a few of the foods in peak condition during autumn which can contribute richness of colour as well as flavour, texture and aroma.

Tomato Soup

What, in this season of mellow fruitfulness, could be more appropriate than a lovely red Tomato Soup? [Microwave]

Melt half the butter in a large pan; add the carrots and onion and cook gently for about 5 minutes until beginning to soften. Add the tomatoes, cover and cook gently again to soften the tomatoes. Add the stock, bacon rinds, sugar, tomato purée, herbs and seasoning, then bring up to the boil and simmer gently until all the vegetables are quite soft. Remove from the heat, put through a mouli-légumes or sieve, discard the tomato skins and bacon rinds and return the soup to the rinsed pan. Blend remaining butter and flour together to make a beurre manié and and add to the soup in small pieces. Stir until melted, then bring up to the boil and cook, stirring or whisking until thickened. Adjust the seasoning before serving in warm bowls, garnished with a swirl of cream and a scattering of freshly chopped basil or flat leaf parsley.

Golden Pumpkin Soup

If you are hollowing out a pumpkin for the Hallowe'en lantern, make the most of the flesh in this pretty soup. Be sure to use a good stock for flavour, as pumpkin flesh is very bland. (Use double quantities if you have enough pumpkin.) [Microwave]

Heat butter and oil gently in a heavy-based saucepan and add the onion and pumpkin. Cover tightly and sweat over low heat for 5 minutes, then stir in the stock, orange juice and rind, cinnamon, tomato purée and cider. Season and bring to the boil, then reduce to a simmer and leave to cook gently for 15-20 minutes until tender. Allow to cool slightly, then blend to a smooth purée. Check seasoning and serve scattered with freshly chopped herbs or croûtons.

Black Pudding with Apple Sauce

Black Pudding with Apple Sauce is a time-honoured combination. Drimcong House lifted it into the gourmet class by including oyster and developing the sauce into a gastronomic experience. This much simpler version serves 4-6 as a first course or weekend brunch dish:

Preheat a moderately hot oven, 375°F, 190°C, Gas mark 5. Cut the black pudding into slices about 1/2"/2.5 cm thick. Lay them in overlapping layers in a buttered shallow ovenproof dish, sprinkle with the cider and sugar and bake for 10-15 minutes. Meanwhile make the sauce: put the peeled and sliced apple into a pan with the lemon zest and juice, the water and the cloves. Cook gently until the apples fall, then remove the cloves, beat in the butter and set aside. Serve the hot black pudding with the warm sauce. *Variation:* Bake the black pudding in individual gratin dishes.

Tomato Soup: Serves 6
2 oz/50g butter
2 carrots, peeled and sliced
1 large onion, peeled and chopped
1½ lb/700g ripe, red tomatoes, washed and halved
1½ pints/900ml good chicken stock
A few bacon rinds
1 teaspoon caster sugar
1 tablespoon tomato purée
1 tablespoon freshly chopped basil OR 1 teasp. dried mixed herbs
Sea salt and freshly ground black pepper
1 rounded tablespoon flour
A little cream
Basil or parsley to garnish .

Pumpkin Soup: Serves 4
½ oz/12g butter
1 tablespoon olive oil
1 onion, chopped
12 oz/350g pumpkin flesh, chopped or thinly sliced
¾ pint/450 ml home-made chicken stock
Juice and finely grated zest of ½ orange
½ teaspoon ground cinnamon, or to taste (optional)
1 dessertsp. tomato purée
¼ pint/150 ml dry cider
Sea salt and fresh pepper

Black Pudding & Apple
1 lb/450g black pudding, preferably Clonakilty
¼ pint/150 ml cider
2 tbsp Demerara sugar
1 lb/450g Bramley's apples
Grated zest and juice of ½ lemon
2 tablespoons water
4 whole cloves
1 oz/25g butter.

Twice-Baked Cheese Soufflé

Serves 4-6:

½ pint/300 ml milk
Slice of onion
Pinch of grated nutmeg
1 whole clove
2 oz/50g butter
2 oz/50g flour
Pinch of dry mustard
6 oz/175g Cheddar cheese,
  grated
4 eggs plus 1 extra white
Salt and freshly ground
  black pepper
12 fl oz/350 ml cream.

How could the perfect hot first course be defined? It should be warming and piquant, take the edge off the appetite without ruining the meal that is to follow and, perhaps, have an element of surprise. Best of all, it should be so easy that the cook is not distracted from the pleasure of seeing the guests: twice-baked soufflés are popular in restaurants because of their convenience, so we should take note and follow suit at home. This Twice-Baked Cheese Soufflé from Rathsallagh House would lend itself to variations.

Preheat a moderate oven, 350°F, 180°C, Gas mark 4. Heat the milk slowly with the onion, nutmeg and clove to make an infusion. Butter 4-6 small teacups or ramekins. Make a white sauce with the butter, flour and strained milk, adding the mustard with the flour. Stir in three quarters of the cheese. Separate the eggs and add the yolks to the mixture; season to taste. Whisk whites stiffly, stir in a tablespoon first, then fold the rest in carefully. Divide the mixture between the buttered cups, stand them in a bain marie and bake for 15 minutes, or until risen and set. Remove from the oven and allow to sink and cool. When ready to serve, prepare a hot oven, 425°F, 220°C, Gas mark 7. Turn the soufflés out upside down in buttered shallow dishes, sprinkle with the remaining cheese and pour over with seasoned cream. Bake in the hot oven for 10 minutes. Serve immediately.

Soufflé Surprise

While twice-baked soufflés look and taste marvellous and involve no kind of tension for the cook, there's nothing to beat the real thing — and the best-kept secret in the cookery world has to be how easy hot soufflés are to make. Forget all the hype about the things that can go wrong, the problems of timing and so on — if you want to make a huge (and totally undeserved) impression as a wizard cook, get yourself a reputation for making great soufflés. What most people don't know is that any conventional béchamel-based soufflé can be prepared hours ahead of baking, right down to folding in the egg whites, so there's no need for the traditional last-minute panic at all. For entertaining, a set of individual 4"/10 cm white china soufflé dishes, holding a good ½ pint/300ml each is a great investment — the soufflés only take about 10 minutes to cook, serving is easy (and they won't sink until somebody prods them and lets the air out) and I've even cooked them directly from the freezer, although this takes a little longer — and it does take nerve. All that said, why not try a Soufflé Surprise?

Quick Herby Tomato Sauce

1 onion
1 large clove garlic
½ oz/15g butter
1 lb/450g ripe flavoursome
  tomatoes, plus 2-3 tbsp
  water
(OR 1 x 15 oz/400g tin
  chopped Italian tomatoes,
  with their juice)
1-2 tablespoons tomato
  purée, or to taste (optional)
1 tablespoon freshly
  chopped parsley,
  preferably flat-leaf
1 teaspoon freshly chopped
  marjoram
1 rounded teaspoon
  cornflour
Sea salt, freshly ground
  black pepper and caster
  sugar to taste.

Despite the grand name, it's just a sharp cheese soufflé and the surprise is the bright red tomato sauce that lurks unsuspected at the bottom. Serves 6 as a first course, in one large 8"/20cm (capacity 3-3½ pints/1.8-2.1 litres) soufflé dish or six individual 4"/10 cm (½ pint/300 ml) ones; or serves 3-4 as a main course.

First make the **Quick Herby Tomato Sauce:** [Microwave]

Peel and finely chop the onion; peel the garlic and crush in a little salt. Melt the butter and cook the onion and garlic in it gently for 5 minutes or until softening but not browning. If using fresh tomatoes, blanch them briefly in boiling water to loosen the skins, then peel and chop roughly, removing the core if it is tough. Put the tomatoes, with their juice/water and all remaining ingredients, into a liquidiser and blend thoroughly. Stir this mixture into the onions and garlic and stir over moderate heat for 1 minute, or until the sauce thickens and clears. Taste and adjust the seasoning with salt, pepper or sugar if necessary. Serve as it is if you like a sauce with texture or, for a very smooth purée, return to the blender and process again.

Variation: Depending on use, the herbs can be varied: tarragon, basil, thyme, dill or chives are all specially appropriate to particular dishes and can be used with parsley or singly.

Basic Cheese Soufflé

[Microwave] First prepare the soufflé dish or dishes, by buttering generously right up to the top. Then, if you like a crusty edge, tip a good tablespoon of Parmesan cheese into the dish(es) and tilt around to cover thoroughly. Turn upside down to tap out excess and set the dish(es) aside.

Melt the butter over low heat in a heavy-based saucepan. Stir in the flour and cook gently for a minute, then gradually blend in the milk, stirring all the time, and bring to the boil. (This is quicker and smoother if the milk is warmed first — just pop the measuring jug into the microwave while making the roux — and I find a small metal whisk easier than the traditional wooden spoon.) Simmer the sauce for 2 or 3 minutes until it is thick and smooth, stirring or whisking all the time to prevent it catching. Remove from the heat. Separate the eggs and whisk the yolks lightly with a fork to break up, then gradually beat them into the hot sauce. Season to taste with salt and freshly ground pepper, mustard or nutmeg and pinch of cayenne, then stir in the grated cheese. Whisk the egg whites until stiff, then stir one tablespoonful into the cheese sauce — this loosens it up and makes it easier to fold in the rest of the whites without loss of volume. Fold in remaining whites carefully with a metal spoon. If you want to make a plain cheese soufflé, spoon the prepared mixture into the buttered soufflé dish(es) and sprinkle with the reserved grated cheese. Now *either* cover with clingfilm and keep in the fridge, or any cool place, for 2-3 hours until ready to bake *or* put into a fairly hot oven, preheated to 375°F, 190°C, Gas mark 5. Immediately reduce the temperature to moderate, 350°F, 180°C, Gas mark 4, and bake for about 35-40 minutes or until golden brown and well-risen. Do not over-cook — the soufflé should wobble a bit when shaken, showing that it is still nice and runny inside, like a good omelette. If baking individual soufflés, give them about 10 minutes in a slightly hotter oven, 400°F, 200°C, Gas mark 6.

To make the **Soufflé Surprise** all you have to do is pour a thin layer of the prepared tomato sauce in the bottom of the soufflé dish(es) before spooning in the soufflé mixture. Otherwise, cook as above. Hand the rest of the sauce separately and, if it is a main course, offer some fresh crusty bread and a crisp green side salad. All sorts of other surprises can be devised, of course, and the basic cheese soufflé is very amenable to variations: Blue Cheese makes a wonderful savoury (end of meal) soufflé with chopped walnuts through it and Spinach Soufflé, for example, is based on the same béchamel sauce, but the cheese is omitted and an equivalent amount of cooked, puréed spinach substituted; nutmeg is an appropriate flavouring. Crab Soufflé can be made in the same way, substituting flaked crabmeat for the spinach purée — the variations are endless.

Basic Cheese Soufflé
2 oz/50g butter
1½ oz/40g plain flour
½ pint/300 ml milk
4 eggs, plus an extra white
  if available
Salt and freshly ground
  pepper
½ teaspoon mustard
  powder or grated nutmeg
Pinch of cayenne
3 oz/75g mature Cheddar
  cheese, finely grated
1 oz/25g Parmesan or
  Regato, grated
A little extra grated cheese
  to sprinkle over.

Note: More fundamental variations are based on the nouvelle cuisine concept of a flourless soufflé, which uses vegetable or fruit purées in place of the béchamel. This is a much more fragile combination and certainly wouldn't tolerate the short-cuts with timing outlined for béchamel-based soufflés above.

Salad of Green Lentils

Continental lentils, especially those lovely little round browny-green ones known as Lentilles du Puy, are one of my favourite foods and very common in France, where they are used in delicious everyday one-pot meals like Lentilles au Petit Salé (Lentils with Salt Pork) and, hot or cold, as a side dish. Green lentils have a special affinity with pork and ham dishes of all kinds and with rich poultry like goose or duck. This Salad of Green Lentils is a marvellous dish for entertaining, as it can be made ahead and served cold or reheated as appropriate — served cold, it would help no end to liven up a buffet of cold Christmas meats or, for a dinner party, reheat it gently for a few minutes in the microwave and serve lukewarm — along with a garlicky Potato Gratin and a good green salad. This makes for very sociable, easily served side dishes to accompany any simple roast or grilled meat. Alternatively try serving a small portion of this salad with smoked fish, such as Smoked Fillet of Wicklow Trout, to

Salad of Green Lentils: Serves 8-10

1 lb/450-500g small green Lentilles du Puy or other continental lentils
4 shallots, finely chopped (or 2 medium onions)
6-8 tablespoons olive oil
2 or 3 tablespoons sherry vinegar
Sea salt and freshly ground black pepper
Freshly chopped chives (optional).

make an unusual first course or light meal. Unlike the larger varieties, these small green lentils don't need to be soaked before cooking and they are less inclined to break up and cook to a mush.

Boil the lentils in plenty of lightly salted water for 20-30 minutes until cooked but not breaking up. Drain well and, while they are still hot, put them into a salad bowl. Add the shallots, dress with the oil and vinegar and season well with sea salt and black pepper. Taste as you go — be careful not to make the dressing too vinegary, but it does need a fair amount of salt. Serve the salad warm or cold, scattered with freshly chopped chives if you like. If reheating, taste for seasoning again and adjust if necessary.

Variation: To convert the lentils into a more substantial dish, 12 oz-1 lb/350-450g hot diced streaky rashers and/or fried diced belly of pork can be forked through the warm salad. Served with crusty French bread, this makes a substantial starter for 8-10 or a light meal for 4-6.

Pumpkin au Gratin

Serves 6:

1 lb/450g pumpkin flesh
4 tablespoons water
2 large eggs, separated
2 teaspoons caster sugar
2 oz/50g mature Cheddar, grated
1 oz/25g Parmesan or Regato
Finely grated zest and juice of ½ lemon
½ teaspoon ground cinnamon
Freshly ground black pepper.

Vegetables cooked au gratin always seem particularly appealing especially when the cooking method transforms a vegetable which is pretty but bland into something distinctly desirable, such as Pumpkin au Gratin. Like the Pumpkin Soup and the pie this is an ideal way to use up flesh that has been hollowed out of the Hallowe'en pumpkin lantern.

Chop the pumpkin flesh up fairly small and put into a saucepan with the water. Bring to the boil, cover and simmer for 15-20 minutes until cooked to a purée, then take off the lid and boil hard to allow the water to evaporate. Remove from the heat and leave to cool. When ready to cook, preheat a moderate oven, 350°F, 180°C, Gas mark 4 and butter a large, shallow gratin dish. Separate the eggs and whisk the yolks and caster sugar together until pale and creamy, then add to the pumpkin purée with two thirds of the cheese, the grated lemon zest, half of the lemon juice, the cinnamon and a good grinding of pepper. Mix well. Whisk the egg whites until fairly stiff, then whisk in the remaining lemon juice and whisk a tablespoonful of the mixture into the pumpkin purée. Fold in the rest of the egg whites with a metal spoon, adjust the seasoning if necessary, then turn the mixture into the prepared gratin dish. Dot with butter, sprinkle over the remaining cheese and bake in the preheated oven for about 20 minutes, or until puffy and golden brown.

Brown Tom

Serves 6 as a side dish, 2-3 as a main dish:

2 onions
3 or 4 rashers streaky bacon
6 slices wholemeal yeast bread
2 tablespoons freshly chopped parsley
1 dessertspoon freshly chopped basil
1½ lb/700g ripe well-flavoured tomatoes
1½ oz/40g butter
Sea salt, freshly ground black pepper and caster sugar
A little grated cheese to finish (optional).

Much more useful on a long term basis, however, is the kind of dish that uses everyday, easily available ingredients and doesn't mess them about too much. Such a dish is this old-fashioned tomato gratin, traditionally known as Brown Tom. Not only are the ingredients always to hand, but this is the kind of versatile dish which can be used as a main course, with a green vegetable or salad, or as a side dish to accompany a simple grill.

Preheat a fairly hot oven, 400°F, 200°C, Gas mark 6. Peel and roughly chop the onions; de-rind and chop the rashers, remove the crusts from the bread and put all three ingredients into a food processor (this is best done onto moving blades, through the chute) then add the herbs. Chop fairly finely, but do not over-process. Alternatively, put everything through a mincer. Blanch the tomatoes briefly in boiling water to loosen the skins, then peel and slice them thinly. Butter a shallow gratin dish and spread a layer of the onion and bacon mixture over the base. Arrange a layer of sliced tomatoes on top and season well with salt, a good grinding of black pepper and a light sprinkling of caster sugar. Repeat until all the ingredients are used up, finishing with a layer of bacon and onion crumbs. Sprinkle over the grated cheese, if using, dot with the butter and bake in the hot oven for about half an hour, or until the top is brown and bubbling.

Braised Chestnuts

Braising vegetables in stock is not a cooking method that comes first to mind in Ireland, but it can be very effective. This recipe makes an excellent accompaniment for turkey and other poultry and rich meats like pork or any kind of game. [Microwave]

Have a pan of boiling water ready. Slit the flat sides of the chestnuts, add to the pan of water and boil for 2 or 3 minutes. Drain and peel away the shells and the soft brown skin underneath. Return the chestnuts to the rinsed pan and add the stock, chopped onion, sliced celery and a good seasoning of salt, freshly ground pepper and the sugar. Bring to the boil, cover and simmer gently for 20—30 minutes, or until the chestnuts are tender. Drain and serve.

Variations: Thickly sliced apple, fried gently in butter until golden brown but not breaking up, can be served with chestnuts and makes a particularly good addition with rich meats such as pork. **Chestnut Purée** can be made using the same recipe — when the chestnuts are cooked, drain and set aside. Peel and finely chop an onion and fry gently in a little butter to soften without browning. Mix in the cooked chestnuts and mash into the onion mixture to break them up. Liquidise the mixture, or press through a sieve to make a purée. Blend in an extra knob of butter, season well, especially with pepper, and beat in enough cream or top of the milk to make a smooth, soft purée. Serve hot with roast pheasant, venison or turkey.

Serves 4-6:
1 lb/450g fresh chestnuts
¾ pint/450 ml chicken stock
1 small onion
1 or 2 sticks of celery
1 teaspoon sugar
Sea salt and freshly ground black pepper.

Braised Endive

Especially good braised is chicory, or Belgian Endive. In Ireland we tend to think of it exclusively as a salad vegetable, but it is often used as a hot vegetable on the continent. Again, this dish is particularly good with game, but makes a successful accompaniment to any red meat and rich poultry, such as goose or duck.

Preheat a fairly hot oven, 375°F, 190°C, Gas mark 5. Halve the endives vertically and, if necessary, cut out any tough core. Melt the butter in a shallow flameproof casserole and cook the endives in it over moderate heat until golden on all sides. Add all the remaining ingredients and stir gently to mix through the endives without breaking them up. Bring to the boil, cover with the lid and put into the oven for about 20 minutes or until tender, but still with a slight bite. Remove the endives to a warmed serving dish and boil the juices down to make a sauce. Check the flavouring and adjust the sharpness with extra vinegar, if you like, or add more salt and pepper. Serve hot.

Braised Endive: Serves 6
6 firm, fat heads of Belgian endive
3 oz/75g butter
2 teaspoons light golden brown sugar
Finely grated zest of ½ orange
Juice of 1 orange
¼ pint/150 ml water
3 fl oz/75 ml sherry vinegar
2 cloves garlic, crushed
1 teaspoon dried green peppercorns or coriander seed, crushed
Sea salt and freshly ground black pepper to taste.

Carrot and Apple Salad
with Nuts and Raisins

There's nothing to beat eating vegetables raw if you want to get a real feeling of freshness and flavour. This salad is simplicity itself and makes an excellent alternative to traditional coleslaw as an accompaniment to cold meat or poultry. Cooking apples such as Bramleys Seedling are ideal for salads when they have matured and sweetened in storage, otherwise any crisp dessert apple can be used.

Scrape the carrots, peel and core the apples and grate both coarsely. Put into a salad bowl with the nuts and raisins. Mix the soured cream, sugar, lemon juice and a good seasoning of salt and freshly ground pepper together to make a dressing, add to the bowl and toss well to mix.

Carrot Salad: Serves 6-8:
1 lb/450g carrots
2 large or 4 medium apples
2-3 oz/50-75g walnuts or brazil nuts, roughly chopped
3-4 oz/75-100g raisins
5 fl oz/150 ml soured cream
3-4 teaspoons caster sugar
Juice of 1 small lemon
Sea salt and freshly ground black pepper.

Red Bean and Onion Salad

Serves 4:

1 x 1 lb/450g tin red kidney beans, drained, *or* 8 oz/225 g dried beans, soaked and cooked

2 medium or 1 large mild onion

1 rounded teaspoon mild Dijon mustard

1 small clove garlic, crushed (optional)

Sea salt, freshly ground black pepper, pinch of caster sugar

1 tablespoon vinegar — wine/sherry/cider, as preferred

3-4 tablespoons olive oil.

This is one of our favourite dishes — it is so simple and, although we have it often, nobody ever seems to tire of it. It adapts well to mixing with other pulses and grains too, if there happen to be leftovers — brown rice makes a great addition, for instance and it is then virtually a meal in itself. It is especially good with game and big, red meats — steak and baked potatoes move into a new league when served with this more-ish mixture.

Drain the beans, rinse under the cold tap and leave to drain again. Peel and thinly slice the onions. Put the beans and onions into a fairly large bowl. In a small mixing bowl, whisk together the mustard, crushed garlic (if using), about $\frac{1}{2}$ teaspoon sea salt, a good grinding of black pepper and a pinch of caster sugar. Blend in the vinegar and gradually whisk in the oil to make an emulsion — the amount required depends on the strength of the vinegar. When it suits your taste, pour over the beans and onions and toss. Leave for an hour or two before serving if possible, tossing occasionally — the overall flavour will mature and onion will marinate and mellow in the dressing.

Variation: Segments of fresh orange can be included. This makes a colourful salad and is good with goose or duck. Or a lightly cooked green vegetable, such as blanched broccoli florets, could be included — very useful if you don't want to bother with a hot green vegetable.

Grilled Sweet Peppers

Sweet peppers are available all year round now, but this is their natural season in our climate and they are always particularly abundant and a better price than at other times.

The mistake most often made with peppers is to serve them raw, when they have a disagreeably bitter flavour and can be very indigestible. Grilling the peppers mellows the flavour and alters the texture so that they become smooth and lose their immature wateriness. After grilling, the charred skins are removed to leave behind a delicious smoky taste.

To grill peppers: Preheat a very hot grill. Halve the peppers vertically, remove seeds and membranes. Lay out on the grill pan, skin side up. Put under the hot grill and leave until charred all over — they must really look burnt. Remove from the grill and put into a paper bag or wrap in a tea towel until cool enough to handle. Peel off the charred skin with your fingers, a little at a time, and discard.

The peppers can now be served hot in dishes such as pasta or as an accompaniment to, for example, grilled fish, or they can be left to cool for use in salads. Or try using them as a warm salad side dish, dressed in a flavoursome olive oil dressing with an interesting vinegar — balsamic, perhaps, or sherry. If you have a lot of peppers available, try preserving them in oil: cut the grilled and skinned peppers into long strips and pack into jars, layering with sprigs of fresh herbs and a whole, peeled clove of garlic between the layers. Simply add enough oil to cover — either olive, or a mixture of olive and an unflavoured oil such as sunflower or groundnut (arachide). Seal and store in a cool, dark place for several weeks before using. The peppers can be used for salads, pizzas, or vegetable stews through the winter and the pepper-flavoured oil can be used in salad dressings.

Above: Crystallised Rose Petals, page 100
Previous page: Cheese and Apple Pies, page 75
Above right: Strawberry Cones, page 95
Centre right: Terrine of Summer Fruits with Fresh Orange Jelly, page 88
Bottom right: Hot Marinated Berries Gratinated with Grand Marnier, page 90
Page 112: Barbecues, page 76

As the days get shorter and temperatures drop, we start to think about big, satisfying dishes and a return to roasts and casseroles. Although modern refrigeration means pork is no longer a seasonal meat, it is traditionally at its best in autumn and the root vegetables and fruit in season at this time of year seem to be the natural accompaniments. Root vegetables are at their peak — parsnips, they say, are sweeter after the first frosts — and, of course, apples have a special affinity with pork though they also work well with a variety of meats and poultry. Pulses come back into their own again too as the colder weather sets in.

Pork Kebabs with Barbecue Sauce

A colourful main course which is especially appropriate for Hallowe'en, as it is simple to make and easy to eat — if the youngsters are 'grazing' and prefer to eat on the move, the kebabs can be slipped into a picnic roll or French loaf instead of serving with rice.

Trim the meat and cut into neat pieces for skewering. Peel the onions, wipe and trim the mushrooms. Deseed the peppers and cut up into chunks. Thread meat, onions, peppers, tomatoes and mushrooms onto skewers, brush with olive oil and set aside while preparing the sauce.

Heat the oil in a saucepan and add the onion. Fry gently for a few minutes to soften the onion, then stir in the tomato ketchup, cider, vinegar, sugar, mustard, Worcestershire sauce and salt. Bring up to the boil and simmer for 5 minutes. Blend a little of the hot sauce with the cornflour blend, mix well and return to the saucepan. Bring to the boil and keep stirring, until clear and slightly thickened. Meanwhile, preheat the grill. Set the kebabs under the hot grill, at least 3"/7 cm below the heat and grill on high for the first minute or two, then reduce the heat and cook gently for 15-20 minutes, turning regularly so that the kebabs cook evenly. Serve the kebabs on a mound of rice with the barbecue sauce separately.

Sweet and Sour Pork

Another option for bonfire night or any other evening when a meal that is especially popular with the children is required, is Sweet and Sour Pork. This is a great little stand-by as it can be stretched or dressed up to suit the occasion and it freezes well.

Trim the pork pieces and cut into even-sized chunks. Heat the butter and oil over moderate heat in a large, heavy-based pan and brown the pork pieces in it. Peel and roughly chop the onions, crush the garlic, scrape and chop the carrots, slice the celery thinly and de-seed and finely slice the pepper. Remove the browned meat from the pan with a slotted spoon. Add the prepared vegetables to the fat remaining in the pan and cook gently for 5-10 minutes, turning all the time, until the onion is just softening. If using the pineapple pieces, drain and make the juice up to $^1/_2$ pint/300 ml with water. Return the pork pieces to the pan with the pineapple pieces, if using. Add the water or pineapple juice and water mixture to the pan, then stir in the vinegar, sugar, soy sauce, tomato purée (if using) and seasoning. Cover and simmer gently for $^3/_4$–1 hour, or until the meat is just tender — be careful not to overcook as pork is inclined to break up. Blend the cornflour with a little cold water to make a paste, then add a little of the hot liquid from the pan; stir and return to the saucepan. Bring back up to the boil gently, stirring all the time until the sauce has thickened and cleared. Serve with rice — a few cashew nuts browned in a little butter make a delicious addition — and a green side salad.

Serves 6:
$1^1/_2$ lb/675g lean shoulder pork or pork pieces
About a dozen each: small pickling onions, cherry tomatoes, button mushrooms
1 red and 1 green pepper
Olive oil

For the barbecue sauce:
2 tbsp olive oil
1 onion, finely chopped
$^1/_4$ pint/150 ml tomato ketchup
$^1/_2$ pint/300 ml dry cider
3 tbsp cider vinegar
2 rounded tablespoons light golden brown sugar
2 teaspoons made mustard
2 tablespoons Worcestershire sauce
$^1/_2$ level teaspoon salt
1 rounded tablespoon cornflour, blended with $^1/_4$ pint/150 ml dry cider.

Sweet and Sour Pork: Serves 4
1 lb/450g pork pieces
1 oz/25g butter
1 tablespoon oil
2 onions
1 or 2 cloves garlic
3 carrots
4 sticks celery
1 green pepper
1 small tin pineapple pieces in juice (optional)
Water (see method)
4 tablespoons wine vinegar
2 tablespoons light golden brown sugar
2 tbsp light soy sauce
1 tablespoon tomato purée (optional)
Sea salt and freshly ground black pepper
1 rounded tablespoon cornflour.

Pork Chops: Serves 4
4 lean loin pork chops

Spice Mixture:
Crush together 1 tablespoon
   mixed allspice and juniper
   berries and coriander
   seeds, with a large clove
   of garlic, some sea salt and
   a very generous grinding
   of black pepper
2 oz/50g butter

Sauce:
1 onion
1 oz/15g butter
1 tablespoon olive oil
8 oz/225g cranberries
½ pint/300 ml dry cider
1 tablespoon cider- or wine
   vinegar
4 each of whole juniper and
   allspice berries, coriander
   seeds
1 tablespoon light golden
   brown sugar
Sea salt and freshly ground
   black pepper.

Stuffed Pork Tenderloin:
   Serves 6-8
1½-2 lb/700-900g pork
   fillet
2 oz/50g butter
1 clove garlic (optional)

Stuffing:
4 oz/100g fine white
   breadcrumbs
1 tablespoon fine freshly
   chopped parsley
2 oz/50g mixed dried fruits
1 tablespoon finely chopped
   onion
1 clove garlic (optional)
1 dessertspoon chopped
   tarragon
2 oz/50g melted butter
1 orange
1 egg
Salt and pepper

Sauce:
1 lb/450g fresh, frozen or
   tinned (in juice) apricots
1 tablespoon water
1 tablespoon light golden
   brown sugar
Juice of 1 lemon
½ teaspoon curry powder.

Pork Chops with Cranberry Cider Sauce

Pork chops have a prosaic sort of image but, given the price you pay for them, they deserve to be upgraded — and this is just the dish to do the job. In summer, or for something very special in winter using fruit from the freezer, I make something similar using raspberries, but this late autumn/winter version made with fresh cranberries is also pretty and delicious.

Mix the crushed spices with the garlic and salt, then blend all into the butter. Divide between the four chops and spread onto both sides, working well into the flesh. If there is time, leave for an hour or two at room temperature to allow the flavours to penetrate. Meanwhile, peel and finely chop the onion. Heat the butter and oil in a small pan over moderate heat and cook the onion in it gently, without browning, until just softening. Add the cranberries, cider and vinegar, then crush the spices and add to the pan with the sugar and a seasoning of salt and pepper. Heat through, stirring, until the sugar has dissolved, then bring up to the boil, reduce the heat and simmer for about 15 minutes, until the cranberries have popped and the sauce is thickening. If you like a sauce with texture, leave it as it is, otherwise rub it through a sieve to make a smooth purée. To cook the chops, preheat a hot grill and cook them close to the heat for 7-10 minutes on each side, until they are cooked through and golden brown on both sides. Serve on a bed of mixed long-grain and wild rice, with a little of the sauce spooned over the chops and the rest handed separately. An interesting green salad is the only other necessary accompaniment.

Stuffed Pork Tenderloin with Apricot Sauce

Pork fillet, or tenderloin, is one of the great Irish foods — the meat is lean, tender and succulent and it lends itself admirably to economy in the shape of a good stuffing and an interesting fruity sauce. This recipe for Stuffed Pork Tenderloin with Apricot Sauce is a speciality from Coopershill House, Riverstown, Co. Sligo. When fresh apricots are in season they use them and freeze plenty for the winter, but tinned apricots in natural juice (not syrup) could be used if fresh or frozen fruit is unavailable.

First prepare the stuffing: Mix all the dry ingredients in a bowl, stir in the melted butter, cut up the orange, removing pith and membrane, and add to the stuffing. Beat the egg lightly and use to bind the mixture; season with salt and pepper. Trim all fat off each fillet and remove the transparent membrane. Slit the meat lengthways through half of its thickness, open it out and flatten with the fist or a meat hammer. Spread the stuffing over the fillets, roll them up tightly, lengthways, and either skewer them with small skewers or tie with cotton string. Preheat a moderate oven, 325°F, 170°C, Gas mark 3. Melt the butter in a flameproof dish on the stove. Peel and slice the garlic and fry until brown, then discard. Fry the pork for a few minutes until browned evenly, cover the pan and roast for an hour in the middle of the preheated oven. Remove the lid for the last 10 minutes to allow the meat to brown.

To make the sauce, halve and stone the apricots, add the water and stew until they are tender. Mix in the sugar, lemon juice and curry powder and then blend until smooth.

Before serving, remove skewers or string, and carve into slices. Arrange on a serving dish and spoon a little of the sauce over the meat, serving the remainder separately.

Carbonnade of Beef with a Garlic Crust

Carbonnade of beef was originally a Belgian recipe for beef cooked in beer — the name refers to the long strips of beef which are characteristic of the dish — but has become so popular that other countries have adapted it to make use of their own specialities. This one includes stout, of course — but it is the crusty garlic bread topping that makes it irresistible. If convenient, the flavour of this casserole improves if it can be made the day before, then reheated when the garlic crust is added.

Trim the beef and cut it into strips, about 3"/7.5 cm long, 1½"/4 cm wide and ½"/1 cm thick. Heat the dripping or butter and oil in a large heavy frying pan and quickly brown the slices of beef, then remove with a slotted spoon and set aside. Peel and thinly slice the onions and add to the fat remaining in the frying pan. Cook gently for about 10 minutes, or until golden, then add the crushed or finely chopped garlic and continue to cook gently for a few minutes until softening. Meanwhile, preheat a very moderate oven, 325°F, 170°C, Gas mark 3. Layer the onions and beef in a large, deep casserole, starting with a layer of onions and ending with beef, and seasoning each layer lightly with salt and a grinding of pepper. Stir the flour and sugar into the juices remaining in the frying pan and cook together for a minute or two over moderate heat, then add a little of the stock and blend until smooth. Stir in the rest of the stock, the stout and the vinegar and bring up to the boil. Simmer, stirring, for a few minutes, then put the bouquet garni into the cassserole and pour in the sauce, which should just cover the meat. Cover and cook in the preheated oven on a low shelf for 2½ hours, by which time the meat should be meltingly tender. If convenient, allow the casserole to cool overnight. Next day, preheat a moderate oven, 350°F, 180°C, Gas mark 4 and prepare the garlic crust: melt the butter in a heavy frying pan over low heat and add the crushed garlic. Cut the bread into ½"/1 cm slices and soak in the garlic butter until it has all been absorbed. Arrange the bread on top of the carbonnade and heat through in the oven for half an hour, or until the meat is thoroughly heated and the topping is crisp and golden. Serve direct from the casserole, accompanied by a lightly cooked green vegetable, or followed by a green salad.

Cassoulet

Cassoulet is one of the great classics of French country cooking and is very relevant to the current rediscovery of the value of regional food. This simple, earthy dish makes a wonderfully relaxed meal for family or casual mid-day entertaining once the evenings start to draw in and, although goose would be the traditional poultry ingredient in its native Languedoc, duck or even chicken can be substituted. Although simple, this is not a dish that can be rushed and the beans have to be soaked overnight, so allow plenty of time. The gratin finish is optional, but gives a nice contrasting texture.

Lay the beans out on a work surface and check through them, removing any grit, then rinse in a colander, turn into a large bowl and cover with tepid (ie not icy cold) water. Leave to soak for 12 hours. Drain and rinse the beans and put them, with the piece of pork or bacon on top, into a pan with the chopped garlic. Cover with cold water, salt lightly (depending on the type of pork used) and bring slowly to the boil. Reduce the heat and simmer gently, with the lid on, for at least an hour. Drain, but reserve the cooking liquid. In a large flameproof casserole, heat the dripping or butter and brown the lamb or mutton pieces (if using) and the poultry joints in it, in several batches. Add the beans and pork or bacon to the casserole, with the sugar, chopped celery, bouquet garni, mustard and a

Carbonnade of Beef: Serves 6

3 lb/1.4 Kg round or lean rib steak
4 oz/100g beef dripping or butter
1 tablespoon oil
3 large onions
4 fat cloves garlic
Sea salt and freshly ground black pepper
1 rounded tablespoon plain flour
1 level tablespoon rich dark brown sugar
½ pint/300 ml good beef stock
¾ pint/450 ml stout
1 tablespoon red wine vinegar
Bouquet garni: a bay leaf and a small bunch of parsley and thyme, tied together

Topping:

8 oz/225g butter
3 or 4 cloves garlic
1 French stick.

Cassoulet: Serves 8

10 oz/275g dried haricot beans
1½ lb/700g belly of pork (salted, if possible), in one piece
OR ½ lb/225g streaky bacon and 1 lb/450g mutton or lamb pieces
4 fat cloves garlic
Good dripping, preferably goose or duck fat, or butter
8 small joints poultry: goose, duck or chicken
1 tablespoon rich dark brown sugar
4 sticks celery
1 large bouquet garni
1 tablespoon Dijon mustard, smooth or grainy
Freshly ground black pepper
6-8 oz/175-225g garlic sausage
6 oz/175g good ripe tomatoes, peeled and roughly chopped
1 dessertspoon tomato purée
A pinch of sugar
Browned crumbs to finish (optional).

good seasoning of black pepper. Add enough of the reserved cooking liquor to cover and bring to the boil then cook gently, covered, on top of the stove or in a moderate oven, preheated to 350°F 180°C, Gas mark 4, for about 2¹/2 hours, adding a little extra liquid from time to time as necessary. Add the sausage, cut up, and cook for another hour or until the beans are tender, checking the liquid level frequently. Remove the bouquet garni and also the piece of pork or bacon, which can be sliced for serving and returned to the casserole. Increase the oven temperature to 400°F, 200°C, Gas mark 6 or preheat a grill to gratinate the cassoulet. Cook the tomatoes to a pulp, add the purée and season well with salt, freshly ground black pepper and caster sugar. Spread this mixture over the top of the cassoulet, sprinkle with the crumbs and return to the hot oven, or finish under the grill until the top is crisp and brown. Serve simply with crusty hot French bread and a few bottles of red wine, followed by a crisp green salad and some farmhouse cheeses.

Parsnip Casserole au Gratin

Serves 4-6:

2 lb/900g parsnips
2 onions
1 lb/450g tomatoes
3 fl oz/75 ml olive oil
3 oz/75g butter
3 level tablespoons light
   golden brown sugar
Sea salt and freshly ground
   black pepper
6 oz/175g melting cheese —
   Gruyere/Emmenthal type
   — grated
¹/2 pint/300 ml cream
4 good tablespoons fresh
   white breadcrumbs.

Parsnips are said to be at their best after the first frosts when they are at their peak. They are one of my favourite vegetables and I use them a lot, either wrapped in buttered paper and baked whole with a roast, cut up into chunks and cooked with potatoes around the roast, or mixed with carrots, either left in bâtons or mashed to a purée. This recipe for Parsnip Casserole au Gratin is a parsnip-lover's delight as it is one of those useful, versatile dishes that are equally happy as a vegetarian main course, or as a side dish with a roast.

Preheat a moderate oven, 350°F, 180°C, Gas mark 4. Peel the parsnips. Slice thinly, removing and discarding any hard central core if necessary. Peel the onions and slice thinly. Blanch the tomatoes briefly to loosen the skins, peel, remove the seeds and slice the remaining flesh into rings. Heat the oil in a frying pan and lightly fry the parsnips and onions. Butter a shallow gratin dish and cover the base with a layer of parsnips and onions. Sprinkle with sugar, salt and freshly ground pepper and add a little cream, then cover with a layer of tomatoes. Spread with more cream and some grated cheese and repeat in layers until all the ingredients have been used, finishing with cream and cheese. Sprinkle the breadcrumbs over the top and dot with the remaining butter, then bake in the preheated oven for about 40 minutes, until the parsnips are tender and the top is a bubbling golden brown. Serve straight from the baking dish.

Chicken with Cider and Apples

Serves 4-6:

4-6 chicken joints
1¹/2 tbsp olive oil
4 rashers back bacon
1 large onion
2 or 3 cloves garlic
4 oz/100g small button
   mushrooms
4 red-skinned eating apples,
   eg Cox's
³/4 pint/450 ml dry cider
Finely grated zest and juice
   of ¹/2 lemon
1 teaspoon sugar
Sea salt and freshly ground
   pepper
About 4 oz/100g cherry
   tomatoes
1 tbsp cornflour.

Chicken with Cider and Apples — a colourful autumn casserole, full of the good things the season has to offer and easy to make and serve. [Microwave]

Put the chicken joints into a flameproof casserole with the oil and brown on all sides, then remove with a slotted spoon and set aside. To the fat in the casserole add the bacon cut into 1"/2 cm strips and fry for a few minutes until just crisp, then add the onion and garlic and cook gently for about 3 minutes, without browning.

Add the trimmed mushrooms, whole, and two of the apples, peeled, quartered and thickly sliced. Add ¹/2 pint/300 ml of the cider, the lemon juice and zest with the sugar and salt and pepper to taste. Replace the chicken portions on top of the vegetables and bring to the boil. Reduce the heat and cook gently on top of the stove or in a moderate oven, 350°F, 180°C, Gas mark 4, for about half an hour or until the chicken is cooked through, adding the cherry tomatoes and remaining apples, cored and cut into chunks but left unpeeled, for the last 10 minutes or so. When cooked, remove the chicken and keep warm. Blend the cornflour with the remaining cider and mix with the hot juices and vegetables in the casserole. Bring to the boil over moderate heat, stirring gently and being careful not to break up the tomatoes and apples, until the sauce thickens and clears — if it is too thick, add a little extra cider; adjust the seasoning, arrange on a hot serving dish with the chicken and serve with baked potatoes and a green salad.

Chicken in Nutmeg and Ginger Yogurt Sauce

There is nothing especially autumnal about this wonderfully fragrant dish, but I often find myself coming back to it at this time of year because it is so easy and utterly delicious — it fits in perfectly in a busy season when the social tempo is beginning to take an upturn. Quantities are given for 8, but it can just as easily be scaled down to 4 or up to 12. Ordinary chicken joints make an economical family meal, but using breast fillets immediately upgrades it to a dish for entertaining. [Microwave]

Heat the butter and oil in a large heavy-based casserole. Season the chicken joints with salt and pepper and cook them until golden brown on all sides. Remove from the pan with a slotted spoon and set aside. Slice the onions and cook them gently in the same fat for about 5 minutes, until softening but not browning, then add the crushed garlic. Cook gently for a minute or two, then stir in the stock, nutmeg and ginger. Bring to the boil, stirring, and replace the chicken joints in the casserole. Cover and simmer gently in the sauce for about an hour or, if it is more convenient, cook in a moderate oven, 350°F, 180°C, Gas mark 4 for the same time. I usually do this and bake a pilaf of brown rice at the same time. Wipe and trim the mushrooms and slice, quarter or leave whole according to their size. Add to the casserole and cook for another 15 minutes, then lift the chicken joints out onto a serving dish and keep them warm. Mix the cornflour and water together, add a little of the hot stock, then gradually blend this mixture into the stock. Bring to the boil, stirring until the sauce thickens, then reduce the heat and simmer for a few more minutes. Remove from the heat and stir in the yogurt. Reheat gently without boiling, pour the sauce over the chicken joints and scatter with the toasted almonds. Serve at once with a pilaf of rice and a good green salad.

Note: Although it must be served immediately after the yogurt has been added, this dish can be prepared ahead and holds well up to that point.

Serves 8:
2 oz/50g butter
2 tablespoons oil
Sea salt and freshly ground black pepper
8 chicken joints, any cut
2 large onions
1 or 2 cloves garlic
1 pint/600 ml chicken stock
1 rounded teaspoon freshly grated nutmeg
4 oz/100g stem ginger, drained
8 oz/225g button mushrooms
1 rounded tablespoon cornflour
4 tablespoons water
l large carton, 10 fl oz/300 ml, natural yogurt
4 oz/100g flaked almonds, toasted.

Baked Lamb Chops with a Golden Potato Topping

At this time of year when the price of lamb has come down, we can afford to be more generous with those easy cuts, such as chops. This is a very handy one-pot dish that is served straight from its a casserole — good, satisfying family food and ideal for a busy day.

Peel and thinly slice the potatoes; put into a bowl of cold water. Peel and finely chop the onion. Peel, core and chop the apples. Heat 2 oz/50g of the butter in a heavy pan. Trim any excess fat from the chops and add them to the hot butter; brown them lightly on both sides, removing as soon as the blood starts to run. Preheat a moderate oven, 350°F, 180°C, Gas mark 4. Gently fry the apples and onion in the fats remaining in the frying pan for about 5 minutes. Use half of the remaining butter to grease a wide, shallow gratin dish. Drain the sliced potatoes thoroughly and pat dry with a clean tea towel, then line the base of the dish with half of them. Arrange the chops in a single layer on the bed of potatoes and spread the onion and apple mixture over them. Sprinkle over the sugar and season

Serves 4-6:
2 lb/900g potatoes
l large onion
3 Bramleys, or other cooking apples
3 oz/75g butter
8 lamb chops, any preferred cut
l level dessertspoon Demerara or light golden brown sugar
Salt and freshly ground black pepper
1/3 pint/200 ml chicken stock.

lightly with salt and a few twists of the pepper mill. Arrange the rest of the potatoes in a layer on top and pour the stock over. Melt the remaining ¹/₂ oz/15g butter and brush over the potatoes, then put the dish into the preheated oven and cook for about an hour, or until the potatoes are tender and golden brown. Serve from the baking dish, with very lightly cooked sprouts tossed in a little brown sugar and crushed allspice.

Variation: The same recipe would work very well with pork chops.

Pot-Roast of Pigeons and Carrots with Gin and Juniper

Serves 4:

4 small pigeons, or 2 large ones, halved
Salt and freshly ground black pepper
2 tablespoons olive oil
1 oz/25g butter
4-6 shallots, or 2 onions, sliced
2 teaspoons caster sugar
1 teaspoon juniper berries, crushed
2 teaspooons coriander seeds, crushed
2 lb/900g small carrots, trimmed and scraped
Finely grated zest and juice of 1 orange
1-2 tablespoons sloe (or rowan) jelly
3 fl oz/75 ml Cork Dry Gin (or dry vermouth)
¹/₄ pint/150 ml double cream.

Pigeons can be very dry — when the age of the bird is doubtful, play safe and keep all the moisture in by choosing a gentle cooking method such as pot roasting.

Wash and dry the birds; season with salt and a light grinding of pepper. Heat a very moderate oven, 325°F, 160°F, Gas mark 3. Heat the oil and butter in a flameproof casserole and brown the pigeons, in batches if necessary. Lift the birds out and set aside, then add the sliced shallots or onions to the casserole and cook gently for a few minutes, until browning. Add the caster sugar, crushed juniper berries, coriander seeds and the whole carrots. Season with salt and freshly ground pepper and stir in the grated orange zest and the sloe or rowan jelly. Replace the browned pigeons on top of the vegetables and season lightly with salt and a couple of turns of the pepper mill, then sprinkle with the orange juice and gin, cover with the lid and put the casserole into the preheated oven. Reduce the oven temperature to 300°F, 150°C, Gas mark 2 and cook for about 2¹/₂ hours, or until the pigeons are very tender. Transfer the birds to a warm serving dish. Remove the vegetables with a slotted spoon and arrange around the pigeons. Keep warm. On the hob, add the cream to the juices in the casserole and bring to the boil. Boil for about two minutes, then pour the sauce around the birds, or put into a sauceboat and hand separately. Garnish the pigeons with a few sprigs of fresh herbs — flat-leaf parsley, perhaps, or celery tops — and serve with a Potato Gratin and a lightly cooked green vegetable such as spring cabbage, spinach or broccoli.

Variations: Instead of carrots try using another root vegetable, such as little white 'snowball' turnips (peeled but left whole, with a bit of green top on), or chunks of parsnip. Other dry-fleshed game birds can be cooked in the same way, varying the vegetables and flavourings if you like. For example, when pheasant is in season, allow 1 bird for 2-3 servings and use the same method to make a **Pot-Roast of Pheasant Normandy Style**: omit the juniper and orange, replace the carrots with sliced celery and the gin with Calvados. Halfway through the cooking time, add two or three peeled, cored and sliced firm dessert apples, preferably Cox's. Finish as for the pot-roast of pigeons, but garnish with sprigs of watercress and serve with game chips.

Roast Smoked Pheasant with Cumberland Sauce

Serves 4:

2 whole smoked pheasants
Finely grated zest and juice of 1 orange
¹/₂ glass port
8oz/225g redcurrant jelly
Juice of ¹/₂ lemon
¹/₂ teaspoon freshly ground ginger.

If you are one of the many who feel that farmed pheasants tend to be rather bland, try this recipe from Moyglare Manor, Maynooth, Co Kildare which uses smoked pheasants and has more flavour than most fresh birds.

Preheat a very moderate oven, 300°F, 150°C, Gas mark 2 and roast the pheasants for an hour. Meanwhile, put all the remaining ingredients into a heavy-based saucepan, bring to the boil and simmer for 5 minutes. Allow to cool. Halve the pheasants and serve with the sauce on the side and a selection of seasonal vegetables.

Apple Snow

Apples symbolise all that is best about autumn and, fortunately, their abundance is matched by an unrivalled versatility. One way or another they turn up in all sorts of dishes, savoury as well as sweet, and it is hard to imagine living in a climate where they do not thrive. To anyone with an apple tree, especially a late cropper like the wonderful Bramley's Seedling which is picked at Hallowe'en, they are the very essence of autumn. So perhaps we should start at the beginning, with one of the very simplest of nursery dishes, light-as-a-feather Apple Snow. Bramley's, which 'fall' to the fluffiest of purées, are ideal. [Microwave]

Peel, core and slice the apples. Turn into a saucepan with the water and lemon zest. Cover and simmer gently for about 15 minutes until the apples are falling, then remove from the heat, take out the lemon zest and sweeten to taste with caster sugar. Beat well with a wooden spoon to make a purée or, if a smoother texture is called for, rub through a sieve. Leave to cool. When the purée is cold, whisk the egg whites until stiff and fold into the apple, then whisk together until the mixture is thick and light. Turn into a serving bowl, or divide between six individual dishes and chill until required. Serve with crisp biscuits, such as Almond Tuiles.

Serves 4-6:
1½ lb/700g apples, preferably Bramley's
3 tablespoons water
a little thinly peeled lemon zest
4 oz/100g caster sugar, or to taste
3 egg whites.

Bramble and Apple Mousse

Bramble and Apple Mousse is quite a sophisticated little dish with a wonderful country flavour that should be welcome on any dinner table. [Microwave]

Peel, core and slice the apples. Sort through the brambles and put the fruit into a pan with the water and 3 oz/75g of the sugar. Cover and cook gently for about 15 minutes, until tender. Meanwhile strain the lemon juice into a cup, sprinkle the gelatine over it and leave to soak. When the fruit is ready, remove it from the heat, add the cake of soaked gelatine and stir until dissolved. Rub through a nylon sieve into a mixing bowl. Leave to cool until beginning to set. Whisk the egg whites stiffly, sprinkle in the remaining sugar and whisk again until firm and glossy, then fold the whites gently into the fruit purée to make a smooth mousse. Divide between six serving glasses and chill. Serve with sponge fingers or other crisp biscuits.

Serves 6:
1 lb/450g cooking apples
1 lb/450g blackberries
¼ pint/150 ml water
4oz/100g caster sugar
Juice of 1 lemon
1 sachet powdered gelatine
2 egg whites.

Apple and Hazelnut Crumble

I love a good crumble and it's a toss as to which is better, Bramble and Apple, or just plain apple. This simple apple one is enlivened with an unusual topping.

Preheat a fairly hot oven, 400°F, 200°C, Gas mark 6. Peel, core and slice the apples, then put with the water and sugar into a large, shallow ovenproof dish. Rub the butter into the flour, add the sugar and continue rubbing until it begins to stick together like big crumbs. Fork through the chopped hazelnuts and cover the fruit with this mixture, packing down lightly. Bake in the hot oven for 15 minutes, then reduce the heat to 375°F, 190°C, Gas mark 5 and cook for another 15-20 minutes, until cooked through and golden brown and crisp on top. Serve very hot, with chilled Crème Fraîche.

Serves 6-8:
2-3 lb/900g-1.4 Kg Bramleys
2 tablespoons water
4-6 oz/100-175g light golden brown sugar

Topping:
4 oz/100g butter
6 oz/175g wholemeal flour.
2 oz/50g light golden brown sugar
3 oz/75g hazelnuts, roughly chopped

Apple and Oatmeal Layer Cake

Serves 6:

1-1½ lb/450-700g cooking
    apples
3-4 oz/75-100g sugar
½ teaspoon ground
    cinnamon or cloves
2 oz/50g seedless raisins
4 oz/100g butter
1 tablespoon honey
12 oz/350g flaked oats
1 oz/25g Demerara sugar
 Grated zest and juice of 1
    lemon
1 egg.

Apples and oatmeal make a very satisfying partnership and this cake is a good example — juicy and with plenty of texture. Can be served as a dessert or as a cake, but is best served warm with Crème Fraîche. Makes a 7"/18 cm cake.

Peel, core and slice the apples. Cook with a few tablespoons of water until soft, then sweeten to taste, add spice and beat in the raisins to make a purée. Leave to cool. Butter a 7"/18 cm cake tin, preferably loose-based, and preheat a fairly hot oven, 375°F, 190°C, Gas mark 5. Melt the butter and honey in a saucepan, then stir in the oats, sugar and the grated lemon zest. Lightly whisk the egg, mix with the lemon juice and blend thoroughly into the mixture. Press a third of the oat mixture into the base of the buttered tin, cover with half of the apple mixture and repeat the layers, finishing with a layer of oats. Bake in the preheated oven for about half an hour, until cooked through and golden brown. Serve very hot with chilled cream or vanilla ice cream, or serve cold as a cake.

French Apple Flan

Serves 6-8:

Rich Shortcrust Pastry:

6 oz/175g plain flour
Pinch of salt
4 oz/100g butter
½ oz/15g caster sugar
1 small egg

Filling:

2 lb/900g Bramley cooking
    apples
2-3 tbsp water
3 oz/75g sugar, or to taste
Glaze: 3 tbsp apple jelly
1 tbsp. lemon juice.

The all-time classic apple dessert for any formal meal is French Apple Flan. There are many versions, but the characteristic they share is the impressive spiralling rings of apple slices that, despite being quite easy to do, look so professional. There are no gimmicks to this version which, unlike those that require a mixture of cooking and eating apples, is based entirely on easily-available Bramleys Seedlings. Makes an 8"/20 cm flan, to serve 6-8.

Sieve flour and salt into a mixing bowl, then cut in the butter and rub in until the mixture is like fine breadcrumbs. Mix in the caster sugar. Make a well in the centre and add enough beaten egg to make a fairly stiff dough, including a little cold water if the mixture is too dry. Gather up into a ball, knead lightly on a floured work surface, then wrap and chill for at least half an hour or until required. Meanwhile, select two even medium-sized apples and set aside. Peel, core and roughly chop the remainder, then put into a saucepan with the water and cook for 10-15 minutes until soft. Remove from the heat, add the sugar and beat with a wooden spoon to make a purée. Set aside and leave to cool. Peel and core the two remaining apples, slice thinly and evenly and keep in a bowl of acidulated water until required.

Preheat a fairly hot oven, 400°F, 200°C, Gas mark 6. Roll out the pastry and use to line an 8"/20 cm flan dish or flan ring. Trim the edges and prick the base lightly with a fork. Spoon in the apple purée and smooth the top. Drain the apple slices, pat dry with kitchen paper and arrange neatly in an overlapping pattern on top. Starting with the largest slices, work from the outside so you will end up with the smaller slices in the centre. Warm the apple jelly with the lemon juice, brush this glaze over the apple slices and bake in the centre of the preheated oven for 40-45 minutes, until the apple slices are tender and the pastry is a crisp golden-brown. Remove from the oven and brush over any remaining glaze. Serve hot or cold with whipped cream or Crème Fraîche.

Apple Filo Tart with Calvados

Serves 6:

6 large sheets filo pastry
3 oz/75g butter, melted
2 Bramleys, peeled and
    thinly sliced
Icing sugar, to taste
Ground cinnamon or
    freshly grated nutmeg
    (optional)
Calvados, to sprinkle over.

This Apple Filo Tart with Calvados is just as impressive as a traditional French Apple Tart, but more unusual — and much easier to make.

Preheat a fairly hot oven, 375°F, 190°C, Gas mark 5. Brush the base of a 10"/25 cm tart tin with butter and layer in three sheets of filo pastry, brushing each layer liberally with melted butter. Trim the edges roughly with kitchen scissors and leave the scraps of filo to dry a little so that they

Top: Layered Cinnamon Biscuit with Fresh Cherries and a Cherry Brandy Sauce, page 88
Bottom: French Apple Flan, page 120 (Photo courtesy of the author)

*Above: Cider Brack,
page 126
Right: Black Pudding
with Apple Sauce,
page 103*

curl up at the edges. Scatter half of the apple slices into the tart tin, brushing with more butter and sprinkling with sifted icing sugar — how much depends on personal taste and the tartness of the apples. Top with another three layers of filo pastry, buttering between and trimming with scissors as before, then scatter with the remaining apple slices and sweeten to taste. Casually arrange the pastry trimmings on top and brush or drizzle with the remaining butter. Lay the tart tin on a baking tray and bake in the preheated oven for about 25 minutes, or until the pastry is crisp — keep an eye on it and make sure it doesn't over-brown. Dust with a little more icing sugar and, just before serving, sprinkle the hot tart with a good measure of Calvados.

Apple Pancakes

Drimcong House at Moycullen in Co. Galway, despite the adventurousness and sophistication of many of its dishes, proves the value of simplicity with its delicious recipe for Apple Pancakes.

Put all the batter ingredients into a blender or food processor and blend to make a smooth batter. Use to make pancakes in the usual way (See Winter Desserts) and reserve; there is no need to leave the batter to stand as in traditional hand-beaten recipes. Preheat a very hot grill. Gently toss the apple slices in the sugar, lemon juice and Calvados. Arrange the apple slices on the pancakes, drizzle with the melted butter and brown under the hot grill. Do not fold the pancakes over, but serve them open, with vanilla or yogurt ice cream.

Apple Pancakes: Makes 12
Batter:
2 eggs
2 oz/50g melted butter
3½ oz/90g flour
8 fl oz/225 ml milk
Pinch of salt

Topping:
6 dessert apples, peeled and
  thinly sliced across
2 oz/50g caster sugar
Juice of 2 lemons
2 tablespoons Calvados or
  Cognac.
2 oz/50g melted butter

Fresh Apple Muesli

Although not necessarily a dessert — it is much better known as a breakfast cereal dish — home-made muesli is much nicer than the commercial kind and well worth making. Try this simple recipe to start, then make up your own variations.

Soak the oats in the fruit juice overnight. The next day, core and chop the apples and mix in with the cream, sugar and dried fruit. Divide between six bowls and sprinkle with chopped nuts.

Apple muesli: Serves 6
6 tablespoons medium
  oatmeal or rolled oats
About ⅓ pint/200 ml
  freshly squeezed orange,
  or other fruit juice
3 dessert apples
6 tablespoons thin cream or
  top of the milk
2 tablespoons Demerara
  sugar
3 oz/75g dried fruit —
  seedless raisins and
  sultanas
Chopped toasted hazelnuts.

Apple Brulée

Still on the subject of our most important autumn fruit, my Aunt Helen used to give me a very simple dessert of stewed apple topped with a crushed Rich Tea or digestive biscuit. At the age of four I thought it was delicious — now I like the grown-up version. This ultra-simple recipe for Apple Brulée is ideal if you have stewed apples to use up or, later in the year, if you have a lot of them in the freezer. If using fresh apples cook them the day before so they can be really well chilled: it is the contrast between chilled and bubbling hot ingredients that makes this simple dish.

Peel and core the apples, slice quite thinly and cook very gently in a little water with sugar to taste — try not to cook hard enough to make the apples fall (difficult if you are using Bramleys) as a little texture is enjoyable. When the apples are tender, remove from the heat and leave to cool. Chill. Preheat a very hot grill. Combine the apples and liqueur, divide between six heatproof serving dishes and spoon the soured cream on top. Sprinkle with the sugar and put under the grill until it caramelises — if the heat is fierce enough, it will do so without melting the cream underneath.

Variation: The same recipe can be used with pears, varying the liqueur — Poire William, perhaps, or Armagnac. Children love the drama of the contrast between hot and cold, smooth and crunchy too — in which case use orange juice instead of alcohol.

Apple Brulée: Serves 6
2 lb/900g apples
Sugar to taste
2 tablespoons Calvados or
  orange liqueur
½ pint/300 ml soured
  cream, well-chilled
6 tablespoons light golden
  brown sugar.

Spiced Pumpkin Pie

Serves 6:

4 oz/100g shortcrust pastry (ie 4 oz/100g flour etc)
2 lb/900g pumpkin
2 oz/50g butter
4 oz/100g caster sugar
1 level coffeespoon salt
1 level coffeespoon ground cinnamon
½ level coffeespoon each grated nutmeg and ground cloves
3 eggs
¼ pint/150 ml cream.

Pumpkin is very much part of the American tradition and has really only gained popularity here because it happens to be in season at Hallowe'en and we're always looking for some interesting way to use up the flesh that is hollowed out to make lanterns. That said, this is a very good Spiced Pumpkin Pie, with plenty of pep. Although they call it a pie, it's really an open tart.

Roll out the pastry to line a deep 8"/20 cm pie plate or tart tin. Trim the edges and leave the tin in the fridge while preparing the filling. If the pumpkin has been bought as a wedge, cut away the outer skin and remove the seeds. (If not, less weight will be required). Chop the pumpkin flesh and put into a saucepan with the butter. Cover and cook over low heat until the pumpkin has reduced to a purée, removing the lid towards the end of the cooking time to allow the accumulated juices to evaporate. Remove from the heat and sieve or purée in a liquidiser. Add the sugar, salt, spices, eggs and cream and mix well. Allow to cool. Preheat a fairly hot oven, 400°F, 200°C, Gas mark 6. When it is ready, pour the pumpkin mixture into the prepared pastry crust and bake for about 40 minutes, or until the filling has set. Serve warm or cold, cut into wedges, with whipped cream.

Baked Pears with Chilled Crème Fraîche

Serves 4:

4 firm dessert pears, eg Conference
About 3 tablespoons Demerara sugar
1 oz/25g butter
¼ pint/150 ml chilled Crème Fraîche or double cream.

This simple dessert also depends on contrast for its success. As with all hot fruit desserts, I much prefer the slightly acidic sharpness of Crème Fraîche here, as our sweet cream lacks the bite that gives a perfect contrast, but you could try soured cream, or unsweetened natural yogurt instead.

Preheat a fairly hot oven, 400°F, 200°C, Gas mark 6. Butter a shallow baking dish, large enough to take the halved pears in a single layer. Peel the pears, halve and core them and arrange in the buttered dish. Sprinkle generously with Demerara sugar and dot with the butter, then bake in the preheated oven for about 20 minutes, until the pears are tender and the topping crunchy. Remove from the oven and serve very hot, straight from the dish, with the chilled cream poured over.

Chocolate and Pear Cake

Serves 6-8:

6 large eggs, separated
5 oz/150 g caster sugar
2 oz/50g cocoa powder, sifted
3 oz/75g self-raising flour, sifted
1 lb/450g pears
2 oz/50g dark chocolate
3 tablespoons rum or kirsch
½ pint/300 ml double cream.
Grated chocolate to decorate

The recipe for this light Chocolate and Pear Cake gâteau was given to me at Cloonnabinnia House Hotel, a most hospitable family-run hotel at Moycullen, Co. Galway. [Microwave]

Oil and base-line three 8"/20 cm sandwich tins. Preheat a moderate oven, 350°F, 180°C, Gas mark 4. Whisk the egg yolks and caster sugar together until very pale and thick. Sift cocoa powder and flour together and fold in lightly with a metal spoon. Whisk the egg whites until stiff, then stir a tablespoonful into the cocoa mixture. Fold the remainder in carefully with a metal spoon, losing as little volume as possible. Divide the sponge mixture between the three prepared tins and bake near the centre of the preheated oven for 15-20 minutes, until springy to the touch and shrinking slightly from the tins. Meanwhile, prepare the pears: if they are very ripe and juicy, all that is required is to peel and quarter them, remove the cores and slice thinly. If they are hard, poach the prepared fruit for a few minutes in a little water with sugar to taste; turn into a bowl and leave to cool. Mix the rum or kirsch with 6 tablespoons of the pear juice and spoon over the cakes. Sandwich together with the sliced pears and whipped cream, then decorate the top with grated chocolate.

Variation: When fresh pears are unavailable, dried ones can be used instead.

Crème Caramel

Two classic desserts which are often confused but are equally delicious in their own way and work well as complementary sweets with autumn fruit compôtes, are Crème Caramel and Crème Brulée. In their classic version, both depend on simplicity and contrast of flavour and texture for their success, but the basic flavours can be varied — citrus flavoured sugars with a little grated zest work well, for instance, or a light coffee flavouring is worth trying. But, in my view, the originals are best. [Microwave]

Preheat a very moderate oven, 325°F, 160°C, Gas mark 3. Put the granulated sugar into a heavy-based pan and stir over moderate heat until the sugar dissolves to make a golden brown caramel syrup. Remove from the heat and carefully stir in the water, then return to the heat and stir to make a smooth caramel syrup. Pour into an ungreased hot 1½ pint/900 ml baking dish, or divide between six ramekins. Using oven gloves or a cloth, tilt the hot dish(es) to coat evenly with the hot caramel, then lay in a shallow roasting tin. To make the custard, scald the milk in a small pan, with the vanilla pod if using. Lightly beat the eggs, sugar and vanilla in a bowl and, when it is nearly boiling, remove the vanilla pod and whisk in the hot milk. If a vanilla pod was not used, flavour now with vanilla essence. Pour into the prepared dish, or divide between the ramekins. Fill the roasting tin to a depth of about an inch/2.5 cm with cold water, cover with buttered greaseproof paper and bake in the centre of the preheated oven until the custard has set — about 1-1½ hours if baking one large dish, or about 30 minutes for individual ones. Leave to cool, then chill. To serve, loosen around the edge of the custard with a knife and tip the dish to encourage the custard to shrink away from the sides. Select a serving dish that is flat in the middle but has a deep enough rim to contain the caramel syrup which will be released when the custard is turned out. Invert the serving dish over the baking dish and turn upside down. Serve as it is, or with cream and, perhaps, some light, crisp biscuits such as Langues de Chat.

Serves 6:
3 oz/75g granulated sugar
1 tablespoon water
1 pint/600ml milk
6 eggs
3oz/75g caster sugar
vanilla pod or a few drops
of vanilla essence.

Crème Brulée

Crème Brulée is dramatic in a totally different way, its crunchy topping contrasting with the smooth creamy custard underneath.

Mix the yolks well with the sugar. Put the cream and vanilla pod together in a saucepan, bring up to scalding point, then remove the vanilla and pour the hot cream onto the yolks, blending well. Add vanilla essence now if the vanilla pod was not used. Return the mixture to a double saucepan or a bowl over hot water and cook very carefully, stirring or whisking all the time, until the mixture thickens — it can go up to scalding point (ie just below boiling) but do not allow it to boil. Strain onto a gratin dish, or divide between six individual ones if convenient. Now put into a cool oven 275°F, 140°C, Gas mark 1, just long enough to let a skin form on the top, but do not allow the custard to colour. Cool and then leave to chill for several hours, preferably overnight. To finish, preheat the grill. Sprinkle the custard evenly with sugar so that it is completely covered, but don't make the layer too thick. Grill as close as possible to the heat until the sugar melts and caramelises, which takes 2-3 minutes, then remove from the heat and leave in a cold place for up to 2-3 hours before serving. Because it is so rich, Crème Brulée is traditionally served with fresh or poached fruit; another delicious option is to put two or three teaspoons of a soft fruit such as raspberries into each ramekin before adding the custard.

Serves 6:
4 egg yolks
1 tablespoon caster sugar
1 pint/600 ml cream
1 vanilla pod, or a few
drops of essence
Caster sugar or light golden
brown sugar to finish.

Irish Pear Cake

Irish Pear Cake
8 oz/225g self-raising flour
Pinch of salt
Good pinch of ground
   ginger or cinnamon
4 oz /100g butter, at room
   temperature
4 pears, eg. Conference
6 oz/175g sugar, or to taste
2 eggs
A little milk to mix
Granulated sugar to
   sprinkle over.

This lovely moist cake is ideal for autumn, when there's an abundance of pears. For the same reason it's often served at Hallowe'en although it isn't associated with Hallowe'en customs in the way that Barm Brack is. It can be served cold, as a cake, or warm with cream or custard as a pudding.

Grease an 8"/20 cm deep cake tin. Preheat a fairly hot oven, 375°F, 190°C, Gas mark 5. Sieve the flour, salt and spice into a bowl, cut in the butter and rub in until the mixture is like fine breadcrumbs. Peel and core the pears; slice thinly, add to the rubbed-in mixture with the sugar — the amount depends on how much sweetening the pears need. Mix in the egg and enough milk to make a fairly stiff dough, then turn the mixture into the prepared tin and sprinkle with granulated sugar. Bake in the preheated oven for 50-60 minutes, until crisp, golden brown and springy to the touch.

Variation: **Irish Apple Cake** is made in the same way. When using apples, substitute a pinch of ground cloves for the ginger.

Cider Brack

Cider Brack
8 oz/225g raisins
8 oz/225g sultanas
6 oz/175g rich dark brown
   sugar
1/2 pint/300 ml cider
4 oz/100g mixed peel
Grated zest of l orange
4 oz/100g butter, melted
2 eggs, lightly beaten
l lb/450g plain flour
2 level teaspoons baking
   powder
l teaspoon mixed spice
1/2 teaspoon cinnamon
Pinch of salt
Charms wrapped in
   greaseproof paper or foil
   (optional)
l tablespoon sugar and 2
   tablespoons cider to glaze.

This juicy unyeasted version of the traditional brack is especially delicious toasted and spread with cinnamon butter. The ring signifies an early marriage, of course, but you can also include other objects intended to divine the future: a small silver coin (wealth), a button (bachelorhood), a thimble (spinsterhood), a chip of wood (a stormy marriage) and a rag (poverty) — these days all hygienically wrapped in foil.

Put the raisins, sultanas and brown sugar into a saucepan with the cider. Over gentle heat, bring up slowly to boiling point, stirring occasionally, then allow to cool — leave overnight if convenient.

Preheat a moderate oven 350°F, 180°C, Gas mark 4. Grease and base-line a 9"/22.5 cm round deep cake tin. Add the mixed peel and grated orange zest to the mixture along with the melted butter and lightly beaten eggs. Sieve the dry ingredients together and gradually stir into the fruit mixture. Stir well, making sure all the ingredients are thoroughly mixed together. Add the charms, if using. Turn the mixture into the prepared tin and bake for 1 1/2-2 hours, until the top of the cake feels firm to the touch. Remove from the oven and brush with a glaze made by bringing the cider to the boil in a small pan and dissolving the sugar in it. Return the brack to the oven for about 3 minutes, until the top is shiny brown. Cool in the tin. When cold, remove the lining paper and store in an airtight tin until required. Serve sliced and buttered.

Apricot Tea Bread

Apricot Tea Bread
4 oz/100g dried apricots
8 oz/225g self-raising flour
2 oz/50g slivered almonds
2 oz/50g light golden
   brown sugar
2 oz/50g butter
4 oz/100g golden syrup (4
   level tablespoons)
1 egg
3 fl oz /75 ml milk.

Delicious at any time and an interesting alternative to a brack for a change.

Pour boiling water onto the apricots and leave to soak for about an hour. Preheat a moderate oven, 350°F, 180°C, Gas mark 4 and grease and base-line a 2 lb/900g loaf tin. Drain the soaked apricots and chop up quite finely. Sift the flour into a mixing bowl and stir in the apricots, nuts and sugar. Melt the butter and syrup together over gentle heat, add the beaten egg and the milk. Blend well and mix into the dry ingredients. Pour into the prepared loaf tin and bake in the preheated oven for an hour, or until the top is golden brown and springy to the touch and the sides are shrinking slightly from the tin. Allow to cool in the tin for a few minutes, then turn out onto a wire rack. When completely cold, store in an airtight tin. Serve plain, or buttered.

AUTUMN Preserves

One man's problem is another's good fortune at this time of year, when over-abundance of home-grown produce can be a headache for one but relatively low market prices good news for another. Either way, it's worth trying to find the time to make some preserves for the winter while so many good things are at their peak. Neither the equipment needed nor the procedure is complicated, but it's wise to bear a few rules in mind before beginning to make chutneys or pickles:

★ Stainless steel, aluminium or unchipped enamelled pans can be used, but not iron, brass or copper (which would react with vinegar).

★ Use a preserving pan or a big saucepan to prevent boiling over, especially if the quantities are large, and get a long-handled spoon for safe stirring.

★ Jars need to have vinegar-proof lids, that is with no bare metal exposed.

★ Weigh ingredients accurately.

★ To ensure good keeping, sterilise jars before use and either seal immediately, while very hot, or when absolutely cold to eliminate the risk of condensation.

★ Store in a cool, dark, dry place and allow to mature for 2-3 months before use.

Note: Sometimes special pickling vinegar, with a higher than 5% acetic acid content, is specified — usually for pickling fruit or vegetables with a high water content. Otherwise, good quality malt vinegar is the most likely option, except where white vinegar is needed for the appearance of light coloured produce such as cauliflower or onions. If quantities are small enough to warrant the extra expense and long-term storage is not a priority, I prefer to use a milder wine or cider vinegar which produces a more subtle, mellow flavour and can usually be used sooner than the harsher variety which needs some time to mature.

Red Tomato Chutney

A surfeit of tomatoes, or simply the fact that they are available very cheaply at the end of the season, is often the incentive needed to get down to chutney-making, so why not begin with this Red Tomato Chutney?

Blanch the tomatoes briefly in boiling water to loosen the skins, then peel and chop. Peel, core and chop the apple.

Peel and chop the onion. Put all the ingredients into a preserving pan or large vinegar-proof saucepan, stir well and bring to the boil. Simmer gently for an hour or until thick and golden brown, stirring from time to time to prevent burning. Put into hot jars; when cold, cover, seal and label. Store in a cool, dark place. Makes about 3 lb/1.4 Kg.

Green Tomato Chutney

Green Tomato Chutney is a very useful preserve at the end of the season when tomatoes have too little sunlight to ripen properly and this recipe comes from Glassdrumman Lodge, Annalong, Co. Down — the chef says it is his mother's recipe and comes highly recommended.

Put all ingredients into a vinegar-proof pan, bring to the boil and cook over gentle heat, stirring from time to time to prevent burning, for about 2 hours or until there is very little free liquid and the chutney looks roughly puréed. Pot, seal and store in a cool, dark place. Makes about 10 lb/4.5 kg.

Red Tomato Chutney
1 lb/450g ripe tomatoes
1 cooking apple
1 large onion or 2 medium onions
1 lb/450g seedless raisins
4 oz/100g light golden brown sugar
½ pint/300 ml vinegar
2 teaspoons salt
2 teaspoons ground ginger
Pinch of cayenne pepper.

Green Tomato Chutney
1½ pints/900 ml malt vinegar
2 lb/900g cooking apples, peeled, cored and sliced
1¼ lb/550g rich dark sugar
10 dried chillies
½ teaspoon cayenne pepper
½ oz/15g salt
4 lb/1.8 Kg green tomatoes, sliced or chopped
1 lb/450g shallots OR 12 oz/350g onions, finely chopped
2 oz/50g fresh garlic, crushed
1 lb/450g raisins.

Marrow and Tomato Chutney

Makes about 6 lb/2.7 Kg:
3 lb/1.4 Kg marrow
3 oz/75g salt
8 oz/225g cooking apples
  or windfalls (prepared
  weight)
8 oz/225g onion
1 red pepper
1 green pepper
1 lb/450g red tomatoes
4 oz/100g dates, stoned
6 oz/175g seedless raisins
1 pint/600ml vinegar
½ oz/15g mustard seed
2 teaspoons grated root
  ginger or dried ground
  ginger
2 teaspoons ground allspice
1 teaspoon ground cinnamon
1 teaspoon ground mace
1 lb/450g Demerara sugar.

Marrows seem to be rather out of fashion these days, with courgettes and other small relations taking the limelight, but they are fun to grow and versatile in the kitchen. This Marrow and Tomato Chutney could also be made with overgrown courgettes and has the virtue of making use of other plentiful fruit and vegetables as well.

Peel the marrow, remove seeds and pith and cut the flesh into small cubes. Arrange in layers in a large bowl, with the 3 oz/75 g salt scattered through them. Cover and leave in a cool place for 24 hours.

Drain the marrow thoroughly, through a colander, then rinse under the cold tap and drain well again. Meanwhile, peel, core and chop the apples, discarding any bruises. Chop the onion quite finely. Remove stems, seeds and membranes from the peppers and chop the flesh. Peel the tomatoes and chop roughly. Put all the ingredients except the marrow and sugar into a preserving pan or heavy-based saucepan and cook over low heat for about 1½ hours until tender. Stir in the sugar and, when it has dissolved, stir in the marrow cubes. Simmer for an hour, until the marrow is soft and most of the liquid has evaporated, stirring occasionally to prevent sticking. Pour into clean, warm wide-necked jars. When cold, cover with vinegar-proof lids (ie with no untreated metal showing), label and store in a cool, dark place until the chutney is mature, in about 2 months.

Apple and Sultana Chutney

9 oz/250g apples
4 oz/100g sultanas
2 oz/50g onions
1 oz/25g almonds, blanched
1 teaspoon white
  peppercorns
Half-teaspoon coriander
  seed
6 oz/175g Demerara sugar
2 teaspoons salt
1 teaspoon ground ginger
Cayenne
¾ pint/450 ml vinegar
Red chillies (optional).

Apple and Sultana Chutney is a favourite in my family and is quite versatile — for a mild chutney add only a little cayenne, for a spicier one increase to taste. The weights are for prepared ingredients.

Prepare and chop the apples, sultanas, onions and almonds. Tie peppercorns and coriander seeds in muslin. Put all ingredients except the chillies into a lined saucepan (ie unchipped enamel) and simmer slowly for 1½-2 hours until most of the liquid has evaporated. Put into warmed glass jars, place one chilli in each jar and cover when cold.

Variation: A **Tomato and Apple Chutney** may be made by using 1 lb/450g ripe tomatoes (skinned) and ½ lb/225g apples with ingredients given above but omitting the sultanas. Makes about 2 lb/1 kg.

Makes about 10 lb/4.5 Kg:
4 lb/1.8 Kg cooking apples
  or windfalls
2 lb/900g pears
3 lb/1.4 Kg ripe tomatoes
4 lb/1.8 Kg light golden
  brown sugar
8 oz/225g sultanas
8 oz/225g seedless raisins
2 pints/1.2 litres vinegar
1 teaspoon ground nutmeg
  or mace
1 teaspoon cayenne pepper
1 teaspoon ground cloves
1 teaspoon ground black
  pepper
2 tablespoons salt
1 teaspoon ground ginger.

Autumn Fruit Chutney

If you have lots of all the autumn fruits, try this delicious spicy Fruit Chutney.

Prepare the apples and pears: peel, core and cut up quite small. (If using windfalls, remove any bruises before weighing.) Skin tomatoes and chop them roughly. Put the prepared fruit into a preserving pan with the other ingredients and stir well over gentle heat until the sugar has completely dissolved. Bring up to boiling point, then reduce the heat and keep at a gentle simmer, stirring from time to time to prevent sticking, for 1½ hours or until thick and golden-brown. Put into warmed jars and leave until cold, then cover and seal.

Apple and Dried Fruit Chutney

This Apple and Dried Fruit Chutney is ideal for tidying up all sorts of ingredients that accumulate during the autumn, like the last of the windfall Bramleys which won't keep through the winter — they are perfect for chutney because they 'fall' during cooking and produce a smooth purée — and oddments of various dried fruit left after baking the Christmas puddings and cakes. I prefer chutneys to be mild and aromatic; if you like a fiery flavour, increase the amount of chilli accordingly.

Chop any larger pieces of dried fruit to match (roughly) small ones such as sultanas. Peel, core and chop the apples. Peel and finely chop the onions, garlic and ginger. Mix everything together in a suitable pan and bring to the boil, stirring, over moderate heat. Simmer, stirring occasionally, for about half an hour or until the mixture is very thick. Pot into clean warm jars; when cold, cover with vinegar-proof lids and label.

Store in a cool, dark place.

Makes about 6 lb/2.7 kg.
1½ lb/700g dried fruit (sultanas, raisins, apricots etc as available)
3 lb/1.4 Kg Bramleys Seedlings
2 large onions
6 fat cloves garlic
2 oz/50g root ginger
1½ lb/700g light golden brown sugar
1 teaspoon crushed chillies
1 tablespoon salt
1½ pints/850 ml cider vinegar.

Apricot Chutney

Of all the commercial chutneys, apricot is the one I find least easy to resist, so I have taken to making my own Apricot Chutney with dried apricots.

Drain the apricots and chop them. Put all ingredients into a preserving pan or large saucepan. Cover and simmer for 1½ hours, or until thick and golden brown, stirring from time to time to prevent sticking. Cool a little then pour into warmed jars and leave until completely cold. Cover and label, then store in a cool, dark place for at least 3 weeks before using.

Variation: For **Peach Chutney**, substitute 8oz/225g dried peaches for the apricots.

Apricot Chutney
Makes about 3 lb/1.4 Kg:
8 oz/225g dried apricots, soaked overnight
12 oz/350g onions, finely chopped
8 oz/225g granulated or light golden brown sugar
Grated zest and juice of 1 orange
4 oz/100g seedless raisins
1 teaspoon salt
1 clove garlic, crushed or finely chopped
1 level tablespoon smooth Dijon mustard
1 coffeespoonful mixed spice
¾ pint/ 450 ml cider vinegar.

Pickled Pears

When there's an abundance of Conference pears bringing the price down in the shops or, if you grow your own and have more than you need, why not use some for piquant Pickled Pears to serve with cold meats or poultry?

Peel and core the pears and cut into quarters. Put the sugar and vinegar into a pan and dissolve the sugar over gentle heat. Put the spices and lemon peel into a piece of muslin, crush them and suspend the muslin bag in the saucepan. Put the pears into the vinegar and simmer until tender. Lift out the pears with a slotted spoon and pack into clean, warm preserving jars. Remove the spice bag and boil the liquid for 10 minutes until syrupy. Cover the fruit and seal at once.

Variation: **Pickled Peaches** can be made in the same way.

Pickled Pears:
Makes about 6 lb/2.7 Kg
4 lb/1.8 Kg pears
2 lb/900g sugar
1 pint/600ml white vinegar
1 oz/25g cloves
1 oz/25g allspice berries
1 oz/25g root ginger
1 oz/25g cinnamon stick
Rind of ½ lemon, peeled in strips.

JELLIES

When the windfalls are beginning to pile up in the kitchen it's time to make the most of their high pectin content and sharp flavour by making some luscious **Savoury Jellies** for the winter. Jellies based on cooking apples, especially under-ripe ones, set very easily. To test for a set, simply pour a small sample of the boiling jelly onto a cold saucer, allow to cool slightly, then push it with a teaspoon; when the surface wrinkles, setting point has been reached and the pan should be removed from the heat immediately. **Yield** depends on the juiciness of the fruit but, as a rough guide, a batch using 3 lb/1.4 Kg sugar will make around 5 lb/2.3 Kg jelly. Savoury jellies keep well in a dark, cool place and are best stored in small jars which will be used fairly quickly once open — it's worth collecting attractive little jars which look nice on the table.

Apple Jelly

4 lb/1.8 Kg green cooking
apples or crab apples
Sugar (see method)
2 pints/1.2 litres water.

Apple Jelly is easy to make and extremely versatile. It's ideal for tarts etc, as a glaze, and in all sorts of recipes; it can often be used as a substitute for jellies which tend to be in short supply such as redcurrant. As the flavour is fairly unassertive, it can also take on other flavourings with subtlety. Crab apples make a pretty pink jelly, cookers tend to come out a deep gold.

Wash the apples, remove bruises and cut the fruit up roughly. Put the pieces into a preserving pan or large saucepan and add the water, which should just barely cover the fruit. Simmer for about 45 minutes until very soft, then transfer to a jelly bag and leave to strain overnight. Measure the juice back into the pan, bring it up to simmering point and add 1 lb/450g sugar per 1 pint/600 ml juice. Stir until dissolved, then bring up to the boil. (At this point any flavourings can be added, tied in muslin — see below.) Boil fast for 5 minutes, then test for a set and repeat every minute or two until a set is obtained. Take the pan from the heat, remove any flavourings, skim and pour at once into heated jars. When completely cold, seal and store in a cool, dark place.

Suggested Flavourings: ★ A few thin strips of lemon or orange peel, tied in muslin. ★ 4 or 5 cloves, tied in muslin. ★ 8 or 9 rose geranium or lemon verbena leaves, tied together.

Quince Jelly

Makes about 6 lb/2.7 Kg:
4 lb/1.8 Kg quinces
Water (see method)
Juice of 1 lemon
Granulated sugar (see
method).

Many a garden has an ornamental quince — but did you know that the rock hard fruits cook down to a pulp as quickly as cooking apples and make a wonderful sharp-flavoured pink jelly that complements any dish with apple in it. When ready to pick, the quinces turn yellow and can be quite hard to find amongst the autumn foliage, but the search is worth the effort.

Wash the quinces, cut up roughly and put into a preserving pan with 4 pints/2.4 litres water. Bring slowly up to the boil and simmer gently for about 1½ hours, or until very soft, mashing them to a pulp as they soften. Ladle the fruit and juices into a scalded jelly bag and leave to drip for half an hour, then remove the pulp from the bag and put into a saucepan with 2 pints/1.2 litres water. This second extraction will get more out of the pectin-rich pulp. Simmer for another half hour, then ladle back into the jelly bag to drip again. When the bag stops dripping, measure all the juices back into the rinsed preserving pan and for every 1 pint/600 ml juice add 1 lb/450g granulated sugar. Add the lemon juice and stir over low heat until the sugar has completely dissolved, then bring up to the boil and boil hard for about 10 minutes, or until setting point is reached. Remove from the heat, skim or stir a knob of butter in if there is a scum, and pour into clean, warmed jars. Leave until cold, then seal and label.

Mint Jelly

3 lb/1.4 Kg windfalls/
green cooking apples
1 pint/600ml water.
½ pint/300 ml cider
2 tablespoons wine- or
cider-vinegar
A good handful of fresh
mint
Sugar (see method)
Green food colouring

Mint Jelly is infinitely superior to mint sauce — advantages include the fact that, unlike its vinegary cousin, it doesn't fight with wine, but it's also very pretty, keeps well and is instantly available whenever you want it. The round-leaved apple mint has the best flavour.

Wash the apples, remove any bruises and cut up roughly. Put into a preserving pan or large saucepan with the water, cider, vinegar and 2 or 3 good sprigs of mint. Simmer to a soft pulp, pour into a jelly bag and leave to drip overnight. Measure the juice and weigh 1 lb/450g sugar per 1 pint/600 ml juice. Heat the juice, stir in the sugar (it will dissolve more easily if warmed first) and dissolve over a low heat. Finely chop 2-3 tablespoons of the youngest mint leaves. When the sugar has dissolved completely, bring to the boil and boil rapidly until setting point is reached. Skim, stir in the chopped mint and a few drops of green colouring, stir once or twice to distribute evenly, then pour into small warmed jars. Leave until completely cold before sealing, then store in a cool place.

Variation: **Herb Jellies** are made in a similar way. Strip the leaves from the stalks of your chosen herb — tarragon, lemon thyme or sage, for example — and cook the stalks with the apples. But, to avoid the herb flavour getting too strong, tie the herb leaves into a muslin bag and add it to the boiling syrup instead of adding chopped leaves — taste the jelly occasionally while it is boiling, so the bag of leaves can be removed before the flavour becomes overpowering. Otherwise, proceed as above. Label carefully, as jellies can look very similar.

Bramble Jelly

Bramble Jelly is probably the most evocative of all the seasonal preserves — who could forget the prickly family expeditions of childhood when, complete with billy cans, we were sent to gather brambles for jams and jellies? Apples, or sometimes sloes, are used in conjunction with the brambles to get them to set properly.

Makes about 5 lb/2.3 Kg:
4 lb/1.8 Kg brambles
2 lb/900g windfalls or sour cooking apples OR sloes
Water (see method)
Granulated sugar (see method).

Pick over the brambles thoroughly and rinse them. Wipe the apples and cut them up (if using windfalls, remove any bruises before weighing); if using sloes, simply rinse them. Put into a preserving pan with about 2 pints/1.2 litres water, or just enough to cover the fruit. Bring up to the boil, then reduce the heat and simmer, uncovered, for about 45 minutes or until tender. Stir the fruit with a wooden spoon as it softens, to break it up. Ladle the fruit and juices into a scalded jelly bag and leave to drip overnight. Measure the juice back into the rinsed preserving pan and for every 1 pint/600 ml juice add 1 lb/450g granulated sugar. Stir over low heat until the sugar is completely dissolved, then bring up to the boil and boil hard for 10 minutes, or until setting point is reached. Remove from the heat, skim or stir in a knob of butter if there is a scum, and pot into clean, warmed jars. Seal and label when cold.

Sloe Gin

While on the subject of sloes, let us not forget that other seasonal speciality that should be made in autumn to give at Christmas: Sloe Gin.

1 lb/450g sloes
4 oz/100g caster sugar
1½ pints/900 ml gin
A few drops of almond essence.

Pick over the sloes, discard any damaged fruit and rinse the rest. Remove the stalks and prick the fruit, then pack alternate layers of fruit and sugar into a wide-necked screw-top jar. Leave for a day or two, shaking or stirring occasionally, until the juices begin to flow, then add the gin and almond essence and seal tightly. Leave in a cool, dark place for about 3 months, shaking from time to time. In December, strain and bottle the liqueur. Although now drinkable, it is very much better to leave it for at least six months before drinking. The sloes which are left behind can be used in the kitchen as a flavouring.

Note: Some recipes for sloe gin contain more sugar than this, some a little less: it is a matter of taste.

Rowan Jelly

Rowan Jelly is perhaps an acquired taste, but its astringent flavour marries well with game and rich meats. Apart from eating it, it's worth making for the sheer pleasure of a day in the mountains, picking the lovely deep orange berries.

2 lb/900g rowan berries (mountain ash)
2 lb/900g windfalls, or crab apples
Sugar (see method)
1 lemon
1½ pints/900ml water.

Strip the berries from their stalks and rinse them in a colander. Wash the apples and cut them up or leave them whole if using crab apples. Put both into a preserving pan or a big saucepan with the thin zest and juice of the lemon and the water, which should barely cover the fruit. Simmer slowly for about 45 minutes, until reduced to a pulp. Pour into a jelly bag and leave to drip overnight. Measure the juice, reheat gently then add and dissolve 1 lb/450g warmed sugar for each 1 pint/600 ml juice. When the sugar is completely dissolved, bring to the boil and boil fast until a set is reached, testing after 5-6 minutes.

Variation: The proportion of apples can be varied — it can even be made without apples at all, but using 2 lemons to 4 lb/1.8 Kg berries. Using more apples produces a milder, less acid jelly.

Candied Citrus Peel

The early autumn is a good time to make a batch of Candied Peel, so that it will be ready and in peak condition when the Christmas baking season begins. Any combination of citrus peels would be useful, but the wider the selection the better — grapefruit, orange, lemon and lime make a good mixture. Select thick-skinned fruit and leave as much pith on the cooked skins as possible, removing only any excess membranes that may be clinging to the pith. Well-scrubbed fruits used for their juice are suitable — simply gather together the halved peels in the freezer until you have a worthwhile batch of, for example, 2 grapefruit (4 halves), 2 lemons (4 halves), 2 limes (4 halves) and 6 oranges (12 halves). Put the peel into a large saucepan, cover with cold water and bring up to the boil. If the mixture contains grapefruit, drain off the hot water and start again with a fresh batch — do this at least once, preferably twice. Simmer uncovered, as if making marmalade, for about 1½ hours, or until the peel is really tender — test all varieties, as they may not cook at the same speed. Drain, reserving the juice. Check all the peels and remove any excess membrane with a tablespoon if necessary, but be careful not to disturb the pith. Measure the cooking liquor and, if necessary, make up to 1 pint/600 ml with water. Add 1 lb/450g granulated sugar per pint/600 ml and dissolve over low heat, then add the peels and bring up to boiling point. Cook for 1 minute to make sure everything is thoroughly heated through, then pour off into a bowl and leave the peel to soak up the syrup for 2 days. Stir gently occasionally, to ensure that the peel is evenly distributed through the syrup. After 2 days, drain the syrup off the peels into a saucepan and add another 8 oz/225g granulated sugar. Stir over gentle heat to dissolve, then add the peel to the pan and simmer gently until it is semi-transparent. Turn into a bowl, or a large preserving jar and leave the peel in the syrup for 2-3 weeks. After this time, drain off the syrup and lay the peel out on a wire rack. Cover lightly with greaseproof paper and leave to dry out. Any remaining syrup can be dribbled into the upturned halves of peel where it will crystallise and help preserve the fruit. Break off or rinse off before chopping up to use in puddings, fruit cakes, mincemeat etc, or slice the candied orange peel thinly to serve as it is or half-dipped in plain chocolate with after-dinner coffee as a sweetmeat. (See Christmas Gifts)

SURE-SET RECIPES

Thrifty Out-of-Season Marmalade

Anybody who has ever used Sure-Set Sugar for making small quantities of quick foolproof preserves will appreciate the confidence that this special sugar and pectin mixture gives when you want to make something which can be tricky (such as strawberry jam, which is notoriously difficult to set), something you just want to be quick and certain of (such as fruit jellies based on juice) or something which is theoretically impossible, such as my Thrifty Out-of-Season Marmalade which is a bit like my father's Super-Economical Marmalade (see Winter Preserves) except that it contains no whole fruit at all... This is a really handy recipe if you run out of home-made marmalade before the new season's marmalade oranges are due in.

After squeezing the breakfast juice, keep the citrus skins in the fridge for a day or two until you have 3 lb/1.4 Kg skins — the equivalent of about 5 grapefruit and 7 oranges. They can go into a bag in the freezer if the collection will take longer than a couple of days. Put the peels into a large saucepan and cover generously with cold water. Bring to the boil and, if there is grapefruit in the mixture, drain off the water and start again with a new batch. Bring to the boil and simmer, uncovered, for 1-1½ hours, or until all the peels are really tender. Remove from the pan with a slotted spoon and, as soon as cool enough to handle, chop roughly and put through a mincer or turn into a food processor and chop fairly finely in several batches, but be careful not to over-process. Turn into a bowl. Measure the cooking liquid left in the saucepan and make up to 1 pint/600 ml with water if necessary; add to the chopped peel — it should make a fairly slushy mixture. Measure back into the rinsed saucepan and add Sure Set Sugar in the proportion of 1 lb/450g per 1 pint/600 ml processed fruit — this should work out at about 3½ pints/2.1 litres to 3½ lb/1.6 Kg sugar. Stir over gentle heat until the sugar has completely dissolved, then bring up to the boil and boil hard until setting point is reached. For a 1 Kg/2lb 3 oz batch of jam or marmalade using Sure-Set the boiling time is exactly 4 minutes from the time the mixture comes to a full boil so, for this slightly larger batch, I allow 5 minutes. Have about a dozen assorted jars warming in the oven — this batch makes about 10 jars, appproximately 8 lb/3.6 Kg marmalade. Not bad for something made entirely as a side product.

Note: Preserves made with Sure-Set seem to boil especially vigorously and have a tendency to splash, so the bigger the saucepan the better — a preserving pan is highly recommended, even for quite small quantities.

Quick Apple Jelly

A short-cut version using fresh juice or pure juice in cartons.

Heat the apple juice and add the Sure-Set, stirring over low heat until it has completely dissolved. Add the lemon juice. Bring to the boil and boil vigorously for 1 minute, timing accurately from the time the mixture is boiling hard. Pour into small, clean, warmed jars and fill right to the top to allow for shrinkage. Leave until absolutely cold before covering. Label and store in a cool, dark place until required.

Variation: For **Quick Mint Jelly**, substitute about ¼ pint/150 ml cider vinegar for some of the apple juice and stir in about 3 tablespoons finely chopped young mint leaves just before potting. A few drops of green colouring can be added at the same time if you like.

1⅓ pints/¾ litre apple juice
2 lb/1 Kg Sure-Set sugar
Juice of 1 lemon

Cranberry and Cider Jelly

Cranberry and Cider Jelly is a versatile jelly which is very quick and easy to make. Store it in small jars which are neat enough to put on the table — dressed up with attractive labels and lid covers they make great little gifts or additions to a home-made hamper for Christmas.

Heat the fruit juice and cider gently and add the Sure-Set, stirring over low heat until it has completely dissolved. Add the lemon juice. Bring to the boil and boil vigorously for 1 minute, timing from the moment it begins to boil hard. Remove from the heat and pour into small, clean, warmed jars. Leave until absolutely cold before covering. Label and store in a cool, dark place until required.

Makes about 3 lb/1.75 Kg jelly.
1 pint/600ml cranberry juice
⅓ pint/200 ml cider
2 lb/1 Kg Sure-Set sugar
Juice of 1 lemon.

CHRISTMAS   Diary of the Big Day

It's inclined to be something of a marathon, so get the day off to a good start with family and friends sharing a brunch of Buck's Fizz (equal parts of champagne/sparkling wine and freshly squeezed orange juice) and establish a good base with a plateful of Croque Monsieur. This delicious French speciality — a hot sandwich of ham and cheese which can be fried or toasted — makes ideal finger food and is highly nutritious.

Croque Monsieur
For 8:

16 slices of white bread
About 1/4 lb/100g butter, at room temperature
8 slices lean cooked ham
8 oz/225g Cheddar cheese, grated or thinly sliced
About 2 oz/ 50g butter and 2 tbsp oil if frying.

Butter the bread and cover half of the slices with the ham and cheese. Top with the remaining bread, press firmly together and trim off the crusts. Cut each sandwich into three fingers. Heat the butter and oil in a frying pan and cook the bread fingers in it until golden brown on both sides. Drain on kitchen paper as they are cooked and serve hot. Alternatively, toast under the grill.

To follow this fairly substantial beginning, I like to make a huge bowl of popcorn which everyone can dip into as they like through the morning — it's easy, healthy and won't ruin the main meal if you have it at lunchtime.

When it comes to dinner, it obviously pays to have all the main preparation done on Christmas Eve. Personally I don't think a first course is necessary before such a big meal but if you feel the occasion demands it, keep it very light and simple — hot baked grapefruit with brown sugar and sherry, perhaps, or melon with Parma ham. Traditionally, the turkey should be stuffed the night before too, and it certainly makes Christmas morning easier, but health scares have led to recommendations that the stuffing be prepared but not actually go into the bird until the morning. I feel that this is probably unnecessary providing you make sure the bird is well cooked, but extra care is advisable if you are using a frozen turkey. Make sure it is completely thawed before cooking (allow 48 hours in a cool place for a small turkey, 3 days for a large one) and, if is still very cold and you are in any doubt, cook the stuffing separately so that the heat can get right into the bird.

A meat thermometer will tell you when the centre is properly cooked, although testing with a skewer in the thigh is quite reliable: if the juices run clear, with no tinges of pink, the bird is cooked.

TURKEY TABLE

For traditional roast turkey, cooked whole on the bone:

Thawing: If using frozen turkey, leave in the bag and allow plenty of time to thaw at cool room temperature. Remove giblets as soon as they are loose and use to make stock for the gravy. When thoroughly thawed, transfer to the fridge; cook as soon as possible.

Stuffing: Stuff fairly loosely to allow fast heat penetration; extra stuffing can be cooked separately for about 1 hour. Stuff and truss just before cooking.

Cooking: Weigh the stuffed bird and calculate the cooking time to be ready half an hour before serving to allow the flesh to firm up so it is easier to slice. Spread the bird with butter, grind pepper over, wrap loosely in foil or put straight into a roasting tin. Cook in a preheated oven 350°F, 180°C, Gas mark 4; about 45 minutes before the end of cooking time, fold back foil to allow browning. Baste regularly.

Testing: Insert a fine skewer into a turkey thigh. If the juices run clear, it is cooked. If the juices are still pinkish, return to the oven to cook a little longer.

Note: Leftover turkey should be cooled quickly and refrigerated; don't leave it standing in a warm room.

TIMING

Small turkey, 8-11 lb / 3.6-5 Kg oven-ready weight: if frozen, allow 18-20 hours thawing time at room temperature; allow 2 1/2-3 hours cooking time without foil, 3 1/2-4 hours if foil wrapped. Provides 10-15 servings.

Medium turkey, 11-15 lb/5-6.8 Kg oven-ready weight: if frozen, allow 20-24 hours thawing time at room temperature; allow 3-3 1/4 hours cooking time without foil, 4-5 hours if foil wrapped. Provides 15-20 servings.

Large turkey, 15-20 lb/6.8-9 Kg oven-ready weight: if frozen, allow 24-30 hours thawing time at room temperature; allow 3-4 hours cooking time without foil, 5-5 1/2 hours if foil wrapped. Provides 20-30 servings.

Hints to get the best from your turkey

If you are choosing your own fresh turkey, look for a broad-breasted bird which will give a high proportion of tender white meat. Another good sign is a flare of white up either side of the breast, as this thin layer of fat will keep it moist during cooking.

Make sure you get the neck and giblets; remove from the body cavity before stuffing and use to make stock for a good gravy.

Traditional forcemeat, flavoured with herbs and lemon, is my favourite stuffing for both ends of the bird. Although you can also use sausagemeat or chestnut stuffing, I find them heavy and prefer the sausages baked and served separately and chestnuts cooked whole and mixed with underdone sprouts. In fact, a lump of butter and a peeled onion is enough to give flavour in the body cavity. Any leftovers can be used to make stuffing balls, which are crisp and easy to serve separately.

For a traditional roast, spread the turkey with soft butter, cover with bacon rashers and buttered paper or a square of double thickness butter muslin. (You can baste through the muslin.) Cook in an oven preheated to 425°F, 220°C, Gas mark 7 for half an hour, then reduce to 350°F, 180°C, Gas mark 4 for a small bird (under 12 lb/5.4 Kg) or 325°F, 160°C, Gas mark 3 for a larger one for the remaining time. Allow 15 minutes per lb/450g and 15 minutes over for the small bird, 12 minutes per lb/450g for larger

birds. A big turkey, 18-20 lb/8-9 Kg, will take 4½-5 hours.

Slow roasting is ideal if you have dinner in the evening and ensures succulence in large turkeys. Set in an oven heated to 325°F, 160°C, Gas mark 3 and allow 25 minutes per lb/450g for turkeys under 12 lb/5.4 Kg, or 20 minutes per lb/450g for a larger one.

On a meat thermom-eter, the bird is cooked when a temperature of 190°F, 90°C is reached.

Sprinkle a heaped table-spoon of flour in the roasting tin underneath the turkey. During roasting, the flour absorbs drippings and colours; this will help make a rich gravy with the giblet and vegetable stocks.

Allow the roast turkey to stand for at least 15 minutes before carving, so that the juices can settle and it will slice better. As long as the skin is not pierced, it will hold in the heat.

Bacon rolls provide a good alternative to ham with hot turkey. The ham can then be cooked ahead and provide more variety at a meal of cold turkey and fresh vegetables on St Stephen's Day. Cranberry sauce and a good gravy is all you need with hot turkey, but sweet pickled fruits such as peaches in brandy are delicious when it is served cold. Cumber-land sauce is lovely too, especially with ham.

Christmas Day Countdown

Based on a 10-12 lb /4.5-5.5 Kg stuffed turkey in foil to serve at 1 pm:

08.30: Put the turkey in to roast.

09.00: Put Christmas Pudding on to steam; check water regularly.

10.30: Put potatoes in to roast. Add finishing touches to table; prepare wines.

11.15: Unwrap turkey, baste and continue cooking. Put plates and serving dishes to warm.

12.30: Put bacon rolls and chipolatas into the oven with the turkey, or cook under a hot grill. Keep warm. Make white sauce — rum or brandy — if using; keep warm. Test turkey with a skewer; if cooked, wrap in foil and keep warm beside the oven or leave in a low oven for 20 minutes to keep warm. Make gravy. Cook vegetables; drain and keep warm. Reheat Bread Sauce, adding a little milk to thin if necessary. Remove Trifle or other sweet from fridge.

12.50: Turn out the Christmas Pudding; cover with foil until ready to serve.

13.00: Put turkey on a carving dish; if serving a large number, carve in the kitchen, transfer to a serving platter, cover and keep warm.

CHRISTMAS and NEW YEAR

DECEMBER — THE PARTY SEASON

After the build-up of preparations throughout the autumn, Christmas and New Year mark the high point of the culinary year. Christmas itself means family get-togethers, lots of hungry mouths to be fed and an ongoing atmosphere of 'special occasions' at every meal. For the cook under pressure, careful planning is the only way to be able to enjoy company and, especially, provide hospitality without adding unnecessary strain to a heavy schedule of other commitments. For the lucky cook who has time to take on a challenge with enjoyment, Christmas and the party season bring a unique chance to spread the wings, gastronomically speaking. A lot of my favourite special occasion recipes come into this section — and, of course, many of them are equally suitable for other times of year. Although this kind of cookery is relatively time-consuming, these are practical recipes and nothing unnecessarily fiddly has been included. What's more, because it's out of the everyday, budget-conscious rut, it is fun. At Christmas, as other times of year, the best ingredients are those at the peak of their season and many of the familiar Christmas foods have become traditional for that very reason. This is the most wonderful time of year to shop for food — there's a bountiful feeling in the air and shops are full of displays to tempt the most hard-hearted to part with their money for food that is out of the ordinary. Game and poultry are especially tempting, but the butchers compete with wonderful hams and succulent roasts that are strictly for special occasions. It is probably at the greengrocers that the sense of excitement is strongest: there are all our quiet under-stated winter vegetables — the leeks and parsnips, cabbages and sprouts, artichokes and onions — jostling for space with the nuts and brightly-coloured citrus fruits that used to be the treat in the toes of Christmas stockings. It's evocative, it's exciting. The dried fruit is at its best too, bringing with it the mystery of the east. Ah, how could anyone resist?

FRESH FOODS IN SEASON include:

Poultry and Game: Duck, goose, grouse, guinea fowl, hare, mallard, partridge, pheasant, pigeon, quail, snipe, teal, venison, and, of course, turkey.

Vegetables: Avocado pears; beetroot; broccoli; brussels sprouts; cabbages; carrots; cauliflower; celeriac; celery; chicory; endive; fennel; garlic; horseradish; Jerusalem artichokes; kale; leeks; lettuces; mushrooms; onions; parsley; parsnips; peppers; potatoes; salsify; savoys; sea kale; shallots; spinach; scallions; swedes; tomatoes (imported); turnips; watercress.

Fruit and Nuts (including imports): Almonds, apples, apricots, bananas, brazil nuts, chestnuts, clementines, coconuts, cranberries, dates, figs, grapefruit, grapes, lemons, mandarins, melons, oranges, pears, pineapples, rhubarb (forced), pomegranates, satsumas, tangerines, walnuts, plus, a very wide range of dried fruits.

SUGGESTED MENUS

Christmas Dinner
Melon and Orange Cocktail;
Roast Goose with Cranberry Port Sauce;
Roast Potatoes;
Glazed Jerusalem Artichokes and Red Cabbage
with Apple;
Christmas Pudding with Rum Butter;
Christmas Ice Cream;
Gaelic Coffee and Petits Fours.

New Year's Eve Party
Mulled Wine and Spiced Beef Canapés;
Coriander Pork with Apricots;
Pilaf of Brown Rice with Toasted Almonds;
Orange and Endive Salad;
Celery, Apple and Walnut Salad;
Ratafia Trifle;
Profiteroles with Chocolate Sauce;
Oranges with Grand Marnier.

Dinner Party for Friends
Crab and Mushroom Ramekins with Olives;
Pheasants in Red Wine;
Game Chips; Boiled Potatoes;
Glazed Turnips; Sprouts with Chestnuts;
Grape Pudding.

New Year's Day Dinner
Pears with Cashel Blue Cream and Walnuts;
Crown Roast of Lamb and Cranberry Stuffing;
New Potatoes (if available) or Roast Potatoes;
Glazed Onions; French Beans or Mangetout;
Mincemeat Meringue Pie;
Bombe Favourite with Raspberry Coulis.

First courses for the festive season — Christmas itself makes for a 'fifth' season for cooks — range from the ultra-simple, which will balance up the quantity and richness of a major meal, to the rather sophisticated dish required to create interest and stimulate the palate at the outset of a formal dinner party. A few of each are given here, but check other chapters for a wider selection. Vegetables for big meals need to be a little different, without being too filling and salads are best kept very simple, with strong, clear flavours. Again, check other sections, including Basic Recipes, for ideas.

Onions à la Grèque

Little button onions are good and easily available at this time of year and Onions à la Grèque is a classic first course which makes the most of them in a dish which can be prepared well ahead. [Microwave]

To peel the onions, cut off the tops and bottoms with a sharp knife and drop the onions into a large pan of boiling water. Leave for 1 minute, then drain and leave until cool enough to handle. The skins will now come off them very easily.

Put all remaining ingredients into a heavy-based pan, season to taste with salt and pepper, then add the onions. Bring to the boil and cook gently for about 20 minutes, or until the onions are just tender. Remove the onions with a slotted spoon and set aside. Note the level of the sauce and boil hard for 10-15 minutes, or until it has reduced by a quarter. Strain the sauce over the onions and leave to cool. Chill well before serving in soup plates, garnished simply with a light scattering of finely chopped parsley.

Serves 6:
1½ lb/700g button or
   pickling onions
1 pint/600 ml dry white
   wine
½ pint/300 ml water
2oz/50g caster sugar
5 tablespoons olive oil
8 juniper berries
Juice of 1 lemon
1 bay leaf
2 tablespoons tomato purée
Small bunch parsley
½ teaspoon freshly
   chopped basil
Salt and freshly ground
   black pepper
Garnish: 3 tablespoons
   freshly chopped parsley.

Pears with Cashel Blue Cream and Walnuts

Pears with Cashel Blue Cream and Walnuts is a piquant first course and very simple to make. Its success depends on the quality of the pears, which must be very succulent.

Salad base for serving, for example: curly endive, oakleaf lettuce, radicchio and, perhaps, a cherry tomato and a scattering of roughly chopped walnuts.

Mash the cream cheese and Cashel Blue together in a mixing bowl with a good grinding of black pepper, then blend in the cream to make a smooth mixture. Add the chopped nuts and mix to distribute evenly. Cover and keep in the fridge until required. Peel and halve the pears and scoop out the core. Put them into a bowl of acidulated water. Whisk all the dressing ingredients together. Arrange a bed of salad on six plates — shallow soup plates are ideal. Drain the pears well and pat dry with kitchen paper, then turn them in the prepared dressing and arrange, hollow side up on the leaves. Divide the Cashel Blue mixture between the six pears, spoon the dressing over the pears and garnish each half with half a walnut and a sprig of flat-leaf parsley.

Pears with Cashel Blue Cream: Serves 6

4 oz/100g fresh cream
   cheese
3 oz/75g ripe Cashel Blue
Freshly ground black
   pepper
2-3 tablespoons cream
1 oz/25g chopped
   walnuts/pecans
6 ripe pears.
Salad (see method)

Dressing
Juice of 1 lemon
A little finely grated lemon
   zest
Sea salt and freshly ground
   black pepper
Pinch of caster sugar
4 tablespoons olive oil
Walnut or pecan halves and
   a few sprigs of flat-leaf
   parsley to garnish.

Grilled Grapefruit

Another good first course which seems to have disappeared from view in recent years is Grilled Grapefruit — a pity, as the contrast of cold and hot, sweet and sour is very pleasing. Minus the sherry, this has always been especially popular with children and is well worth reviving.

Preheat a hot grill. Halve the grapefruit horizontally, remove any pips

Grilled Grapefruit: Serves 4:

2 large, juicy grapefruit
4 dessertspoons
   medium-dry sherry
   (optional)
Demerara sugar
1 oz/25g butter.

Serves 8 as a starter:

8 oz/225g very fresh button
   mushrooms
2 cloves garlic, peeled and
   crushed
Juice of 1/2 lemon and a
   little grated zest
Dash of Tabasco
4 fl oz/100 ml olive oil
Pinch of caster sugar
Salt and freshly ground
   black pepper
8 oz/225g flaked white
   crabmeat, preferably fresh
5 fl oz/150 ml double cream
1 head Florence fennel,
   trimmed
1 orange, peeled and
   segmented
 3-4 oz/75-100g black olives.

Melon Cocktail: Serves 8

1 large, ripe honeydew
   melon
4 oz/100g caster sugar
2 large juicy oranges,
   peeled and segmented
Finely grated zest and juice
   of 1 large orange
Juice of 1/2 lemon
1-2 tablespoons strawberry
   or raspberry vinegar
   (optional)
Fresh mint leaves to
   decorate.

Glazed Turnips: Serves 6

2 lb/900g small white
   turnips
1 oz/25g unsalted butter or
   oil
1 teaspoon caster sugar
About 1/4 pint/150 ml
   chicken or vegetable stock
A small sprig of thyme
Salt and freshly ground
   black pepper.

and cut out the centre core from each half. Using a grapefruit knife, detach each segment from its surrounding membrane, so it can be lifted out easily. Arrange the grapefruit on the grill pan. Spoon the sherry into the fruit (if using) and sprinkle generously with Demerara sugar. Put a small knob of butter on top of each half and grill until the sugar has melted to make a hot, crunchy caramelised topping. Serve immediately.

Crab and Mushroom Ramekins with Olives

This is an easy and versatile dish which can be made with fresh, frozen or even tinned crabmeat according to availability. Although given here as a first course, it can easily be adapted to make a light main course for lunch or supper.

Trim the mushrooms and slice thinly into a deep bowl. Combine with the garlic, lemon juice and zest, a light dash of Tabasco and the olive oil. Season to taste with sugar, sea salt and freshly ground pepper, mix everything thoroughly together and chill, covered, for at least an hour. When ready to serve, mix the flaked crabmeat with the cream and stir the mixture into the mushrooms. Divide between eight ramekins and put each one on a plate. Reserving the feathery green leaves for garnish, slice the fennel fairly finely and arrange, with the orange segments around the edge of the ramekins. Garnish each ramekin with one or two black olives and a sprig of fennel leaves and scatter any remaining olives around the bases. Serve with warm home-made brown bread.

Melon and Orange Cocktail

Light, fruity first courses make a refreshing start to meals based on a rich and filling main course and they're also a simple and practical choice for the cook. The reputation of fruit cocktails has suffered unfairly because of low standards in hotel dining rooms over the years but, properly made, they can be delicious. This Melon and Orange Cocktail, for example, is juicy, colourful and simplicity itself — the perfect appetiser.

Halve the melon, scoop out the seeds and cut into quarters. Either use a melon baller to scoop out all the flesh from the quarters, or cut again into eighths, slide a sharp knife under each section and detach the flesh from the skin, then cut up into bite-sized dice. Put the balls or dice into a bowl and sprinkle with the caster sugar. Add the orange segments, zest of orange, the strained orange and lemon juice and, if using, the fruit vinegar. Toss well to blend all ingredients thoroughly. Cover and leave in a cool place overnight, or at least for several hours, to allow the juice to run from the melon and blend with the other fruit juices. Chill for at least an hour before serving, garnished with fresh mint leaves, in chilled cocktail glasses.

Glazed Turnips

Turnips are probably about as under-rated as any vegetable could be, yet this recipe for Glazed Turnips proves they can be a gastronomic treat, especially when served with joints of venison, beef or lamb.

If the turnips are very small (not larger than a golf ball), leave them whole. If larger, peel and cut into 1/2"/1.25 cm slices and then across into bâtons. Melt the fat in a large, heavy-based pan, big enough to take the turnips in a single layer. Add the turnips, sprinkle with sugar and cook gently, shaking the pan occasionally, for 5-10 minutes, or until lightly browned. Add a little of the stock, the sprig of thyme and a seasoning of salt and pepper. Cover and cook gently for another 5 minutes or until the turnips are glazed and tender, shaking the pan frequently and adding more stock if necessary.

Facing Page: Stuffed Pork Tenderloin with Apricot Sauce, page 114
Overleaf: Decorating Christmas Cakes, page 168

Jerusalem Artichokes

Jerusalem Artichokes are even more neglected than turnips (if that is possible) but they're one of my favourite winter vegetables. Their knobbly brown exterior hides a flesh of such sweet whiteness that it takes very little help to glaze them — and newer varieties are much easier to peel.

Peel the artichokes, dropping them straight into a bowl of water acidulated with a good dash of lemon juice or vinegar to prevent browning. Cut up so that the pieces are matched for size, otherwise they will cook unevenly. Preheat a moderate oven, 350°F, 180°F, Gas mark 4. Bring a large pan of salted water to the boil, drain the artichokes and boil them for about 5 minutes, or until just tender. Watch them carefully, as they break up easily. Melt the butter in a roasting tin, coat the artichokes in the seasoned flour and roll them around in the butter, then put into the oven for 20-30 minutes, or until golden brown.

Variation: Take a short cut with this recipe: omit the flouring entirely and use ordinary salted butter. If you keep a close eye on it, you can also speed up the process by browning the artichokes at a higher temperature.

Serves 6:
1 ½ lb/700g Jerusalem artichokes
Lemon juice or vinegar, as required
Salt
2 oz/50g unsalted butter
Seasoned flour.

Red Cabbage with Apple

Red Cabbage is one of the most useful and versatile of all the winter vegetables. Like the other hard cabbages, it is ideal for crunchy salads and coleslaws; it can be cooked lightly like its green relations and served crisp and brilliant red but it is the only brassica to survive long cooking with dignity and it can even be cooked ahead and reheated. It combines well with fruit, especially apple and raisins or sultanas, and makes a perfect partner for many robust winter dishes, especially game.

For this recipe, the cabbage is cooked on the hob and it can be used while it is still crunchy, but it could also be cooked gently in a slowish oven, 300-325°F/150-170°C/Gas mark 2-3. Heat the oil and butter over low heat in a large heavy-based pan. Shred the cabbage and turn in the fat, until glistening all over. Peel and chop the onion and add to the pan, then peel and slice the cooking apple and stir in. Cook gently until softening, then stir in the redcurrant jelly and the sugar. When they have dissolved, turn up the heat and quickly stir in the vinegar. Season to taste with salt and freshly ground black pepper, add the crushed allspice and bring back up to the boil. Either serve immediately, for a bright, crunchy side dish, or continue to cook gently until the cabbage and onion have softened and the apple has fallen to form a sauce. Any leftovers may be reheated.

Red Cabbage with Apple: Serves 4-6
4 tablespoons olive oil
1 oz/25g butter
1 small red cabbage
1 onion
1 large cooking apple
1 tablespoon redcurrant jelly
1 tablespoon rich dark brown sugar
2 tablespoons red wine vinegar
Sea salt and freshly ground pepper
3 or 4 allspice berries, crushed (optional).

Hot Devilled Beetroot

Beetroot is another vegetable that tends to be under-rated and is all too often thought of only as a pickle or, at best, a cold salad vegetable. But of course it's much more versatile than we give it credit for: try this Hot Devilled Beetroot, for example — it's especially good with baked ham or gammon.

Cook the unpeeled beetroot gently in salted water for about an hour, or until tender. Drain, peel and keep warm. Add the finely chopped onion to the vinegar and crushed peppercorns in a saucepan and boil, uncovered, over medium heat until reduced to only 1 tablespoon. Stir in the tomato purée, sugar, cayenne, mustard and Worcestershire sauce. Add the stock and bring to the boil. Blend the cornflour with the cold water, stir in a little of the hot liquid then add the mixture to the pan and cook for a few minutes, stirring, until the sauce clears and thickens. Arrange the hot beetroot in a serving dish (halve or quarter them if they are big), cover with the sauce and sprinkle with freshly chopped parsley.

Hint: Cooking times for beetroot vary widely, depending on age and

Hot Devilled Beetroot: Serves 6
2 lb/900g beetroot, preferably small ones
1 onion, peeled and chopped
4 tablespons wine/cider vinegar
1 small coffeespoon black peppercorns (about a dozen)
1 tablespoon tomato purée
1 oz/25g rich dark brown sugar
Pinch of cayenne pepper
1 coffeespoonful mustard powder
1 tablespoon Worcestershire sauce
¾ pint/450 ml beef or vegetable stock
1 rounded tablespoon cornflour
2 tablespoons cold water
Freshly chopped parsley.

size. A very simple test is to pinch the skin between thumb and forefinger: when it comes away easily, the beetroot is ready. DO NOT test like other vegetables with the point of a sharp knife, or the deep red juices will bleed into the cooking water. For the same reason, don't trim stalks off with a knife before cooking, simply twist them off neatly and leave all cutting until the beetroot is fully cooked.

Hot Beetroot with Orange

Serves 3-4:

1 large or 2 medium cooked beetroot
2 oz/50g butter
1 tablespoon olive oil
Thinly peeled and shredded zest of ½ orange
Juice of 1 small orange
1 coffeespoon coriander seeds, crushed
Salt and caster sugar to season.

If you have plain boiled beetroot left over for any reason, it can still be served as a hot side dish as, for instance in Hot Beetroot with Orange.

Peel the beetroot and dice into about ½"/1.2 cm cubes. Heat butter and oil over moderate heat in a heavy-based pan, add the beetroot and heat through with the orange zest and juice. Stir in the crushed coriander seeds and season to taste with salt and sugar. When all ingredients are thoroughly heated through but not boiling, serve quickly to catch the freshness of the flavours.

Hint: If you prefer a more subtle orange flavour, blanch the shredded zest in boiling water for a minute, then drain and refresh under the cold tap before using.

Spiced Parsnips

Serves 6:

2 lb/900g parsnips
2 oz/50g butter or dripping
1 tablespoon oil, preferably olive
1 level dessertspoon light golden brown sugar
1 teaspoon each, ground cumin and ground coriander
1 large clove garlic, crushed in ½ tsp salt
Finely grated zest of 1 orange
Freshly ground black pepper
Freshly chopped coriander (optional).

Parsnips are particularly good roasted. For simple family meals, I very often chop them up into large chunks and mix them in with the potatoes around any kind of joint. For grander occasions, try dressing them up to make Spiced Parsnips.

Have ready a hot oven, 400-425°F/200-220°C/Gas mark 6-7. (This is not crucial — a cooler or hotter oven can be used to suit the main dish.) Peel the parsnips and cut into large, even-sized chunks about the size of a small potato. Parboil in lightly salted water for 5 minutes, or until just changing texture. Turn into a colander and leave to drain. Put the butter or dripping and oil into a roasting tin and heat in the oven. Meanwhile, mix together the sugar, spices, crushed garlic and grated orange zest. Turn the chunks of parsnip in the hot fat, sprinkle evenly with the spice mixture and turn to mix well. Put into the hot oven and cook, turning occasionally, for ¾-1 hour, or until the parsnips are crisp and golden-brown on the outside and tender in the middle. Lift out with a slotted spoon and transfer to a warmed serving dish, season lightly with salt and freshly ground pepper and sprinkle with freshly chopped coriander leaves, if using.

Variation: A mild curry powder could be used instead of the ground cumin and coriander if preferred.

Caramel Onions with Cloves

Serves 4-6:

1 ½lb/700g button onions, or shallots
About ¼ oz/7g whole cloves (30 cloves)
Good pinch of salt
1 ½ oz/40g butter
2 level tablespoons caster sugar.

Like the Onions à la Grèque given above, Caramel Onions with Cloves makes the most of those delicious little button onions. Shallots could be used instead for this hot side dish, if preferred, but they are more unevenly sized. Serve with turkey, or other poultry.

Put the onions into a bowl, cover with boiling water and leave to stand for a few minutes. Drain off the water and, as soon as they are cool enough to handle, the skins will come off easily. Stick cloves into half of the onions. Put the onions into a heavy-based pan, add just enough cold water to cover and a good pinch of salt. Bring slowly to the boil, then drain thoroughly. Add the butter and sugar to the pan, cover, and cook over gentle heat for about 15 minutes, or until golden brown, turning occasionally.

Chicory and Orange Salad with Walnuts

Salads often seem to me to be more enjoyable in winter, when cool, colourful side dishes provide a perfect foil for hearty main courses and the tangy seasonal salad ingredients tend to be crisp and characterful. Chicory and Orange Salad with Walnuts is one of my favourites and, although it makes a good accompaniment to most game or meat, whether hot or cold, it goes especially well with pâtés and terrines and rich meats such as pork or duck. The nuts are optional.

Trim the root ends and any brown leaves from the chicory. Rinse and shake off excess water, then slice the chicory horizontally and put into a salad bowl. Peel the oranges and remove all pith, then halve vertically and remove any hard core. Slice horizontally with a sharp saw-edged knife and remove any pips.

Put the oranges into the bowl with the chicory and scatter on the walnuts. Whisk the dressing ingredients together in a small bowl; taste for seasoning and adjust as necessary. Just before serving, add enough dressing to make the salad glisten without leaving a pool in the bottom of the bowl, toss well and serve.

Variation: Another salad that is similar in character but sharper and more peppery is **Watercress and Grapefruit Salad with Toasted Pine Kernels**. Make more or less as above, but be careful with the dressing — zest of grapefruit is not to everybody's taste, so use lemon juice and zest instead in the dressing. Orange also combines well with watercress and the nuts are variable — walnuts, slivered brazils, toasted hazelnuts or almonds are all good.

Celery and Apple Salad with Walnuts

Celery and Apple Salad with Walnuts is a variation on the great American classic, Waldorf Salad and can also be served as a first course, although (like the previous salads) it also works especially well with rich meats like pork and duck.

Wash and core the apples, but do not peel them unless the skin is tough. Dice the apples. Mix together the lemon juice, caster sugar and 1 tablespoon of the mayonnaise and put this dressing into a salad bowl with the chopped apples. Mix well so that the apples will not brown. Trim the celery, remove any coarse outer stalks and discard (to the stock pot); check any remaining large stalks for coarse strings and remove if necessary, then slice fairly finely. Add to the salad bowl along with the rest of the mayonnaise, the yogurt and 2 oz/50g of the roughly chopped walnuts. Mix well, taste for seasoning and add salt and freshly ground black pepper to taste. Chill before serving with the remaining 1 oz/25g walnuts scattered over the salad.

Serves 6:
4 heads Belgian endive
 (chicory)
3 large, juicy oranges
2-3 oz/50-75g walnuts,
 roughly chopped
 (optional)

Dressing:
2 tablespoons strained
 lemon or orange juice
A little finely grated zest of
 orange
1 teaspoon smooth Dijon
 mustard
Salt, freshly ground pepper,
 caster sugar to taste
4 tablespoons olive oil.

Note: The names chicory and endive are confusing, but Belgian endive is a broad-leaved chicory, a smooth, tight salading with pale green tips on the leaves. Its cousin, curly endive (or chicorée frisée) has a similar bitter flavour but is a much larger plant with very curly leaves that are green on the outside and a pale creamy yellow in the centre.

Celery and Apple Salad:
 Serves 6
4 crisp eating apples (about
 1 lb/450g), preferably
 red-skinned
2 tablespoons lemon juice
1 teaspoon caster sugar
5 tablespoons mayonnaise
1 good head of celery
5 tablespoons natural yogurt
3 oz/75g walnuts, roughly
 chopped
Salt and freshly ground
 black pepper.

Tradition takes the spotlight for Christmas main courses, although it can be nice to give a new twist to the old familiars if the family will allow it, which is unlikely in the case of Christmas Dinner. Apart from the main festive meal of the season however, there are usually plenty of other, less tradition-bound opportunities for celebration and the suggestions given below would cover a wide variety of occasions, ranging from family feasts, to dinner parties and buffet parties.

Spiced Beef

Serves 8 as a main course (many more as a party snack):

4 lb/1.8 Kg tailend or lean silverside
8 oz/225g salt
4 oz/100g brown sugar
1 rounded teaspoon saltpetre
2 pints/1.15 litres water, approximately
1 level tablespoon coarsely ground black pepper
1 level tablespoon juniper berries, crushed
2 teaspoons ground ginger
3 teaspoons ground cloves
1 teaspoon grated nutmeg
2 teaspoons ground mace
3 teaspoons allspice, crushed
1 teaspoon freshly chopped thyme
2 crushed bayleaves
1 small onion, finely chopped
1/2 pint/300 ml stout (optional).

Serves about 8 as a main course, (more as a starter or party snack)

4 lb/1.8 Kg corned beef, silverside or tailend
1 tablespoon coarsely ground black pepper
2 teaspooons ground ginger
1 tablespoon juniper berries, crushed
1 tablespoon coriander seeds, crushed
1 teaspoon ground cloves
3 teaspoons allspice
3 tablespoons rich dark brown sugar
2 bay leaves, crushed
1 small onion, finely chopped
1/2 pint/300 ml stout.

Spiced Beef is one of the most traditional of all Christmas foods in Ireland and, although you can buy it ready-spiced from the butcher, it is easy to do it at home as long as you allow enough time — this traditional method takes about 10 days, although there is a quicker one given below. Saltpetre, used in the traditional version, is a preservative available from chemists. As well as being an essential part of the Christmas buffet and a great antidote to a surfeit of turkey, spiced beef makes an easy, tasty and nourishing snack to hand around at drinks parties — just slice it very thinly and serve on squares of lightly buttered dark home-made wholemeal bread. Delicious!

Put the beef into a large saucepan with the salt, sugar, salpetre and enough water to cover. Bring slowly to the boil. Boil for 10 minutes, then turn off the heat and leave to cool. When cold, transfer to a suitable container and leave the meat in the fridge for 5 or 6 days to pickle, turning daily. Remove the meat from the pickle and leave to drain well. Meanwhile, thoroughly mix all the spices, the bay leaves and chopped onion in a bowl. Discard the pickling liquid and rub the spice mixture into the meat, then return to the fridge for 3-4 days, turning and rubbing in the spice mixture daily.

To cook, put the spiced beef into a pan, just cover with cold water, cover with a lid and bring slowly to the boil. Reduce the heat to a simmer and cook very gently for about 3 1/2 hours, adding the stout for the last half hour. Can be served hot with vegetables but is much more popular served cold, in which case leave to cool in the cooking liquid, then drain well, wrap in foil and store in the fridge until required. It will be easier to slice thinly if the cooked meat is compressed by putting it into a container it fits quite neatly, covering it with foil and a weight and leaving overnight before slicing.

Quick Spiced Beef

Quick Spiced Beef takes the short cut of omitting the initial pickling stage, so it takes about half the time of the traditional version. Using this method the meat stays pink all the way through, making it especially attractive.

First spice the beef by mixing the spices, sugar, bay leaves, and onion together and rubbing this mixture into the meat. Put into a suitable container and leave in the fridge for several days, turning and rubbing every day.

To cook, put the meat into a pan with just enough water to cover it, cover tightly and bring slowly to the boil. Reduce the heat and simmer gently for about 3 1/2 hours, adding the stout for the last hour. When the meat is cooked, leave it to cool in its liquid, then drain well, weight as above if you like, then wrap in foil and keep in the fridge until required.

Whole Glazed Ham

Cooking a whole ham is not something to be taken on lightly these days, but if you have a lot of people to feed over Christmas and the New Year it is a sound investment. The cooking is not difficult and it will provide a lot of easy meals over a busy period. Trust your butcher, make your order well in advance and try, if at all possible, to get a joint from a free-range animal — once you have tasted the difference in flavour and texture, you will understand why it is worth the effort. A whole ham will weigh anything from 10-20lb/4.5-9Kg, but is most likely to be around 12-15 lb/5.4 -6.8 Kg which, allowing ½lb/225g per portion, will give about 24-30 servings. Ask your butcher how long to soak the ham. Most hams available today need only overnight soaking in cold water, then a change of water for cooking but, if you are lucky enough to get a well hung, home-cured ham it could need up to 4 days, with frequent changes. Although consumer demand has resulted in farmers producing leaner animals, a good layer of fat is essential for the flavour and succulence of the meat.

1 x whole ham, fresh or lightly smoked
2 tablespoons Dijon mustard, smooth or wholegrain
4-5 tablespoons Demerara sugar
¼ teaspoon ground cloves
Pineapple pieces or glacé cherries and whole cloves to decorate (optional).

Weigh the ham and calculate the cooking time: 20 minutes per lb/450g and 20 minutes over for joints up to 10 lb/4.5 Kg; 15 minutes per lb/450g and 15 minutes over for joints of 10-15 lb/4.5-6.8 Kg. Joints over 15 lbs/6.8 Kg will not need the extra 15 minutes. After making a note of the weight, cover the ham generously with cold water and soak overnight (or longer if necessary). To cook, put into a very large pan, on a trivet or upturned plate so that it is not resting on the bottom, cover well with fresh cold water and bring gently to the boil — this will take 1-2 hours. If a white froth rises to the top of the water it is probably still too salty — taste it and, if necessary, discard it, cover with fresh cold water and start cooking again. Start timing when the water comes to the boil, subtracting 30 minutes from your original calculation if you have had to change the water. Simmer very gently, checking regularly to make sure that the water is just trembling throughout the cooking time.

To glaze, preheat a hot oven, 400°F/200°C/Gas mark 6. 15 minutes before the end of the calculated cooking time, remove the ham from its liquor, allow to cool for a few minutes to make it easier to handle, then carefully cut off the skin with a small, sharp knife. Score the fat lightly into diamonds. Mix the mustard, brown sugar and ground cloves together to make a glaze and spread it evenly all over the surface of the joint. It can now be left as it is or, for an especially festive presentation, each diamond can be studded with a clove stuck through a pineapple piece or halved glacé cherry, or simply with whole cloves. Bake in the hot oven, for 20-30 minutes or until the joint is nicely brown and glazed. Watch carefully: baste if necessary, and make sure the dripping glaze does not scorch on the bottom of the pan. Serve hot or cold, with Raisin Cider Sauce or Cumberland Sauce.

Variations: If the ham is only to be served cold, boil it until fully cooked, remove the skin and, while still warm, cover the fat with lightly toasted fine breadcrumbs. Another option, if it is to be used whole as part of a buffet display, is to glaze it as above but without any extra decorations. When cold, decorate alternate diamonds with halved glacé cherries or pieces of pineapple, spiked with whole cloves.

Raisin Cider Sauce

Raisin Cider Sauce makes a very good accompaniment to ham when it is served hot. [Microwave]

Makes about ¾ pint/450 ml:
2 oz/50g brown sugar
1 ½ level tablespoons cornflour
Pinch of salt
½ pint/300 ml cider
2 oz/50g raisins
6-8 whole cloves
2"/2.5 cm stick of cinnamon
½ oz/15g butter.

Mix together the sugar, cornflour and salt and put into a saucepan with the cider, chopped raisins, cloves and cinnamon. Bring up to the boil over gentle heat and simmer, stirring, for 10 minutes, then beat in the butter. Remove the spices and serve very hot.

Variation: To make Apple and Raisin Cider Sauce, include a peeled and finely chopped Bramley apple along with the chopped raisins.

Gammon with Spiced Peaches

Serves 6-8:

1 piece of corner gammon,
 3-4 lb/1.4-1.8 Kg
12 oz/350g dried peaches,
 halved
3/4 pint/450 ml water
8-10 whole cloves
6 oz/175g Demerara sugar
4 fl oz/100 ml cider vinegar
2 x 1"/2.5 cm pieces
 cinnamon stick
Glaze: About 2 tablespoons
 apricot jam
1/2 teaspoon mixed spice
 (optional).

Where numbers over Christmas are likely to be smaller, a corner of gammon, usually weighing 3-4 lb/1.4-1.8 Kg, is probably ideal. This delicious Gammon with Spiced Peaches comes complete with its own sauce.

Weigh the gammon and estimate the cooking time, allowing 20 minutes per lb/450g. Cover generously with cold water and leave overnight to soak. Meanwhile, halve the peaches and leave them to soak in the water for several hours, or overnight, then turn them into a saucepan, add the cloves, sugar, vinegar and cinnamon stick and bring to the boil. Reduce the heat, cover and simmer for 10-15 minutes, or until the peaches are tender. Remove the whole spices and set aside about a third of the peaches, then put the remaining fruit and the spiced cooking liquid into a food processor or blender and purée to make a sauce.

To cook the gammon, drain off the soaking water and place the joint in a large pan, skin side down and preferably set on a trivet or upturned plate so the meat is not resting on the bottom of the pan. Add enough fresh cold water to cover generously, bring up slowly to the boil and then cook for the calculated time, checking regularly to make sure that the water is simmering gently all the time. Towards the end of the cooking time, preheat a hot oven, 400°F, 200°C, Gas mark 6. When the joint is cooked, lift it out of its cooking liquor and transfer to a roasting tin. Using a small sharp knife, trim away the rind and mark the fat lightly in diamonds. Spread with the apricot jam, which can be blended with the mixed spice if you like, and bake in the preheated oven for 15-20 minutes until browned and glazed. Serve hot or cold, with the reserved peaches and sauce.

Variation: Other dried fruits can be used, as available, including the mixture sold as 'Dried Fruit Salad'.

Roast Goose with Orange and Walnut Stuffing

Serves 8:

1 goose, weighing about 10
 lb/4.5 Kg
1/2 lemon
Salt and freshly ground
 pepper

Orange and Walnut Stuffing:

3 onions, finely chopped
4 oz/100g butter
12 oz/350g fresh white
 breadcrumbs
3 tablespoons freshly
 chopped parsley
Grated zest and juice of 3
 oranges
3 oz/75g chopped walnuts.

Although turkey has become traditional for Christmas Dinner in Ireland and is now by far the most popular choice, there are other special occasions to cater for over Christmas and the New Year — and a growing minority who prefer to cook something different on Christmas Day. Admittedly, where the numbers are large there's nothing to beat turkey for value and convenience but for smaller groups — say up to about 8 or 10 — the choice is much wider. Goose, for example, is traditional both here and in Scotland for New Year and it's now in great demand again although, weight for weight, it won't feed nearly as many people as a turkey. Unlike other poultry, which is almost all intensively farmed, geese are still free-range, seasonal birds available only from late September until January and various traditions have built up around this seasonality: the old one of the Michaelmas Goose given to the landlord as a sweetener on the quarterly rent day in September, is one example and, of course, its special position as a real treat for festive Christmas and New Year occasions, is due to the fact that it is at the height of its season. When buying an oven-ready bird, it will usually have to be ordered and you need to allow a good 1 lb/450g, per person, in comparison with 12 oz/325g oven-ready turkey. Farmyard geese have big bones and they are very fatty, which makes them very succulent and tender, but the uncooked bird looks deceptively big: an average goose, weighing about 10 lb/4.5 Kg, will only feed 8, whereas a comparable turkey will give 12 servings. The difference is mainly caused by weight loss during cooking as the fat melts down, but this isn't wasteful as you will be left with all that wonderful goose fat for cooking with long after Christmas has been forgotten. To balance the natural richness of goose, choose a stuffing which introduces a balancing sharpness of flavour and will absorb fat during cooking: potato and apple is very traditional here in Ireland, for example, and there's a local tradition in Normandy which should interest us, as it combines black pudding and apples — or you could try this Roast Goose with Orange and Walnut Stuffing.

Remove giblets and neck from the goose cavity and set aside for making stock. Rinse the bird inside and out and pat dry. Rub the skin all over with the cut lemon, then season inside and out with salt and pepper. Using a fork, prick the skin all over without piercing the meat, to help the fat drain off during cooking.

To make the stuffing, cook the onions gently in the butter until softened but not brown. In a bowl, gently stir the butter, softened onion and the juice of 2 of the oranges into the other ingredients with a fork. Preheat a hot oven, 425°F, 220°C, Gas mark 7. Spoon this mixture loosely into the body and neck cavities of the goose. (If there is any left over it can be wrapped in buttered foil and cooked alongside the the bird for the last hour or so of cooking time.) Truss or close with a skewer and make a note of the weight of the bird after stuffing. Place the goose breast side up on a rack in a roasting tin with 3 or 4 tablespoons of water in it. Cook for 20 minutes, then turn the goose upside down and reduce the oven temperature to 350°F, 180°C, Gas mark 4 and continue cooking, allowing 15 minutes per 1 lb/450g. After an hour, turn the goose breast side up again and leave it that way for the rest of the cooking time. Do not baste the bird, but use a baster or a ladle to remove the fat as it accumulates in the tin — this will probably need to be done several times. For the last 15–20 minutes increase the temperature to 450°F, 230°C, Gas mark 8 to get a really crisp, deep golden skin.

Hint: **Goose fat** is a much-prized cooking fat, producing incomparably crisp and flavoursome results in many dishes, especially when searing meats or sautéeing potatoes for example — and, of course, it gives authenticity to classic country dishes such as Cassoulet. Reserve it carefully when cooking the goose then, when there is time, warm it until liquid and strain through several thickness of muslin to remove any impurities. Kept in jars in the fridge, it will keep well for months. (**Duck fat**, although not quite so special, especially if the birds are intensively reared, can be used in the same way.)

Cranberry-Port Sauce

Serve the goose with Apple Sauce, or this Cranberry-Port Sauce, which can be made several days ahead, keeps well in the fridge and is excellent with lamb and pork as well as all kinds of poultry.

Sort through the cranberries and remove any stalks or discoloured berries. Put cranberries, port, sugar, orange juice, orange zest and ginger into a stainless or enamelled pan. Bring to the boil over medium heat, stirring to dissolve the sugar. Reduce the heat and simmer gently for 10–15 minutes until the cranberries have popped and the sauce has thickened slightly. Stir in the redcurrant jelly and set aside to cool. Keep in the fridge until required, but allow to come up to room temperature before serving.

Note: Vegetable and fruit combinations such as Red Cabbage and Apple go especially well with roast goose and, if you have any leftovers, serve cold roast goose with Cumberland Sauce and a salad with fruit in it, such as Orange and Endive or Celery, Apple and Walnut.

Makes about 1/4 pints/750 ml:
1 lb/450g fresh cranberries
6 fl oz/175 ml port
4 oz/100g caster sugar
Finely grated zest and juice of 1 small orange
1 or 2 pieces preserved ginger in syrup, drained and chopped
2 tablespoons redcurrant jelly.

Roast Duckling with Sweet and Sour Grapefruit

Duckling is always a treat and, like goose, the sharpness of fruit used in stuffings, sauces or accompanying dishes will balance its natural richness. If you are able to get a real free-range bird, it should provide a memorable meal without requiring any fancy tricks in the kitchen — a little freshly grated citrus zest and juice and a dash of Grand Marnier or Cointreau in the gravy, perhaps, but that is all. But most of the birds on the Irish market are intensively reared and the advantages of easy availability and relative cheapness have, of course, the down side of blandness, so they need some imagination to make the meal special. The traditional accompaniments, like black cherries or orange, are still extremely good if made with integrity (ie not black cherry jam or marmalade in place of the fresh fruits), but this

Keep the precious duck fat — preserve it and use it in the same way as goose fat.

Variations: This is a very versatile dish, easily adapted to other citrus fruits and others with a sharp flavour, such as pineapple — fresh pineapple can be used with pineapple, orange or lemon juice, or use tinned pineapple in juice (not syrup).

Serves 8

Two 4-5 lb/1.9-2.3 Kg fresh
  ducklings, quartered
Salt and freshly ground
  black pepper
2-3 tablespoons clear honey
1-2 tablespoons hot water
1 onion, roughly sliced

Sauce:

Juice of 2 grapefruit made
  up to 3/4 pint/450 ml with
  stock
2 tablespoons cider vinegar
3 oz/75g light golden
  brown sugar
1 tablespoon rich soy sauce
2 level tablespoons
  arrowroot or cornflour
salt, if necessary, and
  freshly ground pepper
2 grapefruit, peeled and
  segmented
Sprigs of watercress and
  extra grapefruit segments
  to garnish.

Roast Duckling with Sweet and Sour Grapefruit is a little more unusual for a special occasion. It's a perfect dish for entertaining, as the birds are divided into serving portions before cooking.

Preheat a moderate oven, 350°F, 180°C, Gas mark 4.

Wipe and trim the duckling portions, then prick the skin all over with a fork to help release the fat during cooking. Season generously with salt and rub well into the skin, then add a light grinding of pepper. Arrange the duckling joints, skin side up, on a rack in a roasting tin, with the giblets underneath on the base of the tin. Cook in the preheated oven for an hour, then remove the giblets and put into a small pan. Pour off the fat which will have accumulated in the roasting tin. Blend the honey with the hot water and brush generously over the duckling portions, then return them to the oven. Brush again with the honey mixture once or twice during the remaining cooking time, so that the skins will be glazed and golden brown. Meanwhile, add the chopped onion to the giblets, just cover with cold water, season and bring to the boil; simmer for 30 minutes to make a stock.

When the ducklings are cooked, remove from the roasting tin to a serving dish and keep hot while you make the sauce. Strain the duck stock. Put the grapefruit juice into a measuring jug, make up to 3/4 pint/450 ml with stock and add the vinegar, sugar and soy sauce. Pour away any fat in the roasting tin, leaving behind only the dark sediment. Turn the contents of the measuring jug into the roasting tin and set over a low heat. Stir well to dislodge any sediment sticking to the tin. Measure the arrowroot or cornflour into the jug, add enough cold water to make a thin, smooth paste, then blend in a little of the hot liquid from the roasting tin. Turn this mixture into the tin and bring gently to the boil, stirring all the time. Simmer for a couple of minutes until the sauce thickens and clears. Taste for seasoning and sharpness and, if the sauce is too thick, add a little extra stock. Add the grapefruit segments and stir around for a minute or so to heat through, then pour the sauce around the duck portions, garnish with watercress and some fresh grapefruit segments and serve immediately. A mixture of white and wild rice makes a good accompaniment to the duckling, also a colourful, spicy side dish like Orange and Watercress Salad with Toasted Pine Kernels.

Pheasants in Red Wine

Pheasant in Wine: Serves 6

3 small-medium pheasants,
  halved
3 oz/75g belly of pork,
  diced
2 oz/50g unsalted butter
Salt and freshly ground
  black pepper
16 button onions
3 fl oz/75 ml brandy
1 bottle red wine
1/4 pint/150 ml chicken
  stock
1 bouquet garni
2 cloves garlic
1 level tablespoon rich dark
  brown sugar
4 oz/100g mushrooms
Beurre manié for thickening
  the sauce, made by
  working 1 oz/25g plain
  flour and 1 oz/25g
  unsalted butter to a paste.

Game is the other big treat for many people at this time of year and, although wild game may not be so easily attainable, farmed birds such as quail, guinea fowl and pheasant are widely available. Unlike farmyard poultry, game birds are very lean — the plus side of this is that they don't lose weight through fat loss during cooking but, of course, the down side is their tendency to dryness, making the choice of cooking method especially important: barding, braising, casseroling — anything that helps make the flesh moist and succulent will make the most of feathered game, whether wild or farmed.

This recipe for Pheasants in Red Wine is really very like the classic Coq au Vin that we see so little of these days — maybe it's due for a come-back. Although given for pheasant, other birds such as guinea fowl or even pigeon would be equally suitable. If cooking pigeon, allow one per person as there is very little except the breast meat on a pigeon. Pheasants, on the other hand, have quite a lot of eating on them — a large one, weighing about 2½ lb/1.1 Kg, is comparable with a small chicken and serves 3-4, while a medium one weighing about 2 lb/900g serves 2-3.

Wipe the pheasants and season with salt and freshly ground pepper. In a heavy casserole, fry the diced pork in half of the butter and set aside, then brown the pheasants slowly in the pork fat and butter. Meanwhile peel the onions, then add to the pan together with the diced pork. Turn the onions

*Above: Old-Fashioned Round Christmas
Pudding, page 166
Right: Hot Beetroot with Orange, page 142
Overleaf: Roast Goose with Orange and
Walnut Stuffing and Cranberry Port Sauce,
page 146
Page 152: Mincemeat Star Pies, page 173*

in the pan until they are glazed. Warm the brandy, pour over the birds and set alight. As soon as the flames have died down, pour over the wine and stock, add the bouquet garni and the crushed garlic and stir in the brown sugar. Increase the heat and bring up slowly to boiling point. Check the seasoning, cover and simmer for 30 minutes. Meanwhile, wipe and trim the mushrooms, cook them in the remaining l oz/25g butter and, after the 30 minutes is up, add to the pan. After another 10 minutes, check the pheasants. When they are tender, transfer to a warmed serving dish and keep hot. Raise the heat and boil the cooking liquid hard until it is reduced to about ¾ pint/450 ml, then remove from the heat and whisk in knobs of the beurre manié until the sauce thickens. Return to the heat, bring slowly to the boil and cook gently for a minute or two before pouring the sauce over the pheasants. Serve with game chips (thinly sliced rounds of potato deep fried for about 3 minutes) or boiled potatoes in their jackets and one or two other simple vegetables such as carrot batons and very lightly cooked brussels sprouts.

Braised Venison

Although many people are wary of cooking it, there is no mystery about venison — the main point to bear in mind is that, like most game, it is a dry meat so the cooking method chosen should compensate for the lack of fat to transform it into a tender, succulent dish. Marinating is the first stage, then the meat is either gently braised or pot-roasted to tenderise it and retain as much moisture as possible or, if you are sure the meat is tender enough for roasting, it can be wrapped in streaky rashers, set in a roasting tin, covered with foil to prevent drying out, then roasted in the same way as beef at 400°F, 200°C, Gas mark 6 for 15-20 minutes per l lb/450g depending how you like it done. Serve with Rowan Jelly.

Gourmets and chefs argue endlessly about the pros and cons of wild versus farmed venison but it must be said that it is only because of the recent upsurge in deer farming that venison is an option for most of us at all and, as farmed animals have a less energetic lifestyle than their mountain cousins and are shot at the right age, farmed venison is more likely to be suitable for roasting than a wild animal. It's also worth mentioning that deer farming is probably one of the most humane methods of meat production currently practised. This recipe for Braised Venison is delicious and a very safe cooking method for first-time venison cooks — it would be ideal for entertaining at any time through the winter.

Put the joint of venison into a deep dish. Put all the marinade ingredients into a saucepan, bring up to the boil and allow to cool. When cold, pour over the meat and leave in a cool place for at least 24 hours and preferably several days, turning occasionally.

Preheat a very moderate oven, 325°F, 160°C, Gas mark 3.

To braise, remove the meat from the marinade and pat dry with kitchen paper. Reserve the marinade. Heat the dripping or an equal mixture of oil and butter in a deep heavy-based oven-proof casserole; add the venison to the hot fat and quickly brown on all sides to seal. Remove and set aside. Reduce the heat and add the sliced braising vegetables to the casserole; cover and cook them gently for about 5 minutes to brown lightly, stirring occasionally. Add the herbs, orange zest, the reserved marinade and the stock, which should just cover the vegetables, and bring up to boiling point, then lay the joint of venison on top of the bed of vegetables, cover the casserole with a lid and put into the oven to braise, allowing 30 minutes per 1 lb/450g and 30 minutes over. When the meat is tender, remove it from the casserole, carve in fairly thick slices as for lamb and arrange on a warm serving dish. Keep warm. Meanwhile, strain the cooking liquor from the casserole into a saucepan and add the orange juice and redcurrant or

Serves 6-8:

Marinade for a 3 lb/1.4 Kg haunch of venison:
l onion, sliced
l bay leaf
2 teaspoons rich dark brown sugar
1 dessertspoon juniper berries, crushed
1 teaspoon allspice berries, crushed
Small bunch parsley stalks, tied together
l large clove garlic, crushed
1½ pint/300 ml red wine
2-3 tablespoons olive oil

To Braise:

2 tablespoons dripping or oil and butter
l onion, sliced
2 or 3 carrots, sliced
3 or 4 sticks of celery, sliced
Bunch of fresh parsley, thyme, marjoram etc, tied together
Pared zest l orange
1½ pint/300 ml stock

To finish:

Juice of the orange
l tablespoon redcurrant or rowan jelly
Salt and freshly ground black pepper
Beurre manié: l oz/25g butter, worked into l oz/25g flour.

Crown Roast of Lamb: Serves 7
Stuffing:
8 oz/225g fresh cranberries
1/4pint/ 150 ml cider or
  water
1 oz/25g caster sugar
1 onion, finely chopped
4 oz/100g mushrooms,
  coarsely chopped
1 oz/25g butter
1 clove garlic, peeled and
  crushed
8 oz/225g minced or finely
  chopped belly of pork
4 tablespoons freshly
  chopped parsley
2 teaspoons freshly
  chopped rosemary or 1
  teaspoon ground, dried
  rosemary
4 oz/100g fresh white
  breadcrumbs
Salt and freshly ground
  black pepper
1 egg, lightly beaten.

Sauce:
1/2 pint/300 ml lamb stock
  (made from the trimmings)
2 tablespoons port
1 tablespoon redcurrant jelly
1 rounded teaspoon
  cornflour or arrowroot,
  dissolved in a little water
Salt and freshly ground
  pepper.

Serves 12
3 lb/1.4 Kg scallops or
  queens (weight after
  shelling)
1 large or 2 medium onions
3 tablespoons oil
3 level tablespoons curry
  powder, or to taste
3 level tablespoons plain
  flour
3 teaspoons concentrated
  tomato purée
3/4 pint/450 ml water
3 tablespoons sweet chutney
Juice of 1 1/2 lemons
6 oz/175g butter
1/4pint/150 ml double
  cream.

rowan jelly. Gradually add knobs of the beurre manié to the pan, stir or whisk until melted and blended, then bring up to the boil again and cook for a minute or two, stirring or whisking, until the sauce thickens. Spoon a little of the sauce over the venison and hand the rest separately.

Crown Roast of Lamb with Cranberry Stuffing and Port and Redcurrant Sauce

Red meat makes a very welcome contrast to what is inclined to be surfeit of poultry over the Christmas season. A simple roast of sirloin with Yorkshire pudding will always draw sighs of contentment, but lamb (which is a good size at this time of year) lends itself especially well to dressing up, and goes well with the seasonal fruit and nut trimmings. Crown Roast, for example, is an extremely festive roast for any special occasion. Get the butcher to trim and chine two fair ends (7 cutlets in each) and shape them into a crown, and to give you the trimmings for stock.

Sort through the cranberries to remove any stalks or discoloured berries, then put them into a saucepan with the cider or water and sugar. Bring to the boil and cook, uncovered, over a fairly high heat until the berries have popped and the cooking liquid has boiled down and thickened.

In a separate pan, gently cook the onion and mushrooms in the butter until softening and lightly coloured, then add the garlic and cook for another minute or so. Turn the cranberry mixture and the onions and mushrooms into a bowl and mix with the minced pork, parsley, rosemary and breadcrumbs. Season with salt and pepper and fork in the beaten egg to bind the stuffing.

Preheat a fairly hot oven, 375°F, 190°C, Gas mark 5. Spoon the stuffing into the centre of the crown, press down lightly and level off with the back of the spoon. (If there is too much stuffing, shape the excess into balls and arrange around the joint.) Wrap foil around the cutlet bones to prevent them from burning during roasting. Weigh the stuffed joint and calculate the cooking time, allowing 30 minutes per lb/450g. Melt 1 or 2 tablespoons of lamb dripping or vegetable oil in a roasting tin and lay the stuffed crown on it. Put on a fairly low shelf of the preheated oven and cook for 10 minutes, then reduce the temperature to 350°F, 180°C, Gas mark 4 and continue cooking, basting frequently. When cooked, transfer the roast to a serving dish, replace the foil with cutlet frills and keep warm.

To make the sauce, pour off as much fat as possible from the roasting tin and add the stock to the pan juices. Bring to the boil, add the port and redcurrant jelly and simmer gently for a few minutes. Blend in the cornflour or arrowroot, season to taste and bring back to the boil. Simmer for a minute or two, stirring, until the sauce has thickened and cleared. Hand the sauce separately. Good accompaniments include Spiced Roast Parsnips and Glazed Onions.

Scallops in Curry Sauce

Scallops in Curry Sauce is a good winter party dish and easy to eat with a fork. Frozen scallops, available from specialist suppliers such as Sawyers of Chatham Street, Dublin, 2, are very handy for this as you don't have to rely on being able to get them at the last minute. Allow about 4 oz/100g per head.

Cut the scallops into thick slices, leaving the coral (if any) whole and set aside. Peel and finely chop the onion. Heat the oil in a saucepan over low heat. Add the onion and fry gently for 5 minutes to soften but not brown. Add the curry powder and cook for 1 minute, stirring occasionally, to draw out the flavour, then stir in the flour. Add the tomato purée and the water. Bring to the boil and add the chutney (chop any large pieces of fruit) and lemon juice, then simmer for 5 minutes. Strain the curry sauce and reserve. Melt the butter in a frying pan over moderate heat. When hot and foaming, add the scallops (including coral, if available) and fry for 2-3 minutes. Stir in the curry sauce and bring to the boil. Remove from the heat and stir in the cream. Serve with hot buttered rice and offer a selection of salads separately.

Variation: If scallops are unavailable, peeled prawns (fresh or frozen) can be used instead.

Leg of Lamb with Chestnut Stuffing and Spiced Cranberry Cider Sauce

Less expensive than crown roast, and still very much in the festive mood.

Preheat a moderate oven, 350°F, 180°C, Gas mark 4. Mix the onion, sultanas and breadcrumbs together. If using whole chestnuts, drain and chop finely. Mix chestnuts, lemon zest and seasoning with the other stuffing ingredients and use to stuff the leg. Tie the lamb very securely with cotton string, put into a roasting tin and cook in the preheated oven for about 2 hours. When cooked to your liking, transfer the joint to a serving dish and keep warm. Pour excess fat from the roasting tin and add the onion and garlic to the remaining pan juices. Cook over gentle heat to soften without browning. Sort through the cranberries and add them to the roasting tin with the cider and the sugar. Stir over moderate heat to dissolve the sugar, then stir in the vinegar, wine or port and the redcurrant jelly and bring to the boil. Add the spices and seasoning, then boil for a few minutes, stirring, until the sauce has reduced and thickened a little. Check the seasoning before serving as it is or, if a smooth sauce is preferred, liquidised or rubbed through a sieve. Hand the sauce separately.

Leg of Lamb: Serves 8

1 whole leg of lamb, boned by the butcher

Stuffing:

1 onion, finely chopped
2 oz/50g sultanas
4 oz/100g fresh white breadcrumbs
1 can (8-10 oz/250-300g) unsweetened chestnuts, whole or puréed
Finely grated zest of 1 lemon
Salt and freshly ground pepper.

Sauce:

1 onion, finely chopped
1 clove garlic, crushed
8 oz/225g fresh cranberries
1¼ pint/150 ml cider
1 oz/25g caster sugar
1 tablespoon red wine vinegar
1 tablespoon red wine or port
1 tablespoon redcurrant jelly
4 juniper berries
4 allspice berries crushed together
4 black peppercorns
Sea salt to taste.

Beef with Fresh Pineapple

Entertaining over the Christmas season isn't necessarily formal and, for New Year's Eve especially, good casseroles are hard to beat. This unusual Beef with Fresh Pineapple has delicious oriental flavours and can be kept warm without spoiling.

Cut the meat into bite-sized pieces. Heat the oil in a large heavy-based casserole and brown the meat in it, in batches if necessary. Remove with a slotted spoon and set aside. Peel and chop the onions, then cook them gently in the oil remaining in the casserole until softening and beginning to brown. Replace the meat in the casserole. Preheat a very moderate oven, 325°F, 160°F, Gas mark 3. Wash and trim the celery, discarding any coarse outer stems; slice finely. Remove the skin and hard core from the pineapple, then cut it into slices and chop up into bite-sized chunks. Add the celery and pineapple to the casserole. In a measuring jug, combine the pineapple or orange juice, cornflour, sugar, soy sauce, ketchup, vinegar and stock. Mix well, then add to the casserole, add a grinding of pepper and stir to mix all the casserole ingredients thoroughly. Over low heat, bring the casserole gently to the boil, then cover and transfer to the preheated oven. Cook for 2 hours, or until the meat is tender, reducing the heat to 300°F, 150°C, Gas mark 2 after the first hour. When cooked, check the casserole for seasoning, sharpness and consistency and make any necessary adjustments, then turn right down to 250°F, 130°C, Gas mark ½ and leave until ready to serve. Serve with rice spiked with roughly chopped walnuts and a selection of salads such as Celery, Apple and Walnut Salad and Chicory and Orange Salad.

Beef with Pineapple: Serves 12

4 lb/1.8 Kg round steak
About 4 tablespoons oil
3 onions
1 head good quality celery
1 ripe pineapple
½pint/300 ml pineapple juice or fresh orange juice
4 level tablespoons cornflour
2 tablespoons light golden brown sugar
2 tablespoons soy sauce
2 tablespoons tomato ketchup
4 tablespoons cider vinegar
1½ pints/850 ml stock (preferably beef, but a good home-made household or chicken stock is preferable to using cubes).

Pork with Apricots and Coriander

Pork with Apricots: Serves 12

8-12 oz/225-350g dried
  apricots, halved
1 tablespoon light golden
  brown sugar
Finely grated zest and juice
  of 2 lemons
1"/2.5 cm cinnamon stick
1 pint/600 ml cider
Butter and oil for frying
4 lb/1.8 Kg pork pieces,
  trimmed and cubed
6 onions, peeled and sliced
6 cloves garlic, peeled and
  crushed
1½lb/700g carrots, peeled
  and sliced
Inside stems of 1 head
  celery, trimmed and sliced
4 teaspoons coriander
  seeds, crushed
Sea salt and freshly ground
  black pepper.

My own favourite party casserole is Pork with Apricots and Coriander, a wonderfully subtle aromatic dish which always has people coming back for more.

Put the apricots into a pan with the sugar, lemon rind and juice, cinnamon sticks and cider, bring slowly to boiling point, then remove from the heat. Cover with a lid and leave to infuse. Preheat a very moderate oven, 325°F, 160°C, Gas mark 3. Heat about 1 oz/25g butter and 2 tablespoons oil in a flameproof casserole and brown the pork pieces in it, in batches if necessary. Remove the meat with a slotted spoon and set aside. Add the onions and garlic to the fat remaining in the casserole (add a little more if necessary) and cook gently, stirring occasionally, for a few minutes until the onions are softening and just beginning to brown. Stir in the carrots and celery, then the crushed coriander. Turn gently for a minute or two, then add the apricot and cider mixture and season to taste with salt and freshly ground pepper. Bring up to boiling point, then cover closely and cook in the oven for about an hour, or until the meat is tender. Be careful to avoid over-cooking, especially if you want to keep it warm for some time, as pork has a tendency to break up. When the casserole is cooked, remove the cinnamon stick and check seasoning and consistency — add some extra cider if it has dried up too much — then leave on a very low setting 200°F, 100°C, Gas mark ¼, until ready to serve. We love this with a Pilaf of Brown Rice which can be cooked in the oven at the same time as the casserole and, for wonderful flavour and a good crunchy contrast to the casserole, fork in 2-4 oz/50-100g toasted flaked almonds per 1 lb/450g rice (raw weight).

Lamb Pilaf

Lamb Pilaf: Serves 12

3 lb/1.4 Kg lean, boned
  lamb
About 2½ fl oz/60 ml oil
About 3 oz/ 75g butter
3 large onions
3 fat cloves garlic, or to taste
2 lb/ 1 Kg long-grain
  brown rice
6 oz/175g mushrooms
3 tsp crushed coriander
  seeds
1½ tsp turmeric
About 1"/2.5 cm fresh root
  ginger, or stem ginger,
  finely chopped
Sea salt and freshly ground
  black pepper
3 pints/1.8 litres stock or
  water
3 oz/75g raisins
3 oz/75g sultanas
6 oz/175g blanched split (or
  flaked) almonds
Freshly chopped coriander
  leaves or parsley to
  garnish.

Lamb Pilaf is a wonderfully fragrant meal-in-a-pot, easy both to make and to eat. Serve it with poppodums and a selection of chutneys — which will also go well with the curried scallops — as well as salads.

Dice the meat fairly small. Heat the oil and butter in a large flameproof casserole and brown the meat in it in batches, then set aside. Add the onions and garlic and cook gently until just softening, then return the meat to the casserole. Stir in the rice and the sliced mushrooms; cook for a few minutes, stirring. Add the spices and seasonings. Pour in the stock and bring to the boil. Cover, and simmer very gently for half an hour, then fork in the raisins and sultanas and add the almonds — which may be browned on a baking tray in the oven for a better flavour if you like — and continue cooking gently for another 30-40 minutes, or until all the stock has been absorbed and the meat is tender. Garnish with the freshly chopped coriander or parsley and serve with poppodums, chutneys and a selection of salads.

Variation: Instead of cooking on top of the stove, the pilaf may be baked in a moderate oven, 300°F/150°C, Gas Mark 2 for ¾-1 hour, if more convenient.

Aside from the traditional plum pudding and, perhaps, trifle that most families make, the Christmas party season is the high point of the year for glamorous desserts and puddings, including ice creams. In addition to the selection of favourites given here, there are more irresistible recipes in other sections of this book, especially Summer Desserts and Ices.

Traditional Christmas Pudding

It's a pity that old-fashioned plum puddings are now seen exclusively as a Christmas speciality, as they're really much more enjoyable at other times when there is less competition on the table. Relegation to seasonal status is very much a late twentieth century development — it is interesting to note that plum pudding was on the menu when the Titanic went down in April 1912. Half a century later, impervious to the fact that the fashion regarding this particular dish now put it firmly into the Christmas season, my own family always used to have the last pudding for lunch on Easter Sunday — and it was always the best. Maybe it's time to start reversing the trend, as a really good Traditional Christmas Pudding is a treat at any time throughout the colder part of the year. This favourite version is especially light, as it contains only breadcrumbs and no flour. [Microwave]

Sort through the dried fruit to remove any stalks or pieces of grit. Wash, dry, and halve the cherries. If using whole candied peel, cut up finely with a very sharp knife. Blanch and sliver the almonds. Remove crusts from a day-old white loaf and make crumbs in a food processor or blender. Peel and grate the carrot and apple. In a large bowl, mix all dry ingredients, including apple, carrot and grated lemon and orange zest. Warm the treacle slightly in the microwave or small pan to make it runny and add the orange and lemon juice, whiskey, rum or brandy and the lightly beaten eggs. Mix the liquids well, add to the pudding mixture and stir to mix thoroughly. Cover the bowl with a tea towel and leave in a cool place overnight. Next day, butter two 2-pint/l-litre pudding basins and put a buttered disc of greaseproof paper in the base of each. Also prepare buttered double greaseproof circles a little larger than the top of the bowls and double plain greaseproof circles about 4"/10 cm bigger than the top of the bowls. Give the pudding mixture a good stir, spoon into the prepared bowls and tap sharply on the worktop to eliminate air pockets. Smooth down the top with the back of a tablespoon, cover with the smaller buttered circles of greaseproof paper and tuck in neatly around the edge, then lay over the larger pieces and tie down firmly with good string — allow enough for a handle if possible, as it will be much easier and safer to handle the hot puddings later on. Trim the excess paper a bit if it is very bulky, then top off with a piece of foil and tuck it firmly under the rim of the bowl.

Cook by one of the following methods, then reheat when required by steaming/boiling for a further 2–3 hours:

To boil: stand puddings on trivets in deep saucepans, pour in enough boiling water to come two-thirds of the way up the sides, cover tightly and boil for 5-6 hours, making sure the water never goes off the boil and topping up regularly to keep up a level at least half way up the bowl.

Steam for 5-6 hours over pans of simmering water, making sure it does not go off the boil and topping up with boiling water as necessary.

Oven-steam: this method does not require regular topping up, making it suitable for overnight cooking — and it also keeps the kitchen free of steam. Preheat a very moderate oven, 300°F, 150°C, Gas mark 2; stand the

Makes two 2-pint/1 litre puddings, each serving 8.

12 oz/350g raisins
8 oz/225g currants
8 oz/225g sultanas
4 oz/100g glacé cherries
4 oz/100g candied peel
3 oz/75g blanched, slivered almonds
14 oz/400g fresh white breadcrumbs
1 good carrot, about 6 oz/185g, scraped and coarsely grated
1 large Bramley apple, 6-8 oz/175-225g, peeled and finely chopped or coarsely grated
1 small coffeespoon salt
l teaspoon ground mixed spice
1 teaspoon ground cinnamon
1 teaspoon finely grated nutmeg
1/2 teaspoon ground ginger
1/2 teaspoon ground cloves
8 oz/225g shredded suet
8 oz/225g Demerara sugar
Finely grated zest and juice of l orange and l lemon
2 tablespoons black treacle
4 fl oz/100 ml whiskey, rum or brandy
4 eggs, lightly whisked.

Hint: Although a steamed pudding can very easily be under-cooked (if the cooking water is allowed to go off the boil unnoticed) it is hard to imagine one being over-done if cooked by conventional methods, so err on the side of generosity when timing — but make sure the pan is not allowed to boil dry.

puddings in a deep roasting tin, three-quarters fill with boiling water, then cover completely with foil to prevent steam escaping. Cook in the preheated oven for about 6 hours, or overnight, reducing the temperature to 280°F/140°C/Gas mark 1 if it will be unattended for more than 6 hours.

Pressure cooking is also very suitable and faster, although only one pudding can be cooked at a time. Consult your pressure cooker instruction leaflet for details as they vary.

Microwave cooking is also successful, especially in a ring mould. Adjust time to suit the power of your machine, based on the fact that half of the above mixture takes 16 minutes in a 700 watt microwave on full power, plus an extra 2 minutes at the end when turned out upside down on a plate. In my experience microwaved puddings do not have the same keeping qualities as traditionally cooked ones, so I suggest either making them nearer the time of use or freezing them until required, then defrost and reheat on full power, allowing 1 minute per lb/450g.

Variations: This mixture can be used to make 1 large, 1 medium and 1 small pudding, if more convenient; adjust cooking times according to size.

Hints: ★ Warm the spoon before measuring out treacle or honey, then it will slide off easily, without waste. If treacle or honey has to be weighed, avoid a sticky situation by reversing the usual procedure: put the tin or jar on the scales and weigh the amount removed. If you need to warm the treacle to make it easier to mix with other liquids, this is most conveniently done in a small jug in the microwave; otherwise use a small saucepan.

★ Grating the zest from citrus fruits is easiest if the skin is lightly frozen, so put it into the freezer while assembling other ingredients. On the other hand, you get most juice if the fruit is slightly warm — so pop it into the microwave for a few moments between grating and juicing.

Wholefood Plum Pudding

Wholefood Plum Pudding is more unusual than the traditional pudding, but equally delicious — it's a rich golden brown, but it will darken with longer cooking in the same way as the traditional mixture.

Chop the dates, figs, apricots, almonds, brazils and walnuts. Toast the pine kernels in a hot oven for a few minutes until golden brown. Put into a large bowl with the raisins, currants, breadcrumbs and spices. Wash and dry the cherries if they are very sticky, then halve them and add to the bowl. If using whole candied peel, chop finely with a very sharp knife, then add to the mixture. Add the sugar, salt and finely grated lemon zest, then mix everything together thoroughly. Melt the butter and honey together, whisk eggs lightly and add to the honey mixture then add all the liquids, including the lemon juice, to the dry ingredients and stir thoroughly. Butter one large or two medium pudding bowls, base-line with a disc of buttered greaseproof paper and three-quarters fill with the mixture, pressing down to eliminate air pockets. Cover as in the previous recipe and steam or oven-steam for 4-6 hours, depending on the size of the pudding. Store in a cool place until required then, to re-heat, steam for another 2-3 hours.

Apart from a few specialities like plum puddings and mince pies, **Cold Desserts** *are generally more popular than hot over the Christmas party season. They can often be prepared well ahead, making life easier for the cook, but they also tend to be more glamorous and fruit-based desserts and ices make a refreshing contrast to hot main courses. Because they are always in demand, most of the following dishes are de rigueur in our house at Christmas time. In fact, although I omit them at my peril, we never eat them all at the planned time and the ones which keep well in the freezer are a wonderful encouragement to entertain in the dull days of January and February.*

Quantities make one large (3-pint/1.8 litres) or two medium (1½ pint/850 ml), giving a total of 12-14 servings:

2 oz/50g dried dates, stoned
4 oz/100g dried figs
4 oz/100g dried apricots
4 oz/100g almonds, blanched
2 oz/50g shelled Brazil nuts
2 oz/50g shelled walnuts
1 oz/25g pine kernels
8 oz/225g seedless raisins
4 oz/100g currants
6 oz/175g wholemeal breadcrumbs (yeast bread)
1 teaspoon mixed spice
½ teaspoon each ground cinnamon and grated nutmeg
½ coffeespoon ground cloves
4 oz/100g glacé cherries
4 oz/100g candied peel
4 oz/100g rich dark brown sugar
Pinch of salt
Grated zest and juice of 1 lemon
4 oz/100g butter
4 oz/100g honey
3 large eggs.

*The very mention of **chestnuts** is evocative to anyone old enough to remember them being roasted in the streets at this time of year and, although we seem to make less and less use of fresh chestnuts here (largely because of their high price, I suspect) they are an important part of Christmas celebrations on the continent, especially in France. Fortunately tinned chestnuts — whole and puréed, sweetened and unsweetened — are widely available in Ireland now and make a very convenient ingredient for many traditional dishes, sweet and savoury.*

Chestnut Yule Log

Chestnut Yule Log is everything that a Christmas dessert should be — it includes traditional ingredients, looks festive, is easy to make and will satisfy anyone who complains that you didn't bake a Chocolate Yule Log this year. This very rich dessert will serve 10 and can be frozen, although it will keep in foil for up to a week in the fridge. [Microwave]

4 oz/100g bar Bournville chocolate
6 oz/175g unsalted butter, at room temperature
4 oz/100g caster sugar
1 lb/450g can unsweetened chestnut purée
½ teaspoon vanilla essence
Dash of brandy
Icing sugar to dust over.

Melt the chocolate in a bowl in the microwave, or over hot water, then beat in the softened butter, a little at a time, until it is well blended. Add the sugar, chestnut purée, vanilla essence and brandy and beat thoroughly until the mixture is cool and thick. Oil a sheet of kitchen foil, turn the chestnut mixture onto it and form into a log shape; chill until firm. Using a fork, mark bark and knots along the length of the log and rings on the ends. Sift over a light sprinkling of icing sugar 'snow' and decorate with holly. Serve thinly sliced, with lightly sweetened chilled whipped cream.

Variation: If preferred, the log can be completely enclosed in whipped cream 'snow' and then decorated — this presentation may be neater than serving cream separately at a party.

Charlotte Malakoff

A top ten of favourite classic desserts would have to include Charlotte Malakoff. Made with equal quantities of butter, sugar, whipped cream and ground almonds, it is probably the richest of the moulded desserts known as charlottes and I am always especially pleased to find there is still one in the freezer in February, when it is really appreciated. Although a few charlottes are served hot (notably the famous apple one served in a crisp crust of overlapping browned buttered bread) they are mostly elaborate cold sweets, typical of the nineteenth century — and due for a revival. Rich desserts like this need to be balanced up with something refreshingly sharp-flavoured and colourful such as a compôte of fresh fruit, or a fruit coulis. Quantities given will fill one large (2-pint/1.2 litre) or two small (1-pint/600 ml) moulds, serving a total of 12. The real charlotte mould is tall and shaped like a wine bucket, but any suitable container can be used.

8 oz/225g sponge fingers or boudoir biscuits, or as required (see method)
4 tablespoons brandy, or as required
Water, as required
8 oz/225g unsalted butter, at room temperature
8 oz/225g caster or light golden brown sugar
8 oz/225g ground almonds
½ pint/300 ml cream.

First trim as many sponge fingers as required into long triangles to fit the base of the charlotte mould(s) in a flower shape. Mix 2 tablespoons of the brandy with an equal quantity of water and dip the smooth sides of the prepared sponge fingers into this mixture, then arrange them rounded (sugared) sides down, to make a flower-shaped base-lining. In the same way, dip whole sponge fingers in the brandy mixture and stand them round the sides of the mould, sugared side out; use triangular trimmings from the base to fill in any gaps. Don't worry if the sponge fingers are higher than the mould — it's easier to trim them later, after the filling has set. Cream the butter and sugar until light and very fluffy, add any remaining brandy (plus an extra dash if it seems on the mean side) and the ground almonds. Whip the cream lightly and fold it into the almond mixture, then turn into the lined mould(s) and tap sharply on the worktop several times to remove any air pockets. Freeze uncovered for 24 hours, then remove from the freezer and trim the sponge fingers level with the almond filling. If the mould is needed for something else, the charlotte can now be turned out safely and wrapped in clingfilm and foil before returning to the freezer. When required, allow to thaw (in the mould) for 6 hours at room temperature, then turn out onto a flat plate and decorate with star-piped Chantilly Cream and crystallized fruits or flowers.

Meringues

Makes 24 half shells:
4 egg whites, at room temperature
8 oz/225g caster sugar.

Meringues are the most useful Christmas standby or party pudding as they keep so well — not just a few days, but for weeks in an airtight tin. Large discs of meringue can be assembled quickly and easily with fruit and cream or other fillings to make glamorous desserts but simple, old-fashioned meringue shells, paired together with cream or ice cream and served on their own at tea time or with fresh fruit or Melba Sauce for dessert have a timeless appeal of their own.

Preheat a cool oven, 300°F/150°C/Gas mark 2. Line 2 very large (oven-sized) or 4 standard baking sheets with non-stick baking parchment, or grease them with white cooking fat, dust with flour and tap sharply to remove any excess. Whisk egg whites until stiff but not dry, then add half of the sugar, a tablespooon at a time and continue whisking until the meringue is smooth and glossy. Using a large metal spoon, gently fold in the remaining sugar, mixing thoroughly with as little loss of volume as possible. Spoon or pipe the mixture onto the prepared baking trays, keeping the sizes as even as possible. Put into the oven and immediately reduce the temperature to 200°F/110°C Gas mark 1/4 and leave to dry out for 2-3 hours, until pale beige, crisp, moving the sheets around occasionally to make sure they bake evenly. If extra space is wanted for filling them with cream or ice cream, remove the meringues halfway through the cooking time and gently press in the bases to make a hollow. Return to the oven, on their sides, to finish drying out. Cool the meringues on a wire rack. When completely cold, store in an airtight tin until required.

Variations:
A little **extra caster sugar** sprinkled over the meringues before baking will colour attractively, glisten and make them very crisp. Demerara sugar or coffee crystals are especially effective and very crunchy. Hundreds and thousands make a colourful topping for children's parties.

Nutty Meringues are very easily made by adding 1 oz/25g finely ground nuts — almonds, toasted hazelnuts or walnuts — with the second half of the sugar.

To make **Chocolate Meringues,** fold grated or chopped plain chocolate (or chocolate chips) into the meringue after all the sugar has been incorporated — up to 2 oz/50g per egg white.

To make delicious **Brown Sugar Meringues** whisk the egg whites with a pinch of cream of tartar until they stand in stiff peaks, then fold in light golden brown sugar (2 oz/50g per egg white). Bake at a slightly higher temperature — 250°F, 130°C, Gas mark 1/2 — for 1-11/2 hours, or until completely dry.

HINTS FOR PERFECT MERINGUES:
★ Eggs should not be too fresh — 2-3-day-old eggs are more acid and whisk up better than new-laid ones. Never use straight from the fridge and, preferably, separate them the day before — this allows some of the moisture to evaporate, giving more volume.

★ Best volume is gained by using a copper bowl and a balloon whisk. Most cooks now opt for an electric whisk, but try to use a metal bowl (eg stainless steel) rather than glass, ceramic or plastic.

★ It is vital to have everything totally grease-free when making meringue. Make sure there is no trace of yolk in the egg whites and that both bowl and whisk are absolutely clean — rubbing round the mixing bowl with a cut lemon before beginning is a good idea as the acid helps stabilise the beaten whites. Alternatively, add a pinch of cream of tartar, which is also acidic and helps make a crisp meringue.

★ Don't use damp sugar and do take care with the mixing: after gradually whisking in the first half, fold in the remainder very lightly using a metal spoon in a cutting and lifting action. Just stirring it in will make the meringue collapse.

★ If a soft, spongy texture is required (in a Pavlova, for example, or a pie topping), add a little vinegar to the meringue.

★ Steam is disastrous for meringues, so always bake them on their own. Once cooked, uncovered meringues will attract moisture from the atmosphere so store them in an airtight tin as soon as they are cold.

★ If you like them to have a nice gooey texture, crisp on the outside but beginning to soften in the middle, fill meringue shells an hour or two before serving.

Meringue Sitric

At the King Sitric Seafood Restaurant, Howth, Co. Dublin, egg yolk is used in most of the sauces, which posed a question — what to do with all those whites? No problem, said the owner-chef, we'll create a speciality house dessert, based on enormous meringues — and so he did: Meringue Sitric. The secret of these cunning hollow meringues is the special wooden dome-shaped moulds with an outside ledge they are piped around, but space for the ice cream can also be made in more modest domestic meringues by removing them from the oven before they are fully baked and pressing the base in gently to make a hollow, then finishing baking as usual.

Make a batch of basic meringue (2 oz/50g caster sugar per egg white) and, if you have the special wooden moulds, use a plain tube to pipe around the outside ledge and up in a continuing spiral until the meringue is about 2"/5 cm high. Place in a preheated very cool oven, 275°F, 140°C, Gas mark 1, bake for 2½ hours, then remove from the moulds and return to the oven for another hour to dry out. If you do not have wooden moulds, pipe large meringues onto baking sheets lined with baking parchment and bake at the lowest oven setting, 225°F, 110°C, Gas mark ¼ for 2-2½ hours or until the meringues can be lifted off the parchment quite easily but are still soft in the centre. Gently push the base in with a spoon or other implement to create a hollow and return to the oven on their sides to finish drying out. They will then make a quite respectable substitute for the King Sitric's real 'moulded' meringues.

To serve a full Meringue Sitric: Place a small rosette of whipped cream on a 10"/25 cm plate and lay a ball of vanilla ice cream on top. Arrange a half meringue on each side of the ice cream, fitting it into the shell cavities. Pipe some more whipped cream over the joining seam, cover generously with hot chocolate sauce and sprinkle with flaked almonds.

Basic meringue mixture
Vanilla Ice Cream
Whipped Cream
Hot chocolate sauce
Flaked almonds, toasted or plain.

Although I generally prefer to use fresh, local produce in its natural season, there are one or two **summer fruits** which freeze so well, have such piquancy and colour — and, in short, evoke the best of summer so wonderfully — that they are utterly irresistible in the depths of winter and, especially, as a contrast to traditional Christmas food. Top of my list would be **raspberries** and **blackcurrants**: raspberries not only keep their flavour and colour, making them perfect for ices, coulis and other sauces, but actually defrost so gracefully that they can be used whole in, for example, a Vacherin or a very more-ish Hazelnut Meringue Cake (see below). Blackcurrants, on the other hand, are at their best puréed and used in mousses, ice creams and so on, where their sharp, piquant flavour and rich colouring bring drama to the table. In a similar way other soft fruits such as loganberries, blackberries, redcurrants, bilberries and blueberries provide colour in winter and less obvious contenders, like gooseberries and rhubarb, are valued for their sharpness of flavour.

Hints for successful meringue:

— use eggs at room temperature, not straight from the fridge

— have Bakewell-lined baking sheets ready before beginning

— preheat oven beforehand and use the prepared mixture immediately

Raspberry Vacherin

Raspberry Vacherin is a favourite all-year treat for any special occasion in our house. Raspberries freeze so well that this is one of the few out of season dishes that we find as seriously tempting at Christmas time as in high summer. I make it with the ordinary **basic meringue** *mixture (not Meringue Cuite, which has to be whisked over hot water) and have never had any problem with it. Serves 6-8.*

Preheat a cool oven, 300°F, 150°C, Gas mark 2. Line two baking sheets with non-stick baking parchment (a little dot of white cooking fat under the corners will hold it down) and lightly draw in two circles, about

4 egg whites
8 oz/225g caster sugar
About 1 lb/450g raspberries
Caster sugar to taste
½ pint/300 ml cream
Vanilla essence or liqueur, eg kirsch or Crème de Framboise.

9"/23cm and 7½"/20 cm diameter. Have ready a piping bag fitted with a ½"/2 cm star nozzle. Whisk the egg whites until stiff peaks form then, keeping the machine running, add half of the sugar, a tablespoon at a time and keep whisking until the mixture has a smooth, close texture and stands in stiff peaks when the whisk is lifted. Using a metal spoon, carefully fold in the remaining sugar to mix thoroughly without loss of volume. Use most of the mixture to spread or pipe inside the prepared circles, then put the remaining meringue into the piping bag and use to pipe out onto the surrounding baking parchment a number of miniature meringues — ideally 9 will look best. Cook in the preheated oven for 50-60 minutes, until lightly coloured and quite dry. (The small ones will take less time.) Peel off the parchment, cool the meringues on wire racks and, when quite cold, store immediately in airtight tins. When required, whip the cream until soft peaks form, sweeten lightly and flavour with a few drops of vanilla essence or other flavouring. Lay the larger meringue circle on a serving dish, spread with about three-quarters of the fruit, keeping the best berries back to decorate the top. Add the smaller meringue circle, spread with the remaining cream, arrange the small meringues around the edge and use the remaining fruit to decorate the top. Dust lightly with icing sugar.

Variations: The possibilities are endless — a plain meringue, filled simply with Crème Chantilly is delicious served with **Melba Sauce:** rub 8 oz/ 225g raspberries through a nylon sieve and beat 3-4 heaped tablespoons in, a little at a time, until the purée thickens. Alternatively, as raspberries and strawberries bring out the best in each other, fill the meringue with strawberries instead of raspberries and hand a Melba Sauce, perhaps sharpened with the juice of half a lemon, separately. Also, the Hazelnut Meringue Cake given below is wonderful filled with fresh raspberries. Many other fruits can be used instead of raspberries, of course — other soft fruits, cooked or raw as appropriate, are ideal at this time of year but the choice round the year is virtually unlimited.

Crookedwood House, near Mullingar, makes a **Chocolate and Orange Meringue Gateau**. It is very similar to my Raspberry Vacherin, but uses an extra egg white (5 whites, 10 oz/275g sugar). The mixture is used to make two meringue circles and about 8 small meringues, cooked as above. For the filling: whip ½ pint/300 ml cream and fold in 6 dessertspoons of best quality dark chocolate, grated, and 2 dessertspoons of orange liqueur such as Grand Marnier or Orange Curacao. Use half to sandwich the meringue layers, then spread the rest on top and decorate with the miniature meringues and some fresh orange segments. They serve the gateau with **Rich Chocolate Sauce**, made very simply by warming ½ lb/225g good dark chocolate with ½ pint/300 ml cream. The sauce can be kept warm in a bain marie until required, or cooled and reheated if more convenient: it is not at all tricky.

Hazelnut Meringue Cake

Hazelnut Meringue Cake is a classic and a great way to round off a party at any time of year, but there is something especially delicious about this raspberry filling in winter. Hazelnuts also have a special affinity with apricots, so poached fresh or dried apricots could be used instead of the raspberries, and with chocolate — see variations given below.

Preheat a fairly moderate oven, 350°F/ 180°C, Gas mark 4. Lay the hazelnuts in a single layer on a baking tray and toast in the oven for about 10 minutes, until crisp and aromatic. Cool a little, then pour them onto a clean tea towel and remove the outer skins by gathering it up to make a bag and rubbing the nuts together vigorously; grind finely in a coffee grinder or Mouli grater. Raise the oven temperature to 375˚F, 190˚C, Gas mark 5. Butter the sides of two 8"-9"/20-22cm sandwich tins and dust with flour, then base-line the tins with non-stick baking parchment. Whisk the egg whites until stiff, then gradually beat in the caster sugar. Continue beating until very stiff, smooth and glossy, adding the vanilla and vinegar or lemon juice. Lastly, carefully fold in the ground nuts with a metal spoon, losing as little volume as possible.

Divide the mixture equally between the prepared tins, spread level and bake for 30-40 minutes. Leave to cool in the tins, then loosen the sides and peel the base lining paper away. Store in an airtight tin until required. To serve, whip the cream until soft peaks form and sandwich the layers with the cream and raspberries. Dust with icing sugar and chill for several hours — the filling will become firm and the meringue layers soften, making the cake easier to cut. Serve with Melba Sauce.

Variations: Two other classic combinations work equally well:

Hazelnut Meringue Cake with Apricot Cream: Make the hazelnut meringue in exactly the same way as above, but omit the cream and raspberry filling and replace it with this apricot cream:

Cook the apricots gently in the liquid they were soaked in plus a strip of lemon rind for flavouring. When they are tender, purée in a blender or food processor and leave to cool. Squeeze the juice from the lemon and strain. Put the water into a small pan with the sugar and heat gently to dissolve, then add the lemon juice, bring up to the boil and boil for 3 minutes. Whip the cream, sweeten and mix in a little of the apricot purée. Sandwich the cake with this apricot cream and dust the top with icing sugar. Blend the sugar syrup with the remaining apricot purée to make a sauce and hand it separately.

Gâteau Ganache: Instead of whipped cream and fruit, the same hazelnut meringue base can be used with a luscious chocolate cream filling and served with chocolate sauce to make another classic.

Break up the chocolate, put it into a pan with a little of the water and melt very gently over low heat. Add the rest of the water and the sugar, heat gently to dissolve then raise the heat, bring up just to boiling point and allow to simmer, uncovered, for 10-15 minutes. Turn into a bowl and leave to cool. When cold, whip the cream and fold in 2 or 3 tablespoons of the chocolate sauce. Use this chocolate cream to sandwich the two layers of hazelnut meringue, then wrap in foil, put a light weight on top and leave in the fridge overnight. To serve, decorate with piped cream, chocolate caraque or simply a dusting of icing sugar and hand the chocolate sauce separately.

Profiteroles

Profiteroles seem to enjoy perennial popularity and, as they keep for a few days (unfilled) in an airtight tin and much longer in the freezer, they make a wonderful Christmas standby and a very practical glamorous dessert for any occasion. They can be filled simply with sweetened whipped cream, chocolate cream or various combinations of finely chopped fruit or nuts. A particularly irresistible combination with chocolate sauce is to mix a little Grand Marnier and a pinch of freshly grated orange zest into the cream filling. Serve with the chocolate sauce given in the previous recipe, or Quick Chocolate Sauce.

Sift the flour. Put the butter, water, salt and sugar into a medium saucepan and heat gently until the butter has melted. Bring to a fast boil and immediately tip in all the flour. Beat with a wooden spoon for 1 minute

Serves 6-8:
4½ oz/125g whole
  hazelnuts
4 egg whites
9 oz/250g caster sugar
Few drops vanilla essence
½ teaspoon vinegar or
  lemon juice
Icing sugar, to dust over

Filling:
¼ pint/150 ml double
  cream
8 oz/225g raspberries
Icing sugar for dusting.

Hazelnut Meringue Cake with Apricot Cream
2 x hazelnut meringue
  cakes, as above
4 oz/100g dried apricots,
  soaked (or use a no-soak
  variety)
½ lemon
¼ pint/150 ml water
4 oz/100g granulated sugar
¼ pint/150 ml cream.

Gâteau Ganache
2 x hazelnut meringue
  cakes, as above
6 oz/175g Bournville
  chocolate
½ pint/300 ml water
4 oz granulated sugar

Makes about 24 profiteroles (or 12 choux buns or éclairs):

2½ oz/65g strong white flour
2 oz/50g butter
¼ pint/150 ml cold water
Pinch of salt
1 level teaspoon caster sugar
2 eggs, possibly plus 1 yolk (see method)
beaten egg for glazing

Filling:

½ pint/300 ml double cream
1 level tablespoon vanilla sugar
1 tablespoon Grand Marnier (optional)
½ teaspoon finely grated orange zest (optional).

over the heat, until the mixture forms a ball and leaves the sides of the pan clean. Remove from the heat and leave to cool for about five minutes, or until the side of the pan is cool enough to hold comfortably. Beat the eggs lightly and add to the pastry gradually, beating well after each addition until the eggs have been thoroughly absorbed and the pastry is smooth and glossy and just stiff enough to hold its own shape. Chill until ready to use, then preheat a hot oven, 425°F/220°C/Gas mark 7 and grease two baking sheets. Pipe or spoon the mixture into small heaps (a teaspoon is just right for profiteroles, use a dessertspoon for choux buns) and bake in the preheated oven for about 15 minutes, or until puffed out, golden brown and absolutely dry — test by pinching the sides, which should not feel at all soft or the pastry will collapse when removed from the oven. If in doubt, make a vent in each one with a sharp knife to let the steam out, then return to the oven for another few minutes to dry out completely. Leave until absolutely cold before filling or storing in an airtight tin.

To serve, whip the cream lightly, add vanilla sugar and any other flavourings and continue whipping until soft peaks form.

Either make a small hole in each one with a sharp pointed knife and pipe the filling in, or cut a slit in the side of each one and spoon it in — this is the most practical method if chopped fruit or nuts have been included in the filling. Pile the profiteroles onto a serving dish, pour over the cold chocolate sauce and sprinkle with chopped nuts or candied julienne strips of orange peel.

Snaffles Grape Pudding

Grape Pudding — grapes covered with chilled whipped cream and a caramelized sugar topping — was so popular as a dinner party dessert in the late '60s and early '70s that it became a cliché and disappeared from menus completely. A pity, as it's a super little dish if handled with flair. The secret of getting the top to caramelise before the cream melts is to make sure the cream is really cold and the grill really hot before bringing the two together. (The dish can have a short spell in the freezer before finishing if you like — some people even used to stand the whole dish in a bed of ice before putting it under the grill.) If you need further encouragement to make this refreshing and amusing sweet, just remember that it was a speciality of that wonderful basement Dublin restaurant of the '60s, Snaffles, where it was known (of course) as Snaffles Grape Pudding.

Serves 8:

1 lb/450g green (or mixed green and black) grapes
1 pint/600 ml double cream
3 rounded tablespoons Demerara sugar.

If you are fussy the grapes can be peeled but, unless the skins are unusually tough, this is not really necessary. Halve and deseed them, then divide between 8 fireproof ramekins or arrange on the base of a shallow gratin dish. Whisk the cream until thick, spoon over the grapes to cover and level with the back of the spoon. Chill thoroughly for several hours so that the grapes are really cold and the cream very firm — if the fridge is not cold enough, put into the freezer for the last half hour. Preheat a very hot grill. Sprinkle the sugar evenly over the top and put under the hot grill just long enough for the sugar to melt, turning the dish if necessary so that the whole top has caramelized. Unless serving immediately (the contrast of hot and cold is an experience) put back into the fridge immediately and chill again so that the sugar topping is really crisp and the cream has firmed up again before serving.

Old-Fashioned Sherry Trifle

Christmas wouldn't be Christmas without a good old-fashioned trifle. Tinakilly House, at Rathnew, Co Wicklow puts on a magnificent Victorian Christmas programme each year and this Old-Fashioned Sherry Trifle, made with home-made sponge cake, fresh or poached fruit and rich egg custard is one of their specialities.

First make the custard. Set aside, stirring occasionally until cold. Halve the sponge cake horizontally, spread with raspberry jam and make a sandwich. Cut into slices and use to line the bottom and the lower sides of a large glass dessert bowl. Sprinkle generously with the sherry. Peel and slice the fruit, then spread it over the sponge to make an even layer. Strain the custard on top, cover with a plate and leave to cool. Chill. Before serving, whip the cream and spread it over the custard, then decorate with the traditional blanched split almonds, angelica and glacé cherries if you like.

Serves 6-8:

Custard: ¾ pint mixture of egg custard (¾ pint/ 425ml milk and 3 eggs)
1 small sponge cake (2 eggs etc)
Raspberry jam
¼ pint/150 ml medium or sweet sherry
1lb/450g fruit, eg pears and bananas
½ pint/300ml cream
Blanched almonds, glacé cherries and angelica to decorate (optional).

Ratafia Trifle

I usually make a traditional sherry trifle, but when someone gave me a bottle of Amaretto di Saronno recently it prompted me to try this rather special Ratafia Trifle, which is said to date from the eighteenth century.

First make the custard. Leave to cool. Split the sponges in half, spread generously with the apricot jam and cut up into pieces about 1"/2.5 cm square. Arrange in the base of a deep glass trifle bowl and sprinkle the Amaretto over.

When the custard is cold, spread it over the trifle sponges, cover with a plate or some clingfilm and chill well for several hours, or overnight. To serve, whip the cream stiffly and decorate the top with big piped swirls of whipped cream, ratafia biscuits and almonds.

Hint: If an egg custard threatens to curdle, put in an ice cube to lower the temperature quickly.

Ratafia Trifle: Serves 8-10

1 x 3-egg mixture sponge OR 2 packets trifle sponges
8 oz/225g apricot jam
3 fl oz/75 ml Amaretto di Saronno (about 2 miniatures)

Custard:

1 pint/600 ml milk etc (See Sauces)

Topping:

½ pint/300 ml cream
1 packet (3-4 oz/75-100g) ratafia biscuits/ miniature macaroons
1 packet (3-4 oz/75-100g) chocolate-covered almonds, if available
2 oz/50g whole almonds, blanched.

Oranges with Grand Marnier

Oranges with Grand Marnier makes a delicious and refreshing dessert after such a substantial main course.

Using a potato peeler, remove the zest from two of the oranges and set aside. Peel the oranges, removing all trace of pith, and cut crosswise into thin slices. Arrange in a serving dish. Shred the reserved zest of orange, then blanch to remove bitterness: cover with cold water, bring to the boil and drain. Return to the pan, cover with fresh water, bring to the boil and simmer, covered, for 10-15 minutes, or until tender. Drain and reserve the zest. Put the sugar and water into a saucepan, stir over low heat until the sugar has dissolved, then add the cooked zest and simmer for about 5 minutes, or until the zest is glazed and candied. Draw off the heat, add the lemon juice and allow to cool. Stir in the Grand Marnier, pour the syrup over the orange slices and chill well before serving with vanilla ice cream.

Variation: **Oranges in Cointreau** is a simpler version — omit the candied peel and serve sliced oranges in a syrup as above but with less sugar (to taste, about 3-4 oz/75-100g) and Cointreau in place of the Grand Marnier.

Oranges with Grand Marnier: Serves 8

8 oranges
6 oz/175g caster sugar
¼ pint/150 ml water
Juice of 1 lemon
3 tablespoons Grand Marnier.

1 lb/450g raisins
1 lb/450g sultanas
1 lb/450g currants
12 oz/350g chopped
  candied peel
1¼ lb/550g shredded suet
1 lb/450g self-raising flour
1 lb/450g white
  breadcrumbs
14 oz/400g Demerara sugar
2 teaspoons mixed spice
4 oz/100g ground almonds
6 eggs
2 oz/50g black treacle
1 pint/600ml Guinness
2–3 fl oz/50–75 ml brandy
2 square yards/metres
  muslin
melted butter and flour, as
  required
A stick to suspend the
  pudding

Old-Fashioned Round Christmas Pudding

The Park Hotel, Kenmare, Co. Kerry, was kind enough to share the secret of their Old-Fashioned Round Christmas Pudding. This makes a huge spherical pudding in the Victorian style and is suspended in a big pot of boiling water for cooking, a method which would have suited the three-legged pot over an open hearth very well, and it is the butter and flour mixture which forms a seal and prevents the water from penetrating the pudding and making it soggy.

In a very large bowl, mix all the dry ingredients together thoroughly. In a separate bowl, whisk the eggs together lightly; warm the treacle until it is liquid, then mix with the eggs and add to the dry ingredients with the other liquids. Mix well and set aside. The mixture can conveniently be left overnight at this stage. When ready to proceed, prepare a large pot (such as a stock pot) of boiling water.

Soak one of the muslin squares in melted butter, then remove and sprinkle with flour to coat the muslin evenly. Lay it out on a board, butter side up, place the pudding mixture on top and tie up firmly to make a ball shape. Take the second square of muslin and tie it round the pudding, to seal in the flour on the outside of the inner muslin, and to attach it to the stick so that the pudding can be suspended from the top of the pan. Submerge the pudding in the pot of boiling water, bring back up to the boil, then simmer for 8 hours. Top up with boiling water as required to keep the pudding covered and do not allow the water to go off the simmer. When cooked, remove and leave the pudding suspended in a cool dry place for several months to mature. When required, heat in the same way, suspended over boiling water, for 4 hours. To serve, remove the muslin, place on a heated serving dish, decorate with holly and flame with brandy. Serve in the traditional way with brandy butter, or with whipped cream. Serves at least 20.

Traditional Christmas Cake

Baking really starts off the Christmas preparations and, having tried countless traditional and other festive recipes over the years, this is a selection of the ones I have found most interesting and/or successful. Although most of the preparation is done in December, if you like a traditional plum pudding or rich fruit cake at Christmas (or, like us, as a treat to look forward to in the dreary dark days of January and February), it's important to to get down to baking in good time. Rich cakes need at least a month to mature and they get better all the time, so it's worth making a mental note to make the puddings and fruit cakes by about Hallowe'en. This traditional recipe has been a favourite of mine for years and I always make at least one for my own house and another as a gift.

8 oz/225g plain flour and a pinch of salt
1 flat coffeespoonful each: nutmeg, cinnamon, cloves and ginger
12 oz/350g currants
12 oz/350g sultanas
8 oz/225g raisins
2 oz/50g almonds, blanched and shredded
4 oz/100g glacé cherries, halved
4 oz/100g cut mixed peel, preferably home-made
8 oz/225g butter, at room temperature
8 oz/225g rich dark brown sugar
1 tablespoon black treacle
Grated zest of 1 orange and 1 lemon
1 teaspoon vanilla essence OR 1 coffeespoon each rose and orange flower water
4 large eggs
1/4 pint/150 ml brandy, whiskey or sherry.

Prepare an 8"/20 cm round or 7"/18 cm square loose-based cake tin by lining with three layers of greased greaseproof paper, extending 2"/ 5 cm over the top of the tin. Tie a thick band of folded newspaper around the outside of the tin to protect the sides of the cake from overcooking.

Sift flour, salt and spices. Sort through fruit and mix in a large bowl with the almonds, cherries, peel and a tablespoonful of flour taken from the measured amount. Cream butter and sugar until light and fluffy, then add the treacle, zests and essences. Beat well. Add eggs one by one, including a dessertspoonful of flour and beating well after each addition. Fold in remaining fruit and flour and 2 tablespoons of the brandy, whiskey or sherry. Mix well. Put the mixture into the prepared tin, smooth down well with the back of a tablespoon, leaving slightly hollow in the centre. At this stage, the cake can be left overnight or until it is convenient to start baking.

Preheat a fairly slow oven, 325°F, 170°C, Gas mark 3, and bake for about 1½ hours or until just beginning to brown, then reduce the heat to 300°F, 150°C, Gas mark 2 and continue to bake for another 3 hours or until cooked. Oven temperatures vary and the times and temperatures given have always worked for me but, if it's your first time trying the recipe, keep an eye on it and be prepared to adjust the temperature and/or timing to suit your oven. In any case, protect the top of the cake from overbrowning by covering loosely with foil or brown paper if necessary towards the end of the cooking time. When cooked, the top of the cake will feel springy to the touch and a skewer thrust into the centre will come out clean, without any uncooked mixture on it.

Cool the cake in the tin, then remove papers and turn upside down. Using a skewer, make small holes all over the base of the cake and pour in the remaining brandy or other alcohol. Repeat this process if possible in a month's time, before applying the almond paste. When thoroughly drained, wrap the cake in a double layer of greaseproof paper, then a layer of foil. Seal and store in an airtight tin in a cool place until about a fortnight before Christmas or whenever you are ready to apply the almond paste

Variation: **Miniature Christmas Cakes** make an ideal gift, especially for an older relation living alone who wouldn't want to bother with baking a cake. The mixture given above can be divided to make three small cakes 4"/10 cm in diameter before decoration — keep big (1 lb 13 oz/825g) fruit cans for this: cleaned, dried and lined they make ideal small cake tins. The small cakes take about 1½ hours to bake and can be decorated in much the same way as a full size one. Miniature bread (loaf): this and other shapes can be used and decorated in simple, original ways.

Decorating Christmas Cakes

Rich fruit cakes made during the autumn need to be taken out a week or two before Christmas for decoration. There's a much more flexible attitude to cake decoration at the moment and very welcome it is too, as it encourages people to do their own thing in a creative atmosphere without worrying too much about the rules. Casual 'snow scene' decorations are quick and easy to do and ideal for family celebrations as even the tiniest tots can join in — but the fact that it's fun can also spark the beginning of an interest in more disciplined and skilful decorative work. Although stiffly piped geometrical designs and seasonal motifs in red, green and white have been out of fashion for the last couple of decades, there's been a new vogue for theme cakes in all sorts of tricky designs and there's a great deal of highly skilled work going into special occasion cakes of all kinds at the moment — in fact, we might even be in for a revival of the intricate icing of the '50s...

For most of us, though, it's back to the familiar snow scene — or, perhaps, one or two equally easy but slightly less predictable seasonal cake treatments. Although I quite enjoy a little of a good lemony white icing, Royal Icing usually does nothing for me — it's just something to dig through to get to the treasure of more-ish almond paste and wonderfully mature, boozy rich fruit cake underneath. So, once the children are old enough not to demand the return of Santa, his Reindeer et al, I shall either stick to the sort of Crunchy Fruit and Nut Topping given below (easiest option), or cover the cake with almond paste and toast it in the same way as for Simnel Cake (easy, but much more fattening) or decorate the top with Glazed Nuts and Glacé Fruits (quite easy and attractive — can also go on top of almond paste if you like. See Cider Brack, page 126 for glaze).

Almond Paste

For the traditional (and still most popular) decoration for rich Christmas cakes, Almond Paste is applied a few days before the icing.

Almond paste for top and sides of an 8"/20 cm round or 7"/18 cm square cake. This is a moderate amount — almond paste addicts should double the quantities for a deep layer.

12 oz/350g ground almonds
6 oz/175g sifted icing sugar
6 oz/175g caster sugar
2 tsp lemon juice
A few drops of natural almond essence
1 tablespoon golden or navy rum (optional)
1 standard egg.

Mix ground almonds with sifted icing sugar and caster sugar. Blend lemon juice, almond essence and rum and add to the mixture, together with enough egg to mix to a smooth paste. (This is very quickly and easily done in a Kenwood mixer.)

Gather together with the fingers, turn onto a work surface which has been dusted with icing sugar and knead until smooth. Cut off about a third of the ball and roll out to fit the sides of the cake, using a piece of string as a guide for the length and width of the strip. Brush the sides of the cake with warmed apricot jam or lightly beaten egg white and apply the almond paste in two strips, blending the joins with the fingers. Roll out the remaining almond paste to fit the top of the cake — this is easily done using the cake tin and string as guides. Brush the top of the cake with warmed apricot jam and invert onto the rolled-out almond paste. Press down gently but firmly to stick it in place, and work around the top edge with a palette knife to make a neat join. Use a straight-edge glass to roll around the outside of the cake, sticking the almond paste on firmly and giving a clean line. Leave cake upside down overnight. Next day, put right way up, cover lightly with tissue and leave for at least a day to dry out a little before applying *Light White Icing* (see below).

Quick All-in-One Fruit Cake
with Crunchy Topping

This easy and attractive cake can be made anything up to a couple of days before Christmas and doesn't need any further decoration.

Butter and base-line an 8"/20cm round or 7"/18cm square loose-based cake tin. Preheat a cool oven, 300°F/150°C/Gas mark 2.

Put all the cake ingredients into a large mixing bowl and mix by hand with a wooden spoon for a minute or two until all ingredients are thoroughly blended and there are no streaks of butter showing through the mixture. Turn into the prepared tin and level the top with the back of a tablespoon.

Mix the topping ingredients — quartered cherries, mixed peel and flaked almonds — and scatter evenly over the top of the cake.

Bake in the centre of the preheated oven for an hour, then reduce the temperature to 280°F/140°C/Gas mark 1 and continue baking for another hour or until a skewer thrust into the centre of the cake comes out clean, without any trace of uncooked mixture. Leave the cake in the tin to cool. When cold, turn out, remove papers and wrap loosely in fresh greaseproof paper. Store in an airtight tin until required. This cake improves if it can be kept for a week or so, but it can be used the day after baking if necessary. It keeps indefinitely.

Variation: If you like almond paste but don't want to be bothered applying it to the cake in the usual way, you can have the best of both worlds with this cake — simply put a layer in the centre of the uncooked cake mixture, in the same way as for Easter Simnel Cake. For other suggestions on decorating Christmas cakes, see below.

Hint: Although testing with a skewer is the surest way of knowing whether a cake is cooked, experienced bakers can usually tell at a glance: a cake which is ready to take from the oven will have stopped 'singing', be shrinking slightly from the sides of the tin and the top will feel firm and springy to the touch. On the other hand, exceptionally large rich cakes which have very long cooking times (such as the bottom layer of a wedding cake) are best tested by removing a plug from the centre. Gadgets for doing this are available from specialist kitchen shops.

White Christmas Cake with Light White Icing

Traditional as it is, rich fruit cake is not to everyone's taste but there are plenty of alternatives. For example, you could try this lighter but still festive alternative, using crystallized fruits. Using the ingredients given as a guideline, the fruits used can be varied according to availability and personal preference.

Butter an 8"/20 cm round or 7"/18 cm square loose-based cake tin and line with a double layer of buttered greaseproof paper. (This is most easily done by melting the butter and brushing it on.) Tie a folded band of newspaper or heavy brown paper around the outside of the tin, making it an inch/2.5 cm or so higher than the tin to protect the top of the cake. Soak the sultanas in the brandy or sherry overnight, or at least for several hours.

Preheat a moderate oven, 350°F/180°C/Gas mark 4.

Sift the flour and salt together. Quarter the glacé cherries, washing and drying them first if they are very sticky, and chop the pineapple, ginger, angelica, walnuts and candied peel. (If you haven't got home-candied peel, try to get whole citron peel from a specialist shop.) Beat the eggs with an electric mixer until very thick and foamy. Meanwhile, cream the butter with the lemon zest and sugar until light and fluffy. Add the beaten eggs, a little at a time, beating well after each addition and adding a little flour if the mixture curdles. Lightly stir in the chopped fruit and nuts and finally the sultanas and brandy or sherry. The mixture should be a bit stiffer than dropping consistency — if it is too stiff, add a little extra brandy or sherry, but be careful not to make it too soft, or the fruit will sink.

Spoon the mixture into the prepared tin, smooth the top with the back

6 oz/175g butter, at warm room temperature
7 oz/200g rich dark brown sugar
8 oz/225g plain flour
Pinch of salt
1 coffeespoon each ground cloves, ginger, cinnamon, nutmeg
$\frac{1}{2}$ level teaspoon baking powder
8 oz/225g currants
5 oz/150g each, sultanas and raisins
4 oz/100g glacé cherries, halved
4 oz/100g chopped candied peel
Finely grated zest of 1 orange
1 tablespoon black treacle
3 large eggs
2 oz/50g almonds, blanched and slivered (OR use flaked almonds)
2 oz/50g ground almonds
$\frac{1}{2}$ teaspoon vanilla essence
Few drops natural almond essence
4 tablespoons whiskey, brandy or cider

Topping:
2 oz/50g glacé cherries, quartered
2 oz/50g chopped candied peel
1 oz/25g flaked almonds.

White Christmas Cake
8 oz/225g plain flour
$\frac{1}{4}$ teaspoon salt
8 oz/225g glacé cherries
4 oz/100g crystallised pineapple
2 oz/50g crystallized ginger
2 oz/50g angelica
4 oz/100g walnuts
6 oz/175g candied peel
4 large eggs
8 oz/225g butter, at room temperature
Finely grated zest and juice of 1 lemon
8 oz/225g caster sugar.
8 oz/225g golden (yellow) sultanas
3-4 tablespoons brandy or sherry.

of a tablespoon and make quite a deep hollow from the centre up to the sides of the tin so that it will rise evenly. Bake just below the centre of the preheated oven for about 1½ hours, then reduce the temperature to 275°F/140°C/Gas mark 1 and bake for another 2½ -3 hours, or until the cake is nicely browned and springy to the touch and the sides are shrinking slightly from the tin. (If in doubt, test with a skewer.) During the second half of the baking time, check the cake regularly and, if it is getting too brown, protect the top by laying a piece of foil or double greaseproof paper lightly over it. When it is cooked, remove from the oven but leave in the tin to cool for at least an hour, then turn out carefully, remove the papers and leave on a wire rack until completely cold. Store in an airtight tin.

Note on Decoration: This cake can be served just as it is, but if you want a more festive appearance, why not decorate the top with whole crystallised fruits? Melted apricot jam will hold them in place and they look very glamorous — all you need to finish it off is a couple of lengths of red and green satin ribbon to tie around the sides. Another possibility is to brush over the cake with melted apricot jam, allow it to set, then cover with **White Christmas Icing**, a softer, lighter version of the traditional Royal Icing. The glycerine (available from chemists) will keep the icing from becoming brittle but if you like it firm on the outside and still fairly soft underneath, don't make the icing until a few days before Christmas. More lemon juice can be added for extra flavour if you like, but it tends to make the icing harden in storage so extra glycerine may be needed.

Light White Icing

2 egg whites
About 1 lb/450g icing sugar, sifted
2 teaspoons lemon juice
2 teaspoons glycerine.

Whisk the egg whites lightly together in a large bowl. Work about half of the sifted icing sugar into the egg whites with the lemon juice and glycerine. Gradually beat in enough of the remaining sugar until the icing is thick enough to coat the back of the spoon without running off. Spread roughly over the top and sides of the cake, then flick into peaks. Decorate simply with a few sprigs of holly or other seasonal decoration and, when the icing is dry, tie a red satin ribbon around the cake and finish with a double bow.

Rum and Raisin Cake with Lemon Icing

For a special occasion or an alternative Christmas cake, try this luscious Rum and Raisin Cake. The subtle flavours of lemon and rum are reminiscent of hot toddies and the crunchy topping is absolutely irresistible.

8 oz/225g raisins
Grated zest of 1 lemon
¼ pint/150 ml golden rum
6 oz/175g softened butter
6 oz/175g light golden brown sugar
3 eggs
6 oz/175g plain flour
Pinch of salt
Pinch of ground cinnamon
1 teaspoon baking powder

Icing:

Juice of 1 lemon
8 oz/225g icing sugar
A little warm water
Crystallised lemon slices or fruit, to decorate (optional).

Put the raisins and grated lemon zest into a bowl with the rum and leave overnight to soak. Grease and base-line a deep 7"/18 cm cake tin and preheat a moderate oven, 350°F, 180°C, Gas mark 4. Cream the butter and sugar until light and fluffy. Separate the eggs and sift the flour, salt, cinnamon and baking powder together into a bowl. Beat the yolks into the butter and sugar one by one, including a spoonful of flour and beating well after each addition. Gradually add the raisin and rum mixture, alternating with the remaining flour. Do not overbeat at this stage. Finally, whisk the egg whites until stiff and fold them into the mixture with a metal spoon. Turn into the preheated oven and bake for about 1½ hours, or until well-risen and springy to the touch — test with a skewer, which should come out clean, if you are uncertain. Turn out and cool on a wire rack.

Meanwhile, make a **lemon icing** by mixing the lemon juice with the sieved icing sugar and just enough warm water to make a pouring consistency. Put a dinner plate under the cake rack to catch the drips and pour the icing over the cake a tablespoonful at a time, letting it dribble naturally down the sides. Don't worry if a lot ends up on the plate underneath, just scoop it up and put it on top again. When the icing has set, it can be decorated with crystallised lemon slices, or other crystallised fruit, if you like.

Chocolate Yule Log with Vanilla and Chocolate Butter Icings

But the most popular of all the seasonal cakes, especially with children, is usually the Yule Log. Although now no more than a symbol of the great logs which were once brought in to the hearth to burn throughout the festive period, this small cake is one of the most attractive Christmas foods and very versatile. If it's for family tea times and mainly for children, it can be filled with whipped cream or butter icing, then covered with chocolate icing or simply dusted with icing sugar 'snow'. Or it can be a much richer and definitely adult affair flavoured with rum or filled with brandy-flavoured chestnut cream, when it becomes the traditional French alternative to our kind of Christmas cake, the Bûche de Noël. The basic **Chocolate Swiss Roll** *is common to both.*

Grease and base-line a swiss roll tin about 13"x9"/31cmx23cm, allowing enough paper to extend beyond each end by about an inch/2.5 cm. Preheat a hot oven, 425°F/220°C Gas mark 7. Sift flour and cocoa powder together several times and set aside on a sheet of greaseproof paper in a warm place. Whisk eggs and sugar in an electric mixer, or using a hand whisk in a bowl set over a pan of hot water, until the mixture is very thick and foamy. If whisking by hand, this may take about 10 minutes; then remove the basin from the heat, set on a damp cloth to hold it steady, and whisk for another 2 or 3 minutes. Sift the flour over the mixture, about a third at a time, and gradually fold in gently with a metal spoon, losing as little volume as possible. Pour the mixture into the prepared tin, spread level and bake in the centre of the preheated oven for for 12-15 minutes, until well-risen and springy to the touch. Lay a damp tea towel on a work surface and cover it with a sheet of greaseproof paper sprinkled evenly with caster sugar. Peel off the lining paper and, using a sharp knife, trim off the crisp edges from the cake to make it easier to roll. Roll up immediately, using the cloth as a guide and leaving the greaseproof paper inside to prevent the cake sticking together and make it easier to unroll for filling when cold.

For a family Yule Log, either fill with slightly sweetened whipped cream or with **butter icing**, which is most effective if vanilla is used for the filling and chocolate for the outside 'bark', but chocolate can be used for both if preferred.

Vanilla Butter Icing:

Cream the butter, gradually add the sieved sugar and beat well until smooth and creamy. Add a few drops of vanilla essence.

Chocolate Butter Icing:

Put the coffee essence, cocoa and hot water into a cup or small bowl and mix well until smooth. Cream the butter, gradually work in the sieved sugar and beat until smooth and creamy, then add the cocoa mixture.

To assemble the Yule Log:

Carefully unroll the cold swiss roll and spread the Vanilla Butter Icing over the cake. Re-roll carefully, then use a palette knife to spread the Chocolate Butter Icing over the outside of the swiss roll and, using a fork or palette knife, mark circles on the ends and, along the top and sides, lines and knots to look like bark. Sprinkle lightly with icing sugar 'snow' and decorate with holly.

Chocolate Swiss Roll
2 oz/50g self-raising flour
1 oz/25g cocoa powder
3 eggs
3½ oz/90g caster sugar
Extra caster sugar for rolling.

Vanilla Butter Icing:
3 oz/75g butter, at room temperature
4 oz/100g icing sugar
Vanilla essence.

Chocolate Butter Icing:
½ teaspoon coffee essence
1 level tablespoon cocoa powder
1 tablespoon hot water
2 oz/50g butter, at room temperature
4-6 oz/100-175g icing sugar, as required.

Bûche de Noël with Chestnut Brandy Cream

Chestnut Brandy Cream:

2 tablespoons finely
  ground coffee
Scant 4 fl oz/90 ml milk
8 oz/225g unsweetened
  chestnut purée
2 oz/50g caster sugar
5 fl oz/150 ml carton
  double cream
2-3 tablespoons brandy.

Of the more adult versions, the most sophisticated is the Bûche de Noël, which is more of a dessert than a cake. Use the basic Chocolate Swiss Roll and Chocolate Butter Icing given above, but fill it with this delicious Chestnut Brandy Cream:

Put the coffee and milk into a small pan, bring almost to the boil, then remove the pan from the heat and leave for 5 minutes to infuse. Strain through a fine sieve. Sieve the chestnut purée into a bowl, beat in the hot coffee-flavoured milk and the sugar until smooth. In a separate bowl, whisk the cream until stiff, then stir into the chestnut mixture with the brandy. Spread evenly over the inside of the swiss roll to fill, re-roll carefully, cover with Chocolate Butter Icing and decorate as above.

Chocolate Rum Log

Rum-Flavoured Chocolate Icing:

3 level tablespoons cocoa
  powder
3 tablespoons very hot water
6 oz/175g unsalted butter,
  at room temperature
1 lb/450g icing sugar
3-4 tablespoons rum, or to
  taste
Extra rum to sprinkle over
  cake.

Another delicious variation which is not quite as rich as the Bûche de Noël is Chocolate Rum Log, also based on the same Chocolate Swiss Roll. This rum-flavoured chocolate icing is enough to fill and cover the log generously.

Mix the cocoa and hot water together in a mixing bowl to make a smooth paste and leave to cool. Carefully unroll the swiss roll and sprinkle it lightly with rum. Add the butter and half of the icing sugar to the cocoa mixture and beat well to mix, then gradually beat in the rest of the icing sugar. Spread about half of the icing evenly over the inside of the swiss roll, then roll up carefully. Sprinkle the outside lightly with rum, then spread with the remaining icing, mark the 'bark' with lines and knots, dust lightly with icing sugar snow and decorate with holly.

Mincemeat

Mincemeat

1 lb/450g raisins (seedless
  or de-seeded)
1 lb/450g sultanas
1 lb/450g currants
8 oz/225g chopped candied
  peel, preferably
  home-made
3 large Bramleys or 6
  dessert apples, peeled,
  cored and chopped finely
2 lb/900g sugar, preferably
  brown
12 oz/325g shredded suet
4 oz/100g almonds,
  blanched and slivered
1 tsp each: grated nutmeg,
  ground cloves, ground
  cinnamon
Grated zest and juice of 3
  lemons and 3 oranges
Sherry or brandy (see
  method).

Mincemeat is very easy to make and there's no comparison between home-made and commercial versions. It needs a couple of weeks maturing time, so make it as near the beginning of December as possible. Although mincemeat is really a short-term preserve and should ideally be used up within a few months, it keeps surprisingly well if you are generous with the alcohol, keep it in a dark, cool place — and if you use the right apples. Although I have a weakness for home-grown Bramleys Seedlings, which make an especially juicy and not too sweet mincemeat for almost immediate use, juicy cooking apples sometimes cause fermentation so a drier dessert apple such as Cox's Orange Pippin is a better choice if you want it to last — it can't be guaranteed, but I have known mincemeat last from one Christmas to the next. As well as its most obvious use in mince pies, which seem to be as popular as ever, mincemeat is a versatile filling in lots of other delicious recipes (see below) and, if prettily presented, makes a very acceptable small gift coming up to Christmas.

Put the dried fruit, chopped peel, chopped apples, sugar, suet, almonds and spices into a large bowl and mix together thoroughly. Finely grate the zest from the lemons and oranges and mix in with the other dry ingredients. Squeeze the juice from the oranges and lemons, strain into a measuring jug and make up to 1 pint/600 ml with sherry or brandy. Add liquid to the fruit mixture and stir well. Cover and set aside in a cool place for 24 hours, stirring from time to time. Finally, stir thoroughly and pack into clean, dry screw-top jars, pressing down to eliminate air pockets. A dessertspoonful of brandy can be used to top up if available, but is not essential. Lay a waxed disc on top, cover, label and store in a cool place for at least a fortnight. Stir well before use as the fruit settles in the bottom of the jars — in fact, if you are sure they are properly sealed, it is a good idea to turn them upside down occasionally during storage so that the juices are evenly distributed. Makes about 10 jars.

Mince Pies with One-Stage Sweet Pastry

*Mince Pies are just about the most convenient of all the traditional Christmas foods, as they can be made up at any time and kept in the freezer, uncooked, to have hot from the oven at very short notice whenever you like. My preference is definitely for short pastry but, that said, there's plenty of variety to be had. A simple Pâté Sucrée is always delicious, especially if made with butter, or try foolproof **One-stage (Fork) Pastry**, a smooth sweetened pastry which is exceptionally easy to handle and cooks to a light, crisp golden-brown.*

Put the butter or margarine into a bowl with half of the flour and the water. Cream with a fork until thoroughly mixed. Sift together the remaining flour and icing sugar and, still using a fork, gradually work into the mixture to form a manageable dough. Turn out onto a floured work surface and knead lightly until smooth. Wrap in clingfilm and chill for 30 minutes before use.

One-Stage Pastry:

This quantity is enough for about 24 mince pies (depending on thickness of pastry):

8 oz/225g butter or block margarine, at room temperature
12 oz/350g plain flour
3 tablespoons very cold water
1 oz/25g icing sugar.

Mincemeat Star Pies

Some people find the proportion of pastry to mincemeat too high in traditional mince pies, but Mincemeat Star Pies are lighter and very attractive. For trays of standard 2½"/6.3 cm bun/tartlet tins you need three cutters — a 3"-3½"/7.5-8.9 cm round fluted cutter for the bases, a 2"- 2½"/5.5-6.3 cm round fluted cutter for half of the lids and a 2"/5cm star-shaped cutter for the rest of the lids.

Roll out the pastry to about ⅛"/0.3 cm thick. In case there is any re-rolling to be done, always make the lids first: stamp out 12 circles with the 2½"/6.3 cm round fluted cutter then, using the 2"/5 cm star-shaped cutter, remove a star shape from the centre of each one. Set aside. Next stamp out 24 bases, using the 3½"/8.9 cm round fluted cutter and re-rolling as necessary. Use these to line the bases of 24 bun tins, then place about a teaspoonful of mincemeat in each one — be careful not to overfill, especially if the mincemeat is very juicy. Next, using a pastry brush dipped in cold water, dampen the edges of the lids with the star-shapes in the centre and press the edges down gently onto the pastry bases. (An upturned egg cup can be useful for this.) Lay the remaining small star-shaped lids on top of the mincemeat in the other 12 tarts and press down lightly. Either open-freeze, then wrap and store in the freezer until required, or bake immediately in a preheated hot oven, 425°F/220°C/ Gas mark 7 for about 20 minutes, or until the pastry is a light golden-brown. Using a round-bladed knife, ease the pies from the tins and onto a rack. Dust with icing sugar and serve warm with chilled whippped cream or Rum Butter.

Note: If the mince pies have been frozen, put straight from the freezer into a hot oven, as for fresh mince pies, but allow about 10 minutes extra cooking time.

1 quantity One-stage pastry (see above)
About 1 lb/450g mincemeat
Icing sugar to decorate.

Traditional Mince Pies with Almond Pastry

Apart from using different shapes, interesting variations on traditional mince pies can easily be created with flavourings, such as in this Almond Pastry.

The method for the pastry is traditional: sift the flour into a mixing bowl, add the ground almonds and then cut in the butter. Either mix with a pastry blender or rub in lightly with the fingertips until the mixture looks like fine breadcrumbs. Add the sifted icing sugar and the finely grated lemon zest and mix well. Beat the egg lightly with the almond essence, cold water and lemon juice. Stir into the flour mixture and mix to a rough dough with a fork. Turn out onto a floured surface and knead lightly until smooth. Cover and leave in a cool place for 30 minutes to rest. Roll out to a thickness of about ⅛" /0.3 cm and, if using standard 2½"/6.3 cm tartlet

Almond Pastry:

10 oz/275g plain flour
2 oz/50g ground almonds
6 oz/175g butter
3 oz/75g icing sugar
Finely grated zest of ½ lemon
Yolk of 1 large egg, lightly beaten
1 coffeespoon natural almond essence (or to taste)
3 tablespoons very cold water
1 tablespoon lemon juice

Filling:

1 lb/450g approx mincemeat
1 egg white, beaten lightly, to glaze
Caster sugar to sprinkle over
About 1 oz/25g blanched, split almonds to decorate.

tins, use a 2"/5.5 cm round fluted cutter to stamp out 24 pastry lids and a 3"/7.5 cm one for the bases, gathering up the trimmings and re-rolling as necessary. Line tins with pastry and half fill each with about 1 teaspoonful of mincemeat. Dampen the undersides of the pastry lids, lay over the mincemeat and press down lightly with an upturned egg cup to seal the edges. Brush the tops with lightly beaten egg white, sprinkle over a little caster sugar and press half an almond into each lid. Put into a preheated hot oven, 425°F/220°C/Gas mark 7 and immediately reduce the temperature to 400°F/200°C/Gas mark 6. Bake for about 20 minutes, until golden brown. Serve hot with Rum or Brandy Butter, or with chilled whipped cream, which can be slightly sweetened if you like and flavoured with a dash of rum or brandy, or with orange flower water and/or a little grated orange zest. Make 24.

Mincemeat Meringue Pie with Orange Pastry

Serves 8-10:

Orange Pastry:
9 oz/250g plain flour
4½ oz/125g butter
2½ oz/60g caster sugar
Finely grated zest of ½ orange
3 egg yolks, lightly beaten
Juice of 1 orange, as required (see method)

Filling:
1 lb/450g home-made mincemeat
2 oz/50g ground almonds
Finely grated zest of ½ orange
Orange juice (see method)
2 tablespoons Cointreau or Grand Marnier

Topping:
3 egg whites
6 oz/175g caster sugar
Caster sugar for dredging
Optional, for decoration: candied orange peel and angelica; blanched split almonds, toasted.

There's much more to mincemeat than individual mince pies: home-made mincemeat is one of the tastiest and most versatile stand-bys you can have in the store cupboard, whether for quick family desserts or entertaining. This Mincemeat Meringue Pie, for example, with its unusual orange pastry base and Cointreau-flavoured filling makes an excellent hot or cold dinner party dessert, while a quicker simplified version is ideal for family meals.

First make the pastry: put the flour, roughly chopped butter and sugar into the bowl of a food processor and process for a few seconds until the mixture looks like coarse breadcrumbs. Add the finely grated zest of orange, egg yolks and 1 tablespoon orange juice. Continue to process, adding a little extra orange juice if necessary, until the mixture forms a ball around the centre of the chopping knife. Remove the pastry, wrap in clingfilm and leave in the fridge for at least 10 minutes before rolling.

Meanwhile, preheat a fairly hot oven, 400°F/200°C/Gas mark 6. Mix together the mincemeat, ground almonds, grated orange zest, whatever orange juice remains from the pastry and the Cointreau or Grand Marnier. Put this mixture aside, while rolling out the pastry to line a 9"-10"/22-25 cm fluted flan ring or deep tart tin with removable base. Prick the pastry with a fork, lay a sheet of greaseproof over it and weigh down with baking beans. Bake blind for 10 minutes. Remove the beans and paper and cook for another 10 minutes, or until a light golden brown. Remove from the oven and reduce the oven temperature to 300°F, 150°C, Gas mark 2.

Leave the pastry shell to cool slightly, while making the meringue: whisk the egg whites until stiff, then add half of the sugar and continue whisking until thick and glossy. Lightly but thoroughly, fold in the remaining sugar with a metal spoon, losing as little volume as possible. Spread the prepared mincemeat mixture over the base of the flan and spoon or pipe the meringue on top. Spike with angelica and pieces of candied orange peel (or glacé cherries), sprinkle with caster sugar and bake for 20-30 minutes until golden-brown, reducing the temperature to 275°F, 140°C, Gas mark 1 after 10 minutes. Can be served hot or cold, but it's best of all served hot with chilled whipped cream or Cumberland Butter.

Variations: For a simpler dessert at other times of year, ordinary shortcrust pastry can be used or even a biscuit crust, using half butter to crushed digestive biscuits. The meringue can be omitted, if preferred, in which case the cooking temperature can be higher (350°F/180°C/ Gas mark 4) and the time shorter (10-15 minutes). For family meals, omit the liqueur; a little orange flower water makes a delicious addition to lightly sweetened whipped cream to serve with the hot or cold tart.

Edible Gifts and Miscellaneous Christmas Ideas

Whether you are planning to make up hampers for all your friends or simply like to take along a small gift for your hostess when invited out to dinner, edible gifts are a pleasure both to make and receive at any time of year, but making them for Christmas presents carries the added bonus that you are doing something enjoyable in the peace of your own kitchen instead of fighting your way through the Christmas crowds in the shops. There are plenty to choose from in this chapter, but check through the index for other ideas as there are lots of suitable recipes throughout the book, especially in the sections on preserves.

Farmhouse Pâté

Farmhouse Pâté is a very useful standby at this time of year: this kind of robust pâté can be made well ahead for Christmas and it freezes well, which can be a special bonus point if brought as a gift to a house already well stocked for Christmas. It's a particularly versatile dish which will keep well in the fridge and can be used as a starter, a light meal served with soup, salad and brown bread or, served on savoury biscuits, as a snack to hand around at parties. Cranberry or Cumberland Sauce both complement the flavour of this pâté. [Microwave]

Remove any skin and bones from the belly of pork, trim the liver and mince both coarsely, then pass the slice of bread through to clean the mincer. Alternatively, use a food processor or electric chopper, but be careful not over-process.

Melt the butter and soften the finely chopped onion and crushed garlic in it, without colouring. Remove from the heat and mix thoroughly with the pork mixture, all the herbs, spices and seasonings. Mix together the lightly beaten egg, brandy or sherry and the tomato purée; blend into the pork mixture. Remove any bones from the streaky rashers, cut off the rinds and flatten the rashers by stretching along a chopping board with the back of a knife. Reserve a few rashers and use the rest to line a terrine or other suitable container(s). Spoon in the well-mixed pâté mixture, level off and top with the reserved rashers. Cover with foil or a lid, set the dish in a roasting tin containing about 1"/2.5 cm of cold water and cook in a preheated moderate oven 350°F, 180°C, Gas mark 4, for 2½ hours if making one large pâté, proportionately less if smaller dishes are used. Remove from the roasting pan and cool, then leave overnight under a light weight; when cold, decorate with a bay leaf, run a little melted unsalted or clarified butter over the top and refrigerate. Freezes well and keeps for at least a week in the refrigerator. (If freezing for more than a few weeks remove the bacon rashers, as they tend to go rancid during long storage.)

Makes one large (2-pint/1.2 litre) pâté or several smaller ones:

2 lb/900g belly of pork
1 lb/450g pig's liver
1 slice day old bread
1 oz/25g butter
1 large onion, finely chopped
2 cloves garlic, crushed
1 teaspoon dried mixed herbs
2 tablespoons freshly chopped parsley
½ teaspoon crushed allspice
¼ teaspoon grated nutmeg
Salt, freshly ground pepper
1 egg
1 small glass brandy or sherry
1 tablespoon tomato purée
About 8 oz/225g streaky bacon rashers to line terrine
Bay leaf to decorate
Clarified butter or lard to seal.

Chicken Liver Pâté

Chicken Liver Pâté has suffered from an image problem because it became a bit of a cliché in the 1960s and, since then, has so often been badly prepared and presented in hotels. Also, chicken livers suddenly became harder to get, but it's worth persevering because this simple, quickly made pâté is too delicious to abandon. Country people should have easy access to fresh chicken livers — in the cities they are available frozen from specialist outlets.

Defrosted raw chicken livers should not be re-frozen but, in the unlikely event that you should wish to freeze cooked ones, that is quite safe. This smooth pâté does not freeze well, but it keeps much better than you might expect — for at least a week in the fridge before the seal is broken and for several days afterwards, if it is being used up gradually. Try to keep the open surface as small as possible, as it is

Makes several small pâtés:

2 onions
2 large cloves garlic or to taste
8 oz/225g butter
1 lb/450g chicken livers
1 dessertspoon freshly chopped mixed herbs — parsley, thyme, rosemary etc OR 1 teaspoon mixed dried herbs
Salt, freshly ground black pepper
2 or 3 tablespoons brandy
Clarified butter to seal.

contact with the air that causes it to turn an unattractive grey colour. [Microwave]

Chop the onions and garlic finely. Melt 2 oz/50g of the butter over gentle heat, add the onion and garlic and cook gently until just turning colour. Check through and trim the chicken livers; add to the pan with the herbs and cook together for about 3 minutes, until the livers have browned on the outside but are still pink in the middle. Cool. Dice the remaining butter. Turn the chicken liver mixture into a blender or food processor and, gradually working in the cubes of butter by dropping them down the chute onto the moving blades, blend the mixture to a smooth purée. Add the brandy at the end, check the seasoning, then turn out into china or earthenware pots. Lay a bay leaf on top of each one if you wish, then seal with melted clarified or unsalted butter. Cool and chill. Will keep in the fridge for at least a week.

*While savoury contributions are especially welcome at a time when we all tend to over-indulge on sweeter treats, seasonal **PRESERVES** tend to be much better keepers and will still be there to enjoy in the austere days of January and February. Refer to the Index for a wide range of preserves suitable for gifts.*

Alcholic Prunes

3 lb/1-2Kg pitted prunes (best quality)
1 lb/450g light golden brown sugar
Zest of 1 large lemon, peeled and cut into thin strips
1 pint/½ litre sherry, brandy or vermouth (cheapest available).

Alcholic Prunes is an old favourite because it's not only delicious but easy and not too expensive. Most dried fruits taste wonderful when plumped out with brandy, sherry or whatever so try other combinations if you prefer — dried apricots are especially delicious with amaretto, for example. They can be eaten as sweetmeats, warmed gently in their juices and served with cream, or used in fruit tarts. Make them in good time to allow time for the luscious liquids to be absorbed and don't pack jars too tightly to allow for swelling. Use proper preserving jars if possible to prevent evaporation and the fruit will keep for six months in a cool, dark place.

Put the prunes into a large saucepan, cover with cold water and bring slowly to the boil then simmer, covered, for about 5 minutes. Remove from the heat and allow to cool for about 10 minutes, then strain, retaining about ¾ pint/450ml of the cooking liquor. Pack the prunes loosely into preserving jars. Combine the prune liquid, sugar and lemon zest over a low heat until the sugar is completely dissolved. Boil gently for 5 minutes. Remove from the heat and pour over the fruit, distributing evenly between the jars. Fill the jars with liquor, making sure the prunes are completely covered and the jars filled to the top. Seal. Shake jars once a week to distribute ingredients.

Bitter Chocolate Brazils, Stuffed Dates, Walnut and Almond Pairs

*For many people, **Home-made Sweets** and **Petits Fours** are the perfect gift. If you have some pretty little boxes and plenty of petits fours cases, it's easy to make up an attractive selection that you couldn't get in a shop. Some of the best are extraordinarily simple — there's nothing to beat **Bitter Chocolate Brazils** (roasted brazil nuts dipped in melted bitter or plain dessert chocolate), for instance, and some, such as **Stuffed Dates** (stones removed, almond paste inserted) and **Walnut and Almond Pairs** (nut halves paired together with almond paste) are just a good way of using up almond paste left over from the Christmas cake.*

A range of edible gifts, page 175
Previous page: (top) Bûche de Noël with Chestnut Brandy Cream, page 172
and (bottom) Traditional Mince Pies, page 173

Granny Campbell's Fudge

Then there are the old favourites: Granny Campbell's Fudge has been an essential part of Christmas in our family for several generations and, as this makes a big batch, there's always enough of this dark, gooey fudge to help out with the gift boxes too.

In a large, heavy-based pan, heat the butter and water together gently until the butter melts, then add the sugar and stir over low heat until it has dissolved. Raise the heat, bring the mixture up to the boil and boil hard until strands 'crack' when tested in a saucer of cold water. Remove from the heat, beat in the condensed milk with a wooden spoon and return to a moderate heat, stirring, for a few minutes. Remove from the heat, add vanilla to taste and beat again with a wooden spoon until glossy and of pouring consistency. Pour the mixture into a buttered shallow oblong tin, about 11"x7"/28 cm x 18 cm, and leave to cool. When cold, cut into cubes and store in an airtight tin until required. Pack in petits fours cases to serve.

6 oz/175g butter
1/4 pint/150 ml water
2 lb/900g rich dark brown sugar
1 tin (14 oz/397g) condensed milk
1/2 tsp vanilla essence, or to taste.

Basic Vanilla Fudge

By working on variations to this more orthodox Basic Vanilla Fudge, a whole range of different sweets can be made.

Put all ingredients except the flavouring into a large, heavy-based saucepan and stir over low heat until the sugar dissolves. Bring to the boil and allow to boil, stirring occasionally, for about 15 minutes or until it reaches 240°F/120°C on a sugar thermometer, when a little of the mixture will form a soft ball if dropped into a bowl of cold water. Remove from the heat, add the vanilla and cool slightly, then beat with a wooden spoon until the mixture thickens and grains. Pour into a buttered 7"/18 cm square tin. When set, mark into small squares. When cold, turn out and cut up. Pack into a box in petits fours cases.

Endless variations can be made on the basic fudge, including:

Chocolate Fudge: add 4 oz/100g plain chocolate and 1 tablespoon cocoa and dissolve with the other ingredients.

Coffee Fudge: omit the vanilla and add 2 tablespoons coffee essence instead, with 4 oz/100g chopped walnuts if you like.

Almond and Raisin Fudge: Omit vanilla and add 1 teaspoon almond essence with 2 oz/50g chopped blanched almonds and 2 oz/50g chopped seedless raisins.

2 lb/900g granulated sugar
Small tin (6 oz/170g) evaporated milk
Large tin (14 oz/397g) condensed milk
4 oz/100g butter
2 teaspoons vanilla essence.

Turkish Delight

Turkish Delight is another wonderful sweetmeat, yet it is not often made. I especially like the traditional rosewater flavour, but there's also a mint-flavoured one given below.

Put the water into a saucepan and sprinkle the gelatine over. Add the granulated sugar and heat gently until both the gelatine and sugar have dissolved. Bring to the boil and boil gently for 20 minutes. Remove from the heat and set aside for 10 minutes, then add the rosewater and just enough red colouring to turn the mixture a delicate shade of rose pink. Pour into a wetted tin, about 6-7"/15-18 cm square, and leave in a cool place for 24 hours. Sift the icing sugar and cornflour together onto a piece of greaseproof paper laid out on a work surface, then turn the Turkish Delight out onto this mixture — if it sticks, dip briefly in hot water to release. Coat well with the sugar and cornflour mixture, then cut into cubes with a sharp knife, coating each square generously before packing in a tin or the traditional wooden box for storage.

Variation: **Peppermint Turkish Delight (Crème de Menthe Jellies)** is made in the same way — replace the rosewater and the red colouring

Makes about 1 lb/450g:
1/4 pint/150 ml hot water
1 oz/25g (2 sachets) powdered gelatine
1 lb/450g granulated sugar
1 tablespoon rosewater
A few drops red food colouring
2 oz/50g icing sugar
1 oz/25g cornflour.

with a little peppermint essence and a few drops of green food colouring.

Hint: While peppermint flavoured sweets are very acceptable and a selection of them may be even more so, do not mix peppermint sweets in with other flavours, as their strong aroma will taint all the others.

Peppermint Creams

Makes about 12 oz/350g:
8 oz/225g icing sugar
l egg white, lightly beaten
Peppermint oil or essence
A few drops green food
  colouring (optional)
4 oz/100g plain chocolate,
  eg Bournville.

We used to make Peppermint Creams with the leftover Royal Icing in the days when it didn't do to slap every scrap of icing onto the cake somehow, but they are worth making for themselves and I especially enjoy this combination of mint and chocolate.

Sift the icing sugar into a large bowl and gradually add enough egg white to form a stiff paste. Add a few drops of peppermint flavouring and the green colouring, if using. Knead lightly. Dust a work surface with icing sugar and roll the paste out to about ½"/1 cm thick. Using a small plain cutter (about 1"/2.5 cm), stamp out circles of the mixture and transfer to a baking sheet lined with Bakewell paper. Gather up trimmings and re-roll as appropriate. Cover lightly and leave overnight to dry out. Melt the chocolate in a small bowl set over hot water. Using a small fork or cocktail stick to hold them, dip the creams into the chocolate — either coat half the creams completely, or half-coat the whole batch, as preferred. Return the chocolate-coated creams to the non-stick baking parchment and leave to set before storing.

Variations: **Lemon Creams** can be made with the same basic mixture as for peppermint: instead of peppermint essence and green colouring, use lemon essence and a few drops of yellow colouring; let the fondant mellow for an hour, then roll out, cut into wedge-shaped pieces and decorate each with a piece of crystallised lemon or lemon peel. Allow to dry out for 24 hours. **Orange Creams** are very similar and fun to make: mix the finely grated zest of an orange with 2 tbsp orange juice, 2 teaspoons lemon juice with 12 oz/350g icing sugar and enough egg white to make the mixture firm but pliable. Add a few drops of orange colouring, knead well and shape into small balls. Rub on a nutmeg grater to give the texture of orange skin, add a small piece of angelica for the stalk and leave for 24 hours to set and dry.

Chocolate Truffles (1)

Chocolate Truffles (1): Makes about 10 oz/275g
8 oz/225g plain chocolate,
  eg Bournville
l egg yolk
l oz/25g butter
l tablespoon double cream
l tablespoon rum or brandy
Drinking chocolate, cocoa
  or chocolate vermicelli to
  coat.

Probably the most popular of all home-made sweets. This is a particularly dark, chocolatey version and can be flavoured with rum or brandy, as preferred. Although the brandy or rum will help them to keep, the fresh cream content means they must be kept in the fridge. [Microwave]

Melt the chocolate over hot water. Add the other ingredients and beat well to blend thoroughly, then remove from the heat and leave in a cool place for 10 minutes, or until the mixture has set enough to shape into small balls. Roll in chocolate powder or vermicelli and put into paper cases. When cold, pack into an airtight polythene box and keep in the fridge until required.

Chocolate Truffles (2)

Chocolate Truffles (2): Makes about 1 lb/450g
8 oz/225g plain dessert
  chocolate, eg Bournville
2 oz/50g butter
1 egg yolk
2 or 3 tablespoons rum or
  brandy
4 oz/100g ground almonds
3-4 oz/75-100g sieved icing
  sugar
Chocolate powder or
  vermicelli to coat.

An equally good but slightly less rich version, containing ground almonds and no cream. [Microwave]

Melt the chocolate in a good-sized basin over hot water. Remove from the heat, add the butter, egg yolk and rum or brandy and beat well. Add the almonds and mix thoroughly, then stir in enough icing sugar to hold the mixture together for moulding. Form into small balls, roll in the chocolate powder or vermicelli and firm up in the fridge.

Marzipan and Raisin Truffles

These are completely different and fun to make — a good way of using up almond paste if you have a lot to spare, but worth making from scratch anyway as almond paste is so quick and easy to make. [Microwave]

Melt 4 oz/100g of the chocolate in a basin over hot water. Add the raisins and rum. Blend thoroughly and, when firm enough, form into 24 small balls. Chill. Knead the marzipan until pliable, work in the coffee essence and roll out to about ¼"/0.6 cm thick. Using a 2"/5 cm plain cutter, stamp out out 24 rounds, kneading and re-rolling as necessary. Shape the marzipan around the raisins to form balls. Melt remaining chocolate over hot water in a basin small enough to give good depth. Dip each ball in the melted chocolate, drain a little and coat half of them with chocolate vermicelli. Leave the others to dry on baking parchment, then roll in drinking chocolate. Makes 24.

Variation: **Hazelnut Clusters** are a superb and extremely simple variation on the chocolate and raisin mixture given above. The secret is to roast the nuts for full flavour and really crisp texture and to use good plain or bitter dessert chocolate — put about 8 oz/225g whole hazelnuts into a hot oven (about 400-425°F/200-220°C, Gas mark 6-7) and roast for 10 minutes, or until the skins will rub off easily in a tea towel. Leave to cool. Meanwhile, melt 5-6 oz/150-175g good plain chocolate in a bowl set over hot water. When melted but not hot, use two teaspoons to dip the cold nuts into the chocolate, 3 or 4 at a time, then put the clusters onto non-stick parchment, or oiled foil, to set and harden.

Makes about 2 dozen:
8 oz/225g plain chocolate
6 oz/175g seedless raisins
1 tablespoon rum
8 oz/225g ready-made marzipan (almond paste)
1 teaspoonful coffee essence
3 oz/75g chocolate vermicelli
Drinking chocolate.

Chocolate Citrus Candies

Chocolate Citrus Candies are often to be found amongst the petits fours at the best restaurants these days and are easy to make. The basic candy is useful in cooking, of course, but it is quickly transformed into a sweetmeat by coating in sugar or chocolate.

Put the peel into a saucepan with enough cold water to cover and boil for 15 minutes. Drain, cover with fresh cold water and boil again. Repeat, until the peel is tender, then drain and cut into thin pieces. Put the sugar into a heavy-based pan with 5 fl oz/150 ml water and stir over low heat to dissolve. Add the peel and boil for about 35 minutes, or until the syrup is completely absorbed. Drain throughly, then spread out on baking parchment for 12 hours, or roll in sugar if you are using it as a sweet but not with a chocolate coating. If coating, break the chocolate into small pieces and melt carefully in a double boiler or a bowl over a pan of hot water. Spear each piece of peel onto a cocktail stick and dip it into the chocolate. To dry, stick the cocktail sticks into a large potato. When dry, remove the sticks and pack the candies attractively in a box.

Variation: **Chocolate Coated Crystallised Ginger** is also excellent and easy to make: simply scrape off some of the rough sugar coating with a knife before dipping in melted chocolate as above.

Peel from 2 large thick-skinned grapefruit or other citrus fruit, removed in quarters (eat fruit separately)
10 oz/275g sugar
8 oz/225g Bournville chocolate.

Macaroons

Petits Fours and special occasion biscuits overlap to a considerable extent — often the only real difference is the size of, say, a macaroon or a Florentine that makes the difference as to whether it will appear on the tea table or after dinner with the coffee. These Macaroons, for example, are the usual medium size, to serve with tea or as an accompaniment to cold sweets or ices, but all you have to do to convert them into petits fours is make them smaller and, perhaps, intensify the flavouring by replacing the vanilla with almond essence and adding a dash of Amaretto liqueur.

Makes about 2 dozen:

Rice paper
4 oz/100g ground almonds
6 oz/175g caster sugar
2 egg whites
1 tablespoon rice flour,
  cornflour or arrowroot
¼ teaspoon vanilla essence
Split almonds to decorate.

Line two large or three medium baking trays with rice paper. Preheat a moderately hot oven, 375°F, 190°C, Gas mark 5. Mix the almonds and sugar, then add the unbeaten egg whites and cream the mixture very thoroughly together with a wooden spoon. Add the rice flour (or cornflour or arrowroot) and flavouring and mix well. Either fill the mixture into a forcing bag fitted with a ½"/1 cm plain nozzle and pipe into rounds about 2"/5 cm across, or use a teaspoon to pile small mounds of the mixture onto the rice paper and spread out neatly. Press a split almond into the centre of each macaroon, then bake in the preheated oven for 15-20 minutes or until lightly browned, risen and slightly cracked. Cut the rice paper to fit around each macaroon and cool on a wire rack. When cold, store in an airtight tin.

Orange Macaroons

1 orange
9 oz/250g icing sugar
9 oz/250g ground almonds
3 egg whites.

Orange Macaroons are more unusual than almond-flavoured ones — they are delicious on their own, make a good gift, or an ideal crunchy accompaniment to ice cream or a cold sweet. This recipe comes from Blairs Cove House, Durrus, Co Cork, where they serve them with cold sweets such as a strawberry or raspberry bavarois.

Preheat a moderate oven, 350°F, 180°C, Gas mark 4 and grease several baking trays (or line with rice paper). Peel the orange with a vegetable peeler, blanch in boiling water for a minute to remove excess bitterness and refresh under cold water. Drain and cut into thin strips. Put the sifted icing sugar and ground almonds into a mixing bowl and blend together thoroughly. Break the egg whites up lightly with a fork and add to the dry ingredients along with the strips of orange zest. Mix everything together well. Put the mixture out onto the prepared baking trays in blobs, spacing them out well to allow room to spread. Bake in the preheated oven for about 20 minutes, or until golden brown. Remove and cool on wire racks. If using rice paper, cut around the macaroons with scissors and discard the trimmings.

Florentines

Florentines: Makes about 18 full-size biscuits or 3-4 dozen petits fours:

1½ oz/40g unsalted butter
2 oz/50g caster sugar
1 tablespoon flour, sieved
1 tablespoon double cream
1 teaspoon lemon juice
2 oz/50g chopped candied
  orange peel or mixed peel
2½ oz/65g blanched
  almonds, slivered or
  chopped
2½ oz/65g glacé cherries,
  finely chopped
6 oz/175g plain dessert
  chocolate, eg Bournville.

It takes a bit of care to get the technique right when making Florentines for the first time but after that they are quick and easy to make.

Preheat a moderate oven, 350°F, 180°C, Gas mark 4. Line several baking sheets with non-stick baking parchment. Melt the butter with the sugar in a heavy-based pan over moderate heat, stirring all the time — do not allow the mixture to brown. Remove from the heat and beat in the sieved flour, cream and lemon juice. Mix all the chopped fruit and nuts and stir in. Allowing plenty of space (at least 2"/5 cm) between them, put rounded teaspoons of the mixture on the lined baking trays and cook in the preheated oven for 10-15 minutes, or until golden-brown. Keep a close eye on them and be careful not to over-cook. Leave to cool on the baking trays, then carefully peel the baking parchment off and arrange the Florentines upside down on a wire rack. Break up the chocolate and melt in a bowl over hot water then, using a small rounded knife, spread a layer of chocolate on the underside of each biscuit. When half-set, run a fork across the chocolate in wavy lines to make a combed effect. (This is a particular characteristic of Florentines, but can be omitted to save time.) Leave until set and completely cold. Stored in an airtight tin, they will keep for several weeks.

Note: More special occasion biscuits suitable for gifts appear in other sections — Brandysnaps and Almond Tuiles, for example.

Glacé Grapes

Glacé Grapes don't keep well, but they make a delightful small gift to take along to a dinner party and eat on the same day.

Melt the butter in a heavy-based pan, add the syrup and sugar and stir over gentle heat until dissolved. Bring to the boil and boil gently until a little dropped into a bowl of cold water will harden. Remove the pan from the heat and allow the mixture to cool a little. Meanwhile wipe the grapes and, making sure they are dry, cut into little clusters of 2 or 3. Oil one or two baking trays or plates, then, using a fork, dip the clusters, one at a time, into the mixture. Drain them for a moment over the pan, then lay them out on the oiled surfaces and leave until hard and set. Arrange in petits fours cases for serving and pack attractively in a box if using as a gift.

2 oz/50g unsalted butter
8oz/225g golden syrup
4 oz/100g Demerara sugar
8 oz/225g grapes,
  preferably green.

HISTORY OF SUGAR

Although many other plants have been useful suppliers of sugar on a small scale, the most important are *sugar cane* which, despite the dramas involved in the story, has a long history of success in tropical zones, and *sugar beet* which has more recently been produced on a commercial scale in temperate climates. Through the centuries only these two and, to a lesser extent, the sugar maple, a tree from which maple syrup is tapped, have proved to be commercially viable.

The history of sugar cane goes back several thousands of years, originating in the south Pacific where the cane gave rise to a number of legends relating it to the origins of mankind, no less. In Noel Deerr's classic, The History of Sugar (Chapman & Hall, 1949), several similar legends from different islands are quoted – in the Solomon Islands, for example, legend has it that mankind sprang from a variety of cane called tohu nonu: two knots of this sprouted, 'from one coming a man and from the other a woman, who were the parents of all mortal men'. Sugar cane was apparently grown thousands of years ago in India and China too and was known to the Greeks and Romans several hundreds of years before Christ – there is evidence that Alexander the Great's army encountered cane in India in 325 BC and he was probably responsible for its introduction to the Mediterranean, from where it spread to Persia, Egypt, Arabia and East Africa. In later writings, around the beginning of the Christian era, it was referred to as the Indian reed or, because of its crystalline consistency, Indian salt, 'in colour and form like common salt, but in taste and sweetness like honey'. Deerr suggests that the origin of the word saccharon goes back to about this time, saying that it first appeared in Diocorides (c. 50 AD) and Pliny the Elder (c. 23-79 AD) and, only around 95 AD, the first known mention of sugar as an article of commerce is made. The Venetians started importing sugar into Europe in 996 AD and pursued the trade with typical vigour and success until the seventeenth century, when wars of the period created problems resulting in the decline and eventual death of the industry in Venice. In other areas, however, production and commerce went from strength to strength: in 1544, Britain's first refinery was built and, by 1750, there were 120 British refineries at work. From the sixteenth century, manufacture spread throughout tropical America, especially Brazil, which supplied the whole of Europe with sugar in the late sixteenth and early seventeenth centuries, until the West Indies took the lead.

(Continued on page 231)

Drinks and Nibbles for Christmas Parties

Mulled Wine

Hot drinks make a good start to any winter party, even if you then move on to something more conventional. Mulled Wine is always popular and very welcoming in cold weather.

3 small apples, studded with cloves
Peeled zest of 1 lemon
About 3 pints/1.7 litres cheap red wine
8 oz/225g brown sugar
3 cinnamon sticks
$1/2$ pint/300ml brandy.

Put the clove-studded apples into a saucepan with the lemon zest, red wine, brown sugar and cinnamon. Bring to simmering point and heat gently covered (without allowing to boil), for 2-4 minutes to allow the flavours to develop. Remove from the heat, add the brandy and serve at once. Serves 12.

Mulled Red Wine with Orange

This version is one I have been using in various forms for years — it's very adaptable and I prefer it to the more traditional versions as the last thing anyone needs at one of our parties is brandy and there is none in this recipe. In fact, I often increase the amount of water and it seems to make no difference — it still gets a good party atmosphere going on a cold day and guests usually move on to ordinary wine after a few glasses anyway.

Makes about 8 glasses:
$1/2$ pint/300 ml water
Zest and juice of 1 orange
A little grated nutmeg
1"/2.5 cm cinnamon stick
2 whole cloves
4 allspice berries
4-6 oz sugar, to taste
1 bottle cheapest red wine (home-made is fine)
Fresh orange slices to garnish (optional).

Put the water, finely peeled orange zest and orange juice into a pan with the spices and sugar. Bring slowly to the boil, stirring to dissolve the sugar, then infuse gently over low heat for 15 minutes. Strain and return to the pan with the wine. Reheat, but be careful not to boil as this will drive off the alcohol. Serve very hot, garnished with a quarter slice of orange.

Hint: The basic infusion of fruit and spices can be prepared in large quantities ahead of a party — it is then very easy to prepare new batches of the mull, just by adding the wine to a measured amount and reheating. A preserving pan is very useful for a mull, also a slow cooker to keep wine hot without boiling.

Farmer's Bishop

This is an old country drink that always used to be popular in cider-producing areas, when each farm had its own supplies — as indeed they still do in some parts of the west of England. This spicy mull has a good flavour, but is much cheaper than the equivalent wine-based one. It's especially appropriate at Hallowe'en, but good for any winter party.

2 oranges
About 18 whole cloves
$1/2$ pint/300ml water
1 stick cinnamon
A small piece of root ginger
A blade of mace OR $1/2$ teaspoon grated nutmeg
1 dozen allspice berries
3-4 oz/75-100g sugar, or to taste
2 measures whiskey
$13/4$ pints/1 litre cider, preferably still
Quartered orange slices, stuck with cloves, to garnish.

Stick oranges slices with the cloves, quarter them and simmer in the water with the spices until reduced to a quarter of its original volume. Strain off. Return the infusion to the rinsed pan, add the sugar and stir until dissolved, then add the whiskey and cider and bring up almost to boiling point. Serve very hot with a quarter slice of orange in each glass. Serves 10.

Mulled Cider

Mulled Cider is another richly spiced alternative that is economical for large numbers and some people prefer the flavour.

Makes about 16 servings:
6 small red-skinned eating apples, studded with cloves
2 or 3 small cinnamon sticks
3 level teaspoons ground ginger
3 oz/75g light golden brown sugar, or to taste
$1/2$ pint/300 ml water
2 small oranges
$31/2$ pints/2 litres cider.

Put the clove-studded apples, broken cinnamon sticks, ginger, sugar and water into a pan with the zest and juice of 1 of the oranges and heat gently until the sugar has dissolved, then bring to the boil and simmer gently for 5 minutes. Add the cider and heat gently without allowing to boil. Strain into a punch bowl and serve decorated with the remaining orange in quartered slices.

Hint: If you have a slow cooker, use it to keep punches hot between servings.

Cider Cup

Alternatively, you could try this very easy Cider Cup, a warming mull that is traditional at Hallowe'en but equally suitable for any convivial get-together in the colder months.

$13/4$ pints/ 1 litre apple juice
$31/2$ pints/2 litres medium sweet cider
Zest of 2 lemons
3 small cinnamon sticks
6 whole cloves.

Blend all the ingredients together in a saucepan. Heat through over a low heat and infuse for 15 minutes, without allowing to boil. Strain and serve. Makes about 20 glasses.

Mulled Ale

Beer drinkers may well prefer Mulled Ale and, again, it is very easy to make and especially handy for people who make their own beer.

For 3 mugs:
1 pint/600 ml mild draught beer
Grated nutmeg
Pinch each of powdered allspice, ginger, cinnamon, coriander
Twist of lemon zest
1 tablespoon Demerara sugar
1 glass port or brandy.

Bring the beer almost to boiling point, season with the spices and add the lemon and sugar. Stir to dissolve the sugar and, just before serving, add the port or brandy.

Hot Spiced Pineapple Cup

Lastly, a non-alcoholic mull for non-drinkers and drivers.

Serves about 8:
2 x 1 litre/1¾ pint cartons natural pineapple juice
4 tablespoons sugar, or to taste
3-4 tablespoons freshly squeezed lemon juice
1 whole cinnamon stick, broken up into sections
1 dessertspoon of whole coriander seeds

Simmer all the ingredients together for 10-15 minutes to allow the flavours to infuse, then strain. Adjust flavouring with sugar and/or lemon juice and serve very hot.

Nibbles for Drinks Parties

Finger food for cocktail parties needs to be simple to make, easy to eat and very tasty. My favourites are bite-sized pieces of thinly sliced spiced beef served on dark, moist bread, likewise smoked salmon or gravad lax — all gimmick-free food that is as easy to prepare as it is to handle. But sometimes something a little different is wanted and, with the exception of the spare ribs, which are delicious enough to deserve inclusion despite being messy to eat, all of these ideas are easy on the guest as well as the cook.

Spiced Almonds

Spiced Almonds are much tastier than ordinary salted almonds and just as easy to make:

8 oz/225g whole, unblanched almonds
1 oz/25g sea salt
2 heaped teaspoons ground cumin
1 level teaspoon caster sugar.

Blanch the almonds in a bowl of boiling water for a minute or two to loosen the skins, then the nuts will pop out easily. Dry with kitchen paper. Spread the nuts on a lightly greased baking sheet and cook in a moderate oven, preheated to 300°F, 150°C, Gas mark 2, until they are a pale biscuit colour. Be careful not to over-brown as they burn easily and take on a bitter flavour. Sprinkle a sheet of paper with the salt, cumin and sugar, then empty the nuts onto it and swirl them around in the seasoning. Gather up the corners of the paper, twist into a bundle and tie with string. Leave the almonds wrapped up like this until required, but try to make them early on the day of the party if possible.

Spare Ribs with Rum and Ginger

Although they are a bit messy (you need to have plenty of paper napkins and/or finger bowls around), spare ribs always disappear very quickly at drinks parties and this recipe for Spare Ribs with Rum and Ginger is especially more-ish.

Makes about 24-30 pieces:
8-12 pork spare ribs, about 2 lb/900g
Marinade:
2 tbsp soy sauce
4 tbsp apple or orange juice
1 tbsp dark rum
2 tsp rich dark brown sugar
2 pieces stem ginger, drained and finely chopped
2 tbsp red wine vinegar.

Get the butcher to cut the ribs into 3 or 4 small pieces, according to length. Trim off any excess fat and put the ribs into a shallow dish. Mix the marinade ingredients together, pour over the ribs and leave for an hour or two, turning occasionally. When ready to cook, preheat a hot oven, 425°F, 220°C, Gas mark 7 and line a roasting tin with foil. Arrange the ribs in the tin, in a single layer if possible, and pour over the marinade. Roast in the preheated oven, turning often and brushing with the marinade, for 40-45 minutes or until tender.

Variation: This doesn't have to be a cocktail snack — the ribs can be served in larger portions (or in the same way), as part of a Chinese meal or as a course in a conventional meal.

Glazed Cocktail Sausages

Cocktail sausages are easier to eat by far and, however predictable, always disappear as fast as they can be produced. These Glazed Sausages are more unusual and can be made with ordinary cocktail sausages, spicy ones or, best of all, mini frankfurters.

Makes about 36:
1 lb/450g cocktail sausages
6 oz/175g redcurrant jelly
1 tablespoon smooth Dijon mustard
Juice of 1 lemon.

Cook the sausages, as appropriate — ordinary sausages should be grilled or cooked in the oven, frankfurters in hot water — but have them slightly undercooked. Put the redcurrant jelly, mustard and lemon juice into a saucepan and whisk over moderate heat until the jelly has dissolved. Add the drained, cooked sausages to the sauce and cook together over gentle heat for a few minutes.

Chicken Satays

As they are easy to eat, nourishing and very delicious, satays make the perfect finger food. This recipe can be adapted to any other lean, tender meat such as pork or steak, or shellfish such as Prawns, which should be shelled and de-veined.

Makes about 20 'bites':
1 lb/450g boned, skinless chicken breast
Sauce:
2 tablespoons crunchy peanut butter
1 tablespoon peanuts, roughly chopped
1 skinned, crushed clove garlic
2 tablespoons dark soy sauce
1 tablespoon light golden brown sugar
Juice of 1 lemon
1 dessertspoon oil
Pinch of chilli powder
Dash of tabasco
Scant 1/4 pint/150 ml water.

Preheat a moderate oven, 350°F, 180°C, Gas mark 4 and grease one or two baking sheets. Cut the chicken into quite small cubes, about the size of a large dice and thread onto wooden cocktail sticks, leaving a little space between the pieces so that they will cook evenly. Lay them out on the greased baking sheets. To make the sauce, put the peanut butter, peanuts, crushed garlic, soy sauce, brown sugar, lemon juice, oil, chilli powder and Tabasco into a small saucepan and stir over moderate heat until smooth, then gradually work in the water to make a creamy sauce. Brush the chicken pieces with a little of this sauce and cook in the preheated oven for 10-15 minutes, brushing with the sauce again halfway through cooking, until golden brown and tender. Reheat the remaining sauce and serve separately, as a dip for the satays.

Variation: By using larger pieces of meat on longer skewers, this recipe adapts to make a main course for 3-4. Serve with stir-fried vegetables.

Sole Ceviche

Sole Ceviche is the kind of dish which smart caterers put on as a first course for executive lunches, but it is not difficult to do and adapts well as a cocktail snack. The fish is 'cooked' and flavoured in the marinade and, as long as it's very fresh, other firm white fish can be used instead of sole.

Makes about 35 pieces:
1 lb/450g filleted and boned black sole
2 fl oz/50ml fresh lime or lemon juice
2 finely chopped shallots
1 fresh green chilli, very finely chopped
1 tablespoon white rum
1 1/2 tbsp olive oil
1 red and 1 green pepper
Salt and freshly ground black pepper
Cocktail sticks.

Skin the fish fillets and cut the flesh into 1/2" squares. Put the lime or lemon juice, chopped shallots and chilli, rum and oil into a non-metallic mixing bowl, add the fish and stir well to coat throroughly with the marinade. Season to taste with salt and pepper, cover tightly and chill overnight. Deseed the peppers and slice lengthways into 1/2"/1cm strips, then divide to make into 1/2"/1cm squares. Drain the fish cubes, reserving the marinade. Thread the cocktail sticks with a piece of red pepper, a piece of fish and then a piece of green pepper. Put the marinade into quite a deep bowl which is just big enough to hold all the sticks and chill until needed.

Savoury Stuffed Dates

Savoury Stuffed Dates — a good combination of sweet and savoury, which is easy to make and convenient to eat.

Makes about 30:
2 oz/50g streaky bacon
6 oz/175g cream cheese
About 8 shelled walnuts
Salt and finely ground black pepper
8 oz/225g best quality dessert dates.

Grill the bacon until crisp and drain on kitchen paper. Put into a food processor, chop finely, then add the cheese and walnuts and blend for about 5 seconds until the nuts are chopped and all ingredients well blended, then add seasoning to taste and blend again very briefly. Stone the dates and open up each one to make a pocket for the filling. Spoon or pipe the mixture in, arrange on a plate and cover with clingfilm. Keep in the fridge until required.

Walnut and Cashel Blue Bites

An easy, piquant nibble.

Makes about 30.
4 oz/100g Cashel Blue cheese
About 8 oz/225g (30 pairs) shelled walnut halves.

Mash the cheese to a smooth paste with a wooden spoon, then use to sandwich together the pairs of walnuts halves. The same amount of cheese could also be used to fill about 16 dried apricot halves, or about 8 oz/225g green or black grapes, de-pipped and threaded on cocktail sticks. Try similar mixtures on 1"/2.5cm sections of celery too, to make **Celery Logs.**

Garlic Pâté Balls

Garlic Pâté Balls can be very quickly made with a good bought pâté from your local delicatessen counter.

Makes about 24:
8 oz/225g stiff garlic pâté
6-8 gherkins
Petits fours cases.

Take a teaspoonsful of the pâté and shape into small balls. Chop the gherkins very finely and roll the balls in them to coat evenly. Chill well and serve in petits fours cases.

Being a great collector of no-stir ice cream recipes, I usually avoid making the kind that either need to be made in an ice cream machine or require attention during the freezing process. But there are some honourable exceptions and these, generally speaking, contain fruit or nuts which would sink to the bottom of the mixture if not forked through when semi-frozen. A perfect example is **Christmas Ice Pudding**, a traditional alternative to the hot plum pudding which is not difficult to make but, as it is crammed full of fruit and nuts, it is essential to redistribute them during freezing.

Christmas Ice Pudding with Apricot Sauce

Serves 8:

4 oz/100g raisins
4 oz/100g glacé cherries, chopped
1 oz/25g angelica, chopped
2 oz/50g chopped candied peel
2 oz/50g glace pineapple or stem ginger, chopped
Finely grated zest and juice of 1 small lemon
1/4 pint/150 ml Cointreau or Grand Marnier
4 large eggs, separated
4 oz/100g icing sugar
1/2 pint/300 ml cream
2 oz/50g blanched, chopped almonds, toasted
2 oz/50g walnuts, roughly chopped.

Put the raisins, chopped cherries, angelica, candied peel and glacé pineapple or stem ginger into a bowl and stir in the grated lemon zest and juice. Mix well. Pour over the Cointreau or Grand Marnier and leave, covered, in a cool place overnight. Stir occasionally if convenient. Next day, turn the freezer to its lowest setting. Whisk the egg yolks and sugar together until very light and creamy. Whip the cream until soft peaks form and, in a separate bowl, whisk the egg whites stiffly. With a metal spoon, carefully fold cream and beaten egg whites into the yolk mixture to mix well without losing volume. Turn into a large pudding basin, about 2 1/2 pints/1.65 litre capacity, cover with a lid or with foil and freeze for about 1 1/2 hours, or until the mixture has frozen around the edges. Add the chopped nuts to the fruit mixture and stir well, then fold into the egg mixture along with any juices that haven't been absorbed, drawing the frozen edges into the centre with a fork. When the fruit and nuts have been thoroughly blended in, cover and return to the freezer. Check after another hour in case the fruit has sunk to the bottom of the mixture — if so, stir again, otherwise leave for several hours or until frozen firm. When required, the ice cream can be served straight from the freezer or it can safely be turned out and decorated as you like — cover it with whipped cream 'snow' and decorate with holly, for example — then leave it in the fridge; it should not soften too much if used within about half an hour. It is delicious served on its own, or you might try a rather sharp sauce based on dried fruit such as **Apricot Purée**: Soak 8 oz/225g dried apricots in cold water overnight; next morning, drain, cover with fresh cold water and simmer, uncovered, for about half an hour, or until tender. Drain the apricots and purée them in a food processor or blender. Add the finely grated zest and juice of 1 small or 1/2 large lemon, plus enough of the cooking juices to make a sauce of pouring consistency; sweeten to taste with caster sugar, bearing in mind that the sauce must be quite sharp in contrast to the sweet, rich ice cream. Chill and hand separately or pour about 2 tbspn of sauce onto each plate and lay a slice of ice cream on top.

Cassata Slice

Serves 8-10

3/4 pint/450ml cream
1/2 teaspoon finely grated orange zest
4 tablespoons orange juice
2oz/50g caster sugar
2oz/50g sultanas
2oz/50g maraschino or glacé cherries, chopped
2oz/50g almonds, toasted and chopped
20 sponge finger/boudoir biscuits
2 tablespoons Cointreau.

Cassata Slice is an easy but impressive dessert from Roundwood House, Mountrath, Co Laois. It seems to break all the rules, as this kind of ice normally needs to be stirred during freezing to redistribute the heavy fruit and nuts, but it is absolutely delicious.

Line a 2lb/900g loaf tin with clingfilm, allowing enough to hang over the sides. Whip the cream, orange zest and 2 tablespoons of juice together until soft peaks form. Whisk in the sugar, sultanas, cherries and almonds. Dip the sponge fingers in the Cointreau and remaining orange juice and use 8 to line the base of the tin. Spoon the cream mixture on top, cover with the remaining sponge fingers and wrap the overhanging clingfilm over the top. Put the whole tin into a polythene bag, seal and freeze. Remove from the freezer 30 minutes before required and serve in thick slices.

Rum Ice Cream

3 eggs, separated
3 oz/75g caster sugar
1½ tbsp rum
1 tbsp lemon juice
½ pint/300ml cream.

Rum and Christmas are firmly partnered in my mind and I especially like the idea of a Rum Ice Cream Christmas Ice. This is really a semi-freddo (ie it never freezes very hard and can be served straight from the freezer) and is easy to make.

Whisk the egg yolks and sugar until very light and creamy, then whisk in the rum and lemon juice. Beat the cream lightly and fold into the mixture with the stiffly whisked egg whites. Turn into a freezer box or serving dish, cover and freeze. Serve straight from the freezer.

Variation: to make **Rum and Raisin Ice Cream**, soak a couple of ounces of raisins (whole or chopped) in the rum and lemon juice for several hours or overnight. Mix thoroughly with the yolk and sugar mixture before folding in the cream and egg whites. Freeze for about an hour, or until the mixture is becoming icy around the edges, then turn the sides to the centre with a fork. After one stir, the mixture can be left for several hours or until frozen firm. Serves 6-8.

Brown Bread Ice Cream

4 oz/100g wholemeal
  breadcrumbs
4 oz/100g light golden
  brown sugar
2 large eggs, separated
1-2 tablespoons
  medium/sweet sherry
¾ pint/450 ml cream.

Brown Bread Ice Cream is another of those classics that, once tried, are always in demand. The secret is not to have too many breadcrumbs (which makes the ice cream heavy) but to toast them until really crisp and well browned, for really good flavour and texture. Yeast bread produces a better flavour than soda bread.

Preheat a moderately hot oven, 375°F, 190°C, Gas mark 5. Spread the breadcrumbs out on a baking sheet and toast them in the oven for about 15 minutes, or until they are crisp and well browned. Leave to cool. Whisk the sugar and egg yolks together until very light and creamy, then beat in the sherry. Whisk the cream until soft peaks form and, in a separate bowl, whisk the egg whites stiffly. Sprinkle the breadcrumbs over the beaten egg yolks, add the cream and fold both into the mixture with a metal spoon. Finally, losing as little volume as possible, fold in the stiffly beaten egg whites. Turn the mixture into a lidded freezer container, cover and freeze until firm. Serve straight from the freezer. This ice cream is good on its own or as part of a selection and works well with chocolate or fruit sauces.

Rathmullan Brown Bread Ice Cream

Serves 6-8:
3 oz/75g wheaten bread,
  preferably home-made
3 oz/75g Demerara or
  caster sugar

Custard:
½ pint/300 ml milk
3"/7.5cm vanilla pod OR 1
  teaspoon vanilla essence
4 oz/100g sugar (OR use
  vanilla sugar and omit
  vanilla)
6 large egg yolks
½ pint/300 ml cream.

This recipe for Brown Bread Ice Cream comes from Rathmullan House in Co. Donegal and is ideal for a special occasion served, perhaps, with a compôte of dried apricots or mixed dried fruit. The method is traditional, based on custard.

Preheat a moderate grill. Crumble the bread onto a baking tray, sprinkle with the sugar and put under the grill, stirring at least once, until caramelised. Turn out onto a piece of foil and, if a fine crumb is preferred, process when cold. To make the custard, scald the milk with the vanilla pod, if using. Whisk sugar and egg yolks together for about 10 minutes until light and fluffy, then pour in the hot milk and continue beating for another 10 minutes. Turn into a metal bowl and cool quickly over iced water. Whisk the cream to soft peaks, fold in the cold custard and turn into an ice cream maker or freeze in a loaf tin in the deep freeze. When the sides are setting, mix well and fold in the crumbs, then freeze for 4-5 hours.

Black Cherry Parfait

Up at the Roundwood Inn, in the Wicklow Hills, they make some of the best bar food in Ireland — where else, I wonder, could you have a bar meal beginning with home-cured Gravad Lax, followed by a fresh lobster salad and finish off with their dessert speciality of the house, a sophisticated, creamy Triple Liqueur Parfait? Their parfait is based on three separately coloured and flavoured mixtures to produce a striped dessert, but chef Paul Taube has worked out a simplified home version, a Black Cherry Parfait which is quite easy to make and produces an exceptionally smooth, creamy ice for a special occasion.

Drain the cherries, reserving the juice. Remove stones, if necessary. Purée the cherries finely in a food processor. Blend with the reserved juice and boil until reduced to a thick pulp. Cool. Whisk the eggs and sugar in a bowl over hot water until the mixture reaches blood temperature, then remove from the heat and continue whisking until it is cold and the whisk will leave a ribbon trail when lifted. Whip the cream separately until stiff, then add the fruit purée, liqueur and cream to the egg mixture. Fold in lightly but thoroughly to mix well, then turn into a freezer container and freeze until firm.

Serves 10:
1 x 15 oz/425g tin black cherries
3 eggs
4 ozs/100g caster sugar
1 pint/600ml cream
½ wine glass liqueur, eg kirsch.

Rich Lemon Ice Cream

Rich Lemon Ice Cream is a foolproof no-stir recipe which invariably attracts far more credit than it deserves.

Whisk egg yolks and sugar until thick and light, then gradually beat in the finely grated zest and juice of the lemons. Beat the cream until thick but not stiff and fold into the mixture. Turn into a freezer box, cover and freeze. Transfer from the freezer to the fridge about 15 minutes before serving with meringues made from the spare egg whites.

Serves 6-8:
6 egg yolks
8 oz/225g caster sugar
2 lemons
½ pint/300 ml double cream.

Amaretto Bombe

A richly-flavoured, festive variation on my Bombe Favourite.

Whip the cream until thick, then sift in 1 oz/25g of the icing sugar and the vanilla essence. Whisk the egg whites until soft peaks form, then gently fold in the remaining 1 oz/25g sifted icing sugar. Using a metal spoon, carefully fold the egg whites into the cream, then fold in the crushed biscuits and the liqueur. Turn into a 2-pint/1.15 litre mould or freezer box, cover and freeze for several hours or until firm. To serve, turn out and serve in slices on a raspberry or strawberry coulis, or Apricot Sauce.

Serves 8:
1 pint/600 ml whipping cream
2 oz/50g icing sugar
½ tsp vanilla essence
2 egg whites
4 oz/100g amaretti, ratafias, or macaroons crushed
2 tablespoons Amaretto liqueur, or to taste.

Blackcurrant Bombe

Blackcurrants keep their flavour beautifully in the freezer and, although this would obviously be a wonderful summer dessert when the berries are in season, their clear, fresh flavour is especially appreciated in winter — and, along with raspberries, this is one of the few ingredients that I enjoy when out of season. This Blackcurrant Bombe is an all-time Christmas favourite in my family and especially convenient to make at the same time as a standard 4-white batch of meringue, as it uses 4 yolks — and, although it looks spectacular, it is neither extravagant nor difficult. Quantities make one big bombe to serve 12 (see variation below), or a medium-sized one to serve six (as given here) plus six individual sweets. Like the others in this book, it is not a true bombe (which usually consists of several complex layers, classically ice cream on the outside, then water ice and finally a rich mousse in the centre). This one is simply a mousse frozen inside a layer of whipped cream, but it does have the element of surprise which is essential to the bombe — and it is very pretty. As the mousse contains gelatine, it is much more stable than an ordinary ice

Serves 6:
1 lb/450 g blackcurrants
1/2 pint/300 ml water
12 oz/350 g caster sugar
Good squeeze of lemon juice
1-2 tablespoons icing sugar
1 miniature Grand Marnier,
   Cointreau or a few drops
   orange flower water, to
   taste
2-3 tablespoons water
1 sachet gelatine
4 egg yolks
2-3 tablespoons Crème de
   Cassis liqueur (optional).

cream and won't melt, even in a warm room.

Cook the fruit gently with half of the water, 8 oz/225 g sugar and a good squeeze of lemon juice until soft. Purée in a blender, then sieve through a nylon sieve into a measuring jug; the purée should measure about 1/2 pint/300 ml. Leave to cool. Whip 3/4 pint/450 ml of the cream stiffly with icing sugar to taste, and flavour with liqueur or orange flower water. Use to line a 2-pint/1.2 litre fluted brioche tin, or other suitable container, and smooth with the back of a tablespoon to make a hollow, or press a 1 1/2 pint/850 ml pyrex bowl into the cream to make a smooth and even mould. Freeze. Put 2-3 tablespoons cold water into a small Pyrex jug and sprinkle with the gelatine; leave to soak. Whisk the yolks with the remaining sugar and water in an electric mixer until very thick and creamy. Beat in the blackcurrant purée and the cassis. Dissolve the cake of gelatine in a microwave, or over hot water, add in a few tablespoons of the blackcurrant mixture, then add the gelatine to the bowl and fold in gently but thoroughly. Take the brioche tin containing the frozen cream from the freezer and pour in enough of the mixture to come level with the cream. (This should leave about 3/4 pint/450 ml mousse.) Open freeze, then cover with clingfilm and freeze until required. Whip the remaining cream lightly, sweeten and flavour as for the bombe, then divide between six glasses and level the cream in the base with the back of a spoon, or hollow, as for a miniature bombe. Divide the remaining mousse between the cream-lined dishes and chill to serve as a mousse, or freeze.

Variation: To make one very large bombe serving 12 for a family occasion or party, whip the cream with sugar and flavouring to taste, then spoon into a very large (4-pint/2.3 litre) or two 2-pint/1.2 litre basins. Line the basin(s) and fill as above, substituting a large tin of evaporated milk for the 4 egg yolks: whip the *well-chilled* evaporated milk until thick (this takes about 5 minutes in a Kenwood Chef on high speed) by which time it will three-quarters fill the bowl. Slow down, sweeten with sifted icing sugar and whisk until thoroughly mixed, then fold in the blackcurrant purée with a metal spoon, mixing thoroughly without losing volume. Turn into the cream-lined bowl(s), which should be filled to the rim. Replace in the freezer and leave, uncovered, until firm, then cover and store in the freezer until required. Remove from freezer to fridge for an hour or more before serving — turn out and decorate as above.

Flavour variations: A **Bramble Bombe**, made as for blackcurrant with a lemon- or vanilla-flavoured cream is equally dramatic and delicious, or try using home-made or good quality bought ice cream for the outer layer — good combinations include orange or chocolate ice cream with a strawberry mousse, chocolate with nuts or praline, or coffee and chocolate.

Hint: Volume of both cream shell and mousse filling can be increased still further if extra egg whites are available. For the cream, add 1 (unwhisked) white per 1/2 pint/300 ml cream and whip as usual; for the mousse, whisk 2-3 whites, or available, until stiff but not dry and fold in lightly, but thoroughly, at the end. *Note:* As volume is increased, either increase the proportion of gelatine included, or serve colder.

WINTER

January and February

After the excitement of Christmas and the New Year party season has died down, the mood changes abruptly and people tend to go very quiet and home-loving for a couple of months until the days start to brighten. This is no cause for complaint: where, after all, could be more agreeable at this time of year than your own cosy kitchen or fireside? It also gives us every excuse to keep the stock-pot going and indulge in big, flavoursome winter soups and casseroles, with lots of earthy root vegetables and pulses — wonderful comfort food. But there are one or two little culinary highlights on the horizon to get us out of hiding, including **St Valentine's Day**, if you are romantically inclined, **Shrove Tuesday** for the annual pancake binge and the **Chinese New Year**, which provides a great excuse to play around with exotic, hot flavourings while the sleet lashes against the window... For the the same reason, this is my favourite season for entertaining — once the post-Christmas depression has lifted, see what's left in the freezer (an amazing amount usually, including a wide selection of party sweets) and work your menus around using dishes which will otherwise languish in the freezer for months. It's a great way to spend the winter. lst February is St Brigid's Day which is traditionally the first day of Spring in Ireland, but the weather is at odds with this tradition and, in the kitchen at least, spring is still around the corner.

PRODUCE AT ITS BEST IN WINTER

Vegetables: Avocados, beetroot, (purple) broccoli, brussels sprouts, cabbages, carrots, cauliflowers, celeriac, celery, chicory, endive, fennel, garlic, horseradish, Jerusalem artichokes, kale, kohl rabi, leeks, mushrooms, onions, parsnips, peppers, potatoes (including new, imported/grown under glass), radish, salsify, Savoys, scorzonera, shallots, spinach, swedes, turnips.

Fruit: This is the big area of interest at the beginning of the year, with a wide variety of citrus fruits, especially, at their cheapest and best. Apples, brazil nuts, Chinese gooseberries, clementines, cranberries, dates, grapefruit, lemons, mandarins, mangoes, melons, oranges, pears, rhubarb (forced), satsumas, tangerines, walnuts.

Poultry and Game: Chicken, duck, goose, guinea fowl, hare, mallard, partridge, pheasant (January), pigeon, rabbit, snipe, teal, turkey, venison, wild goose, woodcock.

Fish: Except that winter storms may affect availability, the selection is similar to other months. Expect high prices, but availability should include: Clams, cod, coley, crab, Dover (black) sole, Dublin Bay Prawns, lobster, mussels, pike, plaice, prawns, salmon (February), scallops, shrimps, skate, rainbow trout, turbot.

SOME SUGGESTED MENUS

St Valentines's Dinner for Two
Hot Crab with Mushrooms and Gin;
Pork with Coriander and Lime;
Chicory and Orange Salad;
Apricot and Almond Ice Cream Heart with Hazelnut Heart Biscuits.

Chinese New Year Party
Barbecued Spare Ribs; Spring Rolls;
Classic Stir-Fried Beef with Mangetout;
Stir-Fried Prawns with Baby Sweetcorn;
Chicken with Walnuts and Celery;
Chinese Noodles; Fried Rice.

Winter Dinner Party
Marinated Kippers with Freshly-baked Wholemeal Bread;
Loin of Pork with Dried Fruit in Cider, Spiced Parsnips, Steamed Broccoli;
Treacle Tart with Walnuts *or* Snaffles Grape Pudding.

Casual Supper for Friends
Soupe à l'Oignon Gratinée;
Scallops with Two Salads;
Eggless Lemon Cheesecake in a Ginger Crust, served with Raspberry Coulis.

Soupe à l'Oignon Gratinée

Serves 6:
2 tablespoons each butter
    and oil
1/2 lb/700g onions, peeled
    and sliced
l teaspoonful sugar
Salt and freshly ground
    pepper
2 level tablespoons flour
3 1/2 pints/2 litres strong
    beefstock or consommé
1/4 pint/150ml red wine
6 slices French bread
6 heaped tablespoons
    grated Gruyère or mixed
    Parmesan and Gruyère
    cheese
3 tablespoons brandy.

Soupe à l'Oignon Gratinée (French Onion Soup) will always be associated with the markets at les Halles, where the cafés stayed open all night to provide good, hot food for the porters. Although the markets have long since moved out, many of the cafés have survived, albeit in refurbished form — and the soup can still be very good.

Heat the butter and oil in a large saucepan and when hot add the thinly sliced onions. Cook over a low flame turning from time to time until they are soft, then add the salt and sugar. Continue cooking until the onions are an even brown. Sprinkle over the flour, add the stock and red wine and stir until it comes to the boil. Lower the heat, cover and simmer very gently for about an hour. Taste for seasoning and leave until ready to serve, removing any fat when cold. Meanwhile toast the bread or dry out in a warm oven for half an hour. Grate the cheese. Heat the soup to simmering point, add the brandy if using, and pour into individual ovenproof dishes or one large one, float the bread slices on top and add the cheese to each slice. Either put into a preheated hot oven, 450°F, 230°C, Gas mark 8 or brown under the grill until the cheese is bubbling and lightly browned.

Game Soup

Serves about 8:
Carcass or bones of game
l onion
1 carrot
Stick of celery
2 oz/50g butter
Pinch of sugar
Large bouquet garni:
    thyme, parsley, rosemary
    and bay leaf
About a dozen black
    peppercorns
Salt
1 glass port or
    medium-sweet sherry
1 teaspoon redcurrant or
    rowan jelly
1/2 oz/15g flour.

Game Soup is well worth making — any time you have some game, keep the carcass or bones and any leftover meat or gravy.

Strip as much meat as possible off the bones and set aside. Chop the onion, carrot and celery roughly. Melt half of the butter in a large, heavy saucepan and fry the vegetables in it quickly until they are golden brown. Add the bones and the pinch of sugar and continue to fry until the vegetables and bones begin to darken. Add as much water as the pan will hold (at least 3-4 pints/1.8-2.4 litres) and bring slowly to the boil, skimming off any scum which rises. When it has cleared, add the bouquet garni, the peppercorns and some salt, half cover the pan and simmer gently for at least three hours. Taste and boil rapidly for 5-10 minutes to reduce if you feel that the flavour is too weak. Strain the stock into a clean pan and add the reserved meat, cut up or shredded neatly — or it can be liquidised with some of the vegetables from the stockpot if you want a smooth soup. Add the port or sherry and the redcurrant jelly. Taste and adjust the seasoning accordingly. Blend half of the remaining butter with the flour to make a beurre manié and add this, in little dollops to the soup. Whisk it in or stir vigorously until it has dissolved, then bring up to the boil and cook until the soup has thickened a little. Just before serving, add the remaining butter, cut into small pieces, to give it a glaze.

Orange & Grapefruit Starter

Serves 6:
2 grapefruits
2 oranges
1 rounded tablespoon
    chopped celery
OR 1 rounded teaspoon
    chopped mint
1 level tablespoon caster
    sugar.

This pretty first course is from Ballymaloe House, Co. Cork and is as delicious as it is simple to make.

Halve the fruit and cut out the segments, leaving the membrane in the shells, then remove the membranes from the shells to leave a smooth cup. Mix the grapefruit and orange segments with the other ingredients and fill back into the fruit cups and chill before serving.

Variation: If time permits, segments may be removed and carefully replaced in membranes for neat presentation.

Fish Soup

Fish soup isn't made nearly as often as it should be but, with some fresh crusty home-made brown bread, or garlic bread, it can be served like a stew and it makes a meal in a bowl.

Melt butter in a large heavy-based pan and cook the onion and garlic gently in it, until softening but not browned. Add pepper, season and sprinkle over the flour. Cook gently for a couple of minutes, then gradually stir in the stock and add the tomatoes. Bring to the boil over moderate heat, then reduce and simmer gently until the vegetables are soft. Add the milk and bring back up to boiling point. Cut the fish up into bite-sized cubes and add to the pan; simmer for 3 minutes, then add the mussels, if using, and cook for another three or four minutes until the fish is just tender but not breaking up. Serve immediately, scattered with freshly chopped parsley or chives.

Marinated Kipper Salad

Marinated Kippers makes one of the nicest (and easiest) first course salads that I know of — it can be made ahead and keeps well in the fridge for at least a week. It's absolutely delicious served with a nutty home-made brown bread, preferably one with lots of oatmeal in it. Try to find lightly smoked, undyed kippers if possible, as the flavour will be far more subtle. Make at least a day ahead.

Skin the fillets and cutting diagonally across the grain, cut into thin strips about 1"/2.5 cm wide. Arrange in a shallow serving dish. Make the dressing by whisking the salt, pepper, sugar and mustard together and dissolving them in the vinegar, then whisk in the oil to make an emulsion. Pour the dressing over the kipper strips. Lay the bay leaves and a few rings of the thinly sliced onion on top. Cover and leave in the fridge for several hours, then add the remaining onion rings and the juice of $1/2$ lemon and toss the mixture gently to ensure that the dressing reaches all the ingredients. Leave to marinate again, turning the contents occasionally if it is convenient. To serve, sprinkle with the freshly chopped parsley and garnish with the remaining lemon, cut into wedges.

Warm Salad of Chicken Livers

The other first course salad that I simply can't resist is Warm Salad of Chicken Livers. It can in fact be made in exactly the same way as the Warm Salmon Salad with Pine Kernels and often is, or I sometimes make this crunchier version with winter vegetables and iceberg. Unlike some warm salads, where the leaves are heated through and become limp, this one has hot ingredients tossed through a crisp cold salad. Serves 4 as a first course (2 as a light main course).

Wash and dry the lettuce and put into a large salad bowl with the chopped scallions and the parsley. Pour rather more than half (4 fl oz/110 ml) of the oil into a heavy-based pan and have it warming gently. Whisk together 2 tablespoons of the vinegar, the mustard, crushed garlic and seasonings to make a creamy dressing. Set aside. Turn up the heat under the pan containing the olive oil and quickly cook the chicken livers in it until they are crisp and brown on the outside but still pink in the middle, adding the celery after a minute or so. Turn the livers and celery into the salad bowl and deglaze the pan with the remaining tablespoon of sherry vinegar. Tip this into the dressing mixture and quickly mix together. Add the tomatoes and walnuts to the salad, pour on the dressing and toss well. Serve immediately on heated plates.

Fish Soup: Serves 6

1 oz/25g butter
1 onion, finely chopped
1 clove garlic, crushed or finely chopped
1 small red pepper, deseeded and chopped
Seasoning: Salt, freshly ground pepper, $1/2$ tsp sugar and a dash of Tabasco
1 oz/25g flour
1 pint/600ml fish stock
1 tin (1 lb/450g approx) chopped tomatoes in their own juice
$1/2$ pint/300ml milk
8 oz/225g white fish, eg cod, haddock or whiting, filleted and skinned
4 oz/100g smoked haddock or cod
A few mussels (optional)
Chopped parsley
Chives.

Kipper Salad: Serves 6

8-10 kipper fillets
Sea salt and freshly ground black pepper
Pinch of caster sugar
1 teaspoon smooth Dijon mustard
2 tablespoons wine vinegar
4 tablespoons olive oil (or mix olive and sunflower)
2 bay leaves
1 large, mild Spanish onion
$1 1/2$ lemons
1 tablespoon freshly chopped parsley.

Chicken Salad: Serves 4 or 2

1 small-medium iceberg lettuce
$1/2$ small head radicchio
1 bunch of scallions, trimmed and chopped
2 tablespoons freshly chopped flat leaf parsley
7 fl oz/200 ml olive oil
3 tablespoons sherry vinegar
1 heaped teasp mild smooth Dijon mustard, or to taste
1 clove garlic, crushed
Sea salt, freshly ground black pepper, caster sugar
12 oz/350g chicken livers, trimmed
2 sticks celery, finely sliced
8 oz/225g cherry tomatoes
3oz/75g broken walnuts.

8 lambs' kidneys
1 large Spanish onion
Butter or oil for frying
1 tablespoon light golden
  brown sugar
2 tablespoons white wine
  vinegar
½ glass of brandy
½ pint/300 ml
  well-reduced meat stock
1 glass of port
1 oz/25g butter
Salt and freshly ground
  black pepper
Freshly chopped parsley
  and sprigs for garnishing.

Grilled Lambs' Kidneys with Caramelised Onions

This recipe for Grilled Lambs' Kidneys with Caramelised Onions and Rich Port Sauce is a speciality at MacCloskey's Restaurant, Bunratty, Co. Clare. It makes a very substantial first course or light meal for 4.

First, halve the kidneys, remove skin, cores and any fat. Wash well under cold water and leave to soak in fresh cold water. Slice the onion and fry in a little butter or oil over medium heat, then sprinkle in the sugar and cook to dissolve and caramelise. Add the vinegar and brandy and season to taste with salt and pepper. Set aside and keep warm. To prepare the sauce, simply heat the well-reduced beef stock (which should be rich and syrupy) with the port and add the butter in pieces to thicken. Keep warm. Preheat a fairly hot grill. Drain the kidneys, pat dry with kitchen paper and lay, round side up, on the grill pan; cook to the required degree of done-ness, turning as necessary. To serve, arrange the onions in a straight line on warmed dinner plates, lay the kidneys on top (4 halves each, round side up) and finish with the sauce on either side of the onions. Sprinkle with freshly chopped parsley and garnish with some whole sprigs.

Boston Baked Beans: Serves 4-6

12 oz/350g dried haricot
  beans
1 large onion
1 tablespoon sunflower or
  olive oil
1 teaspoon ground mustard
1 dessertspoon black treacle
1 dessertspoon rich dark
  brown sugar
2 tablespoons tomato purée
¼ pint/150 ml tomato juice
  or ¼ pint/150 ml water
  plus an extra tablespoon
  of tomato purée
½ pint/300 ml unsalted
  stock.

Boston Baked Beans

That great American classic, Boston Baked Beans, is the kind of dish you can live on, very healthily, for a very long time — and it's equally happy as a vegetarian main dish, served with freshly baked wholemeal bread to make up the protein content, or as a side dish with a whole range of plainly cooked foods.

Soak the beans in cold water for 12 hours, then drain and rinse. Put them into fresh water and cook in fresh unsalted water for 1-1½ hours until almost tender, then drain again.

Preheat a slow oven, 275°F, 140°C, Gas mark 1. Peel and slice the onion, then heat the oil in a flameproof casserole and cook the onion in it gently for about 5 minutes, without colouring.

Add the beans, mustard, treacle, sugar, tomato purée, juice and stock. Mix well and bring up to the boil. Cover the casserole with a lid and cook in the preheated oven for about 4 hours, stirring occasionally. Test for seasoning before serving and add salt and freshly ground pepper to taste if you like.

Winter Salad: Serves 6-8

¾-1 lb/350-450g hard
  white cabbage, finely
  shredded
1 red and 1 green pepper,
  deseeded and thinly sliced
1 large mild onion, thinly
  sliced
3 or 4 sticks celery, thinly
  sliced
1 large carrot, scraped and
  coarsely grated.

Dressing:

6 tablespoons olive oil
2 tablespoons wine vinegar
  ½ teaspoon dry mustard
  or 1 heaped teaspoon
  smooth Dijon mustard
Sea salt, freshly ground
  pepper and caster sugar.

Winter Salad

Winter Salad is a useful side dish. The ingredients can be varied according to taste and availability, but aim for contrast to the main dish with a crunchy, colourful salad.

Put all the salad ingredients into a large bowl — the onion may be plunged briefly into boiling water then refreshed under the cold tap if a milder flavour is preferred. Whisk all the dressing ingredients together vigorously, add to the salad and mix well. Unlike lettuce salads, which wilt soon after the dressing is added, the robust textures and flavours of this kind of winter salad benefit from marinating in the dressing, so allow some time ahead if possible. For the same reason, leftovers need not be wasted. Check the seasoning just before serving and, if you like, toss through a little freshly chopped parsley or chives.

Above: Warm Salad of Chicken Livers, page 193
Below: Stir-Fried Prawns with Baby Sweetcorn, page 204
Previous Page: Marinated Kipper Salad, page 193

Above: Glazed Cocktail Sausages, Mulled Red Wine with Orange, pages 184 and 185
Right: Valentine's Day: Apricot and Almond Ice Cream with Hazelnut Hearts, pages 209, 210

Top: Pork Plait, page 202   (Photo courtesy of the author)
Left: Fruit Terrine with Yogurt Cream, page 206
Above: Orange and Grapefruit Starters, page 192

Spring Rolls

Have you ever tried making your own Spring Rolls? It's easier than you think now that special spring roll wrappers can be bought from Chinese supermarkets and specialist shops. Otherwise use filo pastry, which is similar but thinner (so you need to use more layers) and is easily available from the freezer cabinets of major supermarkets. These quantities make enough to serve 10 as a first course — it is worth making a big batch, even if not immediately required, as they can be frozen before deep-frying to use another time.

Fry the onion, garlic and ginger gently in the vegetable oil until translucent, then add the carrot, cabbage and beansprouts. Stir-fry for 2 minutes, or until the cabbage is soft. Mix the cornflour with the soy sauce, sesame oil, sugar, seasoning and water. Add to the vegetables and stir well until the sauce has thickened. Roll up neatly in the spring roll wrappers and seal or, keeping the pack of filo covered so that it doesn't dry out, take one sheet at a time, brush with melted butter and fold over to make a double rectangle. Repeat if the sheets are very large. Lay some of the stuffing in an oblong shape in the middle, then roll up to make a neat tubular parcel; seal the open flap well with beaten egg. Continue in this way until you have made 20 rolls and used up all the ingredients. Deep fry in moderately hot oil for about 4 minutes, until crisp and golden brown.

Serves 10:

1 large onion, finely sliced
2 cloves garlic, crushed
1 teaspoon fresh ginger, finely chopped
2 tbsp vegetable oil
2 carrots, coarsely grated or shredded
1/2 small white cabbage or Chinese leaves, finely shredded
8 oz/225g fresh beansprouts
2 teaspoons cornflour
2 tbsp rich soy sauce
1/2 tsp sesame oil
Pinch of sugar, salt and pepper to taste
2 tbsp stock or water
Spring roll wrappers *or* filo pastry, as required
Melted butter
1 beaten egg.

Diced Chicken in Hot Bean Sauce

This recipe was given to me by my friend Deh-Ta Hsiung, a well-known authority on oriental food whos is based in London and author of several user-friendly Chinese cookery books. It is from Sichuan, famous for its richly flavoured and piquant dishes. Crushed yellow bean paste mixed with chilli sauce can be used instead of the chilli bean paste suggested. The chicken should be tender with a touch of hotness, an ideal starter.

Dice the chicken meat into small cubes, mix with a pinch of salt, egg white and cornflour.

Dice the bamboo shoots, finely chop the root ginger and spring onions. Have all the seasonings and sauce ingredients at hand.

First stir-fry the chicken and bamboo shoots for about a minute, then scoop them out of the oil with a perforated spoon. Heat up the oil again, stir-fry the spring onions and ginger and add the chicken and bamboo shoots together with all the seasonings and sauce. Stir to make sure everything is well blended before serving.

Diced Chicken: Serves 4

8 oz/225g boneless chicken
1 teaspoon salt
1/2 egg white, lightly beaten
1 teaspoon cornflour, mixed with a little cold water
8 oz/225g bamboo shoots
1-2 slices root ginger, peeled and finely chopped
2-3 spring onions, finely chopped
3-4 tablespoons oil
1 teaspoon sugar
1 tablespoon soy sauce
2 tbsp rice wine or sherry
1 tbsp chilli bean paste.

This is the peak season for citrus fruits — and, in the case of Seville, or bitter, oranges it is a very short season — only a few weeks long. They are wonderfully useful for giving zest to all kinds of food, including savoury dishes ranging from beef casserole to fish salads, as well as the more obvious desserts, baking and preserves. Citrus zest and juice can often be used in oriental dishes too, to replace or emphasise the flavour of vinegar and other sharp-flavoured ingredients. Seville oranges can be used in small quantities to give zest to all sorts of dishes — wherever sweet oranges are called for, some or all can be replaced with bitter ones for a punchier dish. Duck with bigarade sauce is the classic, but try it with other rich meats and game also, more cautiously, with fish and white meats — the results can be stunning.

Scallops with Two Salads

Serves 4 as a main course, 6 as a light lunch or supper dish, or 8 as a first course:

Crisp Salad:
1 head crisp salading, eg chicory frisée
6-8 oz/175-225g streaky bacon
3-4 oz/75-100g hazelnuts
8 oz/225g cherry tomatoes

Warm Salad:
8 oz/225g pasta shapes, pref. shells in 3 colours
3 peppers, preferably 1 red, 1 green and 1 yellow
8 oz/225g button mushrooms
1 lb/450g scallops or queens, shelled weight
Olive oil as required
Juice of 1 Seville orange and a little finely grated zest
Fresh ground black pepper; sea salt if necessary.

Dressing:
1 tablespoon bitter orange or lemon juice
4 tablespoons olive oil
1 tablespoon hazelnut oil (or an extra spoon of olive oil)
Sea salt and freshly ground pepper to taste.

Shellfish such as mussels and scallops are especially good at the moment and marry well with orange as I discovered with this unusual and versatile dish which combines a warm scallop and pasta salad with a crisp green one.

First make the crisp salad: Wash and dry the lettuce or centre leaves of the frisée; tear up into manageable pieces and put into a salad bowl. De-rind the bacon and put into a hot oven until very crisp. Lay the hazelnuts out on a baking tray and brown in the oven, then rub the skins off. Chop roughly or leave whole, as preferred. Cut up the crispy bacon and add to the salad bowl with the nuts and the cherry tomatoes. Whisk the dressing ingredients together in a small bowl or jar and set aside.

Next boil the pasta in plenty of salted water until just cooked. Drain, toss in a little olive oil and keep warm. De-seed and quarter the peppers and grill skin side up until blackened; peel off the skins and cut each quarter up roughly into three or four pieces. Set aside. Wipe and trim the mushrooms, but leave whole. Rinse the scallops and drain well; slice horizontally two or three times according to size — queens can be left whole. Heat a little olive oil in a heavy-based pan and brown the scallops in it, then add the mushrooms and cook over moderate heat for a couple of minutes, turning occasionally. Add the orange juice, a little grated zest and a good grinding of black pepper, then toss in the chopped peppers and the pasta shells. Warm through, turning gently. Taste for seasoning and add extra orange zest if necessary. Toss the crisp salad in just enough dressing to make the leaves glisten and arrange around the outside of a large platter or individual plates. Pile the warm scallop and pasta salad in the middle and serve immediately with crusty French bread and a glass of wine.

Variations: Time can be saved by omitting stages, eg not charring and peeling the peppers (the flavour is much stronger if used raw) or browning and skinning the nuts. Use walnut oil and walnuts instead of the hazelnuts if preferred. Sweet oranges and lemons can be used at other times of year.

Pork with Ginger and Garlic Sauce

Pork with Ginger: Serves 4
1 lb/450g shoulder pork
2 tablespoons oil
3-4 cloves garlic, finely chopped
1 tablespoon root ginger, finely chopped
2 tablespoons hoisin (barbecue) sauce
2 tablespoons wine vinegar
2 tbsp dark soy sauce.

Pork with Ginger and Garlic Sauce is as delicious as it is economical.

Trim the meat and cut it into finger-size strips. Heat a wok or large frying pan, then add the oil. Add the meat, in batches, and stir-fry quickly. As it browns, transfer to a plate. Add the finely chopped garlic and the ginger and stir-fry for 1 minute. Return the meat to the wok. Mix together the hoisin sauce, vinegar and soy sauce and pour it over the meat in the wok. Cover with a lid, reduce the heat and cook vegetables for about 15 minutes, until tender. Add a little water to the sauce if necessary. Serve with rice and stir-fried vegetables.

Loin of Pork with Dried Fruit in Cider

Iris Sothern of Birr, Co Offaly, won a first prize in a menu competition with this mouthwatering pot-roast, Loin of Pork with Dried Fruit in Cider.

Put the prunes, apricots, mixed spice, orange and lemon juice and zest into a bowl with half of the cider. Cover and leave overnight. Rub the pork with salt, pepper and sage. Melt the butter in a flameproof casserole. Add the pork and brown on all sides. Pour in the soaked fruit mixture. Sprinkle over the brown sugar and crushed garlic. Add in the remaining cider, reserving 1 tablespoon. Bring to the boil, cover and simmer for about 2 hours or transfer to a moderate oven, 170°C, 325°F, Gas mark 3 and cook for the same amount of time. Skim any fat off the surface of the cooking liquid. Bring to the boil, add the apples and cook for another 20 minutes. Transfer the pork to a serving dish or carving board. Carve into thick slices and arrange the pieces of dried fruit on the serving dish with the meat. Dissolve the cornflour in the remaining cider and stir a little of the hot liquid into the cornflour mixture; return to the casserole and simmer for 5 minutes, then pour the sauce over the meat and serve.

Loin of Pork: Serves 6
12 dried stoned prunes
12 dried apricot halves
$1/2$ tsp mixed spice
Juice and zest of half an orange
Juice and zest of half a lemon
1 pint/600ml dry cider
4 lb/1.8kg boned loin of pork, rolled and tied
Salt and black pepper
1 tbsp fresh sage (or $1/2$ tablespoon dried sage)
1 oz/25g butter
1 tbsp brown sugar
1 clove garlic, crushed
2 cooking apples, peeled and sliced
2 teaspoons cornflour.

Jugged Hare

Mount Falcon Castle in Ballina, Co. Mayo has many claims to fame, not least of which is their woodcock shoot in January — when, ironically, the favourite dish of the month is Jugged Hare.

Boil up the bones for stock. Roll the meat in seasoned flour and brown in a little butter, along with the onions and bacon. Take out the meat, add enough flour to soak up the fat and cook for a minute or two over gentle heat, then add enough stock to make a gravy and all the herbs and spices. Bring up to the boil and cook, stirring, for a few minutes. Pour this and the meat into a heavy casserole and simmer over low heat, or cook in a slow oven, 300°F/150°C, Gas mark 2, for 2 hours or until very tender. Add the blood, mashed liver, red wine, marmalade and lemon juice, if needed — keep tasting and adjust the flavouring as necessary until it is right. *Variation:* Port and redcurrant jelly, which is more traditional, can be used instead of the wine and marmalade.

Jugged Hare: Serves 6
1 hare, cut off the bone but left in large pieces; keep the blood and liver
Seasoned flour
2 large onions, peeled and chopped
2 oz/50g streaky bacon rashers, chopped
Butter for frying
Sprig of thyme, bayleaf, parsley, cloves, peppercorns
2 large glasses red wine
2 tablespoons home-made marmalade (see Winter Preserves)
lemon juice, if needed.

Pork with Coriander and Lime

Pork with Coriander and Lime makes a special meal for two and is no trouble at all — ideal for St Valentine's Day, perhaps.

Heat the oil and butter in a heavy pan. Slice the pork steak fairly thinly across the grain and fry on each side for a few minutes until evenly browned. Add the garlic and crushed coriander and cook gently for a few minutes, then add the wine or cider and simmer until reduced by about half. Add the sugar, lime (juice and slices) and a seasoning of salt and pepper. Cook a little longer, until the pork is tender and the sauce has reduced again and thickened slightly. Serve with rice (or new potatoes, when available) and a mixed leaf side salad.

Pork with Coriander
1 tablespoon olive oil
$1/2$ oz/15g butter, approx.
1 pork steak, about 1lb/350-450g
1 large clove garlic, crushed
2 teaspoons coriander seeds, crushed
Scant $1/4$ pint/150 ml white wine or cider
1 tsp brown sugar
1 lime — $1/2$ sliced, $1/2$ squeezed for juice
Sea salt and freshly ground pepper.

Butter Bean Bake

This is an extremely easy, trouble-free winter dish that can either be served as a vegetarian dish, as it is, or with some chopped grilled sausages included if preferred.

If using dried beans, soak in cold water overnight. Drain and rinse. Melt the butter in a large heavy-based casserole and cook the prepared vegetables in it gently for about 10 minutes. Stir in the beans and enough unsalted stock or water to cover by about $1/2$"/1 cm. Bring to the boil, cover and

Butter Bean Bake: Serves 4-6

12 oz/350g butter beans *or*
  2 tins ready-prepared
1 onion, peeled and sliced
1 clove garlic, crushed
2 carrots, peeled and sliced
2 sticks celery, trimmed and
  sliced
2 oz/50g butter
Unsalted stock or water
1 x 14 oz/400g tin chopped
  tomatoes, with their juice
2 tablespoons freshly
  chopped parsley
Sea salt, freshly ground
  pepper and sugar
Chilli powder or cayenne
  pepper
Topping: 4 oz/100g grated
  cheese, mix with handful
  of dry breadcrumbs.

Pork Plait: Serves 4-6

1 x 13 oz/375g packet puff
  pastry, or equivalent
  rough puff
2 eggs, beaten
1 lb/450g lean pork minced
1 large onion, peeled and
  finely chopped
1 or 2 cloves garlic, peeled
  and crushed
1 cooking apple, peeled and
  finely chopped
4 oz/100g fresh white
  breadcrumbs
2 oz/50g mixed dried fruits
2 teaspoons wholegrain
  mustard, preferably
  Meaux type
2 tablespoons freshly
  chopped parsley
1 oz/25g melted butter
Finely grated zest and juice
  of 1 orange
Salt and freshly gound
  black pepper

simmer gently for about 1 hour until tender. (If using canned beans, omit the long cooking and go straight from frying the vegetables to the next stage.) Preheat a fairly hot oven, 400°F, 200°C, Gas mark 6. When the beans are cooked, add the tomatoes and chopped parsley to the pan, season with sea salt, freshly ground black pepper, a little caster sugar and a pinch of chilli powder or cayenne pepper. Turn the mixture into a fairly shallow ovenproof dish, scatter with the grated cheese and crumb mixture and bake in the middle of the oven for about half an hour, until crisp and brown. Serve hot with a side salad and, perhaps, some fresh crusty bread.

Pork Plait

Pork Plait is basically an easy and inexpensive family dish upgraded for guests by serving it with a rather special sauce.

Preheat a hot oven, 400°F, 200°C, Gas mark 6. Roll out the pastry to make an oblong about 12" x 10"/30 x 25 cm. Set aside about a third of the beaten egg. Mix together all of the remaining ingredients and, when mixed thoroughly, distribute neatly along the centre of the pastry rectangle. On each side of the filling, slash the pastry into strips about 1/2"/1.2 cm wide and brush well with beaten egg — this will seal the pastry from the inside and prevent the filling seeping out. Wrap the pastry strips over the filling, alternating strips from the left and from the right, until the filling is completely enclosed. Finish off the end neatly, brush the whole plait thoroughly with the remaining beaten egg to seal and glaze and slide the plait onto a lightly oiled baking sheet. Cook in the centre of the hot oven for 45-50 minutes, keeping an eye on it towards the end of cooking — reduce the heat a little if it is over-browning, or protect lightly with foil. Serve with Apricot Sauce, page 114.

Variations: For family meals a sauce based on easily available fruit such as apples would be more economical. To make **Beef Plait with Tomato Sauce**, substitute 1 lb/450g lean minced beef for the pork, omit the dried fruit and the orange, replace the chopped apple with coarsely grated carrot and include some mixed dried herbs in the mixture. Prepare and cook the plait as above and serve with any of the tomato sauces given elsewhere in this book. **Lamb Plait** is made in the same way as Beef Plait, but use finely chopped rosemary instead of the mixed herbs.

Note: these plaits freeze very well, uncooked, and can be cooked from frozen — reduce the oven temperature to 350°F, 180°C, Gas mark 4 when the pastry has browned and add 20–30 minutes to the original cooking time.

A TASTE OF THE ORIENT:
The Perfect Antidote to Winter

This is a very good time of year to experiment a little with oriental flavourings — there's quite a bit of enjoyable pottering around in the kitchen involved and the results are light, colourful and full of flavour — just what we need to take our minds off the long, dark days before spring.

Marinated Steaks with Shallot Sauce

Marinated Steaks with Shallot Sauce — a treat for Saturday night which is easy to prepare.

Mix all the marinade ingredients well in a large dish. Add the steaks and spoon the marinade onto them. Leave covered for a few hours in the fridge. To cook, remove steaks from the marinade (reserve for use in the sauce) pat dry and place on a preheated large, heavy frying pan. Sprinkle each steak with a little salt and cook over medium heat until the steaks are cooked to your liking. Remove from the pan and keep warm. Add the shallots to the pan, cook until browned, then add the remaining marinade and boil to reduce. When the sauce is a nice rich consistency, add a knob of butter to give it a glaze. Season if necessary and serve immediately with the steaks.

Stir-Fried Beef with Mangetout

Now that mangetout (or sugar peas) seem to be so widely available virtually all year round, dishes like this are very useful to brighten up meals in winter and early spring before the new season's vegetables come in, and a relatively inexpensive cut of meat can be used.

Coat the beef with the marinade and leave for at least an hour. Preheat a wok or pan and stir-fry the beef in a tablespoon of hot oil for 2 minutes. Add the mangetout and continue stir-frying for another 2 minutes. Add the soy sauce, sherry and sesame oil, toss ingredients together to warm through and serve immediately.

Beef and Orange Stir-Fry

A quick and easy dish that makes the most of a complementary partnership.

Cut the beef across the grain into strips 2"/5 cm long and the thickness of a pencil. Put into a mixing bowl with the marinade ingredients; stir until well blended, then leave at room temperature to marinate for at least 20 minutes.

Meanwhile, peel the zest from half of the orange, being careful not to include any pith; shred finely lengthways, blanch in boiling water for 3 minutes, then refresh under running water and drain on kitchen paper. Finely grate the zest from the other half of the orange; squeeze juice and reserve 4 teaspoons. Drain the marinade off the beef. Heat the vegetable oil in a wok until very hot, then stir-fry the beef for 1 minute to brown. Drain off all the oil. Add the grated orange zest and juice, hot chilli sauce, rich soy sauce, rich dark brown sugar and sesame oil. Add the baby corn, peppers, water chestnuts and mushrooms, in that order, stir-frying briefly between additions. Return any remaining marinade to the pan and stir-fry everything together for a minute or two, until all ingredients are thoroughly heated and the sauce has thickened and cleared. (If it needs more liquid, any leftover orange juice may be added.) Transfer to a warmed serving dish, sprinkle the orange strips over the top, arrange boiled rice around the meat and serve immediately.

Marinated Steaks: Serves 4

4 steaks, striploin or sirloin, trimmed

Marinade:

$\frac{1}{2}$ glass red wine
2 tbsp olive oil
l tbsp light soy sauce
l tsp brown sugar
l tbsp wholegrain mustard
l clove garlic, crushed
3 bay leaves
l tsp black peppercorns, crushed

Sauce:

6-8 shallots, chopped
Knob of butter
Salt and freshly ground black pepper.

Stir-Fried Beef: Serves 2-3

6 oz/175g round steak, cut into thin strips against the grain
Half quantity of Marinade given in previous recipe
l tbsp vegetable oil
4 oz/100g mangetout, topped and tailed
l tbsp light soy sauce
l tsp dry sherry
l tsp sesame oil.

Beef and Orange: Serves 4

12 oz/350g lean sirloin steak
l orange
$2\frac{1}{2}$ tbsp vegetable oil
$\frac{1}{4}$ tsp Sharwood's hot chilli sauce
l tsp rich dark brown sugar
l tsp rich soy sauce
$\frac{1}{2}$ tsp sesame oil
3 oz/75g whole baby corn
1 red and 1 green pepper, sliced thinly
l can water chestnuts, drained
3 oz/75g mushrooms, sliced

For the marinade:

2 tsp rich soy sauce (dark)
$1\frac{1}{2}$"/4 cm piece of fresh ginger, peeled and finely chopped
l tsp cornflour
2 tsp dry sherry
l tsp sesame oil.

Chicken with Pineapple and Almonds

Chicken with Pineapple and Almonds: Serves 4-6

1 whole chicken, boned
Seasoned flour
2 oz/60g butter
75-100g/3-4 oz flaked
    almonds
2 medium carrots
1 green pepper
1 small bunch scallions
1 tin (about 1 lb/450g)
    pineapple pieces in juice
Pineapple juice from the
    can, made up to ½
    pint/300ml with water
1 tablespoon dark soy sauce
1 tablespoon honey
1 oz/25g light golden
    brown sugar
4 tablespoons wine or cider
    vinegar
1 tablespoon cornflour
¼ pint/ 150 ml hot chicken
    stock
Sea salt and freshly ground
    black pepper.

A convenient, easily prepared dish which should please anyone who enjoys crunchy nuts in savoury dishes.

Get your butcher to bone the chicken for you (but ask for the bones, for stock). Cut the flesh into small pieces, toss in the seasoned flour and cook gently in 2 oz/50g of the butter until tender. Meanwhile, melt the remaining butter in a small pan and brown the almonds in it; keep warm. Scrape or peel the carrots and shred finely. Deseed and finely slice the green pepper. Trim and slice the scallions. When the chicken is tender, turn onto a serving dish and keep warm. Add carrots, pepper, scallions and pineapple pieces to the pan the chicken was cooked in, then add the pineapple juice, soy sauce, honey, sugar and vinegar. Simmer for 3 minutes. Blend the cornflour with the chicken stock, add to the pan and stir until boiling. When the sauce thickens and clears, adjust the seasoning to taste and pour over the chicken. Scatter with the browned almonds. Serve with rice.

Variation: Instead of using boned chicken, a jointed chicken or chicken portions can be used, but the cooking time will be longer.

Stir-Fried Chicken with Walnuts and Celery

Chicken with Walnuts and Celery: Serves 4

8-10 oz/225-275g breast of
    chicken
1 medium head celery
1 large onion
4 oz/100g walnut pieces
1 dessertspoon cornflour
Pinch of salt
1 small glass dry or
    medium sherry
1 teaspoon sugar
2 teaspoons dark soy sauce,
    or to taste
¼ pint/150 ml stock or
    water, or as required
Oil for frying, 5-6
    tablespoons approx.

This is very versatile, the sort of dish you can dress up or down as required and it is easily extended for larger numbers by adding extra vegetables. It can also be made with pork, using pork steak for a special occasion, or pork pieces for family meals.

Slice the chicken into thin strips. Wash and trim the celery, remove any coarse strings and slice to match the chicken pieces. Peel and slice the onion. Roughly chop the walnuts. Measure out cornflour and salt and mix sherry, sugar, soy sauce and stock or water in a jug. Heat the oil in a wok or heavy-based pan, add the meat and stir-fry over high heat for 2 minutes, then add the onion and stir-fry for another minute. Add the celery and cook, still over high heat, for another two minutes. Reduce the heat to moderate and toss in the walnuts. Mix well, then scatter in the cornflour and salt. Stir to mix, add the sherry mixture and blend in well. Bring to the boil and cook for about a minute, until the sauce is smooth and clears; add a little extra stock or water if the sauce is too thick and check the seasoning before serving with rice or noodles.

Stir-Fried Prawns with Baby Sweetcorn

Stir Fried Prawns: Serves 2-3

4 oz/100g mangetout peas,
    topped and tailed
8 oz/225g baby sweetcorn,
    trimmed and halved
2 tbsp vegetable oil
1 lb/450g prawn tails,
    cooked and shelled
1 clove garlic, crushed
1 tbsp light soy sauce
Pinch of sugar
Salt to taste.

Stir-Fried Prawns with Baby Sweetcorn also has some mangetout in it, making a colourful dish. Alternatively, when prawns are unavailable, try using the same recipe with pork: trim a small pork fillet and slice thinly against the grain. Pork may require a little extra oil.

Blanch the mangetout and baby corn in boiling water for 3 minutes, then drain and keep warm.

Stir-fry the prawns in 2 tablespoons oil for 2 minutes to heat through, then add all the remaining ingredients and stir-fry to heat through thoroughly. Serve immediately with rice or noodles.

Note: If using pork, stir-fry in batches for 3-4 minutes to cook through. If fresh baby sweetcorn is unavailable, use tinned ones but they will not need to be blanched.

Many of the best puddings traditional to Ireland and Britain are hot and hearty — no doubt a reflection of the weather that can be expected for a considerable proportion of the year, as well as our agricultural background. The current revival of interest in traditional and regional food has meant that comfort food like rice pudding and bread and butter pudding has been appearing on the most exalted menus and it is very much the done thing to offer real old-fashioned puddings again. Their traditional appeal, simplicity and practicality is bringing the old favourites back onto bar-food menus again too, which seems especially appropriate. Men in particular seem to welcome this trend (or is it only the men who own up to it?) and there is much lip-smacking at the prospect of treats like Jam Roly-Poly, Spotted Dick or Eve's Pudding.

Treacle Tart with Walnuts

Treacle Tart (which, despite its name, is usually made with golden syrup) has suddenly become quite chic too, with well-known chefs claiming particular variations as house specialities. This version is inspired by a very old combination, but sharpened by the tang of citrus fruit. It's a very practical recipe as the pastry base doesn't have to be baked blind — and really delicious.

Sift the flour and salt into a bowl, cut in the butter and rub in until like fine breadcrumbs. Using a fork, blend in the lightly beaten egg and, if necessary, just enough cold water to make a dough. Gather the pastry into a ball, wrap in clingfilm and leave to rest in the fridge for at least half an hour before rolling, if possible.

Preheat a fairly hot oven, 400°F, 200°C, Gas mark 6. Knead the pastry on a lightly floured surface then roll out and use to line an 8"/20 cm pie plate or tart tin. Prick the base lightly with a fork. Select some of the best walnut halves for decoration, then chop the rest roughly. Mix together the syrup, breadcrumbs, chopped walnuts, lemon rind and juice (this may be easier if the syrup is warmed first) to make a gooey mixture and spread it over the pastry. If you want to have the traditional lattice topping, roll out the pastry trimmings, cut into $\frac{1}{2}$"/1.2 cm wide strips and lay them in an interwoven criss-cross pattern over the tart. Trim the edges neatly, arrange the reserved walnut halves on top and bake in the preheated oven for 25-30 minutes. Serve hot or cold, with custard or cream.

Variation: Orange marries extremely successfully with walnuts and makes an interesting, less sharp alternative to the lemon. Orange-flavoured pastry can easily be made by including a little grated zest with the dry ingredients and using orange juice instead of water to mix.

To serve 6-8:
Pastry:
7oz/200g plain flour
Pinch of salt
5 oz/150g butter, at room temperature
1 small egg
1 or 2 tablespoons very cold water, if necessary

Filling:
4 oz/100g walnut halves
8 oz/225g golden syrup
4 oz/100g fresh white breadcrumbs
Finely grated zest and juice of 1 large juicy lemon.

Frangipane and Apple Tart

This delicious tart is a speciality of the house at Roche's Bistro in Malahide, Co. Dublin. As one would expect, it's a very practical recipe and there are no gimmicks. Like the treacle tart given above, the pastry case does not need to be baked blind which saves a lot of time. This makes an excellent dinner party dessert at any time of year, but especially during the colder months.

First make the pastry: Sift the flour and icing sugar into a bowl, cut in the fat and rub in lightly to make a mixture like fine breadcrumbs. Using a fork, blend in just enough very cold water to make a dough. Roll up into a ball, wrap in clingfilm and chill. Meanwhile make the frangipane filling: Using an electric beater or food processor if available, cream the butter and sugar until light and fluffy, then mix in the whole egg, followed by the yolks, 2 drops of almond essence and the ground almonds. Preheat a

Serves 8:
Pastry:
6 oz/175g flour
2 oz/50g icing sugar
4 oz/100 butter OR
   2oz/50g butter and
   2oz/50g block margarine

Frangipane Filling:
6 oz/175g butter, softened
6 oz/175g caster sugar
1 whole egg and 2 yolks
2 drops almond essence
6 oz/175g ground almonds

Topping:
3 Granny Smiths or other firm eating apples
8 oz/225g apricot jam.

moderately hot oven, 375°F, 190°C, Gas mark 5. Roll out the pastry and use to line a 10"/25 cm loose-based tart tin. Peel and core the apples; slice thinly. Using a fork, lightly prick the bottom of the pastry case, then spread evenly with the frangipane mixture and, beginning from the outside, arrange the apple slices in circles on top. Bake in the preheated oven for about 30 minutes, but keep an eye on it and be prepared to reduce the temperature if the pastry edge seems to be browning too soon. When cooked, remove the tart from the oven and allow it to cool to lukewarm before adding the glaze, otherwise the apple slices may lift. Warm the apricot jam with about a tablespoon of water, strain and spread evenly over the tart. Serve warm or cold, with whipped cream.

Variation: For a **Frangipane and Pear Tart**, which is naturally sweeter, just add a squeeze of lemon juice and scatter the sliced pears lightly with caster sugar before baking. Glaze as for Apple version.

Queen of Puddings

Serves 6:
4 oz/100g white bread,
   without crusts
½ pint/300 ml cream and
½ pint/300 ml milk *or* 1
   pint/600 ml creamy milk
2 oz/50g unsalted butter
3 eggs, separated
Grated zest of 1 lemon
5 oz/150g caster sugar
4 tablespoons home-made
   jam.

Queen of Puddings is probably the most famous of all the grander nursery puddings and its meringue topping ensures that it is the most popular. Strawberry jam is most usual, but any flavour can be used — apricot is especially good.

Preheat a moderate oven, 350°F, 180°C, Gas mark 4. Generously butter a 2-pint/1.2 litre baking dish. Cut up the bread into small cubes, or make into coarse crumbs, and scatter into the baking dish. Warm the milk and butter until the butter melts, then blend in the beaten egg yolks, grated lemon zest and 3 oz/75g of the sugar. Pour this custard over the bread and bake in the preheated oven for 20 minutes, or until set. Whisk the egg whites until stiff and fold in the remaining sugar. Remove the pudding from the oven, spread with the jam and pile the meringue mixture on top. Return to the oven and cook for another 10 minutes, or until the top is lightly browned and crisp. Serve hot, with chilled cream.

Fruit Terrine with Yogurt Cream

Serves 8-10:
6 grapefruit
12 oranges
2 glasses of white wine
1 sachet gelatine

Yogurt Cream:
8 fl oz/225 ml milk
7 fl oz/200 ml cream
7 oz/200g caster sugar
¼ tsp cardamon seeds
¾ pint/450 ml natural
   yogurt.

Citrus fruit makes an excellent winter dessert, full of colour. Although best known for their seafood, Doyle's of Dingle also do delicious desserts and this sparkling Fruit Terrine with Yogurt Cream is one of their specialities.

Peel the fruit and segment over a colander, cutting between the flesh and membranes; collect the juice underneath. Soak the gelatine in enough cold water to cover: add the cake of gelatine to the wine and ⅔ of the fruit juice. Heat gently to mix the gelatine. Leave to cool. Arrange the fruit segments in 8-10 small ramekin dishes (scant 4 fl oz/100 ml capacity), pour over the juice and leave to set. Meanwhile, make the Yogurt Cream.

Heat milk, cream and sugar with the ground cardamon until warm to the touch and until the sugar has dissolved. Remove from the heat and add the yogurt. Strain. To serve: Run a sharp knife around each terrine, turn onto a serving plate and give a sharp tap to unmould. (This is easier if you leave the ramekins in the freezer for 10-15 minutes before serving so that the texture is firmer.) Pour Yogurt Cream around the terrine and decorate with a little flower.

Note: 1 sachet gelatine sets 1 pint/600ml liquid; measure wine and juices and adjust amount used if necessary.

Pancakes

Shrove Tuesday is one of the major culinary landmarks this season and the image it conjures up is very clear: pancakes, pure and simple. Pancakes are very versatile and I'm sure we should make more of them — they can be folded, rolled or stacked, with sweet or savoury fillings, they freeze well and give you a head start when faced with that legendary phenomenon 'unexpected visitors'. Yet, if truth be told, there is absolutely nothing to compare with the delicious simplicity of a sprinkling of caster sugar and a good squeeze of fresh lemon juice. Like all very simple dishes, the important thing is to get the basic techniques right: a good, heavy cast-iron pan is best, it must be preheated and very hot before any fat is added and the best fat is not oil (and certainly not butter, which would be burnt black at the temperature required) but a hard block of white cooking fat such as Frytex, which you smear over the pan very quickly to make a thin film of hot fat just before adding the batter. Keep the batter in a jug beside the hob and use a ladle — the first pancake is always a disaster (but tastes just as delicious — cook's perk) but once the pan is seasoned it will work a treat and you very quickly learn to judge exactly the amount of batter needed to swirl around the pan and just reach the edges.

Put all ingredients into a food processor or liquidiser in the order given and blend for a minute or so, until thoroughly mixed and smooth, with bubbles rising. Traditionally, the batter is left to rest for an hour before use, but I have never found this necessary, perhaps because of the very thorough beating it gets in a food processor.

Before cooking, pour the prepared batter into a jug and have it ready beside the cooker, with a ladle. Also make sure you have all the necessary warmed plates, caster sugar and lemon juice ready to hand as, once you start making the pancakes, you have to keep up the momentum and there's no time for anything else.

To cook, heat a heavy frying pan, preferably cast-iron, over high heat. Smear lightly with white cooking fat, leave a moment until just smoking, then pour on a ladleful of batter. Quickly tilt the pan around — if you have judged the amount of batter correctly, it will just thinly cover the whole of the base of the pan. Cook for about a minute, until the top is set and the bottom browned, then flip (or toss) over and cook the other side for about half a minute. Slide onto a warm plate, put the pan back onto the heat, sprinkle the pancake with caster sugar and lemon juice, roll up quickly and pass to the first taker. Re-grease the pan and continue in the same way until all the batter has been used up. In polite households it may seem more appropriate to keep the pancakes warm and serve everyone at the same time — it is certainly more polite, but they never taste as good.

Crêpes Suzettes

Oranges complement pancakes almost as well as lemons hence the classic party pudding Crêpes Suzette: go ahead with the basic pancake recipe as given and prepare the sauce — both can be made ahead, then baked in the oven just before serving. Keep the pancakes as thin and light as possible. The basic batter given here will make at least 8 pancakes; allow 2 each for the Crêpes Suzettes and freeze any leftovers for another time.

Preheat a moderate oven, 350°F, 180°C, Gas mark 4. To make the sauce, melt the butter with the grated orange zest and caster sugar. Add orange juice and Grand Marnier. Fold the cooked pancakes in quarters and arrange on an ovenproof dish. Heat the prepared sauce very gently and pour over the laid-out pancakes. Cover the dish and bake in the preheated oven for 15 minutes. If you want to flame the pancakes at the table, warm the brandy, light it as you pour it over the crêpes and serve immediately.

Basic Pancake Batter

This makes about 8-10 pancakes, so most families would want to make at least double quantities.

1 egg
4 oz/100g plain flour
1/2pint/300ml milk
Pinch of salt.

Serves 4

3 oz/75g butter
1 teaspoon finely grated zest of orange
4 teaspoons caster sugar
6 fl oz/175 ml strained orange juice
4 tablespoons Grand Marnier or Cointreau
8 pancakes (see previous recipe)
2 tablespoons brandy (optional).

Crêpes Normandes

Crêpes Normandes: Filling:
2 lb/900g pears or dessert
  apples
1/4 pint/150 ml strong
  medium dry cider
2 oz/50g caster sugar, or to
  taste
2-3 tbsp Calvados.

Topping:
Caster sugar
Calvados (optional).

Crêpes Normandes is another variation, also sharp and fruity, but more unusual than Crêpes Suzettes. Include the finely grated zest of an orange or lemon in the pancake batter and otherwise make the pancakes as given.

To make the filling, peel, core and slice the apples or pears and put into a saucepan with the cider and sugar. Simmer gently, until the fruit is just cooked but not breaking up and the juice has reduced to a syrup. Add the Calvados. Preheat a hot grill. Divide the fruit mixture between the pancakes, fold each one into four like a cornet and arrange in a buttered shallow ovenproof serving dish. Sprinkle generously with caster sugar and grill until the sugar has caramelised. Sprinkle with Calvados, set alight and serve immediately, with chilled cream or, preferably, Crème Fraîche.

Spiced Fruit Compôte

Serves 6:
1 lb/450g mixed dried fruit
1/2 pint/300 ml orange juice
2"/5 cm cinnamon stick
2 whole cloves
Small piece stem ginger in
  syrup, finely chopped
1 small glass dark rum, or a
  fruit-based liqueur
  (optional)
Toasted flaked almonds to
  serve.

With constant supplies of fresh fruit from all over the world a fact we have all taken for granted over the last few decades, dried fruit has lost the significance it used to have. But it is so delicious in its own right — and, of course, highly nutritious — that there's no need to see it as an inferior alternative to fresh produce at all. For example, a very good winter fruit salad can be made simply by soaking and simmering a mixture of dried fruits — prunes, apricots, apple rings, peaches, pears — in plain water, perhaps sharpened with a little lemon zest or juice. The same mixture can also be upgraded very easily to make a Spiced Fruit Compôte to serve hot or cold at breakfast or brunch parties, or with the addition of something to give it a bit of a kick, even as an alternative to a rich dessert for dinner.

Put the dried fruit into a bowl. Bring the orange juice just to boiling point and pour over the fruit, adding just enough boiling water to cover. Stir in the spices and leave for about 40 minutes to soak. Transfer to a pan and bring to the boil, then cover and leave to simmer for 20-25 minutes, until the fruit is tender. (Or do this in the microwave if more convenient.) Remove the cinnamon stick and cloves, stir in the rum or liqueur, if using, sprinkle with the toasted almond flakes and serve warm or cold, with natural yogurt, cream, or Carrageen Pudding.

Carrageen Pudding

1/2 oz/15g carrageen
3 pints/ 1.8 litres milk
2 eggs, separated
4 tbsp sugar, or to taste.

At Rathmullan House Hotel, Co. Donegal, clever menu-planning allows for dishes such as a Dried Fruit Compôte or Carrageen Pudding on the dessert menu at dinner to fit in perfectly next morning. The secret is to resist the temptation to give the desserts an alcoholic kick, then they are quite appropriate at breakfast time. This is the Rathmullan Carrageen Pudding and makes about 31/2 pints/2 litres:

Soak the carrageen in tepid water for 10 minutes, then add to the milk, bring slowly to the boil and simmer very gently for 20 minutes. Strain and rub all the jelly through the strainer. Beat in the egg yolks and sugar, then whisk the egg whites stiffly and fold in gently. Turn into a bowl and leave to set. Serve with poached fresh or dried fruit, or wherever appropriate as an alternative to cream.

Caramel Bavarois

Serves 6:
6 oz/175g granulated sugar
5 fl oz/150 ml water
8 fl oz/225 ml milk
7 fl oz/200 ml cream
1 sachet of gelatine
3 tablespoons cold water
3 egg yolks
1 oz/25g caster sugar
10 fl oz/300 ml cream.

Caramel is always a popular flavouring for desserts and Caramel Bavarois, or Bavarian Cream, makes a change from the better-known classic, Crème Caramel. This recipe comes from Caragh Lodge on Caragh Lake in Co. Kerry.

First make the caramel. Put the granulated sugar into a heavy pan with a little water and, when dissolved, cook steadily to a rich brown caramel. Be careful at the next stage, as the caramel will boil up when the water is added: cover the hand holding the pan, add the rest of the water and stir until all the caramel is melted. Add the milk and cream and bring to scalding point (almost on the point of boiling). Soak the gelatine in the 3 tablespoons cold water. Whisk the egg yolks and caster sugar until light and creamy. Blend the hot cream mixture and the creamed yolks and cook over gentle heat until thick, then add the cake of soaked gelatine and stir with a spatula until the mixture thickens slightly again. Cool. When cold, fold in three tablespoons of whipped cream and turn into a mould, or into individual dariole moulds. Chill. To serve, dip the moulds quickly in warm water to release the sides, turn onto a serving dish and pipe with the rest of the whipped cream.

Apricot and Almond Coriander Crumble

Of the individual dried fruits my personal favourite is the apricot, for its sharpness and individuality, versatility and sheer style. Dried fruit and nuts make a natural partnership and this Apricot and Almond Coriander Crumble is a hot pudding that's as delicious as it is wholesome.

Serves 4-6:
8 oz/225g dried apricots
2 x 1"/2.5 cm pieces cinnamon stick
Grated rind and juice of 1 small lemon
2 oz/50g sugar, or to taste
2 oz/50g flaked almonds

The day before, put the apricots into a pan with the cinnamon stick and enough water to cover generously. Bring to the boil, then remove from the heat, add the finely grated lemon zest and the juice, cover and leave to soak overnight.

Preheat a fairly hot oven, 400°F, 200°C, Gas mark 6.

Crumble Topping:
6 oz/175g coarse wholemeal flour
Pinch of salt
3 oz/75g butter
3 oz/75g soft brown or Demerara sugar
1 tsp coriander seeds, crushed
A few tablespoons water.

To make the crumble topping, put the flour and salt into a mixing bowl, cut in the butter and rub in until the mixture resembles coarse breadcrumbs. Mix in the sugar and crushed coriander seeds. Butter a shallow baking dish. Remove the cinnamon stick from the apricots, then layer the apricots, sugar and flaked almonds in the baking dish and pour in the juices. Mix a little water into the crumble mixture, so that it clings together in bigger crumbs, then scatter over the fruit and bake in the pre-heated oven for 30-40 minutes, or until well-browned and crunchy on top. Serve dusted with icing sugar and hand chilled whipped cream or Crème Faîche separately.

Variation: The same recipe can easily be adapted to other fruit and nut combinations, such as **Prune and Walnut Crumble** or **Mixed Dried Fruit** and **Hazelnut Crumble**. The spices and flavourings can remain the same; the nuts could be included with the crumble mixture if preferred.

Apricot and Almond Ice Cream Heart

Apart from Shrove Tuesday, another excuse for a treat occurs on Valentine's Day, when heart-shaped food of all kinds is very much the flavour of the month. This easy Apricot and Almond Ice Cream Heart makes a lovely romantic dessert and looks especially pretty if it is set in a pool of Raspberry Coulis.

Serves 6:
1 x 1 lb/450g tin apricots or 12 oz/350g soaked dried apricots
2 oz/50g sugar
1 teaspoon lemon juice
1-2 tablespoons apricot brandy or Cointreau (optional
½ pint/300 ml cream
2-3 oz/50-75g nib or flaked almonds, toasted.

Drain the apricots and reserve the juice for use in another dish, such as fruit salad. Liquidise the fruit with the sugar, lemon juice and apricot brandy or Cointreau. Whip the cream until it is thick and forming soft peaks. Fold in half to two-thirds of the toasted almonds, turn the mixture in an 8"/20 cm heart-shaped cake tin and open-freeze. When frozen, slip the whole tin into a freezer bag, seal and return to the freezer. To serve, remove from the freezer about half an hour before required, dip the tin briefly into hot water to release, then turn the ice cream out onto a serving dish. Pour the deep red sauce around the ice cream and leave in the fridge to allow the ice cream to soften a little and release its flavours before serving. Serve scattered with the remaining toasted almonds and offer Almond Tuiles separately or, complete the nuts about hearts theme with these very crisp, delicate Hazelnut Hearts in the next recipe.

Hazelnut Hearts

Makes about 2 dozen biscuits:

4 oz/100g hazelnuts
4 oz/100g Demerara sugar
1/2 egg, beaten.

Preheat a moderate oven, 350°F, 180°C, Gas mark 4. Cut out three sheets of non-stick baking parchment to fit available baking sheets. Lay the hazelnuts out on a baking tray and toast them in the oven until the skins darken and loosen and they smell very aromatic. Put them into a tea towel and rub well to remove the loose skins. Grind the nuts or chop very finely. Put the nuts and sugar into a mixing bowl and add the beaten egg, a little at a time, until a pliable dough is produced. Turn half of it onto a sheet of non-stick baking parchment, cover with another sheet and roll out quite thinly between the two layers of paper. Using an oiled heart-shaped cutter about 1 1/2"/4 cm across, cut out as many heart-shapes as possible. As they will be very fragile and difficult to move, the easiest thing is to remove the trimmings from around the hearts and lay the whole sheet, complete with biscuits, on one of the baking trays. Repeat with the other half of the mixture and use the spare sheet of parchment to line a third tray for cooking the trimmings — form these into little balls, lay out on the baking parchment with plenty of room between, and press down with a fork to form a cookie shape. Bake hearts and trimmings in the preheated oven for about 10 minutes, or until golden brown. Leave on the tins to cool a little until they are firm enough to move, then transfer them to wire racks and leave until cold. Store in an airtight tin.

Pear and Grape Compôte

Pear and Grape Compôte:
Serves 4

4 ripe, firm pears, peeled,
  cored and diced
1/2 pint/300 ml orange juice
2 tsp lemon juice
6 oz/175g green seedless
  grapes, halved
2-3 tablespoons Cointreau,
  to taste
3 or 4 tablespoons caster
  sugar, or to taste
2 tablespoons toasted flaked
  almonds to decorate.

In contrast to our traditional hot pudding, hearty winter main courses often create a craving for lighter desserts, such as this Pear and Grape Compôte, that refresh as much as nourish.

Poach the pears in the orange juice and lemon juice for 5 minutes, or until soft but not mushy. The time will depend on the ripeness of the pears. Mix in the prepared grapes, then add the Cointreau and caster sugar to taste. Stir to dissolve the sugar, then leave to cool. Chill. Serve sprinkled with the toasted flaked almonds.

Lemons are terrific value and very good quality at this time of year and it makes a pleasant change to be generous with an ingredient which is usually dear enough to encourage caution. Lemons bring sunshine into the kitchen and into our cooking with their cheerful colouring and lovely tangy flavour — just what we need now that the days are beginning to lengthen again.

Eggless Lemon Cheesecake

To serve at least 12:

1 lb/450g digestive biscuits
8 oz/225g butter
1/2 teaspoon cinnamon or
  mixed spice (optional)
1 large tin evaporated milk,
  well-chilled
4 oz/100g caster sugar
Finely grated zest and juice
  of 3 lemons
1/2 oz/15g (1 sachet)
  powdered gelatine
Boiling water (see method)
1 lb/450g cottage cheese.

This homely Eggless Lemon Cheesecake has been a favourite of mine for years and is much in demand — not only is it light and refreshing, but it's economical and easy. (There is no need to sieve the cottage cheese.) Quantities given will make two 8"-9"/20-22cm cheesecakes, each serving 6, or one big one, 11"-12"/28-30 cm — the exact sizes depend on the depth of the tins or flan dishes. They can be made in the conventional way, or as a pudding, with the biscuit crust scattered over as a crumble topping. Although not particularly seasonal, I find it convenient to make two at Christmas time and freeze at least one until required (open freeze, then put into a freezer bag; to serve, thaw 3-4 hours at room temperature or overnight in the fridge).

Break the biscuits up roughly, put into a heavy duty freezer bag and crush with a rolling pin to make fine crumbs. Melt the butter and stir in the biscuit crumbs and the cinnamon or mixed spice, if using. Divide between two 8"/20 cm flan dishes and, using a tablespoon, press down well around the base and sides to form a biscuit crust.

Whisk the well-chilled evaporated milk until thick — this takes about 5 minutes in a Kenwood Chef on high speed. Reduce speed and whisk in the sugar. Meanwhile, grate lemon zests finely and squeeze the juice, discarding pips. Put the gelatine into a Pyrex jug with the lemon juice and leave to soak for 5 minutes, then add the rest of the juice and make up to ½ pint/300 ml (if necessary), with boiling water. Set the jug in a bowl of hot water and stir until the gelatine has dissolved. In a mixing bowl, stir together the cottage cheese, grated lemon zest and the gelatine and lemon juice mixture. Blend until fairly smooth. Finally, fold this mixture into the thickly whisked and sweetened evaporated milk, mix thoroughly without losing volume, then pour into the prepared biscuit crusts and chill until set. To serve, decorate with whipped cream or grated chocolate and serve with a contrasting fruit sauce, such as Strawberry or Raspberry Coulis, which can be made with fresh or frozen berries, as available, or a deep purple Bramble Sauce.

Variations: The lemon cheesecake mixture works well with a **Ginger Crust** — follow the recipe as above, but use gingernut biscuits instead of digestive and omit the spices. It could also be served in one large or individual chocolate shells instead of the biscuit crust.

SUGAR UTENSILS

An interesting commercial sideline which gave skilled employment and evolved alongside the developing sugar industry, was in specialised tableware and utensils required for cutting, grinding or handling sugar: sugar was made in a cone shape or 'loaf', usually about 3'/91.5 cm high, weighing about 14 lb/6.3 Kg and wrapped in blue paper to make the yellowish sugar seem whiter. Large households bought whole cones and kept them suspended from the ceiling in string cradles, while smaller families would buy pieces cut off the sugar loaf by the grocer. Sugar snippers, like a cross between tongs and scissors, were available in a variety of sizes, ranging from huge ones, big enough to enclose a whole cone of sugar, for use in shops and big houses, down to delicate little silver ones made for the table. Whether for kitchen or table use, the sugar had to be cut up, first using heavy iron snippers mounted on a wooden block in the kitchen, then into smaller pieces with lighter snippers and so on until you could adjust the size of the lumps to suit your taste at the table. For cooking, the lumps were reduced to the required degree of fineness with a pestle and mortar. Silversmiths created a whole range of beautiful containers for sugar and Irish examples from Dublin, Cork, Waterford and Kilkenny go back to the early seventeenth century. The earliest containers were lidded sugar boxes, very like tea boxes, often with their owner's coat of arms, then silver bowls, often three-legged, were made to hold small chips broken off the loaf. Sugar baskets with handles were kept on the table for cube or lump sugar and there were sugar castors, for sprinkling finely ground sugar. These utensils were usually highly ornamental and, of course, they had delightful accessories such as spoons and tongs to go with them. Although examples are now harder to find, there were also many pottery and china sugar utensils made, both for the kitchen and the table and one line is of particular interest as it was not only a huge commercial success, but reflected accurately public revulsion against slavery in the nineteenth century - in gold lettering the range of china sugar basins bore the legend: 'East India Sugar not made by Slaves'. Similarly, during the time coming up to abolition (which, for the British colonies, was in 1838, but it continued elsewhere for much longer), sugar packs were labelled 'Not Made by Slaves' - despite the subject matter, it all seems so reminiscent of many of today's environmental issues that it has a very modern ring to it.

Orange Juice Cake

Orange Juice Cake, a deliciously light and refreshing cake with a good tangy flavour.

Serves 8-10:
5 eggs
7 oz/200g caster sugar
8 oz/225g plain flour
Pinch of salt
2 teaspoons baking powder
1 teaspoon lemon juice
Scant 1/4 pint/150 ml orange juice.

Preheat a moderate oven, 350°F, 180°C, Gas mark 4. Grease and base-line an 8"/20cm cake tin, preferably loose-based.
Separate the eggs and beat the yolks until foamy, then add half of the sugar and keep beating until the sugar has dissolved to make a pale, creamy mixture. Sift the flour, salt and baking powder and add alternately with the fruit juices. Whisk the egg whites until stiff but not dry and fold in the remaining sugar lightly but thoroughly with a metal spoon. Fold the egg whites into the cake mixture in the same way, then turn into the prepared cake tin and bake for an hour, or until the top is springy to the touch and the sides shrinking slightly from the tin. Turn out and cool on a wire rack. When cool, simply sprinkle with sieved icing sugar, or cover with white **glacé icing** made by putting 8 oz/225g icing sugar into a saucepan with 1-1 1/2 table-spoons water, or 1 tbsp water and 1/2 tbsp lemon juice for a sharper flavour. Stir over very low heat until blended, then pour over the cake. (This 'cooked' method gives a good shine to the icing).

Irish Cider Cake

A less expensive alternative to the traditional Irish Whiskey Cake — lighter in flavour but equally moist.

8 oz/225g sultanas
Grated zest of 1 lemon
1/4 pint/150ml medium-sweet cider
6 oz/175g softened butter
6 oz/175g light golden brown sugar or caster sugar
3 eggs
6 oz/175g plain flour
Pinch of salt
Pinch of ground cloves
1 teaspoon baking powder
Icing:
Juice of 1 lemon
8 oz/225g icing sugar
A little warm water
Crystallised lemon slices to decorate (optional).

Put the sultanas, grated lemon zest and cider into a bowl and leave to soak overnight. Grease and base-line a deep 7"/18 cm cake tin, preferably loose-based, and preheat a moderate oven 180°C, 350°C, Gas mark 4. Cream the butter and sugar until light and fluffy. Separate the eggs and sift the flour, salt, cloves and baking powder into a bowl. Beat the yolks into the butter and sugar, one by one, including a spoonful of flour and beating well after each addition. Gradually add the sultana and cider mixture, alternating with the remaining flour. Do not overbeat at this stage. Finally, whisk the egg whites until stiff and fold them into the mixture with a metal spoon. Turn into the prepared tin and bake in the preheated oven for about 1 1/2 hours, or until well-risen and springy to the touch. Test with a skewer, which should come out clean. Cool on a wire rack. Make the icing by mixing the lemon juice with the sieved icing sugar and just enough warm water to make a pouring consistency. Pour the icing over the cold cake, letting it dribble naturally down the sides.

Sweetheart Cake

A lovely heart-shaped cake to make for Valentine's Day.

Makes one 8"/20cm heart-shaped cake:
4 oz/100g butter, at room temperature
4 oz/100g caster sugar
2 eggs, beaten
4 oz/100g glacé cherries, washed and cut up
2 oz/50g chopped almonds
1 tbsp Tia Maria
4 oz/100g self-raising flour
1/2 level teaspoon baking powder.

To decorate:
1/4 pint/150 ml double cream, whipped, mixed with 2 tablespoons Tia Maria
3 tablespoons chocolate vermicelli
Few fresh or crystallised flowers and ribbon.

Preheat a moderate oven, 350°F, 180°C, Gas mark 4. Butter an 8"/20 cm heart-shaped cake tin and base-line if not non-stick. Cream butter and sugar together until very light and fluffy. Add eggs gradually, beating well between additions. Add cherries, almonds and Tia Maria. Sift flour and baking powder together and, using a metal spoon, carefully fold the flour into the creamed mixture. Spoon into the prepared tin and spread evenly. Bake in the centre of the preheated oven for 20-25 minutes until well-risen, golden brown and springy to the touch. Turn out onto a wire rack and cool thoroughly. When cold, split in half and sprinkle with Tia Maria, then spread with about 2 tablespoons of cream and sandwich together. Place on a serving plate, spread remaining cream over the top and sides and decorate with chocolate vermi-celli and flowers.

Devil's Food Cake with Seven-Minute Frosting

Still on the Valentine's theme, if your relationship is a love-hate one, why not make your partner this easy Devil's Food Cake instead?

Makes one 8"/20 cm cake:
6 oz/175g self-raising flour
2 level teaspoons baking powder
6 oz/175g caster sugar
6 oz/175g softened unsalted butter
4 eggs
90 ml/3½ fl oz very hot (not boiling) water
2 oz/50g cocoa powder

Filling:
6 oz/175g icing sugar
2 oz/50g softened unsalted butter
1 oz/25g plain chocolate.

Preheat a very moderate oven, 325°F, 170°C, Gas mark 3, and grease and base-line two 8"/20 cm sandwich tins.
Warm a large mixing bowl and sieve in the flour and baking powder, then add the sugar, soft margarine and the lightly beaten eggs. In a measuring jug, blend together the hot water and the cocoa to make a smooth paste; scrape this into the other ingredients with a spatula, then mix all the ingredients together and beat with a wooden spoon for about 2 minutes until smooth and creamy. Divide the mixture between the prepared tins and bake in the centre of the preheated oven for 35-40 minutes, or until springy to the touch and shrinking slightly from the tins. Remove from the oven, but leave in the tins for a few minutes so that they will be easier to turn out, then cool on a wire rack. To make the filling, sieve the icing sugar into a bowl, add the softened butter and melted chocolate and beat well to make a smooth, soft icing. When the cakes are cold, sandwich them together with the filling and cover with **Seven Minute Frosting**, a simplified version of the classic American Frosting which is not only quicker but, unlike the original, requires neither a sugar thermometer nor a second pair of hands.

Seven Minute Frosting:
2 egg whites
12 oz/350g caster sugar
4 tablespoons/ 60 ml hot water
½ teaspoon cream of tartar.

Put all ingredients into a deep bowl and whisk together with an electric hand whisk to mix thoroughly. Put the bowl over a pan of very hot water; keep over a low heat and continue to whisk for about 7 minutes, or until the mixture is thick enough to stand in peaks. Use immediately and work quickly, spreading thickly all over the cake with a palette knife and flicking up to make peaks.

St Clement's Sandwich Cake

In St Clement's Sandwich Cake, oranges and lemons make a colourful and very refreshing family cake.

Orange Sandwich Cake:
8 oz/225g butter or margarine, at room temperature
8 oz/225g caster sugar
4 eggs
8 oz/225g self-raising flour
Finely grated zest of l orange

Lemon Filling and Icing:
4 oz/100g butter or margarine, at room temperature
10 oz/275g icing sugar
2-3 tablespoons lemon juice
Grated zest of l large lemon.

Decoration:
Fresh orange slices, or segments of the grated orange; angelica.

Preheat a moderate oven, 350°F, 180°C, Gas mark 4. Butter and base-line two 7½"-8"/18-20cm sandwich tins. Put all of the cake ingredients into a mixing bowl and beat with a wooden spoon for 2 or 3 minutes, or until thoroughly blended. Divide between the two tins, smooth down and bake for 25-30 minutes until the cakes feel firm when pressed lightly. Turn out and cool on wire racks. Meanwhile, put all of the icing ingredients into a bowl and beat with a wooden spoon until smooth and light. When the cakes are cold, sandwich with a little of the icing (or split each horizontally and fill three layers) and spread a thin layer over the top of the cake. Turn the remaining icing into a piping bag fitted with a star nozzle and pipe rosettes around the edge. Decorate between rosettes with quartered orange slices, or with fresh orange segments, and angelica.

Sunny Citrus Treats

Now that most foods are available at any time of year, it is difficult to recall the excitement the beginning of a new season used to generate. But there is still one exception to the rule that you can have whatever you like whenever you like: the season for Seville oranges and their other bitter relations is still very much a flash in the pan and that's the way it looks like staying. They start to come in about the second week of January and they'll only be in the shops for two or three weeks, so don't put them at the bottom of the list. Interestingly, although the more common sweet orange was a much later arrival in Europe, the bitter orange — of which the best-known variety, the Seville, comes from Spain — was known to the Greeks and Romans. As far as we know they did not make marmalade with them however — that didn't come along until about 1700 in (of course) Dundee. Do try making your own marmalade: once you do, you'll be hooked for life — even the best of bought can't compare with the fresh tangy flavour of home-made marmalade and it isn't hard to make either. Cold and grey as it may be outside, the aroma of marmalade through the house has a wonderful way of evoking the warmth and colour our oranges have left behind.

Points to bear in mind for success:
- Cooking citrus fruit takes much longer than other fruits because of the thickness of the peel, so much more water is needed to allow for evaporation. By the end of the first cooking stage, the contents of the pan should be reduced by half and the peel must be very soft — once the sugar is added, the peel will not soften any more.
- Pectin and acid content is important to obtain a good set in all jam and marmalade making; lemon juice is added to seville orange marmalade to supply the extra acid needed to get a good set and prevent crystallisation.
- When the sugar is added it must be dissolved over low heat before bringing the temperature up to the boil. Once dissolved, a fast rolling boil is needed to bring the marmalade up to boiling point. To allow for safe fast boiling, the reduced pulp should not come more than halfway up the pan. If you don't have a big heavy-based pan suitable for preserves, why not consider sharing one with friends? Alternatively, you can hire preserving pans or big heavy-duty saucepans.
 -The longer you boil, the darker the colour and more 'mature' the flavour, but over-boiling produces a half-set, syrupy preserve. If your marmalade has reached setting point and you prefer it darker, add a spoonful or two of treacle instead of boiling longer.
- Setting point is reached when a sugar thermometer reaches 221°F, 105°C, or when a little jam cooled on a cold saucer wrinkles when pushed with a finger or spoon.
- To keep well, the marmalade must be poured into jars which are clean, dry and warm, then left until completely cold before covering. Store in a cool, dark place.

Favourite Mincer Marmalade

2 large lemons
3 lb/1.4 Kg bitter oranges
5 pints/3 litres water
6 lb/2.7 Kg granulated
  sugar.

Even if you haven't time to make marmalade at the moment, get the oranges as the season is very short and they freeze well — just make sure that you choose a recipe which involves cooking the oranges whole and freeze them in weighed batches. If they're likely to be in the freezer for a long time, add an extra orange or two per batch to allow for any loss of pectin during storage — or add a couple of sweet oranges or grapefruit at the time if you leave them longer than anticipated. This recipe is the one I normally use, as it is easy and convenient, whether made with fresh or frozen oranges. Quantities given make about 9 lb/4.1 Kg marmalade, but I recommend doubling them if you have a suitable pan.

Squeeze lemons and reserve juice. Scrub oranges and pick the discs off the stalk ends, then put the whole oranges and lemon peel into a large, heavy-based pan and cover with 4 pints/2.3 litres of the water. Cover, bring to the boil and simmer for about 1½ hours, or until the peel is quite

Facing Page: Caramel Bavarois, page 208
Ocverleaf: (top) Aherne's Marmalade, page 218
(bottom) a selection of Marmalades and Preserves

soft. Lift oranges and lemon peel out with a slotted spoon, reserving the liquid. Halve the oranges as soon as they are cool enough to handle and scoop out the flesh and pips into a small pan. Add the remaining 1 pint/600ml of water, bring to the boil and simmer for 10 minutes to extract the pectin from the pith and pips. Cut up the softened peel as coarsely or as finely as you like, or put it through a mincer. (This looks messy at the time, but works out well). Put the prepared peel back into the pan containing the cooking liquid, then add the sugar, lemon juice and the strained juice from the pith and pips mixture. Stir over low heat until dissolved (this will be quicker if the sugar has been warmed in a low oven beforehand), bring to the boil and boil fast for about 15-20 minutes until setting point is reached. Take the pan off the heat and allow to cool for 10-15 minutes, then stir well to distribute the fruit evenly and use a small jug to pour it into clean warm jars. Small waxed discs may be put on top of the marmalade immediately, but don't cover with cellophane or lids until absolutely cold, as this reduces the chance of condensation forming and of mould during storage. Label and store in a cool, dark place.

Seville Orange Marmalade

Seville Orange Marmalade is made by the traditional method, where the orange is shredded before cooking so it looks prettier than my usual short-cut version with minced peel.

    Scrub the oranges well and remove the small disc at the stalk end. Halve the fruit and squeeze the juice; put the pips into a large square of muslin. Quarter the peel and cut away any thick white pith; add it to the pips in the muslin and tie loosely so that it can hang in the pan with the water circulating through it to extract the pectin. Shred the peel finely. Place the peel, orange and lemon juice, the muslin bag of pith and pips and the water in a preserving pan. Bring to the boil and simmer gently for 1½ hours or until the peel is quite tender. Remove the bag of pith and pips and squeeze it well by pressing between two dinner plates. Add the sugar and stir over low heat to dissolve. Bring to the boil and boil fast for a set — about 15-20 minutes. When setting point is reached a sample, spooned onto a cold plate and left a few minutes to cool, should crinkle when pushed with a teaspoon. Allow the marmalade to cool in the pan for 20 minutes, then stir to distribute the peel evenly. Pour into warm, dry jars and cover with wax discs immediately but leave until absolutely cold before sealing, or condensation might form and cause mould in storage. Store in a cool, dark place.

    Variation: **Vintage Marmalade** is made by replacing a quarter of the white sugar with brown. Alternatively, 2 tablespoons black treacle could be added to the mixture above during the final boiling.

Makes about 10 lb/4.5kg.

3 lb/1.4 Kg Seville oranges (or any 'bitters')
Juice of 2 large lemons
5 pints/3 litres water
6 lb/2.7 Kg granulated sugar.

Mixed Fruit Marmalade

Mixed Fruit Marmalade is useful when Seville or bitter oranges are in short supply, as the proportion is smaller but the flavour still good.

    Scrub the fruit and pick off the discs at the stalk end. Halve fruit and squeeze the juice; reserve. Quarter the peels and remove any excess pith. Tie the pith and pips loosely in a square of muslin. Slice the peels as thickly or thinly as you like them, and chop in a liquidiser or food processor — in which case include a little of the measured water with each batch as it is processed. Put the prepared peel, water and fruit juices into the preserving pan; tie the muslin bag of pips and pith to the pan handle and bring the mixture to the boil. Cover loosely and simmer for 1½ hours, or until the peel is really tender. Remove the pan from the heat, remove the muslin bag and press between two plates to squeeze out all the juice, then discard

1 lb/450g bitter oranges
1 lb/450g sweet oranges
2 large lemons
1 grapefruit
6 pints/3.6 litres water
About 6 lb/2.7 Kg granulated sugar.

the bag. Measure fruit and juice and add 1 lb/450g sugar per 1 pint/600 ml of juice and pulp. Bring up to the boil and boil hard for 15-20 minutes, until setting point is reached. Skim, if necessary, or stir in a knob of butter to disperse any small amount of scum. Cool for 15 minutes then stir to distribute the peel evenly before potting. Makes 8-10 lb/3.6-4.5 Kg.

Pressure-cooked Marmalade

Makes about 6½ lb/3 Kg:

2 lb/900g Seville oranges
6 tbsp lemon juice
2 pints/1.15 litres water
4 lb/1.8 Kg sugar.

Pressure-cooked Marmalade is quick to make because the fruit cooking, which takes most time in conventional marmalade, is done under pressure.

Wash the fruit; pare rind thinly. Peel off the pith and cut the fruit up roughly on a plate, to collect the juice. Tie pith and pips in muslin. Cut the rind into thin strips. Place cut-up fruit and juice, rind, pith and pips, lemon juice and 1 pint/600ml of the water into the pressure cooker. Bring to 10lb/4.5kg pressure, cook for 10 minutes, then leave the pan to cool at room temperature until pressure is reduced. Remove the muslin bag, squeezing well; add remaining water and the sugar. Place open pan over a gentle heat and stir until the sugar has dissolved. Bring to the boil and boil rapidly until setting point is reached, then leave to stand for about 15 minutes. Stir to distribute rind, then pot and cover as above.

Note: If freezing oranges, weigh in batches of 3 lb/1.4 Kg and add one or two extra ones to allow for any slight loss of pectin in long storage. Scrub well, remove discs and pack in heavy duty polythene bags. To use, simply cook from frozen — it doesn't take very much longer.

Orange and Ginger Marmalade

Makes about 10 lb/4.5 Kg:

3 lb/1.4 Kg Seville oranges
6 pints/3.6 litres water
2 oz/50g root ginger
Juice of 2 lemons
6 lb/2.7 Kg sugar
8 oz/225g preserved ginger (crystallised), finely chopped
Small knob of butter.

Orange and Ginger Marmalade is a special occasion preserve, but also useful as a sauce, if heated gently and served with ice creams or steamed puddings.

Scrub the oranges and put them into a preserving pan with the water. Lightly bruise the root ginger, tie loosely into a muslin bag and hang from the pan handle. Cover loosely and cook the oranges for about 1½ hours, or until the skins are soft. Lift from the pan with a draining spoon, allow to cool a little, halve and scoop out the pips and pith; add this to the muslin bag containing the root ginger, re-tie and return to the pan. Chop the orange peel finely and add to the pan with the lemon juice and boil, uncovered, for a further 15 minutes. Remove the muslin bag, squeeze between two plates to extract all the juice, then stir in the sugar and chopped ginger over low heat. When the sugar has completely dissolved, bring to the boil and boil hard for about 20 minutes, or until setting point is reached. Allow to cool for a few minutes, stir to redistribute the peel and ginger, then pour into warmed jars. Leave until cold, then cover and label.

Aherne's Marmalade

Makes about 10 lb/4.5.Kg:

3½ lb/1.6 kg seville oranges
1 lemon
10 lb/4.5 kg granulated sugar
8 pints/4.8 litres water

Aherne's of Youghal, the famous seafood restaurant, now has high class accommodation as well and this marmalade is part of the delicious breakfast served to guests. Make Aherne's Marmalade in January, but try to resist using it for six months as it improves with age. Makes about 10 lb/4.5 kg.

Cut up the fruit, remove pips and put into a muslin bag. Liquidise the fruit with a little of the measured water, add the remaining water and leave to soak for 24 hours. Put the fruit into a peserving pan, add the muslin bag and bring tup to the boil, then cook until the peel is tender and the quantity is reduced by ⅓. Remove the bag of pips, add the sugar and stir over gentle heat until it has completely dissolved, then bring back up to the boil and boil hard for 40 minutes, or until setting point is reached. (Test by dropping a teaspoonful onto a cold saucer; if the surface wrinkles when pushed with the spoon, setting point has been reached.) Pour into warm, sterilised jars. Seal and label when very hot or completely cold and store in a cool, dark place until required.

Super Economical Marmalade

Super Economical Marmalade is a recipe devised by my thrifty father for using up the skins of oranges, grapefruit and so on. You need a small 'starter pack' of 4 to 6 bitter oranges (or at least whole sweet oranges) then, after using the flesh of any other citrus fruits, collect the peels in a plastic bag in the freezer until you have a worthwhile amount, say 3 lb/1.4 Kg.

Weigh the whole fruit and the extra peel and allow 3 pints/1.8 litres water per lb/450g. Chop roughly, put into a liquidiser or food processor in small batches along with some water from the measured amount, then put this pulp into a large pan and cook, uncovered, with the remaining water until the peel is very soft — this may take several hours, especially if there is grapefruit in the mixture. When tender, measure the pulp and juice and weigh out l lb/450g granulated sugar per l pint/600 ml. Add the sugar to the pan and stir over low heat until it has completely dissolved, then bring to the boil and boil hard until setting point is reached. Pour into warm, clean jars and leave to cool. When completely cold, seal and label.

Variation: See Sure-Set version under Autumn Preserves.

Thick Cut Whiskey Marmalade

Where large quantities are not a priority it is fun to experiment with a few pots of an unfamiliar preserve — using the foolproof Sure-Set sugar, this can be done quickly and without risk, so the fun element dominates. Readers are always asking me how to make a whiskey-flavoured marmalade, for example and, using traditional methods, the short answer is that it is very difficult to do on a domestic scale — commercially prepared versions are matured in whiskey barrels and that's not something the home cook can often accommodate. The best solution is usually to put a couple of tablespoons of whiskey into each jar before adding the marmalade, so that there is less chance of evaporation than if it is stirred in afterwards or spooned onto the top — coming up from the bottom, the flavour should develop during storage.(Try this with any of the more traditional recipes given above). Another option is to add the whiskey during the final boiling — and this can only work with Sure-Set, because the boiling time is so much shorter than for traditional methods so the flavour has a chance of coming through. Try it in this Thick Cut Whiskey Marmalade.

Makes about 4½ lb/2 Kg:
1 Kg/2 lb Seville Oranges
2 litres/ 4 pints water
1 Kg/ 2 lb Sure-Set Sugar
70 ml/2½ fl oz whiskey.

Scrub the oranges, halve them and squeeze out the juice and pips. Cut the peel into strips and chop. Put the chopped oranges, juice and water into a large pan, bring to the boil and simmer, uncovered, for 2 hours, or until the oranges are soft and the cooking water has evaporated — to use Sure-Set successfully, the fruit should weigh the same after cooking as it did when starting, ie 1 Kg/2 lb. Add the Sure-Set sugar, stir over low heat until it has completely dissolved, then add the whiskey, bring up to the boil and boil *vigorously* for exactly 4 minutes, timing from the moment when the marmalade starts bubbling hard. Pot into heated jars, leave until cold, then cover and label.

Quick Orange Jelly

Makes about 3 lb/1.75Kg jelly:
750 ml/1⅓ pints
  unsweetened orange juice
Juice of l lemon
1 Kg/2 lb Sure-Set sugar.

Jellies of all kinds are always particularly versatile in the kitchen and Sure-Set really comes into its own here because it makes it possible to make a up a quick, small batch of any kind of jelly — single or mixed fruits, plain, spiced or herbed — from your own cooked fruit, dripped through a jelly bag, or simply from any of the vast selection of fruit juices available in cartons at the supermarket. Using apple juice, it is especially useful to make apple and herb jellies when cooking apples are expensive. (See Autumn Preserves.) This Quick Orange Jelly is given using unsweetened orange juice as an alternative to marmalades, but it can be adapted to any flavour.

Heat the fruit juice and add the Sure-Set, stirring over low heat until it has completely dissolved. Add the lemon juice. Bring to the boil and boil *vigorously* for exactly 1 minute, timing from the moment when it starts bubbling hard. Pot up into small warmed jars and leave until cold, then cover and label.

Lemon Curd

Makes about 1lb/450g, which is best potted into small jars:
2 lemons (or equivalent of
  other citrus fruit)
4 oz/100g butter
6 oz/175g granulated sugar
4 egg yolks.

Hint: When cooking egg-based dishes that might curdle, keep a big bowl of very cold water handy. Dip the pan into it at the first sign of curdling. The temperature will usually drop quickly enough to save it. Whisk hard and continue cooking over a lower heat.

Another traditional use for citrus fruits was, of course in curds. Probably because of its versatility in the kitchen, Lemon Curd, given here, has always been the most popular but the basic recipe can be adapted to any other citrus fruits — so experiment. This is a short-term preserve, best refrigerated and usually expected to keep only a few weeks. My own experience leads me to be more optimisitic about its keeping qualities — I have opened perfect jars of curd after many months in a cool cupboard in the garage — but it is probably wiser to err on the side of caution.

Wash and dry the lemons, then grate finely and lightly to remove the zest without any of the white pith underneath. Squeeze the juice and strain it. Melt the butter in a heavy-based pan over gentle heat, then add the sugar, lemon juice and zests, and the beaten egg yolks. Cook, stirring all the time, over gentle heat until the mixture thickens, but do not allow to boil, or it will curdle. Pour into small jars and allow to cool. When absolutely cold, seal and label. Store in the fridge or a very cool cupboard. Keeps for several weeks at least, usually much longer.

Dried Apricot and Almond Jam

Makes about 5 lb/2.3 Kg:
l lb/450g dried apricots
l large or 2 small lemons
About 3½ lb/1.6 Kg sugar
2½ pints/ 1.5 litres cold
  water
2 oz/50g whole almonds.

A favourite winter preserve which is excellent in its own right and in no way inferior to anything made with fresh fruit is Dried Apricot and Almond Jam. We always used to use a recipe from my mother's student days — Plain Cookery Recipes, from the Edinburgh College of Domestic Science — and this is a slightly updated version.

Wash the apricots and chop them up. Peel the zest from the lemon(s) and chop it finely; squeeze the juice and strain it. Put apricots, lemon zest and juice into a large basin, add the water and soak for 24 hours. Measure this pulp and allow l lb/450g of sugar for each pint/600ml. Put the fruit pulp into a preserving pan or large, heavy-based saucepan and simmer for about half an hour until the fruit is tender. Meanwhile, blanch and shred the almonds. Add the sugar and stir over gentle heat until it has dissolved, then boil rapidly, stirring frequently to prevent burning, until setting point is reached and a sample forms a jelly when left to cool on a cold plate for a minute or so. If there is a scum, stir in a small knob of butter to disperse it; skim if necessary. Finally stir in the almonds and pour into hot sterilised jars. Cover with waxed discs, but leave until absolutely cold before sealing, as this reduces the risk of condensation causing mould in storage. Store in a cool, dark place.

Sauces

Whether as an accompaniment or an integral part of a dish, sauces help more than anything else to make the most of food. The potential is unlimited, but this selection of sweet and savoury sauces should make a good basis for a balanced repertoire — individual variations on the basics are endless.

Crème Fraîche

Crème Fraîche is not really a sauce at all, but a cultured dairy product that is used widely in France in dishes which call for cream. It has a rich, slightly sharp flavour which contrasts especially well with fruit. It is cultured in much the same way as yogurt and needs a starter — the most obvious is to use some real French Crème Fraîche and it is worth bringing a pot home if you are visiting France. Otherwise, similar results are possible using either soured cream, yogurt or cultured buttermilk as a starter — of the three buttermilk gives by far the best results and is virtually indistinguishable from the real thing. It also has the advantage of being fairly light on calories — despite its thick texture and rich flavour, Crème Fraîche can have as much as half buttermilk to cream. Like soured cream, Crème Fraîche keeps very well, at least a couple of weeks in the fridge, so it is worth making a fairly big batch.

1/2-1 pint/300-600 ml cream (whipping or double)
2-3 tablespoons (or more) cultured buttermilk (or yogurt, or soured cream)

Heat the cream very gently so that it is just lukewarm (below body temperature, not more than 85°F, 30°C). Mix it with the buttermilk and turn it into a slightly warmed jar or container. Partially cover and leave it at warm room temperature for about 12-24 hours — it will thicken and develop a slightly nutty flavour within about 8 hours, then it continues to mature and ripen. When it is thick and richly flavoured, refrigerate and use as required.

Note: If you have a yogurt-making jar and thermometer, or a wide-neck vacuum flask, simply pour the mixture into the warmed flask and cover it in the usual way — the temperature will be maintained and it can simply be left on a worktop until refrigeration. Although not really necessary, the thermometer takes the guesswork out of the heating. I use a yogurt-making flask and keep the whole lot in the fridge. When nearly finished, the last few tablespoons of the batch can be used as a starter for the next.

Crème Patissière (Confectioners' Custard)

Crème Patissière (Confectioners' Custard) isn't exactly a sauce either, but a classic thickened custard used as a delicious base for fresh fruit in flans, and also instead of cream for for filling cakes, choux buns etc.

Makes enough for a 10-11"/25-28 cm fruit flan, or equivalent:
1/4 pint/150ml cream and 1/2 pint/600 ml *or*
1/2 pint/300 ml creamy milk
1 vanilla pod
1 whole egg
1 egg yolk
2 oz/50g caster sugar
3/4oz/20g plain flour
1/2 oz./15g butter.

To finish:
2-3 tablespoons double cream (optional).

Put the milk and cream into a small pan with the split vanilla pod, bring up to boiling point and simmer very gently for 10-15 minutes to make an infusion; remove from the heat and leave to cool. Strain, reserving the vanilla for re-use. (Rinse, dry and store in a jar of caster sugar.) Put the whole egg and the yolk into a mixing bowl and whisk in the sugar until thick and light, then whisk in the sifted flour and gradually add the creamy milk. Pour the mixture into a small saucepan and bring to the boil, whisking continuously. Simmer over very low heat for 2-3 minutes, whisking continuously; the presence of flour will prevent the custard from separating at this temperature, but if lumps form, remove from the heat and whisk until smooth. Pour the cooked custard into a bowl and stir in the butter. Cover closely with clingfilm to prevent a skin forming and leave to cool. Chill for several hours or overnight. 2-3 tablespoons of double cream may be folded in before use, if you like.

When required, whip the double cream until soft peaks form (if using) and fold into the chilled custard along with the chosen flavouring.

Variations: Coffee-flavoured confectioner's custard, widely used in France as a filling for éclairs, profiteroles and choux buns, is simply made by replacing the liqueur with a teaspoonful of coffee essence, or to taste. Flavoured sugars, such as orange or lemon, can be used to replace the given sugar. A tablespoon of kirsch, sherry, rum or other liqueur may be added.

Crème Anglaise

Makes about ½ pint/300 ml.
½ pint/300 ml whole milk or single cream
1 vanilla pod
2 egg yolks
2 oz/50g caster sugar OR, if a vanilla pod is unavailable, use vanilla sugar or caster sugar and a little vanilla essence.
1 teaspoon cornflour (optional)

Crème Anglaise, also known as Custard Sauce or Egg Custard (to differentiate it from the cornflour-based commercial custard) is the soft pouring sauce, served warm or cold, as an accompaniment to all sorts of puddings and desserts, ranging from steamed puddings to fruit compôtes.

Scald the milk or cream with the vanilla pod. Leave to infuse for 10 minutes, then remove the pod. (Wash, dry and store for re-use.) Meanwhile, blend yolks and sugar in a double saucepan or mixing bowl, adding the cornflour if using. Whisk in the hot milk or cream and put over hot, not boiling, water. Cook gently, stirring or whisking all the time, until the custard becomes creamy and is thick enough to coat the back of a wooden spoon. To serve warm, pour the sauce into a jug and keep in a pan of warm (not hot) water until required. To serve cold, pour into a bowl and sprinkle lightly with caster sugar to prevent a skin forming.

Variations: Flavoured custards can be made by varying the spice used in the infusion — try cinnamon stick instead of vanilla pod to make **Cinnamon Custard** to serve, for example, with poached pears. Another option is to use flavoured sugar, or finely grated zest, to make **Orange Custard**.

Hint: If the custard threatens to curdle, it can usually be saved by turning quickly into a cold bowl and whisking vigorously. Including a teaspoonful of cornflour thickens the sauce slightly and helps to stabilise it. Include the cornflour in trifle custards.

Dark Chocolate Sauce

2 oz/50g cocoa powder
Scant ½ pint/275ml water
6 oz/175g caster sugar
1 oz/25g softened butter.

A good, simple version which does not depend on being able to get good quality chocolate and keeps well in the fridge for up to a fortnight:

Put the cocoa, water and sugar into a saucepan and mix with a wire whisk to make a smooth paste. Bring to the boil and simmer for 3 minutes. Add the butter, bring back to the boil and simmer for another 4 minutes, whisking all the time. Can be kept warm by standing the pan (or a jug) in a pan of warm water. Otherwise, allow to cool and keep in the fridge. To reheat, first add a teaspoon of cold water, then reheat in a bain marie or double saucepan, whisking well.

Sweet Raspberry or Strawberry Sauce

Serves 4:
8 oz/225g raspberries or strawberries
2 oz/50g caster sugar, or to taste
A squeeze of lemon juice.

*Nothing could be simpler than this fresh fruit sauce and nothing prettier or more delicious with fresh fruit or ice cream. In winter the raspberry version, especially, is very successful made with fruit from the freezer. The raspberry version is also known as **Melba Sauce.***

Sort through the fruit, hulling strawberries. Put into a liquidiser with the sugar and blend to make a purée, then pass through a sieve to remove the pips. Sharpen with a squeeze of lemon juice, taste and chill until required.

Blackcurrant Sauce

A colourful, strongly flavoured sauce which can be served hot or cold and is especially good with ice cream, or as a flavouring for natural yogurt. [Microwave]

Measure the water and sugar into a saucepan and heat gently, stirring occasionally, until the sugar has dissolved. Add the blackcurrants, bring to the boil and simmer for 10 minutes or until the fruit is soft. Sieve or liquidise to a thin purée and add the lemon juice. Slake the cornflour in a little water, stir into the fruit purée and return to the rinsed saucepan. Bring gently to the boil, stirring, until the sauce has cleared and thickened. Pour into a jug and serve hot or cold.

¾ pint/450 ml water
6 oz/175g granulated sugar
1 lb/450g blackcurrants
Squeeze of lemon juice
1 teaspoon cornflour.

Variation: If less sugar is used, a little blackcurrrant sauce makes an interesting accompaniment to rich meat or poultry, eg duck breast. **Bramble Sauce** could be made in the same way.

Beurre Blanc (White Butter Sauce)

Beurre Blanc is a very light, white sauce and ideal with fish and vegetables. There are many variations, notably one made with red wine and many including cooking juices (of fish, for example) to replace some or all of the water. The inclusion of cream helps make the sauce more stable and less likely to separate but this is not a sauce to be kept warm. If the reduction has been prepared, finishing the sauce with butter is very quick, so it is much safer and quite simple to do it at the last minute.

Put the shallots, vinegar, wine and water into a small pan and cook until nearly all the liquid has evaporated. Add the cream and reduce a little, then remove the pan from the heat and whisk in the butter a little at a time, until thoroughly blended.

Variation: Despite its reputation Beurre Blanc is not really tricky but, if it does separate, add 2 tablespoons of water and boil vigorously to emulsify the butter and water. The sauce will not be quite as light but quite acceptable — the rescue is in fact a variation on another method of making the sauce, by which 2 tablespoons of water are added after the cream and the butter is then whisked into the mixture while the sauce is boiling.

Beurre Blanc
2 oz/50g finely chopped shallots, or onion
2 tablespoons white wine vinegar
4 tablespoons white wine
6 tablespoons water
2 tablespoons double cream, or Crème Fraîche
6 oz/175g unsalted butter, cubed.

Beurre Fondu

Beurre Fondu, or Melted Butter Sauce, is simpler than Beurre Blanc and used widely in the same way, for fish, poultry and vegetables. [Microwave]

In a small pan, cook the shallots with the water until it has all evaporated, add the cream and reboil. Gradually whisk in the butter, but do not let the sauce boil again. Strain, or leave the shallots in, and season to taste.

2 shallots, finely chopped
1 tablespoon water
1 tablespoon Crème Fraîche or double cream
8 oz/225g cold unsalted butter, cubed.

White Sauce

The ubiquitous white sauce with all its variations is the one most generally used in Irish cookery. Instructions are given for **Béchamel**, which has a better flavour than the simpler version, but a Basic White Sauce can be made in the same way without the infusion

2 oz/50g butter
2 oz/50g plain flour

Infusion:
1 pint/600 ml milk
1 small onion
3 cloves
1 bay leaf.

First make the infusion: Peel the onion and stud it with the the cloves. Rinse out a milk pan with cold water and add the milk, onion and bay leaf. Bring slowly to the boil, then allow to infuse for 15 minutes and strain.

Melt the butter in a saucepan, stir in the flour and cook over low heat for a minute or two, then gradually add the infused milk, stirring all the time to make a smooth sauce. Simmer over low heat for a minute or two. Use as it is, as a coating sauce, or thinned to make a pouring sauce, or as a base for any of the following variations:

Cheese Sauce: Add 2 oz/50g grated mature Cheddar or other hard cheese, ½ teaspoon made mustard and seasoning to taste, including a pinch of cayenne if you like.

Mushroom Sauce: Add 4 oz/100g cooked, sliced button mushrooms sharpened with a squeeze of lemon juice and season to taste. (Replace some of the milk in the basic sauce with chicken stock and/or juices from the mushrooms if possible.)

Mustard Sauce: Add 1-2 tablespoons made smooth Dijon or wholegrain mustard, to taste.

Onion Sauce: Cook a finely chopped onion gently in the butter without browning when making the roux. Stir in the flour and continue as for basic sauce.

Parsley Sauce: Add 3-4 tablespoons freshly chopped parsley and season to taste. If serving with boiled meat, such as bacon, ham or corned beef, replace half of the milk with the meat stock. Fish or vegetable stocks can also be used when appropriate.

Watercress Sauce: Substitute stock for half of the milk after using it to cook a good bunch of watercress, the leaves stripped from their stalks and simmered until tender. Drain, make the sauce, then stir in the cooked chopped leaves and season to taste.

Rum or Brandy Sauce:

Traditional with Christmas pudding, rum or brandy sauce is a variation of white sauce. Make the sauce as above with plain milk and omit all seasonings. Sweeten to taste with about 2 tablespoons of sugar and flavour with about 4 tablespoons of rum or brandy, or to taste.

Many of these sauces, including sweet variations, can also be based on a simple cornflour sauce (2 level tablespoons cornflour per pint/600 ml milk) although the flavour and texture are not quite as good.

Hollandaise Sauce

This warm sauce is generally regarded as being tricky but it's so good with a lot of delicious, simply cooked foods like fresh salmon and asparagus, that it's well worth mastering. The trick is to keep the heat steady and not too high, and to resist the temptation to add the butter too quickly. The blender version, given below, is easier, although (like blender mayonnaise) it doesn't produce the same sauce.

    3 tablespoons white wine
    vinegar
    1 tablespoon water
    6 peppercorns
    1 bay leaf
    3 egg yolks
    6 oz/175g soft butter
    Salt and freshly ground black
    pepper.

In a small pan, boil the vinegar and water with the peppercorns and bayleaf until reduced to 1 tablespoon. Leave to cool. Cream the egg yolks with 1/2 oz/15g butter and a pinch of salt. Strain the vinegar into the eggs and set the bowl over a pan of boiling water. Turn off the heat. Whisk in the remaining butter 1/4 oz/7g at a time, until the sauce is shiny and has the consistency of thick cream. Season with salt and pepper. If the sauce separates, it can usually be saved by removing from the heat and beating in a tablespoon of cold water.

Variations: **Mustard Sauce**, for serving with grilled steaks or oily fish, is made by adding Dijon mustard to taste.

Mousseline Sauce, for asparagus, artichokes and so on, is made by folding about 2 tablespoons whipped cream into the finished sauce.

Blender Hollandaise

Although this quick version doesn't quite have the bite of real hollandaise, it's a fair substitute. Also, if it doesn't work (ie if the butter wasn't hot enough), you can always rescue it by heating over hot water.

    3 egg yolks
    2 tablespoons lemon juice
    Salt and freshly ground pepper
    4 oz/100g butter, preferably
    unsalted or clarified.

Put the egg yolks into the blender with the lemon juice and a seasoning of salt and pepper. Blend for a few seconds. Heat the butter until very hot then run the blender at high speed and gradually add the butter in a thin stream. Blend for about 30 seconds until thick and fluffy.

Mayonnaise

Real mayonnaise isn't hard to make, it just takes a bit of patience. Use top quality ingredients for best results. Everything should be at room temperature. You can save a curdled mayonnaise by whisking in a teaspoon of tepid water and whisking hard until thick and shiny, or starting off again with another yolk in a fresh bowl and gradually whisking in the curdled batch. It's worth making mayonnaise in some quantity as it will keep in the fridge for up to 3 weeks.

    1 egg yolk
    1/4 level tsp salt
    1/2 level tsp dry mustard
    Pinch of caster sugar (optional)
    Black pepper
    1/4 pint/150 ml olive oil
    1 tbsp wine vinegar or lemon
    juice.

Using a small whisk, beat the egg yolk in a bowl until thick, then whisk in the salt, mustard, (sugar)

and some freshly ground black pepper. Add the oil, drop by drop at first, whisking vigorously all the time so that each additon is absorbed before the next is added. As the mayonnaise thickens and becomes shiny, the oil can be added faster. Finally, blend in the vinegar.

Variations: The flavour can be varied by using flavoured vinegars — **tarragon** or **garlic** for example — or by using **lemon juice** instead of vinegar. Chopped herbs — **parsley, chives, tarragon**, crushed garlic — can also be added to the finished mayonnaise or 1/4 pint/150 ml whipped cream can be folded in. **Curry** flavouring gives a lift to food that could be bland, such as chicken salad, and **lime** gives an interesting twist in many cases where lemon is usual. To make a **lighter mayonnaise**, combine with an equal quantity of a good natural yogurt.

Tartare Sauce: Add 3 finely chopped cocktail gherkins, a teaspoon of finely chopped chives, 2 teaspoons of chopped capers and a squeeze of lemon juice.

Blender Mayonnaise

This easy mayonnaise is quick to make and produces a lighter texture and paler colour than the traditional method. Have all ingredients at room temperature.

    1/2 pint/300 ml sunflower oil
    or half olive, half sunflower
    4 yolks or 2 whole eggs
    1/2 teaspoon mustard powder
    or 1 heaped teaspoon mild
    Dijon mustard
    2 tablespoons cider or white wine
    vinegar, or lemon juice
    1/2 teaspoon salt
    Freshly ground pepper.

Measure the oil into a jug. Put the eggs, mustard, 1 tablespoon of the vinegar and the salt into a blender or food processor. Cover and blend for a few seconds. Remove the centre cap from the lid and, with the motor running, slowly pour in the oil — the mayonnaise will begin to thicken when the blades are covered. When it is very thick, add the remaining vinegar, then continue to process until all the oil has been used. If it is too thick or too thin for your taste, adjust with a little more vinegar or oil. Check the seasoning, then spoon the mayonnaise into a screw-top jar and keep in the fridge until required.

Variations: Any number of flavourings can be added, as for hand-made mayonnaise, but the bland background of Blender Mayonnaise seems especially suitable for strong variations like **Mustard Mayonnaise**: Increase the mustard to 2½ teaspoons, mixed with a little water if using powder. Mix with other ingredients in the blender before adding the oil.

Oil and Vinegar Dressings

If pressed to name a favourite dish, I would have to nominate the salad — not the tired old mixed salad which is still commonplace in so many mediocre restaurants, but those wonderful mixtures of colour, flavour and texture which somehow combine creativity and discipline to lift a meal out of the ordinary. Adding a crunch factor — chopped nuts, toasted pine kernels etc — and using different dressings are simple ways of providing variety. Always use the best possible oil, especially as dressings with a high oil to vinegar ratio are kinder both to the food they are intended to complement and whatever you are drinking with it.

Basic Dressing

Not too strongly flavoured, so it won't dominate other ingredients

1 heaped teaspoon mild Dijon
mustard
1 level teaspoon salt
A good grinding of black
pepper, about 6 twists of the
mill
2 fl oz/50 ml good wine or
cider vinegar
8-10 fl oz/225-300 ml
groundnut or sunflower oil.

Put the mustard, salt, pepper and vinegar into a bowl and whisk vigorously, then gradually whisk

in the oil. Taste and adjust seasoning if necessary.

Variations: Add finely chopped fresh herbs, either mixed or a single variety: try mint as a dressing for new potatoes; chives for cucumber salad; mixed herbs for mixed leaves. Add a clove of garlic, crushed or very finely chopped. Or an ounce or so (25g) of crumbled blue cheese — delicious with steak.

Olive Oil Dressing

This simple dressing is ideal for tomato and basil salad. Use all olive oil rather than a mixture if preferred.

2½ fl oz/60ml olive oil
2½ fl oz/60ml groundnut oil
1 fl oz/25 ml red wine vinegar
½ teaspoon salt.

Combine all ingredients well by whisking in a bowl or shaking vigorously in a screw-top jar.

Walnut Dressing

Walnut oil is robust enough to complement bitter salads like chicory and endive. Include a few nuts with the leaves too. As walnut oil is expensive and strongly flavoured, dilute it with a neutral oil like groundnut or sunflower.

2½ fl oz/60ml walnut oil
5 fl oz/150 ml sunflower or
groundnut oil
1½ fl oz/35 ml red wine
vinegar
¾ tsp salt
¾ tsp English mustard
powder OR 1 heaped teaspoon
Dijon mustard
A good grinding of black
pepper.

Combine all ingredients in a bowl and whisk vigorously to blend. If using English mustard, mix it with a little water first. Taste, adjust seasoning if necessary and store in a screw-top jar.

Variation: **Hazelnut Dressing** is made in exactly the same way, substituting hazelnut oil, or a mixture and some roughly chopped or sliced roasted hazelnuts — the flavour is especially delicious, not quite as assertive as walnut but very aromatic.

Linda's Salad Dressing

This comes from The Old Rectory, Wicklow, where Linda Saunders specialises in using a wide variety of organically grown salad leaves, vegetables and flowers. This is the dresing she serves with her famous salads.

10 fl oz/300 ml sunflower oil
5 fl oz/150 ml tarragon vinegar
5 teaspoons brown sugar
3 teaspoons Dijon mustard
2 teaspoons wholegrain
mustard
1 teaspoon honey
½ teaspoon finely chopped
mixed fresh herbs.

This recipe is simplicity itself: just put all ingredients into a screw-top jar and shake really well to form an emulsion, then serve. To make **Linda's Garden of Ireland Salad**, you need a selection of organically-grown salad leaves and edible flowers: lollo rosso, radicchio, oakleaf, chicory frisée, rocket, lamb's lettuce, dandelion, young spinach or sorrel leaves, nasturtium leaves (especially the variegated form, 'Alaska') and flowers like viola, nasturtium or calendula.

Tucker's Dressing

Our friend Brian is an enthusiastic cook and this is his favourite salad dressing. Lea and Perrins Sauce is the secret ingredient that gives it special character — it must have 'cut'.

5 fl oz/150 ml olive oil
1 dessertspoon white wine
vinegar
A wedge of lemon squeezed (a
good teaspoonful of juice)
1 good teaspoon smooth Dijon
mustard
1 teaspoon caster sugar
1 teaspoon Lea and Perrins
sauce
1 clove garlic, crushed
Salt and freshly ground pepper.

Put all ingredients into a bowl or jar and whisk together or shake vigorously to form an emulsion. Taste and check seasoning.

Herby Fresh Tomato Sauce

If you grow your own **tomatoes**, you may well be faced with a glut at the end of the growing season — if not, they should be cheap and plentiful in the shops anyway, so make the most of them. To keep them for cooking in the winter, the easiest method by far is freezing: if you have time, it's well worth reducing them to a purée or making sauces, which will freeze well, otherwise, simply wash them and put them whole into a freezer bag and seal them. When required, the skins come off in seconds and they can be used in the same way as whole fresh tomatoes in soups, sauces and stews.

If it is to be used fresh, tomato sauce can be thickened with flour or cornflour as preferred, but make sure you use cornflour if it's for freezing. [Microwave]

1 lb/450g ripe tomatoes
1 oz/25g butter
1 tbsp oil, preferably olive
1 onion, finely chopped
1 or 2 cloves garlic, crushed or finely chopped
½ pint/300 ml chicken stock
Small bunch of fresh herbs — parsley, thyme, bay leaf — tied together
Pared zest and juice of ½ lemon
1 heaped teaspoonful cornflour
1 tablespoon freshly chopped parsley
Sea salt and freshly ground pepper.

Immerse the tomatoes briefly in boiling water to loosen skins; peel and chop roughly, removing the core if it is tough. Heat the butter and oil gently over moderate heat and cook the onion and garlic in it until softened but not browning. Add the tomatoes, stock, bunch of herbs, lemon zest and juice; season lightly, bring up to the boil, then reduce the heat and simmer for 10-15 minutes. Mix the cornflour with a little cold water in a cup and add a few tablespoons of the hot sauce; stir well and add to the pan. Cook, stirring, until the sauce clears and thickens, then remove the pan from the heat and stir in the chopped parsley. Taste, and adjust seasoning as required — for a more piquant sauce, more like a barbecue sauce, a dash of Worcestershire sauce can be added. Serves 4-6.

Note: For freezing, beware of over-seasoning — it is better to under-season the fresh sauce and adjust as necessary when used from the freezer. The same rule is useful for herbs and spices, which can change flavour and piquancy during long storage.

Variation: **Tomato and Basil Sauce** is especially delicious — make as above but omit the other herbs and replace with a tablespoon of freshly chopped basil at the end of the cooking time, or more to taste if you like. Best used fresh.

Quick Tomato Sauce

This is one of the most useful sauces of all — it's quick and easy to make, colourful, tasty and goes with all kinds of things. Use this as a basic recipe and vary it to suit the food it's to accompany. In winter, when fresh tomatoes are flavourless and expensive, I make it with tinned chopped tomatoes. [Microwave]

1 onion
1 clove garlic, crushed
½ oz/12g butter
1 lb/450g tomatoes, skinned, plus 2-3 tbsp water
1-2 tablespoons tomato purée (optional)
2 teaspoons freshly chopped basil or marjoram OR 1 teaspoon dried herbs
1 teaspoon cornflour
Sea salt and freshly ground black pepper; pinch of caster sugar.

Chop the onion finely and crush the garlic; cook gently in the butter without colouring until softened. Meanwhile, blend all other ingredients thoroughly in a liquidiser. Stir the tomato mixture into the onions, bring to the boil and cook, stirring for 1 minute or until the sauce thickens and clears.

Variation: Instead of fresh or tinned tomatoes, try using sun-dried ones — soak about 8 oz/225g sun-dried tomatoes in enough tepid water to cover them generously for about an hour, or until they have absorbed plenty of water and are tender. Use as above, with their soaking liquid.

Horseradish Sauce

Based on soured cream, this is very easy to make if you have access to fresh horseradish and is far superior to the bought variety. Serve with oily fish as well as beef.

3 rounded tablespoons freshly grated horseradish
1 small carton (5 fl oz/150 ml) soured cream
Sea salt and black pepper to taste
Pinch of dry mustard.

Fold the grated horseradish into the cream and season to taste.

Mint Sauce

Bought mint sauce is inexcusably awful and the fresh variety very easy to make. At the end of the summer, before the mint dies down, sort through it and chop all the best leaves finely in a food processor. Pack tightly into freezer boxes or heavy duty bags, freeze and use by the spoonful like fresh mint through the winter.

Large handful of mint leaves
1 level tablespoon caster sugar
4 tablespoons cider wine vinegar.

Chop the mint finely and put it into a small jug with the caster sugar. Add about 2 tablespoons boiling water and stir to dissolve the sugar, then add the vinegar. Leave to stand for about half an hour before serving with lamb. Serves 6-8.

Apple Sauce

This is the 'correct' method for apple sauce. I usually just cook the apples to a mush in a small pan or in a jug in the microwave and mash them with a fork — no sugar, no butter. Use Bramleys if possible, as they 'fall' nicely and have a good flavour. A little grated lemon zest is an improvement. [Microwave]

l lb/450g cooking apples
l oz/25g unsalted butter
Caster sugar to taste.

Peel, core and slice the apples. Put them into a small pan with 2 or 3 tablespoons of water and cook gently for about 10 minutes. Sieve or liquidise to make a purée, stir in the butter and caster sugar to taste. Do not oversweeten as the sauce is used to offset the richness of foods like pork and goose. *Variations:* Other fruit sauces, such as rhubarb and gooseberry, are made in much the same way and are especially good with oily fish like herrings and mackerel. They do need sweetening, but not to excess. Serves 6.

Cranberry Sauce

Traditional at Christmas with turkey and good with poultry, pork or game (especially venison) at any time. [Microwave]

l lb/450g fresh cranberries
6 oz/175g caster sugar
1/4 pint/150 ml water.

Pick over the cranberries. Put the sugar and water into a saucepan and stir over low heat until the sugar has dissolved. Add the cranberries and bring to the boil, then simmer, uncovered, for about 5 minutes or until the skins pop. Allow to cool slightly, then turn into a serving dish. Serve warm or cold, when the juices will have set to a light jelly. *Variation:* **Cranberry Sauce with Orange and Cider** — include the finely grated zest of 1 orange with the sugar and substitute cider for the water.

Cumberland Sauce

Cumberland Sauce is one of the all-time greats, giving a terrific lift to hot and cold meats, especially ham and pork, venison and poultry. It complements many terrines and pâtés — a simple Chicken Liver Pâté becomes positively glamorous when served on a lovely translucent pool of Cumberland Sauce:

8 oz/225g redcurrant jelly
Zest of one orange
Juice of l orange and 1 lemon
l glass of port or red wine
1 rounded teaspoon arrowroot
1 tablespoon Grand Marnier (optional).

Using a vegetable peeler, thinly pare the zest from an orange. Cut it into fine shreds, blanch for 5 minutes in boiling water then strain and refresh under the cold tap. Drain well. Squeeze the juice from the orange and the lemon, strain and put into a saucepan with the redcurrant jelly. Bring to the boil and simmer for 3 minutes, then add the port or wine. Blend the arrowroot with a tablespoon of water and stir in; bring back up to the boil and cook gently, stirring, until the sauce thickens a little and clears. Add the shredded orange zest and the Grand Marnier, if using, and leave to cool. Serve at room temperature, with hot or cold meats.

Bread Sauce

Also traditional with turkey at Christmas, but useful for poultry all year round.

l small onion
2 or 3 cloves
l small bay leaf
1/2 pint/300 ml milk
2 oz/50g soft white breadcrumbs
1/2 oz/12g butter
Salt and freshly ground black pepper
A pinch of grated nutmeg (optional)
l tablespoon cream or top of the milk.

Peel the onion, stick it with the cloves and put into a milk pan with the bay leaf and the milk. Bring it just to boiling point, then take the pan off the heat and leave it to infuse for 15 minutes. Strain and discard the onion and bayleaf. Add the breadcrumbs and set the pan in a warm place or on a simmering mat over very low heat for about 1/4 hour until the breadcrumbs have soaked up the milk. Add the butter, season with salt, pepper and the nutmeg if using, and stir until smooth. If it is too thin, simmer the sauce very gently for about 5 minutes, stirring frequently as it burns very easily. Just before serving, stir in the cream.

Rum Butter is my favourite accompaniment to Christmas Pudding and mince pies and dead easy to make: simply beat 6 oz/175g unsalted butter until soft and light, then gradually beat in the same weight of light golden brown sugar and 2 or 3 tablespoons of navy rum. *Variations:* A little lemon juice, grated lemon zest and some freshly grated nutmeg can be included, making **Cumberland Rum Butter. Brandy Butter** is made in the same way but using icing sugar instead of soft brown. If you like a citrus flavouring in brandy butter, use orange instead of the lemon.

Basic Recipes

It is useful to have quick and easy access to a range of basic recipes which are in constant use. In this section you will find, for example, some of my favourite potato and rice side dishes, a range of stocks and some everyday pastries. See also the index for basic recipes in the main text.

Potato Gratin

1½-2lb/700-900g potatoes
1 clove garlic, or to taste
2 oz/50g butter
salt and freshly ground
    pepper
1 egg
½ pint/300 ml single
    cream or creamy milk
Freshly grated Parmesan or
    Regato to scatter over.

My own most enduring favourite potato dish is, perhaps, a cliché — but it's a very popular one and I've never known leftovers, whether for a family meal or when entertaining. This version of Potato Gratin serves 4-5 as a side dish — for dinner parties for 8-10 it's very easy to make one for each end of the table — or, with 4-6 oz/100-150g chopped cooked ham included and, perhaps, a chopped onion, it makes a great lunch or supper dish to serve with a side salad.

Preheat a moderately hot oven, 375°F, 190°C, Gas mark 5. Peel the potatoes, slice thinly into a bowl of cold water, then drain and pat dry. Crush or finely chop the garlic and scatter half of it into the base of a baking dish generously buttered with about half of the butter — an 8"/20 cm china flan dish is ideal. Arrange half of the potatoes in the dish, scatter with remaining garlic and season with salt and pepper. In a small jug or bowl, whisk the egg and cream or milk lightly and add a good seasoning of salt and pepper (also an extra clove of garlic, crushed, if you like). Pour half of this mixture over the layer of potatoes. Arrange the rest of the potatoes on top, pour over the remaining egg mixture, plus some extra salt and pepper if necessary, then dot over the remaining butter and sprinkle with the grated cheese. Bake in the preheated oven for a good hour, or until the top is crisp and brown and the potatoes are tender when tested with a knife.

Game Chips

Light, crisp Game Chips are useful and easy — they are really just plain potato crisps or fancy latticed ones, depending on your mood and the occasion.

For plain game chips, also known simply as crisps, peel the potatoes and slice very thinly, preferably using a mandolin slicer. Soak in cold water to remove the surface starch, then drain and pat dry. Fry once only in hot fat for about 3 minutes, until golden brown and crisp. Remove carefully from the fat, drain, spinkle with salt and serve on a folded napkin.

Latticed game chips, also known as waffled potatoes or pommes gaufrette, are cut with the serrated blade of the mandolin, turning the potato through 90° with each cut so that the slices are latticed. Cook as for crisps.

Perfect Pilaf

½ oz/15g butter
1 tablespoon olive oil
1 lb/450g packet brown rice
    (1 pint/600 ml by volume)
1½ pints/850 ml hot
    chicken stock
Sea salt and freshly ground
    pepper.

As gratin is to potato, so pilaf is to rice and this Perfect Pilaf is my preferred method of cooking rice as a side dish or as the basis for a main course (containing, for example, lamb, garlic, dried fruit, nuts and spices). Although I use white rice when required for specific dishes, eg risotto, this is a brown rice dish and I like to use the rather fat long-grained types sold under the Kelkin or Lifeforce labels. Additions such as slivered garlic, walnuts or toasted almonds or pine kernels, raisins and so on can be included as appropriate. Any leftover pilaf makes a good basis for a salad with, say, finely sliced onion and red beans, dressed with a mustardy olive oil vinaigrette.

Hint: Measured by volume, a 1 lb/450g pack of rice = 1 pint/600ml. Allow 2-4 oz/50-100g per person, depending on its use in the meal.

Preheat a moderate oven, 350°F, 180°C, Gas mark 4. In a heavy flameproof casserole, melt the butter and oil over moderate heat. Add the rice and stir around with a wooden spoon for a few minutes, until the rice, thoroughly coated with the butter and oil, is browning and beginning to 'pop'. Add the hot stock, bring up to the boil, add a seasoning of salt and pepper, stir well, cover and put into the oven. Cook for about 45 minutes, or until all the stock has been absorbed and the top is getting crunchy.

The pilaf goes well with virtually any casserole; we use it often in place of baked potatoes. It can be cooked on the hob over gentle heat, but the texture is not quite the same.

NB: In the absence of fresh chicken stock, use a cube, plus 1½ pints/850 ml boiling water, but go easy on the salt.

Stocks

Fresh stocks are very little trouble, but they make all the difference to all kinds of dishes. There are six basic stocks but, for practical purposes in the home, most needs are covered by a good chicken stock and fish stocks, although a general household one is also included in case you have meat trimmings or want a particular meat flavour for a soup or sauce. Vegetables, especially white ones such as onions and celery, contribute a lot to the flavour of stocks, but potatoes should be avoided, as they will make the stock cloudy, and strongly-flavoured root vegetables such as turnips should be used with care as they may overpower other flavours. Green vegetables, especially brassicas, should not be included. Salt is better added at the time of use, depending on other ingredients and the concentration. Vegetable Stock can be specially made if required in large quantities (in a vegetarian household, for example) but in most kitchens it is adequate to collect the stock as it is produced when cooking vegetables, keep it in a jug in the fridge and use for gravies etc as required. A stockpot can be kept going quite easily and almost indefinitely if it is boiled up every day. [Microwave]

Household Stock

General Household Stock can be used for any meat or poultry or a mixture although single flavours are often more successful than a hotchpotch. Bones and meat trimmings used may be cooked or raw. The yield depends on the amount of reduction during the long simmering. [Microwave]

Break or chop the bones into manageable pieces, then wipe them thoroughly. Prepare the vegetables and chop them roughly. Put everything into a stockpot or large saucepan and cover generously with cold water. Bring slowly to the boil, then reduce the heat and simmer, uncovered, for 3 or 4 hours. Strain and leave to cool. When cold, skim off the fat. Refrigerate and use within 3 days, re-boiling before use. Alternatively, freeze until required, or keep the stockpot going.

2-2½ lb/1 Kg bones of any meat or poultry, or meat trimmings, giblets and bacon rinds
1 lb/450g mixed vegetables — onions, carrots, leeks, celery
A bunch of fresh herbs as available — parsley, thyme, a bayleaf, tied together
A few black peppercorns.

Chicken/Game Stock

Chicken Stock can very easily be adapted to make a Game Stock, by using a game bird instead of a chicken. The amount made varies according to the amount of reduction during the long simmering. [Microwave]

Prepare the vegetables and chop roughly. Put everything into a large pan, cover generously with 5 or 6 pints/about 3 litres water and bring slowly up to the boil. Reduce the heat and simmer gently for 3 or 4 hours, then strain through a fine sieve. Leave to cool. When cold, skim any fat off the top. Keep the stock in the fridge and use within 3 days, re-boiling before use. Alternatively, freeze until required, or keep the stockpot going. For use in sauces, the stock can be reduced by hard boiling to give a concentrated flavour.

Note: Microwaved poultry stock can be made in 30 minutes.

2 onions
1 leek
2 carrots
2 or 3 sticks of celery
Carcass and giblets of 1 chicken
A few peppercorns
A bunch of herbs (parsley, thyme and a bayleaf) tied together.

Fish Stock

1½ lb/700g white fish bones and trimmings
1½ pints/850 ml water
½ pint/300ml dry white wine or cider (optional, but make up with extra water if not using)
1 onion, sliced
1 carrot, chopped
1 stick of celery or 1 leek, sliced
Broken parsley stalks
A few peppercorns, roughly crushed.

Fish Stock is very quick to make. Unlike meat and poultry stocks, which benefit from long simmering to draw out the flavours, fish stock develops a bitter flavour if cooked for a long time. Any white fish bones and trimmings can be used for a basic stock. Oily fish, such as mackerel or herring, are unsuitable for stock and salmon should only be used to make stock for salmon dishes. Cod and haddock trimmings make the stock cloudy, so avoid them if clarity is important. [Microwave]

Put all ingredients except the peppercorns into a large saucepan and bring to the boil. Reduce the heat and simmer, uncovered, for about 20 minutes, adding the peppercorns for the last 5 or 10 minutes. Strain through a fine nylon sieve and allow to cool. Keep in the fridge and use within 2 days, otherwise freeze and use as required. Small quantities are often useful — freeze in yogurt tubs and ice cube trays.

Variation: For a **Court Bouillon**, used for poaching whole fish and, well-reduced, in sauces, omit the fish bones from the stock but include the wine, plus two tablespoons of lemon juice or white wine vinegar and a bay leaf. For a richer flavour, the proportion of vegetables may also be increased. Makes about 2 pints/1.1 litres.

Note: Microwaved fish stock takes 10-15 minutes.

Clarified Butter

Clarified Butter has a much higher burning point than ordinary butter and, having had impurities removed, it is suitable for sealing the tops of pâtés and so on. It is expensive for cooking, as 8 oz/225g butter makes only about 5 oz/150g clarified butter. Concentrated butter can be used instead and even ordinary unsalted butter makes a reasonable substitute. When you need the real thing, however, this is how to make it: [Microwave]

Melt 8 oz/225g salted butter in a small pan over gentle heat and cook, without stirring, until the butter begins to foam. Continue, without browning, until the foaming stops. Remove the pan from the heat and leave until the milky deposits have sunk to the bottom, leaving a clear yellow liquid. Pour this carefully through muslin into a bowl, leaving all the deposits behind.

PASTRIES

Instructions are given here for making a range of pastries by hand but they can also be made very successfully in a food mixer — the cutting action of a food processor is especially good for pastry. Butter is recommended for its fine flavour but, for the basic shortcrust, a mixture of yellow and white fats is best. Do not use soft tub fats, or reduced fat butters. If making pastry by hand, remove the butter from the fridge half an hour beforehand; if using a machine, use fats directly from the fridge.
Note: See Index for other pastries.

Shortcrust Pastry

Makes a 9"/23cm plate pie:
9 oz/250g plain flour
4½ oz/125 g butter, or half butter and half white fat
2 fl oz/50 ml very cold water.

Shortcrust Pastry is the general purpose pastry most often used for pies, tarts and so on. Keep everything cool when making pastry, handle as little as possible and chill for 20-30 minutes before rolling.

Weigh and measure ingredients accurately. Sieve the flour into a large bowl, add the butter and cut into small pieces. Rub butter into flour with finger tips, or using a pastry blender, lifting the mixture as much as possible to aerate. Add 2 fl oz/ 50 ml chilled water, mix with a knife or fork until the mixture clings together, then turn onto a floured worktop and knead lightly once or twice until smooth. Wrap in greaseproof paper or foil and leave in the fridge to relax for 20 minutes before using.

Sweet Flan Pastry

This richer, sweet version of shortcrust is the very light, crisp pastry used for open fruit tarts.

Weigh ingredients accurately. Sieve the flour into a bowl, add the butter and cut into small pieces. Lightly rub fat into flour, incorporating as much air as possible; add the sugar and mix well. Make a well in the centre, add the beaten egg and lemon juice then mix with a knife until the dough clings together. Chill.

9 oz/250g plain flour
4½ oz/125g butter
2½ oz/60g caster sugar
1 egg or 2 yolks
2 teaspoons lemon juice or water.

Rough Puff Pastry

Rough Puff Pastry is easier to make than home-made puff pastry and much nicer than the bought variety. It's the cold air which is folded into the pastry which acts as a raising agent and makes it very light. It's equally suitable for sweet and savoury dishes.

Sieve the flour and salt into a bowl; add the lemon juice and the butter broken into pieces the size of a walnut; add enough cold water to bind the ingredients together. Turn onto a floured board and roll the pastry into a long strip. Fold it into three and press the edges together. Half turn the pastry, rib it with the rolling pin to equalize the air in it and again roll it into a strip. Fold in three, and repeat this until the pastry has four rolls, folds and half-turns. It is then ready for use.

Note: Half fat to flour is the basic recipe, three-quarters makes a richer pastry.

8 oz/225g flour
½ teaspoonful salt
Few drops of lemon juice
4-6 oz/100-175g butter
Cold water.

(Continued from page 183)

After Britain took over from the Spaniards in 1656, Jamaica became a great sugar-producing country - and from about that time, and for the next two centuries, sugar became central to issues of imperial and class ambitions, power politics and economics. Having gradually found its way into British and Irish kitchens and drawing rooms as a rare and costly commodity, it was seen from the late seventeenth century as a taxable luxury, like alcohol and tobacco, and a convenient way for finance ministers to balance their budgets. In the House of Commons, arguments over sugar constantly raged to and fro and it was a very messy issue, involving slavery, self-interest, economics, imperial responsibilities and foreign policy. Even employment at home was an issue, not only in refineries and other businesses directly connected with the sugar industry, but in the fashionable coffee houses of the day, which both provided employment and 'were much frequented by persons of the lower ranks of society, free from intoxicating drinks, and supplied with newspapers and periodicals highly farourable to the morals of the working classes, and aiding in the diffusion of knowledge'. (Deerr, *The History of Sugar*)

SUGAR BEET

Sugar beet, on the other hand, has an earlier definite record than cane, going back to about 2000 BC, but it has only recently been developed into a commercially viable plant - firstly stimulated by demand in Europe during the blockades of the Napoleonic wars, then in England when importation became difficult during World War I, but also, during the nineteenth century, as public reaction against slavery created the demand for an alternative source of sugar.

A Miscellany of Useful Information, Glossary, Hints etc.

A

Acidulated water: cold water with lemon juice or vinegar added, in the proportion of $1/2$ pint/300 ml water to 1 teaspoon acid, to prevent the discoloration of certain fruits and vegetables.

Agar-agar: Seaweed-based alternative to gelatines, suitable for vegetarians.

Al dente: cooked but still firm to the bite. Originally used to describe correctly cooked pasta, but the term is gradually coming into more general use.

Al Fresco: literally 'in the open air', but also used to describe a state of mind or attitude — optimism, given our climatic, accompanied by that holiday feeling ...

Allumettes: vegetables or fruit cut into strips like matchsticks.

Amandine: Cooked or coated with almonds.

A point: Of meat — medium cooked.

Arrowroot: Starch used for thickening sauces; when boiled it clears to leave a translucent sauce.

Aspic: Clear jelly produced from the cooked juices of meat, poultry or fish after cooling.

Au Bleu: Of meat — cooked very rare; of fish — cooked immediately after being caught (when it will turn blue).

B

Bain Marie: A large pan of hot water, such as a roasting tin, in which smaller dishes are put for cooking, or to keep food warm. The term is also used for a double saucepan with hot water in the bottom half.

Bard: to cover lean meat, game or poultry with thin slices of pork fat or bacon to prevent drying out during cooking.

Baste: To moisten food during cooking, most usually using a spoon or bulb baster to redistribute pan juices over roasting meat or poultry, but also to use oils or sauces to flavour food during grilling or barbecueing and prevent it drying out.

Beans: Dried beans and other pulses tend to be under-rated: they are inexpensive, an excellent source of protein, dietary fibre, carbohydrate, calcium and phosphorous. They are also low in calories (only 95 per 4 oz/100g) — and delicious. To get the best from them: Soak according to variety, average 8-10 hours, or overnight. (Lentils do not need pre-soaking.) Rinse and cook in fresh unsalted water, only adding salt at the end of the cooking time. Cooking in salted water toughens the skins of beans and lengthens the cooking time. Boil beans hard for the first 10 minutes of cooking time to ensure that any harmful toxins that may exist are destroyed — this is especially important for red kidney beans. Like pasta, most beans are very successfully partnered by tomato-based sauces, but they are also particularly delicious cold and make wonderful salads.

Beat: To mix food with a wooden spoon, whisk or electric mixer to introduce air and make it lighter and fluffier.

Beurre Manié: Equal parts of butter and flour, worked together to make a paste and added to soups and sauce in small knobs to thicken and enrich them.

Bind: Add eggs, cream, melted fat or a roux (see below) to hold a mixture together.

Bisque: Thick creamy shell-fish soup, based on a stock made from the shells.

Blanch: To immerse briefly in boiling water a) to loosen the skin from fruit, vegetables and nuts; b) to remove strong or bitter flavours; c) to preserve the colour of food and kill enzymes before freezing.

Blanquette: A stew of lamb, veal, rabbit or poultry in a creamy sauce, accompanied by onions and mushrooms.

Blend: Combine ingredients with a spoon, beater or liquidiser to produce a uniform mixture.

Bordelaise (à la): cooked with Bordeaux wine, usually with shallots, typically in Entrecôte Bordelaise.

Bouquet Garni: A bunch of herbs including parsley, thyme, marjoram and bay tied with string, or a mixture in a muslin bag, used for flavouring stocks, soups, stews etc.

Bourguignonne (à la): cooked in the Burgundy style, with red wine, glazed pickling onions, mushrooms and bacon. Snails (escargots) cooked à la bourguignonne are served in garlic butter.

Brandade: Fish dish of puréed salt cod, flavoured with garlic and often served with puréed potatoes or French bread.

Braise: To brown whole or large pieces of meat, poultry or game in hot fat then cook slowly in a covered casserole with vegetables and a little liquid, typically in a pot roast. Suits tough cuts of meat and older birds, producing tender flesh and rich gravy.

Brine: Salt and water solution used for pickling and preserving.

Bruise: To crush ingredients such as garlic or ginger lightly to help release their flavour.

Brochette: Skewer on which chunks of fish, meat or vegetables are threaded for grilling or barbecueing.

Butter: May seem too obvious an ingredient to be worthy of comment but there are one or two points worth noting. The first is that the growing number of 'easy-spread' and 'Low-fat' butters can spell trouble — they are fine for spreading on toast, but their high water content can ruin a recipe. For cooking purposes the best choice is unsalted butter, because of its purity — where clarified butter is called for you can usually get away with using unsalted butter instead and, of course, it will not introduce unwanted flavours, especially salt. Using unsalted butter, the flavouring added is entirely in the hands of the cook. Its purity also means it burns less readily than ordinary butter. If you must use ordinary salted butter for cooking, however, make sure it is real butter and not just a spread.

C

Cakes and Biscuits: Never store cakes and biscuits in the same tin, or the biscuits will absorb moisture from the cake and lose their crispness.

Cake Tins: The size and capacity of cake tins is often not marked, even on ordinary plain round or square ones, so shopping for bakeware can be surprisingly difficult unless you buy one of the few (and usually more expensive) branded types which come with information. When it comes to novelty shapes — numbers, hearts, hexagons and crescents, for example, the problem gets even more complicated. The solution is to measure the liquid capacity of the tin. Simply fill the tin with water to the level you want the cake to rise to and measure the water. Then, for each pint/600 ml of water, using any recipe based on an ordinary sandwich mixture, allow 1 egg, 2 oz/ 50g butter, 2 oz/50g caster sugar and 2 oz/ 50g self-raising flour. With this as the guide to the amount, you can then work out the proportions for your chosen recipe. For fruit cake mixtures the method is the same, but for every 1 pint/600 ml capacity allow 1½ eggs, 3 oz/75g butter, 3 oz/75g sugar and 3 oz/75g plain flour plus 5 oz/ 150g currants, 2 oz/50g seedless raisins, 2 oz / 50g sultanas and 1½ oz/40g glacé cherries.

Canapés: Biscuits or small pieces of bread or toast topped with a savoury mixture and served with drinks.

Candied Julienne Strips of Citrus Peel: makes an attractive and delicious garnish for poached fruits, mousses, sorbets and many other cold sweets. Any citrus fruit can be used: remove the zest with a vegetable peeler, cut into julienne strips, blanch for 2 minutes and drain. Heat 1 oz/25g sugar with 2 tablespoons water in a small pan, stir until the sugar has dissolved, then add the blanched julienne strips from 1 orange or 2 lemons. Simmer together until the zest is transparent and the water has evaporated. Lift the zest out of the pan with a slotted spoon and drain. Store in an airtight container until required — it will keep for a couple of days. Small amounts can be frozen for use at any time.

Capers: Pickled flower buds of a Mediterranean bush, used in sauces and garnished. (Pickled nasturtium seeds are sometimes used as a substitute.)

Caramelise: a) To grill a sugar topping until brown b) to glaze food in butter with sugar c) to cook meat juices to a dark glaze. In confectionery, the term means to cook sugar syrup or sugar to the caramel stage.

Carbonnade: Meat stew made with beer or stout.

Cassoulet: Stew of haricot beans, pork, lamb, goose or duck, sausage, vegetables and herbs.

Chantilly: Whipped cream, lightly sweetened and usually flavoured with vanilla.

Charlotte: Moulded dessert — hot, made of buttered sliced bread and filled with fruit; b) cold, sponge fingers filled with cream and fruit or a set custard.

Charlotte Mould: Tall mould with sloping sides used for making charlottes and other desserts or moulded dishes.

Chowder: Fish dish halfway between a soup and a stew.

Chiffonade: Garnish made of shredded lettuce, sorrel and spinach used to garnish soups and cold dishes.

Clarify: To remove impurities from a liquid, usually a) to clear butter by melting it and straining off the pure oil so that impurites (milk solids, salt, water) are left behind in the sediment or b) to clear stock by simmering with egg white.

Compôte: Dried or fresh fruit cooked in a sugar syrup and served cold.

Concassé: Coarsely chopped — usually refers to tomatoes.

Confit: Food made into a preserve by very long, slow cooking; usually refers to duck or goose, which is cooked in its own fat and then sealed with a layer of it to exclude air. Can also refer to vegetables, such as onions.

Conserve: Whole fruit preserved by boiling in sugar syrup and used in the same way as jam.

Coulis: Thin sauce of puréed fruit or vegetables, raw or cooked according to variety. Usually smooth, but can have texture.

Cream: To beat fat and sugar together until the sugar has dissolved and the mixture becomes pale, light and fluffy.

Crème Brulée: Cream custard with a crunchy caramelised topping.

Crème Caramel: Egg custard cooked with caramel in a mould and served cold: when turned out, the liquid caramel becomes a topping.

Crème Fraîche: Thick, slightly acidic cultured cream used widely in France. Although unavailable in Ireland, a very similar substitute can be made at home.

Crudités: Raw vegetables either a) cut into sticks and served with dips as a cocktail snack or first course or b) coarsely grated raw vegetables served with salad dressing as a first course or side salad.

Curdle: Separation of a mixture into solid

Rough Guide to Baking Times for Fruit Cakes:
These approximate times are based on a cool oven temperature, 300°F, 150°C, Gas mark 2.
For fan-assisted ovens the temperatures are lower, consult manufacturer's instructions.

Round Tins:	Capacity	Cooking Time
5"/12.5 cm	1 pint/600 ml	2-2½ hrs
6"/15 cm	1½ pints/900ml	2½-3 hrs
7"/18 cm	2 pints/1.2 litres	3-3½ hrs
8"/20 cm	2½ pints/1.8 litres	3½-4 hrs
9"/23 cm	4 pints/2.4 litres	4-4½ hrs
10"/25.5 cm	5 pints/3.6 litres	6-6½ hrs
11"/28 cm	8 pints/4.8 litres	7-7½ hrs
12"/30.5 cm	10 pints/6 litres	8-8½ hrs

To calculate the approximate cooking times for square tins, simply go down one size, eg a 5"/12.5 cm square tin is equivalent to a 6"/15 cm round one.

(curds) and liquid, most often caused by overheating egg and cream mixtures, or overbeating when eggs are added to a creamed mixture.

Cure: To preserve food by drying, salting or smoking.

D

Darne: Thick slice cut from round fish, often salmon.

Deglaze: To dissolve solids on the bottom of a pan by adding liquid, such as wine or stock, then scraping and stirring vigorously to extract their flavours for use in a sauce.

Devil: To prepare fish, meat or poultry with highly seasoned or hot ingredients such as mustard, Worcestershire sauce or cayenne pepper, before grilling or roasting.

Dice: To cut food, usually vegetables, into small cubes.

Dredge: To sift an ingredient, usually sugar or flour, fairly thickly over food.

Dried Grated Rinds: of citrus fruit, especially orange and lemon, are very handy for quick zesty flavouring of dozens of dishes, sweet and savoury. Simply grate the rind finely to give thin shreds of zest (it need not be quite as fine as for flavouring sugars) and dry out in a cool oven until crisp. Cool and store in airtight jars — making a citrus mixture would take less space, but is more useful to have the choice of individual flavourings. Keep the jars handy and add a pinch to casseroles, salad dressings, gravies and sauces, cakes and puddings — anything that would be enhanced by a citrus flavour. (See also **Zest**).

Dropping consistency: texture of mixture when it will drop off a spoon if flicked.

Dust: To sprinkle lightly with sugar, flour, spice or seasoning.

E

Emulsion: Mixture of ingredients that normally separate, eg oil and vinegar or lemon juice, using emulsifying agents, such as mustard or egg yolk.

En croûte: Encased in pastry.

En papillotte: Wrapped, cooked and served in buttered or oiled paper or foil.

Entrée: a) Most often, the main course or fully garnished main dish; b) Third course in a formal meal, coming between the fish course and the main meat course.

Entremet: Pudding or sweet course.

Escalope: Thin slice of meat which is beaten flat and pan-fried.

Essence: Concentrated flavouring liquid.

F

Fillet: a) to take a section of fish, poultry or meat off the bone; b) prime cut that has been removed from the bone.

Filo: Paper-thin middle eastern pastry, very like strudel pastry, cooked in multiple layers with melted butter or oil between them to produce a very crisp, light shell. Widely available in frozen pre-packs and used from the freezer.

Fines Herbes: A mixture of fresh chervil, chives and tarragon, sometimes with parsley included also, used raw or towards the end of cooking so they are warmed but still fresh-tasting. Classic flavouring for omelettes.

Flake: a) To separate cooked food, especially fish to that it falls into natural divisions or flakes; b) to grate food such as chocolate or cheese into thin slivers.

Flambé: Flamed, usually by tossing food in burning alcohol.

Flavoured Butters: Are indispensable and can be kept in the freezer to use as required on grilled meats, steamed fish or vegetables, on rice or pasta, or in hot breads. As well as garlic, any fresh herbs in season can be used — tarragon, rosemary, coriander, flat-leaf parsley, chives etc — or any other useful seasonings, such as green peppercorn, wholegrain mustard, allspice and juniper and so on. The amount used depends on the ingredient, its strength and personal taste but, as a rough guide, use 4-5 tablespoons fresh finely chopped herb in a 6 oz/175g batch. Blend ingredients, form into a fairly narrow roll and wrap tightly in clingfilm or foil. Keeps for a month in the fridge, much longer in the freezer. For freezing, it is advisable to store all the rolls together in an airtight freezer box or bag, to avoid the possibility of the strong flavours contaminating other foods. **Garlic**

Butter: Crush or finely chop 2-4 cloves garlic and mash with 6 oz/175g butter. **Coriander Butter**: Chop a large bunch of leaves finely, to produce 4-5 tablespoons when chopped; blend with 6 oz/175g butter. **Green Peppercorn Butter**: Crush 3 tablespoons green peppercorns (drained, if in brine) and blend with 1 tablespoon smooth Dijon mustard, 1 tablespoon lemon juice and 6 oz/175g butter. (**Wholegrain Mustard Butter** is made in the same way, substituting crushed mixed yellow and black mustard seeds for the green peppercorns; or **Black Peppercorn Butter**, substituting roughly crushed black peppercorns.) **Anchovy Butter:** Drain a small (2 oz/50g) tin of anchovy fillets and sieve them or mash very finely, then work into 4 oz/100g butter and season to taste with freshly ground black pepper.

Flavoured Sugars: Extremely useful to have prepared. The simplest and most versatile is **Vanilla Sugar** — just leave a vanilla pod in a jar full of caster sugar. The sugar will absorb the flavour of the pod and be ready for use whenever vanilla flavouring is required. **Orange and Lemon Flavoured Sugars:** Grate the zest of an orange or lemon very finely and mix with 4 oz/100g caster sugar. Blend with a wooden spoon until the sugar is coloured, then spread out on a sheet of greaseproof paper or foil and leave in a warm place until dried out. Crush any lumps and store in a screw-top jar. *Uses:* Use in any recipe including sugar where a citrus flavour is appropriate, such as fruit compôtes or pies, flavouring plain sponge cakes, ice creams, custards and egg-based cold sweets such as Crème Caramel, instead of plain caster sugar on pancakes and so on.

Florentine: a) Made or garnished with spinach; b) Thin, crisp biscuit made of nuts and glacé fruits, spread with melted chocolate.

Flower Waters: Rose Water is distilled from rose petals and was widely used in this part of the world until Victorian times, when it became unfashionable. It has always been an important ingredient in middle-eastern and Indian cookery, however, and is currently undergoing a revival in western kitchens. It is available from chemists and specialist Greek shops and has recently come into supermarkets as part of the 'English Provender' range. Use with discretion in sorbets, desserts, Turkish Delight, curries and spicy casseroles. **Orange-flower Water** has similar uses. Flower waters are very volatile, so they are usually supplied in dark bottles and should be kept tightly sealed, away from heat and light. Their perfume can be overpowering, so use very sparingly at first.

Foie gras: Liver of specially fattened goose or duck; traditionally preserved, usually in pâté with truffles, but increasingly being used fresh.

Fold in: To incorporate ingredients, usually whisked egg whites or cream, into a mixture with minimum loss of volume, usually using a large metal spoon or spatula.

Fondue: a) Swiss dish of hot melted cheese and white wine eaten by dipping pieces of bread or crudités into a communal pot; b) **Fondue Bourguignonne** is a variation: diners cook chunks of steak at the table by spearing it onto long forks and dipping it into a central pot of hot oil.

Fool: Cold sweet made of puréed fruit and whipped cream, or a mixture of whipped cream and egg custard.

Frangipane: Sweet almond and egg filling cooked in a pastry case. Can also be used as a binding in a sweet panada.

Fricassée: a) Dish in which poultry, fish or vegetables are bound by a white sauce; b) old-fashioned white stew of chicken in a creamy sauce, served cold.

Fromage Frais: Fresh French cheese with a light, creamy texture and refreshing, but neutral flavour. It can be used in savoury salads, mixed with chopped scallions, herbs or nuts to serve with lettuce or salad greens, or as a savoury at the end of a meal, sprinkled with garlic and parsley or seasoned with black pepper or cumin. It is also used plain, or sweetened with a little caster sugar, to serve with fresh or poached fruit instead of cream. **Fromage Blanc** is very similar to Fromage Frais, but smoother in texture.

Frost; a) To coat a cake with icing; b) To dip the rim of a glass in egg white and caster sugar and chill until set.

Fumet: Stock or broth, usually of fish but can also apply to meat or vegetables, concentrated by reduction.

G

Galantine: Boned, stuffed and re-shaped dish, usually of poultry but can also be of game or meat, glazed with aspic and served cold.

Galette: a) Flat pastry cake traditionally baked in France for Twelfth Night; b) Traditionally understood to mean a flat cake of sliced or mashed potato, now more correctly extended to mean any sweet or savoury dish that is a flat round shape.

Ganache: A creamy chocolate mixture, a little like fudge but smoother and not as sweet, used as an icing or filling for cake and a centre for chocolates.

Garam Masala: Aromatic blend of whole roasted spices, typically coriander seed, cumin, cloves, cardamom and cinnamon, ground and used in Indian cookery in a similar way to the hotter curry spices.

Garnish: a) Completing a dish with edible ingredients which may or may not be decorative but make it into a complete dish and give it a particular character; b) Edible decorative extras, eg sprigs of herbs.

Gelatine: Six sheets of **Leaf Gelatine** equal 1 oz/25g powdered gelatine. To use, wash in cold water then soak in a bowl of cold water for 15-20 minutes until soft. Squeeze the softened gelatine lightly to remove surplus water, then put it into a bowl with the measured amount of liquid used in the recipe. Place the bowl over a pan of hot water and heat, without boiling, over a low heat until dissolved. **Powdered Gelatine** is usually sold in 2 oz/50g packets of 5 sachets, each containing 11g/0.4 oz or 3 level teaspoons — enough to set 1 pint/600 ml liquid for moulding in the fridge. 2 level teaspoons will set the same amount of liquid to be spooned into serving glasses. Fruit purées and ingredients of a similar consistency, such as moulds and mousses, need 1 level teaspoon per 1/2pint/300 ml purée for setting in glasses. Hot weather affects gelatine, so allow a little extra to compensate. Similarly, if a tall or complicated mould is used, allow extra gelatine to give a firmer set. Some fresh fruit, such as pineapple, contain enzymes which prevent gelatine working. However, these enzymes are destroyed in cooked and canned fruit, so they can be used in jellies.

Ghee: Indian clarified butter, traditionally made from the milk of the water buffalo.

Giblets: Edible internal organs and trimmings of poultry and game, used for making stock.

Glacé: Glazed, frozen or iced.

Glace de Viande: a) Residue on the bottom of the pan after frying or roasting meat. b) Meat stock concentrated by reduction.

Glaze: Shiny finish given to food, typically by brushing with beaten egg or milk before cooking, or coating with melted jelly or aspic when cold.

Gluten; A protein in flour that is developed and makes dough elastic when it is kneaded. 'Strong' flour has a higher gluten content than ordinary plain or cream flour and is better for baking bread, especially yeast bread, and some pastries.

Goujons: a) Originally, gudgeons — small fish fried and served as a garnish; b) Now taken to mean thick, longish slices of fish, usually crumbed and deep-fried and often served as a cocktail snack or buffet dish.

Gratin: Dish finished with a crisp breadcrumb or cheese crust and browned in the oven or under the grill.

Grissini: Italian bread sticks.

H

Hang: Suspend meat or game in a cool, dry place to tenderise the flesh and develop the flavour.

Hard sauce: Butter-based sauce, flavoured with whiskey, brandy or rum, that hardens when chilled and melts when served with hot puddings.

Haricot: Dried bean of haricot bean plant.

Haricot Vert: Green bean, typically French bean.

Hazelnuts: Usually need to be skinned before use; this is done by toasting the nuts under a grill, or roasting in the oven — which also greatly enhances their flavour. Place the shelled nuts in a single layer on a shallow grill pan or roasting tin and toast under a medium grill or roast in a fairly hot oven for 5-10 minutes, or until the skins are dry and the nuts begin to colour. Cool slightly, then turn the nuts onto a clean tea towel and rub them together in the cloth to remove the skins. The nuts will be crisp and aromatic — perfect for use in salads and many other dishes.

Herbs: A personal selection of indispensible herbs would include: parsley, thyme, mint, chives, rosemary, oregano (or marjoram), chevril, sorrel, lovage, French tarragon, basil, coriander leaves: horseradish, while not exactly a herb is an important flavouring. Fresh herbs can always be used more generously, but the amount varies enormously according to pungency.

Hull: To remove the stalk and its surrounding green calyx from soft fruit such as strawberries.

I

Ice Creams: To turn out ice creams and other frozen puddings cleanly, rinse a cloth in very hot water, ring out and use to cover the mould for a few seconds, then shake to release. Repeat if necessary. Metal moulds are good conductors of heat and usually easier to turn out.

Infuse: To soak herbs, spices or other flavourings in a hot liquid, to flavour it. The time varies from as little as two to about fifteen minutes depending on the ingredients used and the strength required.

J

Jardinière, à la: Garnish of garden vegetables, usually cooked, possibly diced and probably arranged in separate groups.

Julienne: Matchsticks of vegetables or rind, usually used as a garnish.

L

Langouste: Crawfish

Langoustine: Norway lobster or Dublin Bay Prawn.

Langue de Chat: Crisp finger-shaped biscuit served with ices and cold sweets.

Lard: a) Natural, unrefined pork fat; b) to thread strips of fat (lardons) through very lean meat with a needle to keep it moist while cooking.

Légumes: a) Vegetables; b) family of plants with seed pods such as peas and beans.

Lyonnaise, à la: In the Lyonnaise style, usually with onions.

M

Macedoine: Mixture of fruit or vegetables.

Macerate: To steep food in liquid to soften it; often refers to vegetables, or fruit which is steeped in syrup or liqueur.

Magret: Boned breast fillet of duck.

Marinate: To soak food in a marinade, usually a mixture of wine, oil, vinegar and herbs, to tenderise and flavour it.

Marinière, à la: a) Mussels cooked in white wine and herbs, served in the shells with the sauce as a soup; b) Fish cooked in white wine and garnished with mussels.

Mascarpone: Rich, creamy Italian fresh cheese, used mainly in desserts.

Mayonnaise: Hand-made mayonnaise is not difficult, but it can't be rushed — if the oil is added too quickly, the mixture will curdle. Curdled mayonnaise can be saved by starting again with another egg yolk in a fresh bowl. Beat the curdled mixture into it it very gradually until it becomes smooth, then continue adding oil as usual.

Medallions: Small circular cuts, usually of meat but can also refer to fish or pâté.

Meunière, à la: In the style of the miller's wife, ie coated with flour before cooking — typically in Sole à la Meuniere which is floured, cooked in butter, seasoned and sprinkled with lemon juice and freshly chopped parsley.

Mirepoix: Mixture of finely chopped vegetables, sometimes with ham, which is fried in butter and used as a base for brown sauces and stews.

Mousseline: Purée of raw fish, poultry or white meat into which unwhisked egg white and often cream are gradually beaten typically to make quenelles, also a sauce.

Mustards: are going through an interesting phase with, for example, several brands of Irish-made speciality mustards now in strong competition. But the most useful mustards are the classics: smooth, mild Dijon Mustard is simply indispensable and very good value if you buy large jars — such as the Bornier brand, available in 850g/ 1 lb 14 oz jars at a fraction of the price relative to a lot of small ones. The other great mustard is of course the coarse, grainy Moutarde de Meaux and an old-fashioned 500g/1 lb stone jar of the classic from Pommery will set you back a great deal less than you think. With these two

— and a jar of loose whole seeds, yellow and black, which are also surprisingly inexpensive — there is no limit to what you can do.

Mustard Seeds, types of: The darker the seeds, the more pungent the flavour — black mustard is strongest, but the slightly milder brown seeds are more easily available. Yellow and white seeds are mildest of all. Its pungent flavour is only released after the seeds have been ground and mixed with water so, for example, dry mustard added to a sauce will be weaker than if it had been mixed with water first. It is useful to have a selection of whole mustard seeds to grind as required, giving extra character in flavour and texture to a wide variety of dishes, in the same way as using different types of pepper.

N

Navarin: Stew of lamb and spring vegetables

Niçoise: In the Nice style — garnished with tomatoes, onion, garlic and black olives.

Noisette: a) Flavoured with hazelnuts, or cooked to a deep, rich nutty brown; b) lamb taken from the boned loin or rack then rolled, tied and cut into neat little slices.

Normande: in the Normandy style a) for meat and poultry: a sauce with cream, apple and Calvados; b) for fish: garnished with shrimp, mussels and mushrooms in a white wine sauce.

Nouilles: Noodles.

Nuts: Like other nuts, the flavour of **coconut** is greatly enhanced by toasting. To do this, cook dessicated coconut in a dry frying pan over moderate heat, stirring all the time so that it browns evenly OR spread out on a piece of foil and brown under the grill, stirring occasionally — watch carefully as it tends to darken very suddenly. Allow to cool, then keep in a screw-top jar until required.

O

Oeufs Mollets: Soft-boiled eggs, with a soft yolk and just-set white.

Offal: Edible internal organs of meat, poultry and game, such as liver, kidneys, heart .

Oils deserve a word of explanation: Light oils, which are suitable for delicately flavoured foods or in any dish where the oil is not a feature to be noticed, include sunflower oil, peanut oil (also known as groundnut or arachide) and safflower oil. Corn oil is slightly heavier, but very suitable for all-purpose use in the kitchen. Olive oils vary enormously in colour, texture and flavour depending mainly on their country of origin — Greece, Portugal and Spain, for example, are well-known for the robust flavours of their oils, while Italy and Provence produce finer, more delicately flavoured oils. Quality, and therefore the cost, is also very much influenced by whether the oil is taken from the first pressing — it is a complex subject and very much a matter of personal taste and means. A good all-round branded oil such as Lesieur Extra Virgin Olive Oil, or an equivalent from another reliable manufacturer is probably the best buy for everyday use and is interesting enough to make good salad dressings without having so much character that it dominates other ingredients. From such a base, the interested cook can sample and compare.

P

Panada: Thick sauce usually based on flour, bread or starchy vegetables such as potatoes, used to bind ingredients, notably for quenelles or as a base for soufflés.

Par-cook/par-boil: To cook food briefly to reduce cooking time, or when it is to be finished by another method.

Parfait: Very smooth, creamy frozen dessert made of whipped cream and fruit purée.

Parsley, types of: The common curly-leaved parsley is most popular with cooks because it keeps well, is easy to chop and makes an attractive, if predictable, garnish. However, the less common flat-leaf French parsley has more flavour and is becoming more widely available.

Paupiette: A thin slice of meat, poultry or fish, spread with a stuffing and rolled, then cooked in a sauce. Also known as an 'olive', as in Beef Olives.

Pectin: A gelling substance necessary to the setting of preserves which occurs naturally, but in varying quantities in fruit and vegetables. Those with a high pectin content include cooking apples, Seville (marmalade) oranges, gooseberries.

Pepper, types of: Black, white and green peppercorns all come from the same plant. **Black pepper** is the dried unripe berry and has a fairly mild, aromatic flavour which is best when freshly ground. **White pepper** is the ripened berry, dried after the outer casing has been removed and has a hotter, less aromatic flavour. **Green peppercorns** are the unripe berries, preserved in brine or freeze-dried: they have a sharp, slightly acidic taste without the heat of the dried berries and are often used in sauces to complement rich meats and shellfish. If preserved in brine, simply rinse and add directly to the sauce; if the berries are freeze-dried, crush them in a pestle and mortar before use. **Pink peppercorns** are unrelated to the others and are piquant rather than peppery. They are used mainly for their decorative value, sometimes in combination with green peppercorns as the flavours marry well.

Petits fours: a) Traditionally, tiny sponge cakes iced and decorated to serve with coffee at the end of a meal; b) Nowadays extended to include small biscuits, sweetmeats, fruits dipped in sugar or chocolate, glacé fruits and other tasty titbits that help round off a meal with style and novelty.

Pickle: To preserve meat or vegetables in brine or a vinegar-based solution.

Pilaf, Pilau: a) Near-eastern dish of cooked rice mixed with spiced meat, poultry or fish; b) Now often used to describe a method of cooking rice: first it is fried in butter or oil, then a measured amount of stock or water added and brought to the boil. The casserole is closed tightly and cooked in the oven or on the hob until all the liquid has evaporated.

Pimento: Sweet pepper.

Pine kernels: Do not have skins that need to be removed but, like hazelnuts, their texture and flavour is greatly improved by toasting or roasting them, or by frying gently in a little butter or olive oil and butter. They have a tendency to turn colour very suddenly and are easily burnt, so watch them carefully and remove when they are an even deep golden-brown.

Pistachio Nuts: Shelled pistachios need to be blanched to remove the skin before use in cooking: put them into boiling water with a pinch of bicarbonate of soda to enhance their natural green colouring, then drain, refresh in cold water and ease off the skins by pinching each nut between thumb and forefinger, in the same way as for almonds. Dry before use. Unsalted ones are often hard to find. To use salted ones in cooking, shell them and allow to stand in boiling water for 10 minutes. Then peel off the skins and dry in a very cool oven, 250°F, 130°C, Gas mark ½, for 15 minutes, or longer if necessary. When thoroughly dried, the pistachios can be stored in a screw-top jar.

Pith: The spongey white, bitter-tasting layer between the fruit and the zest in citrus fruits.

Poach: To cook gently in liquid that is maintained at a temperature just below simmering point, so that it trembles without bubbling. An ideal cooking method for delicate foods that break up easily such as fish and fruit. Also used for casseroles with very long, slow cooking times so that the maximum flavour is obtained without the food breaking up.

Pot-roast: To braise a large piece of seared meat slowly in a covered pot with flavourings and a little liquid.

Praline: Sweet made by caramelising unblanched almonds in boiling sugar. When cold and set, it is broken up and stored for use in ice creams and desserts.

Printanier: Garnish of spring vegetables.

Prosciutto: Raw smoked Italian ham, served very thinly sliced, often with fruit, as a first course.

Purée: To mash, sieve or liquidise food to a smooth consistency.

Q

Quark: Low-fat curd cheese originating from Austria and Germany but now widely manufactured.

Quenelles: Light savoury dumplings made of meat or fish, based on a panada; usually poached and served in a delicate sauce.

Quiche: Originally an Alsatian tart with a savoury filling based on cream and eggs; now used for any kind of savoury flan.

R

Ragout: A well-seasoned rich stew containing meat, vegetables and wine. Now often applied to any stewed mixture.

Ramekin: a) Individual ovenproof dish used for baking and as a mould; b) small pastry case with a cream cheese filling.

Ratafia: a) Flavouring made from bitter almonds; b) liqueur made from fruit kernels; c) tiny macaroon.

Reduce: To concentrate a liquid by boiling and evaporation.

Refresh: To cool hot vegetables in cold water, or in a colander under the tap, to stop the cooking process and retain their bright colour, texture and flavour. Also used for shellfish.

Render: Slow cooking of meat or poultry trimmings to extract the fat for cooking purposes, notably of goose and duck. Also means to clear frying fat by heating it.

Rennet: Animal extract used to make cheese curd and to set junkets.

Rice: It is a myth that rice is tricky to cook correctly. My own preferred method is the pilaf (See Basic Recipes), a variation of the simple **absorption method** which ensures that plain rice will be cooked perfectly every time: use long grain rice and allow 2 oz/50g per person. Tip the weighed rice into a measuring jug and allow twice its volume in stock or water. Bring the liquid to the boil in a saucepan, salt lightly and add the rice. Bring back up to boiling point, stir once and cover closely. Cook over gentle heat 15 minutes if using white rice, 40 minutes for brown. Remove from the heat. The liquid should all have been absorbed and the rice just cooked, al dente. Leave to stand for about 5 minutes and fluff with fork before serving. The same method works well in a moderate oven, 350°F, 180°C, Gas mark 4; allow 30-40 minutes in a closely covered casserole for white rice, an hour for brown. Alternatively, the **excess water method** is equally reliable although, as it involves draining and rinsing, it is slightly more trouble: use a large pan and allow 2 oz/50g rice and 1 pint/600 ml water per person. Bring the water to the boil with 1/4 teaspoon salt per person, add the rice and boil for 12-15 minutes for white rice, 25 minutes for brown, until the grains are just tender. Drain in a sieve, rinse with boiling water and drain well again. Turn into a bowl and serve.

Rice paper: Edible white paper, glossy on one side, made from the pith of a Chinese tree and used as a base for macaroons and similar dishes.

Ricotta: Sweet-smelling, light coloured fresh Italian cheese which can be made with whole or semi-skimmed milk. When young its moist, light texture and neutral flavour make it especially suitable to use in pasta fillings and in combination with other foods — ricotta and spinach is a classic combination, for example.

Roulade: a) A roll of meat such as pork or veal, spread with stuffing, rolled and braised or poached; b) Now more often means a very light sweet or savoury mixture baked in a swiss roll tin, spread with a contrasting filling, rolled and cut in diagonal slices.

Roux: Mixture of equal amounts of fat (usually butter) and flour, cooked together as a base for sauces.

Rub in: To mix butter or other fat into flour by rubbing between the fingertips until the mixture resembles breadcrumbs.

S

Saffron: The dried stigma of the autumn-flowering saffron crocus produces a powerfully aromatic, very expensive spice which colours food yellow as well as flavouring it. Used sparingly it has an unmistakable, slightly peppery flavour but can be overpowering if used in quantity. It is an essential ingredient of dishes such as paella, risotto alla milanaise, bouillabaisse and Cornish saffron cakes and, although other spices — most often turmeric — can reproduce the colour, the flavour of saffron is unique.

Saignant: Of meat, very under-done.

Salmi: Game stew made by first roasting then cooking it in a wine sauce.

Salsa: a) In Italy, pasta sauces; b) In Mexico, uncooked sauces served as an accompaniment, usually to corn chips.

Salt: Like so many other foods, has come under a lot of criticism lately on health grounds but, used in moderation, it is essential to good cookery. Although ordinary table and cooking salt is cheaper and flows more freely, sea salt has a milder but more characterful flavour and is worth the small amount extra. My personal preference is for Maldon Sea Salt, from Essex — it comes in delicious, crunchy little crystals fine enough to crush with your fingers so it is served in a small bowl and no salt mill is required.

Sauces: If a sauce becomes lumpy, beating vigorously with a wire whisk will usually clear it. If the sauce has already boiled the lumps may be too hard to whisk out, but it can still be saved by straining, or by blending in a food processor or liquidiser. Don't try to keep sauces warm over long periods. Instead, allow the sauce to cool completely and reheat it in a double saucepan, or in a bowl over a pan of hot water. To prevent a skin forming, dot the surface with tiny flakes of butter, or lay a piece of buttered greaseproof paper over the sauce.

Sauté: a) To fry food rapidly in butter or oil, turning or shaking constantly, until evenly browned; b) A dish where sautéed ingredients have extra vegetables, wine, stock and flavourings added and the food steams in its own juices, to produce a tender texture and richly flavoured sauce.

Savarin: Rich yeast cake cooked in a ring mould, drenched in a liqueur-flavoured syrup and served cold, with cream.

Savoury: A traditional meal-ending of highly seasoned savoury dishes, rather like the cheese course but with made-up dishes like Camembert Ice Cream or Angels on Horseback (oysters wrapped in bacon).

Scald: a) To heat milk or cream to just below boiling point; b) To plunge vegetables briefly into boiling water, to loosen the skins; c) To rinse a dish with boiling water.

Score: To cut the surface of food at regular intervals either a) to allow more even heat penetration, as when grilling whole fish, for example or b) to produce a crisper finish, as for pork crackling; c) the term is also used to describe a pattern of squares or diamonds used to decorate a pastry crust, or a cooked ham.

Sear: To brown the surface of meat very quickly over high heat to heighten the flavour and seal in the juices.

Seasoned flour: Flour ready seasoned with salt and pepper for use when coating foods or in sauces etc.

Shred: Tear or cut into long thin strips; used of salad greens (torn) and vegetables (cut).

Singe: To flame poultry or pork to remove all traces of feathers or hair before cooking.

Skim: To remove any fat, scum or froth from a liquid with a metal skimming spoon or ladle.

Sous-vide: A relatively new process whereby cook-chill food is prepared, vacuum-sealed and then cooked 'sous-vide'/ 'under vacuum', in a system of very fast heating and cooking which is designed to retain the moisture, flavour, colour and aroma of fresh food. However, to serve it safely, careful handling by trained personnel is essential and it is banned in many countries because of lack of confidence that these safety requirements will be met.

Souse: To cover food, particularly oily fish such as herrings, in wine vinegar and spices and cook slowly, then leave to cool in the juices. Similar to pickling.

Spices: a personal selection of indispensable spices would include: peppercorns, mustard seeds, coriander seeds, cumin, nutmeg (whole, or mace), cinnamon (sticks and ground), cardamom (whole pods), cloves, allspice, cayenne, paprika, juniper, ginger (in various forms: fresh root, preserved stem, crystallised, ground), star anise, fennel seeds, sesame seeds.

Spring-form mould: baking tin with hinged sides held together by a metal clip — when released, delicate cakes or pies can be removed without difficulty.

Steep: To soak food in large quantities of cold or tepid water to draw out impurities, such as excess salt in ham, and to soften foods, such as pulses, and reduce the cooking time.

Sterilise: To destroy germs by exposing food or utensils to heat, or to chemical sterilising fluids.

Stew: To simmer food gently in a covered casserole.

Stir-fry: To cook small pieces of food fast in very little oil, usually in a wok, turning and tossing with a pair of wooden spatulas, or similar, over high heat. Everything must be prepared before cooking begins and ingredients are added in order, according to how much cooking is required.

Stock: Keeping a big old black stockpot going from Christmas onwards is one of my most enjoyable amusements — if the spring is cold so there's an ongoing demand for warming soups and sauces, it can be kept going indefinitely. The current record stands at nearly five months — you have to take a bit out every now and then to make room for new carcasses and vegetables but basically it's the Christmas stockpot and, as long as it is properly boiled up every day, it's grand. Apart from the boiling, which prevents it going off, the rules of my pot are very simple: poultry and feathered game only go into it (to avoid confusion of flavours) and 'pot herb' flavouring vegetables — onion, carrot, celery and herbs such as parsley and thyme — no green vegetables.

SUGAR AND ITS USES A SUMMARY

As a Preservative:

Jam: sugar combines with pectin and acid in the fruit to form a set and also prevents moulding.

Bottling: helps maintain the texture and flavour of the fruit.

Freezing: sugar prolongs the 'freshness' by slowing down enzyme activity.

To Add Texture:

Lightness: it gives sponges, cakes and meringues essential lightness by trapping air.

Creamy Smoothness: added to custards and sauces, sugar helps prevent a skin forming by stopping protein coagulation.

Shape and texture: Sugar helps give shape and texture to confectionery and ice creams. It also gives body to fruit sauces or 'coulis' and soft drinks.

Flavour and Colour:

Flavour: Sugar enhances flavours in other foods and, in some cases, adds flavour of its own.

Colour: It bakes golden-brown in cakes and pastry and, when sprinkled over or melted and brushed over toppings, creates a glaze or carmelised crunchy topping when finished under heat.

For Fermentation:

Yeast Cookery: Sugar is essential for fermentation in bread and enriched yeast doughs as well as in beer and wine-making.

Types of Sugar and Their Uses:

Granulated Sugar is the ideal general purpose sugar, for use in hot drinks, with cereals and in cookery — it is suitable for any recipe where the liquid content and/or cooking time allow it to dissolve completely. It is ideal for rubbing in cake mixture and those made by the melting method and topping where some crunch is desirable such as crumbles.

Caster Sugar has finer crystals than granulated and so dissolves more quickly and seems sweeter. It incorporates more air than other types of sugar and used in baking this creates more volume and a light result. It is ideal for cakes made by the creaming method, meringues, sweetening whipped cream, sifting over stewed fruit and making flavoured sugars.

Icing Sugar is ground to a very fine powder, so the crystalline structure is broken up. It is ideal for making jam from fruit with a low pectin content such as strawberries, or jellies from low-pectin juice or commercially prepared juices, or for any small, quantity of quick jam, jelly or marmalade.

Light Golden Brown Sugar is a soft, fine sugar with similar uses to caster sugar. It has cane molasses added to it, giving a distinctive but delicate flavour to butter creams, cakes, shortbread, and biscuits. It is ideal for almond paste and rum butter, either on its own or mixed with caster or icing sugar.

Rich Dark Brown Sugar is also made from white sugar with cane molasses and, like light golden brown sugar, it is fine grained and creams easily. It adds rich colour and a deeper flavour to cakes, puddings and biscuits and is an essential ingredient in rich fruit cakes and plum puddings. It can give a great lift to familiar recipes, like chutneys, either on its own or mixed with other sugars.

Demerara Sugar is a crunchy sugar with big light brown molasses-covered crystals. Its definite but subtle flavour enhances coffee and is perfect in cooking where granulated sugar would be too bland. It adds flavour and a soft golden tone to cakes, puddings and sauces and is ideal where a good crunch is called for, as in ham glazes and mincemeat.

Sugar Cubes, sometimes called loaf sugar, used to be cubes cut from the loaf of sugar. Nowadays they are made from granulated or demerara sugar moistened with sugar syrup and moulded into cubes. Mostly used in drinks, they are traditional in recipes such as lemon curd, as the zest could be rubbed onto the sugar and infuse it with colour and flavour without the pieces of peel which are inevitable if the zest is grated, however finely; also used in the same way for flavouring sauces, ice creams etc. Try dipping cubes in warm brandy then ignite to flame a Christmas Pudding.

Sugar Syrups: simple sugar syrups of various densities are used for fruit salads, moistening cakes, glazing pastries, poaching fruits and making sorbets. For poaching fruit, make a light syrup of 4oz/100g caster sugar dissolved over low heat in ½pint/300ml water and then brought to the boil and cooked for about a minute until clear. For fruit salad, make a heavier syrup with 4oz/ 100g caster sugar to ¼ pint/150ml water and the juice of ½ lemon. For candying peel the density is gradually increased from one stage to the next (see recipe). For sorbets, the density varies according to the recipe, but the basic proportion is 1lb/450g sugar to 13 fl oz/375ml water. For all sugar syrups, as in jam and marmalade making, it is very important to be sure the sugar has dissolved completely before bringing it to the boil, or the syrup will be cloudy and inclined to crystallise.

Sweat: To cook food in very little fat and no liquid over a very gentle heat so that it will not brown. A very close-fitting lid must be used, or else greaseproof paper or foil is laid under the lid so that the food steams in its own juices. It is usually then added to another dish.

Syrup: A liquid made by boiling sugar with water or fruit juice.

T

Tempura: Japanese style of deep-frying lightly-battered pieces of fish, poultry, meat or vegetables. They are served with individual bowls of soy sauce, for dipping.

Terrine: a) Earthenware or cast iron dish used for cooking and serving pâté; b) Food cooked in a terrine, typically a firm pâté that slices well.

Tian: Shallow Provencale earthenware dish, especially useful for serving big main course salads and baking gratins.

Timbale: Cup-shaped earthenware or metal mould, or a dish prepared in it.

Truss: To tie a bird or joint of meat into a neat shape with string or skewers so that it will cook evenly and be easier to serve.

U

Unleavened bread: Bread which is made without raising agent and, when baked is thin, flat and round.

V

Vanilla Sugar: Sugar which is flavoured by storing it in a closed jar with a vanilla pod.

Vegetables: Remember that in many vegetables valuable nutrients are in or just below the skin. If possible only wash or scrub before cooking, otherwise just scrape or peel as thinly as possible with a vegetable peeler. For the same reason, try to avoid leaving vegetables soaking for a long time. Storing vegetables correctly makes it possible to keep them in good condition much longer. Root vegetables should be stored in a cool, airy place — mine keep extremely well in a basket hanging in an open porch at the back door. Avoid washing them until required, if possible. Most salad ingredients are best washed, dried in a salad spinner and stored loosely in a polythene bag in the salad drawer of the fridge. Tomatoes keep better and have more flavour if stored in a cool place rather than the fridge, if possible. Use paper bags rather than polythene for most vegetables, especially tomatoes and mushrooms.

Velouté: a) White sauce made with chicken, veal or fish stock; b) creamy soup.

Vinaigrette: Mixture of oil and vinegar, seasoned with salt and pepper and sometimes flavoured with fresh herbs.

Vinegar: Clear liquid consisting of varying proportions of acetic acid and made by fermenting wine, cider or malt beer. Vinegars have become similarly complicated in recent years. Once vinegar simply meant **malt vinegar**, or white vinegar — now there are **herb- and fruit-flavoured vinegars** based on red and white wines, **cider vinegars, sherry vinegars** and, the most recent fad, hyper-expensive **Italian balsamic vinegar**, Aceto Balsamico, a wine vinegar which is aged for a very long time in various kinds of wood so that it loses the harshness characteristic of vinegar and becomes very dark and almost sweet — the manufacturers of the Fini brand of Modena, suggest marinating strawberries in it for 15 minutes, then adding sugar to taste, mixing well and serving, which should give an idea of how different from ordinary vinegar this product is. Like olive oils, it varies a lot in quality and price, so buy from a reliable shop where somebody knowledgeable can advise.

W

Whey: Liquid which separates from the curd when milk curdles; used in cheese-making.

Whip: To beat eggs until frothy and cream until thick.

Wild Rice: This is not actually a rice at all but a special variety of long, thin, dark brown grass seed which is highly sought after (and therefore very expensive) and cooked in the same way as rice, or more often because of its very high cost, mixed in with rice. It has an interesting nutty flavour and, both in appearance and texture as well as flavour, adds greatly to the interest of a plain rice dish.

Y

Yeast: Fungus cells that multiply rapidly under favourable conditions to cause dough to rise. Can be used fresh or dry but dried brewer's yeast, used for wine- and beer-making, is not suitable for baking.

Yogurt: Curdled milk which has been cultured with beneficial bacteria and has many uses in the kitchen.

Z

Zest: Coloured outer skin of citrus fruit containing the essential oils which make the peeled or grated zest invaluable for flavouring. Also used, blanched or candied, for decoration. Where 'finely grated zest' is called for, often in sauces or icings, use the finest grater and a very light touch. Grated rind, on the other hand, can be slightly coarser although no white pith should be included. In practice, the terms are often interchangeable. (See also **Dried Grated Rinds**.)

INDEX